Interpreting Classical Economics

This book is the third volume of previously published essays from Heinz D. Kurz and Neri Salvadori, following *Understanding Classical Economics* (1998) and *Classical Economics and Modern Theory* (2003), both published by Routledge. This new collection can be read in isolation but perhaps more fruitfully in conjunction with the previous texts, providing modern interpretations of the classical economists and comparing their analyses with that of contemporary mainstream economics.

The essays in the new volume are split between three parts, the first section dealing with classical economics and modern theory focusing specifically on the differences in the analytical structure and content of the theory of value and distribution of Ricardo, on the one hand, and Say and Walras, on the other. The second part is devoted to Piero Sraffa's contribution, drawing from his hitherto unpublished papers. The final part assesses linear theory of production, concentrating on comparative studies of the contributions of von Neumann, Arrow-Debreu, Georgescu-Roegen and Sraffa.

This new volume will be of interest to economic theorists and methodologists in Europe, Asia and America and particularly academics and researchers engaged with theories of production, value, distribution, economic growth and the history of economic thought.

Heinz D. Kurz is Professor of Economics at the University of Graz, Austria.

Neri Salvadori is Professor of Economics at the University of Pisa, Italy.

Routledge Studies in the History of Economics

1 **Economics as Literature**
Willie Henderson

2 **Socialism and Marginalism in Economics 1870–1930**
Edited by Ian Steedman

3 **Hayek's Political Economy**
The socio-economics of order
Steve Fleetwood

4 **On the Origins of Classical Economics**
Distribution and value from William Petty to Adam Smith
Tony Aspromourgos

5 **The Economics of Joan Robinson**
Edited by Maria Cristina Marcuzzo, Luigi Pasinetti and Alesandro Roncaglia

6 **The Evolutionist Economics of Léon Walras**
Albert Jolink

7 **Keynes and the 'Classics'**
A study in language, epistemology and mistaken identities
Michel Verdon

8 **The History of Game Theory, Vol 1**
From the beginnings to 1945
Robert W. Dimand and Mary Ann Dimand

9 **The Economics of W. S. Jevons**
Sandra Peart

10 **Gandhi's Economic Thought**
Ajit K Dasgupta

11 **Equilibrium and Economic Theory**
Edited by Giovanni Caravale

12 **Austrian Economics in Debate**
Edited by Willem Keizer, Bert Tieben and Rudy van Zijp

13 **Ancient Economic Thought**
Edited by B. B. Price

14 **The Political Economy of Social Credit and Guild Socialism**
Frances Hutchinson and Brian Burkitt

15 **Economic Careers**
Economics and economists in Britain 1930–1970
Keith Tribe

16 **Understanding 'Classical' Economics**
Studies in long-period theory
Heinz Kurz and Neri Salvadori

17 **History of Environmental Economic Thought**
E. Kula

18 **Economic Thought in Communist and Post-Communist Europe**
Edited by Hans-Jürgen Wagener

19 **Studies in the History of French Political Economy**
From Bodin to Walras
Edited by Gilbert Faccarello

20 **The Economics of John Rae**
Edited by O. F. Hamouda, C. Lee and D. Mair

21 **Keynes and the Neoclassical Synthesis**
Einsteinian versus Newtonian macroeconomics
Teodoro Dario Togati

22 **Historical Perspectives on Macroeconomics**
Sixty years after the 'General Theory'
Edited by Philippe Fontaine and Albert Jolink

23 **The Founding of Institutional Economics**
The leisure class and sovereignty
Edited by Warren J. Samuels

24 **Evolution of Austrian Economics**
From Menger to Lachmann
Sandye Gloria

25 **Marx's Concept of Money: the God of Commodities**
Anitra Nelson

26 **The Economics of James Steuart**
Edited by Ramón Tortajada

27 **The Development of Economics in Europe since 1945**
Edited by A. W. Bob Coats

28 **The Canon in the History of Economics**
Critical essays
Edited by Michalis Psalidopoulos

29 **Money and Growth**
Selected papers of Allyn Abbott Young
Edited by Perry G. Mehrling and Roger J. Sandilands

30 **The Social Economics of Jean-Baptiste Say**
Markets & virtue
Evelyn L. Forget

31 **The Foundations of Laissez-Faire**
The economics of Pierre de Boisguilbert
Gilbert Faccarello

32 **John Ruskin's Political Economy**
Willie Henderson

33 **Contributions to the History of Economic Thought**
Essays in honour of RDC Black
Edited by Antoin E Murphy and Renee Prendergast

34 Towards an Unknown Marx
A commentary on the manuscripts of 1861–63
Enrique Dussel

35 Economics and Interdisciplinary Exchange
Edited by Guido Erreygers

36 Economics as the Art of Thought
Essays in memory of G L S Shackle
Edited by Stephen F Frowen and Peter Earl

37 The Decline of Ricardian Economics
Politics and economics in Post-Ricardian theory
Susan Pashkoff

38 Piero Sraffa
His Life, thought and cultural heritage
Alessandro Roncaglia

39 Equilibrium and Disequilibrium in Economic Theory
The Marshall-Walras divide
Michel de Vroey

40 The German Historical School
The historical and ethical approach to economics
Edited by Yuichi Shionoya

41 Reflections on the Classical Canon in Economics
Essays in honor of Samuel Hollander
Edited by Sandra Peart and Evelyn Forget

42 Piero Sraffa's Political Economy
A centenary estimate
Edited by Terenzio Cozzi and Roberto Marchionatti

43 The Contribution of Joseph Schumpeter to Economics
Economic development and institutional change
Richard Arena and Cecile Dangel

44 On the Development of Long-run Neo-Classical Theory
Tom Kompas

45 F.A. Hayek as a Political Economist
Economic analysis and values
Edited by Jack Birner, Pierre Garrouste and Thierry Aimar

46 Pareto, Economics and Society
The mechanical analogy
Michael McLure

47 The Cambridge Controversies in Capital Theory
A study in the logic of theory development
Jack Birner

48 Economics Broadly Considered
Essays in honor of Warren J Samuels
Edited by Steven G Medema, Jeff Biddle and John B Davis

49 Physicians and Political Economy
Six studies of the work of doctor-economists
Edited by Peter Groenewegen

50 **The Spread of Political Economy and the Professionalisation of Economists**
Economic societies in Europe, America and Japan in the Nineteenth Century
Massimo Augello and Marco Guidi

51 **Historians of Economics & Economic Thought**
The construction of disciplinary memory
Steven G Medema and Warren J Samuels

52 **Competing Economic Theories**
Essays in memory of Giovanni Caravale
Sergio Nisticò and Domenico Tosato

53 **Economic Thought and Policy in Less Developed Europe**
The 19th Century
Edited by Michalis Psalidopoulos and Maria-Eugenia Almedia Mata

54 **Family Fictions and Family Facts**
Harriet Martineau, Adolphe Quetelet and the population question in England 1798–1859
Brian Cooper

55 **Eighteeth-Century Economics**
Peter Groenewegen

56 **The Rise of Political Economy in the Scottish Enlightenment**
Edited by Tatsuya Sakamoto and Hideo Tanaka

57 **Classics and Moderns in Economics Volume I**
Essays on Nineteenth and Twentieth Century Economic Thought
Peter Groenewegen

58 **Classics and Moderns in Economics Volume II**
Essays on Nineteenth and Twentieth Century Economic Thought
Peter Groenewegen

59 **Marshall's Evolutionary Economics**
Tiziano Raffaelli

60 **Money, Time and Rationality in Max Weber**
Austrian Connections
Stephen D. Parsons

61 **Classical Macroeconomics**
Some modern variations and distortions
James C.W. Ahiakpor

62 **The Historical School of Economics in England and Japan**
Tamotsu Nishizawa

63 **Classical Economics and Modern Theory**
Studies in Long-Period Analysis
Heinz D. Kurz and Neri Salvadori

64 **A Bibliography of Female Economic Thought to 1940**
Kirsten K. Madden, Janet A. Sietz and Michele Pujol

65 **Economics, Economists and Expectations**
From Microfoundations to Macroeconomics
Warren Young, Robert Leeson and William Darity Jnr.

66 **The Political Economy of Public Finance in Britain, 1767–1873**
Takuo Dome

67 **Essays in the History of Economics**
Warren J. Samuels, Willie Henderson, Kirk D. Johnson and Marianne Johnson

68 **History and Political Economy**
Essays in Honour of P.D. Groenewegen
Edited by Tony Aspromourgos and John Lodewijks

69 **The Tradition of Free Trade**
Lars Magnusson

70 **Evolution of the Market Process**
Austrian and Swedish Economics
Edited by Michel Bellet, Sandye Gloria-Palermo & Abdallah Zouache

71 **Consumption as an Investment**
The fear of goods from Hesiod to Adam Smith
Cosimo Perrotta

72 **Jean-Baptiste Say and the Classical Canon in Economics**
The British Connection in French Classicism
Samuel Hollander

73 **Knut Wicksell on Poverty**
No Place is too Exalted
Knut Wicksell

74 **Economists in Cambridge**
A Study Through Their Correspondence 1907–1946
Edited by M.C. Marcuzzo and A. Rosselli

75 **The Experiment in the History of Economics**
Edited by Philippe Fontaine and Robert Leonard

76 **At the Origins of Mathematical Economics**
The Economics of A.N. Isnard (1748–1803)
Richard van den Berg

77 **Money and Exchange**
Folktales and Reality
Sasan Fayazmanesh

78 **Economic Development and Social Change**
Historical Roots and Modern Perspectives
George Stathakis and Gianni Vaggi

79 **Ethical Codes and income distribution**
A Study of John Bates Clark and Thorstein Veblen
Guglielmo Forges Davanzati

80 **Evaluating Adam Smith**
Creating the Wealth of Nations
Willie Henderson

81 **Civil Happiness**
Economics and Human Flourishing in Historical Perspective
Luigino Bruni

82 **New Voices on Adam Smith**
Edited by Leonidas Montes and Eric Schliesser

83 Making Chicago Price Theory
Milton Friedman – George Stigler Correspondence, 1945–1957
Edited by J. Daniel Hammond and Claire H. Hammond

84 William Stanley Jevons and the Cutting Edge of Economics
Bert Mosselmans

85 A History of Econometrics in France
From Nature to Models
Philippe Le Gall

86 Money and Markets
A Doctrinal Approach
Edited by Alberto Giacomin and Maria Cristina Marcuzzo

87 Considerations on the Fundamental Principles of Pure Political Economy
Vilfredo Pareto (Edited by Roberto Marchionatti and Fiorenzo Mornati)

88 The Years of High Econometrics
A Short History of the Generation that Reinvented Economics
Francisco Louçã

89 Interpreting Classical Economics
Studies in long-period analysis
Heinz D. Kurz and Neri Salvadori
With Christian Gehrke, Giuseppe Freni and Fausto Gozzi

Interpreting Classical Economics

Studies in long-period analysis

Heinz D. Kurz and Neri Salvadori

With Christian Gehrke, Giuseppe Freni and Fausto Gozzi

Routledge
Taylor & Francis Group
LONDON AND NEW YORK

First published 2007
by Routledge
2 Park Square, Milton Park, Abingdon, Oxfordshire OX14 4RN

Simultaneously published in the USA and Canada
by Routledge
711 Third Avenue, New York, NY 10017

First issued in paperback 2014

Routledge is an imprint of the Taylor & Francis Group, an informa business

Typeset in Times New Roman by
Newgen Imaging Systems (P) Ltd, Chennai, India

British Library Cataloguing in Publication Data
A catalogue record for this book is available
from the British Library

Library of Congress Cataloging in Publication Data
A catalog record for this book has been requested

ISBN13: 978–0–415–42880–4 (hbk)
ISBN13: 978-1-138-01063-5 (pbk)

Contents

Acknowledgements

We are grateful to the following publications for allowing us to reproduce articles which originally appeared in their pages: *The European Journal of the History of Economic Thought* for 'Say and Ricardo on Value and Distribution'; *Scottish Journal of Political Economy* for 'Ricardo on Agricultural Improvements: A Note'; *History of Political Economy* for 'One Theory or Two? Walras's Critique of Ricardo'; Ashgate for 'Is Ricardian Extensive Rent a Nash Equilibrium?' in Richard Arena and Neri Salvadori (eds), *Money, Credit and the Role of the State: Essays in Honour of Augusto Graziani* (Aldershot, UK, and Burlington, VT, USA: Ashgate, 2004); *The European Journal of the History of Economic Thought* for 'Keynes and Sraffa's Difficulties with J. H. Hollander'; *Économies et Sociétés. Histoire de la pensée économique* for ' "Man from the Moon". On Sraffa's Objectivism'; Elsevier for 'The Agents of Production are the Commodities Themselves. On the Classical Theory of Production, Distribution and Value', *Structural Change and Economic Dynamics* Vol. 17(1), January 2006, pp. 1–26; The President of the Accademia Nazionale dei Lincei for 'On the Collaboration between Sraffa and Besicovitch: The Cases of Fixed Capital and Non-Basics in Joint Production', *Atti dei Convegni Lincei*, Volume 200 (Rome: Accademia Nazionale dei Lincei, 2004); *Acta Oeconomica* for 'Von Neumann, the Classical Economists and Arrow-Debreu: Some Notes'; Elsevier for 'Fund-Flow versus Flow-Flow in Production Theory: Reflections on Georgescu-Roegen's Contribution', *Journal of Economic Behavior and Organization* Vol. 51(4), August 2003, pp. 487–505; Edward Elgar for 'Endogenous Growth in a Multi-Sector Economy' in Neri Salvadori (ed.), *The Theory of Economic Growth: A Classical Perspective*, Cheltenham: Edward Elgar, 2003. Publication details and dates of all these articles are given in the text.

1 Interpreting classical economics: studies in long-period analysis

An introduction

Heinz D. Kurz and Neri Salvadori

This volume contains a set of chapters written by the two of us, by one of us alone, or by one of us in collaboration with some other co-author. With the exception of this introduction all chapters have been previously published. The collection is a follow-up to two other volumes with essays from us, the 1998 volume entitled *Understanding 'Classical' Economics. Studies in Long-period Theory* (Kurz and Salvadori, 1998) and the 2003 volume entitled *Classical Economics and Modern Theory. Studies in Long-period Analysis* (Kurz and Salvadori, 2003). In order to get a more complete picture of what we mean by 'classical' economics and why we think it necessary to resurrect and develop the standpoint of the classical economists and those working in their tradition, we ask the interested reader to kindly also consult our previous books. Since some of the chapters reprinted in this volume contain a continuation of arguments developed in chapters published in the earlier two volumes – occasionally directly in response to critics of our work – the reader might find it useful to have the previous volumes at hand when reading this one.

The material is subdivided in three parts. Part I deals with 'Classical economics and modern theory' and has four chapters. Chapter 2 grew out of a paper given at the 'Colloque international Jean-Baptiste Say', Institut des Sciences de l'Homme, Lyon, 26–28 October 2000. The chapter focuses attention on the differences of opinion between Ricardo and Say in the theory of value and distribution – the main field in dispute between the two. It is shown that whilst at the beginning of their encounter Say acknowledged Ricardo's authority in political economy, already at the time of his notes to the French edition of Ricardo's *Principles*, published in 1819, he changed his attitude. After Ricardo's death he openly attacked Ricardo and apparently was intent to diminish the latter's achievements. However, there is clear evidence that Say's reception of Ricardo's surplus-based approach to the theory of value and distribution abounds with misunderstandings. These concern, in particular, the distinction between 'value' and 'riches', the theory of value and the problem of the measure of value, and the explanation of rents and profits. Desirous of establishing himself as an original thinker, Say re-defined the scope, method and content of political economy, opting for a more inductive approach. When confronted with Ricardo's criticism of his interpretations and views he frequently responded in an evasive way. Ricardo felt with an ever increasing astonishment, which was to turn into disenchantment, that the substance of Say's respective arguments, which he thought erroneous or misleading, was basically left untouched. Therefore, his belief in Say's ability to understand his, Ricardo's, doctrine gradually vanished. Chapter 3 discusses the numerical examples of land saving and capital saving agricultural improvements Ricardo provided in chapter 2, 'On rent', of the *Principles*. His illustrations of the second kind of improvements in particular met with fierce criticism, beginning with Edwin Cannan. It is maintained that Ricardo was not wrong in any substantive sense and that he could only be criticized for having changed the definition of rent as regards the timing of its payment from *post* to *ante factum*. Chapter 4 scrutinizes Léon Walras's 'Exposition and refutation of the English theory', by which Walras meant first and foremost Ricardo's theory, in lessons 38–40 of part 7 of his *Eléments d'économie politique pure*. While Walras succeeded in pointing out some weaknesses and unnecessarily restrictive assumptions in Ricardo's theory of differential rent, he made a number of mistakes and misunderstood specific elements of Ricardo's theory. He was not aware of the fact that singularly restrictive assumptions must hold in corn production in order for marginal productivity curves of capital with regard to each quality of land to exist. His objection that Ricardo tried 'to determine two unknowns with one equation', involving that his system was underdetermined, is untenable. More important, Walras failed to see that the classical approach to the theory of value and distribution is fundamentally different from his own demand and supply approach. He treated Ricardo's theory as if it were just an early and rude version of his own elaborate neoclassical general equilibrium theory. He missed the fact that the data of the classical theory are different from those of the marginalist one and in particular that profits and wages are not treated in a symmetrical manner. Chapter 5 raises the question of whether Ricardian extensive rent is a Nash equilibrium. Following Ricardo and the other Classical authors, none of the modern contributors to the analysis of extensive rent has given a role to the distribution of land ownership among landlords. In this chapter, on the contrary, it is argued that if the demand for agricultural commodities and the distribution of marginal land ownership is such that demand can be satisfied only if the owner of the largest plot of that land rents out at least a part of his or her land, then a positive rent is possible (if landlords behave in a strategic way). In the analysis provided only two cases are explored: that in which each owner has the same amount of marginal land and that in which there are just two owners.

Part II is devoted to 'Sraffa's contributions' and has four chapters. Chapter 6 deals with an important aspect of Sraffa's preparation of *The Works and Correspondence of David Ricardo* (Ricardo, 1951–1973). As is well known, the publication of the edition was delayed for a considerable time. One of the reasons for the delay was that Jacob H. Hollander, a then leading authority on Ricardo, effectively obstructed the progress of the edition for many years, first by not disclosing to Sraffa the 'Ricardiana' he had acquired, and then, after Sraffa had provided compelling evidence that they must have been in his possession, by refusing Sraffa access to them. How and why Hollander did so requires an intricate story to be unravelled, using hitherto unknown material from several archives. An early version of the paper was presented at a session of the *HES* meeting at the University of British Columbia in Vancouver, 30 June–3 July 2000, and at the *HETSA* meeting at Wesley College, Sydney, 4–7 July 2000. Chapter 7 is devoted to a discussion of Sraffa's 'objectivist' point of view in the theory of value and distribution. The paper was first given at the IXth conference of the Association Charles Gide devoted to the theme 'Agréger, répartir, échanger: la valeur d'Aristote à Sraffa, Shapley et Debreu' at BETA, Université Luis Pasteur, in Strasbourg, 27–29 September 2001. The objectivist point of view, Sraffa was to discover, had been anticipated by the classical economists, whose analysis he was keen to revive by shedding the weaknesses of its earlier formulations and elaborating on their strengths. The chapter draws on Sraffa's hitherto unpublished papers kept at Trinity College Library, Cambridge, focusing attention on the first period of his interpretative and constructive work, 1927–1931. A follow-up to the chapter providing a more detailed discussion of the various facets of this fascinating topic and especially Sraffa's concern with the relationship between economics and the laws established by the natural sciences is Kurz and Salvadori (2005) which is reprinted in Kurz, Pasinetti and Salvadori (2007). An early version of Chapter 8 was given on the occasion of a conference at the Max Planck Institute for Research into Economic Systems in Jena, Germany, 29 November–1 December 2001, devoted to alternative approaches to the theory of production. The emphasis in the chapter is on the characteristic features of the Classical theory, including its objectivist orientation; its explanation of all property incomes in terms of the social surplus generated in production conceived of as a circular flow; and its treatment of wages conceived of either as an inventory of commodities or as a share in the social product as a given magnitude. Chapter 9 adds to our previous discussion of Sraffa's collaboration with his 'mathematical friends' (Frank Ramsey, Alister Watson and Abram S. Besicovitch); see Kurz and Salvadori (2003, chapter 10). The chapter was originally given at the conference 'Piero Sraffa' organized by the Italian Academy of Science, the Accademia Nazionale dei Lincei, in Rome, 11–12 February 2003. In it we discuss two problems Sraffa faced in the course of preparing his 1960 book: (i) the problem of fixed capital which turned out to be a veritable touchstone to his objectivist approach, because whereas in the case of circulating capital goods the process of value transfer to the product and the physical 'destruction' of the input are one and the same thing, in the case of fixed capital items this is typically not so; (ii) the problem of carrying over the distinction between basic and non-basic commodities from systems with only single production to those with joint production. While with Besicovitch's help Sraffa was able to solve the first problem in terms of the joint-products approach we encounter in chapter X of Sraffa (1960) as early as late summer 1943, he became aware of the second problem only in spring 1957 when he was putting together his book from his old notes. The problem turned out to be intricate and necessitated substantial changes in the structure and content of the book. Sraffa and Besicovitch worked hard on this problem from August to November 1957 and there is a further result found by Besicovitch in December 1957 which was not included in the book, whose manuscript was complete by the end of January 1958.

Part III is entitled 'Linear theory of production: an assessment' and has three chapters. Chapter 10 compares the classical theory of value and distribution with von Neumann's model of equiproportionate growth on the one hand and the Arrow-Debreu model of intertemporal general equilibrium on the other. The chapter is based on a paper given on the occasion of a conference on John von Neumann hosted by the Hungarian Academy of Sciences in Budapest, 5 November 2003. It is argued that von Neumann's model shares all important features of the classical theory of value and distribution in terms of method of analysis, analytical structure and economic content and differs in important respects from the Arrow-Debreu model of intertemporal general equilibrium. It is also shown that setting aside some purely formal aspects there are no connections between the von Neumann model and the Arrow-Debreu model. More specifically, it is argued that von Neumann's assumption that each and every commodity enters and/or exits each and every process of production and the assumption of Arrow-Debreu that each agent possesses an initial endowment that allows the agent to survive are not equivalent, as has been maintained in the literature. A claim by Arrow and Debreu (1954) according to which an assumption of the latter plays the 'same role' as an assumption of the former is scrutinized and rejected. The paper is a follow-up to Kurz and Salvadori (1998, chapter 2) and Kurz and Salvadori (2003, chapter 11). Chapter 11 is the result of revising and merging two papers given at the conference 'L' Oeuvre Scientifique de Nicholas Georgescu-Roegen' in Strasbourg, 6–7 November 1998. The chapter discusses Georgescu-Roegen's contribution to production theory, comparing it with the contributions of John von Neumann and Piero Sraffa. The emphasis is on the problem of the choice of technique. It is shown that Georgescu-Roegen's fund-flow approach, in which fixed capital is treated as an 'immutable agent', can be misleading and cannot address issues that are easily handled by the alternative flow-flow approach that reduces fixed capital to circulating within a joint-products framework. The latter allows for an adequate treatment of wear and tear of machines as well as of the problem of capital utilization in both its extensive (the number of hours a fixed capital item is worked per day) and intensive (the speed at which a machine is operated) dimension.

In previous papers (Kurz and Salvadori, 1998, chapter 4; 2003, chapters 6, 7) we have shown that new growth theory essentially formalizes within the framework of steady-state intertemporal equilibrium theory a set of ideas that have been around for a long time and were particularly stressed by the Classical economists. We have shown that several of the models of the 'new' growth theory dispense with the traditional neoclassical determination of the rate of profits in terms of the supply of and the demand for 'capital'. In addition many of them eliminate simple labour from the picture and put in its stead 'human capital' or 'knowledge', that is, something that a modern audience can accept as a producible (and accumulable) factor of production. Finally, the conditions of production of this surrogate of 'labour' play exactly the same role played in the Classical economists' analyses by the assumption of a given real wage rate. One of us has also elaborated a linear multisector model of 'endogenous' growth with heterogeneous capital goods (see Kurz and Salvadori, 2003, Ch. 8). The purpose of this exercise was to show that this kind of model is exempt from the capital theory critique put forward against the conventional long-period neoclassical growth model *à la* Solow. This confirms the claim that at least some of the new growth models are somewhat extraneous to neoclassical analysis and actually exhibit the logical structure of classical theory. In addition it was shown that the use of an intertemporal analysis to establish a correct long-period position is not necessary and that the adoption of the long-period method may speed up the elaboration of new scientific results. This model was further elaborated in collaboration with Giuseppe Freni and Fausto Gozzi and also by these two scholars alone or in collaboration with others (see in particular Freni, Gozzi, and Salvadori, 2006; Kurz and Salvadori, 2003, Ch. 9). Chapter 12 belongs to this strand of research. It was originally delivered at the Conference 'Old and New Growth Theories: An Assessmen', Pisa, 5–7 October 2001. It can be read as an analysis of the problems that the extension to a multi-sector economy poses for endogenous growth theorists, but it can also be read both as a restatement of some solutions proposed by the theory of production of Classical orientation and as a complement to this theory when the growth rate is negative and depreciation is by evaporation. It provides also a comparison with the linear models of production developed in the sixties and the seventies.

Finally, we should like to draw the reader's attention to some further works that contribute to the strand of thought explored in this volume. The problem of economic growth as seen from a classical perspective is dealt with in Kurz and Salvadori (2006). Sraffa's critical assessment in his papers composed in 1943 of Ladislaus von Bortkiewicz's essay on 'Wertrechnung und Preisrechnung im Marxschen System' (Bortkiewicz, 1906–7) against the background of his own achievements up until then is discussed in some detail in Gehrke and Kurz (2006). For a collection of essays dealing with Sraffa's legacy in economics, using archival material from Sraffa's hitherto unpublished papers, see Kurz, Pasinetti and Salvadori (2007).

References

Arrow, Kenneth J. and Debreu, Gérard. (1954). 'Existence of an equilibrium for a competitive economy', *Econometrica*, **22**, July, pp. 265–90.

Freni, Giuseppe, Gozzi, Fausto and Salvadori, Neri (2001). 'A multisector "AK model" with endogenous growth: existence and characterization of optimal paths and steady state analysis', *Studi e Ricerche del Dipartimento di Scienze Economiche dell'Università di Pisa*, n. 75, http://www.dse.ec.unipi.it/ricerca/collana_studi.asp#FSG

Freni, Giuseppe, Gozzi, Fausto and Salvadori, Neri (2006). 'Existence of optimal strategies in linear multisector models', *Economic Theory*, **29**(1), Sept., pp. 25–48.

Gehrke, Christian and Kurz, Heinz D. (2006). 'Sraffa on von Bortkiewicz: reconstructing the classical theory of value and distribution'. *History of Political Economy*, **38:1**, pp. 91–141.

Kurz, Heinz D. and Salvadori, Neri (1998). *Understanding 'Classical' Economics. Studies in Long-period Theory*. London and New York: Routledge.

Kurz, Heinz D. and Salvadori, Neri (2003). *Classical Economics and Modern Theory. Studies in Long-period Analysis*. London and New York: Routledge.

Kurz, Heinz D. and Salvadori, Neri (2005). 'Representing the production and circulation of commodities in material terms: on Sraffa's objectivism', *Review of Political Economy*, **17:3**, July, pp. 69–97.

Kurz, Heinz D. and Salvadori, Neri (2006). 'Endogenous growth in a stylised "Classical" model', in G. Stathakis and G. Vaggi (eds), *Economic Development and Social Change. Historical Roots and Modern Perspectives*, London: Routledge, pp. 106–124.

Kurz, Heinz D., Pasinetti, Luigi L. and Salvadori, Neri (eds) (2007). *Piero Sraffa: The Man and the Scholar. Exploring his Unpublished Papers*. London: Routledge.

Ricardo, David (1951–1973). *The Works and Correspondence of David Ricardo*, 11 volumes, edited by P. Sraffa with the collaboration of M.H. Dobb, Cambridge: Cambridge University Press.

Sraffa, Piero (1960). *Production of Commodities by Means of Commodities*. Cambridge: Cambridge University Press.

Part I

Classical economics and modern theory

2 Say and Ricardo on value and distribution*

Christian Gehrke and Heinz D. Kurz

1. Say's *Treatise*: bringing Smith to the continent

When Jean-Baptiste Say published his *Traité d'économie politique* (henceforth *Treatise* or *T*) in 1803, economic thinking in England was largely shaped by Smith's *Wealth of Nations*, while in France and some other parts of Continental Europe physiocratic ideas were still predominant. Say, who admittedly had adopted (and adapted) the economics of Adam Smith for the main parts of his *Treatise*, can be credited with having established certain Smithian ideas on the Continent.[1]

However, while Say had indeed borrowed much of his economics from Smith, he had not followed the Scotsman in every respect and had not confined himself to merely popularizing the latter's ideas. First, there were other, mostly French authors, especially Condorcet, Condillac and Turgot (see, for example, *T*: xxxii–xxxvi), who exerted an important influence on Say's thinking. Secondly, beginning with the second edition of the *Treatise* Say put forward criticisms of Smith's *Wealth of Nations*. He stressed five 'principal imperfections' of Smith's doctrine: (1) 'To the labour of man alone he ascribes the power of producing value. This is an error' (*T*: xl); (2) 'By the exclusive restriction of the term *wealth* to values fixed and realized in material substances, Dr Smith has narrowed the boundary of this science' (*T*: xli–xlii, emphasis in the original);[2] (3) 'On the subject of commercial production [he] presents us with only obscure and indistinct notions' (*T*: xlii); (4) 'His work does not furnish a satisfactory or well connected account of the manner in which wealth is distributed in society' (*T*: xlii); and (5) 'By not characterizing the two different kinds of consumption, namely, unproductive and reproductive, he does not satisfactorily demonstrate, that the consumption of values saved and accumulated in order to form capital, is as perfect as the consumption of values which are dissipated' (*T*: xlii–xliii). Say had thus departed from Smith in several respects of his analysis, and in particular with regard to that part which was at the very centre of economic theory: the theory of value and distribution. Say's conceptualization, although undoubtedly inspired by Smith's, was markedly different from it. With its emphasis on 'utility' and on 'supply and

* Reprinted with permission from *Euro. J. History of Economic Thought*, **8:4**, 2001.

demand', the theory of value expounded by Say stressed some elements of Smith's to the neglect of others, with the result that an entirely different theory emerged. As seen below, the same can also be said of Say's explanation of interest and profit.

When Ricardo took up the Smithian heritage in England, he could draw not only on the *WN* but also on the exposition and elaboration of Smithian economics contained in Say's *Treatise*. While Ricardo praised certain aspects of Say's analysis, from the beginning he was critical of other aspects and especially of Say's theory of value and distribution. Early on he pointed out difficulties, inconsistencies and contradictions in Say's analysis, which, in Ricardo's judgement, the latter was incapable of resolving in the successive editions of the *Treatise*.

This paper deals with the differences of opinion between Ricardo and Say in the theory of value and distribution – the main field in dispute between them. Attention is focused on those aspects which, in our interpretation, concern fundamental issues in controversy between the two authors, while other aspects which are considered to be only peripheral to the main theme are set aside. In particular, Say's concept of the 'entrepreneur' will be referred to only in passing (see, therefore, Steiner 1996: 30–35 and 1998b), and we shall not deal with the similar, but by no means identical, views of Say and Ricardo with regard to the 'law of markets'.[3] Since during the time of their acquaintance until Ricardo's untimely death in 1823 Say variously expressed his wish to learn from his British counterpart and to absorb his doctrine,[4] our question will essentially be whether he made progress in this regard. With the possible exception of the law of markets there is indeed no presumption that Say exerted any influence on Ricardo, whilst we have Say's word that things were different the other way round. The question then is to what did this influence amount. Accordingly Ricardo's analysis will serve as a measuring rod of Say's analytical achievements in the theory of value and distribution.[5] Whenever possible we shall let the two authors speak for themselves and keep our comments and interpretation to a minimum.

The structure of the paper is the following. In Section 2 we provide a brief account of Say's first encounters with Ricardo and of the latter's criticism of his work in 1814 and 1815. Significant differences in terms of scope, method and content of the analyses of the two economists are pointed out in Section 3, while Section 4 identifies the main areas of disagreement between Ricardo and Say. In Section 5 we document Ricardo's reactions to Say's attempts to come to grips with his criticisms in the successive editions of his *Treatise*. Section 6 turns to Say's concepts of 'value' and 'riches' which Ricardo considered mistaken. Section 7 deals with the different views of the two authors in the theory of value, the problem of the measure of value and Ricardo's criticism of Say's distinction between 'gross' and 'net revenue'. Section 8 addresses their opposing views in the theory of income distribution, focusing attention on the explanation of rents and profits. Section 9 contains some concluding remarks.

2. The first encounters between Say and Ricardo

Ricardo and Say first met in December 1814,[6] when Say visited Ricardo at Gatcombe Park and the two together went to see Bentham and James Mill at

Ford Abbey. Their meeting had been arranged by Mill, who had informed Ricardo on 24 November 1814:

> Mons. Say, the author of the excellent book with which you are well acquainted, entitled *Economie Politique*, is in this island. It would be a thousand pities that you and he should not see one another.
>
> (Ricardo, *Works*, vol. VI: 156–7)

Say had been commissioned by the French Government to study economic conditions in England and bring back such information as might find useful application in France.[7] Ricardo reported on their meeting in a letter to Malthus of 18 December 1814:

> Monsr. Say . . . does not appear to me to be ready in conversation on the subject on which he has very ably written – and indeed in his book there are many points which I think are very far from being satisfactorily established – yet he is an unaffected agreeable man, and I found him an instructive companion.
>
> (Ricardo, *Works*, vol. VI: 161)[8]

In the same letter Ricardo also expressed his agreement with what was later to become one of Say's best-known propositions:

> Mr. Say, in the new edition of his book [*Traité*, second edition, 1814], . . . supports, I think, very a[bly] the doctrine that demand is regulated by production. Dema[nd] is always an exchange of one commodity for another. . . . Accumulation necessarily increases production and as necessarily increases consumption.
>
> (Ricardo, *Works*, vol. VI: 163–4)

But on the occasion of this meeting Ricardo (and Mill) must also have raised objections to some of Say's 'definitions', because Ricardo was to write to James Mill on 30 August 1815: 'Have you seen Mr Say's Catéchisme D'Economie Politique? . . . I like it very much though he has not altered the definitions to which you and I objected last year' (Ricardo, *Works*, vol. VI: 264–5; see also ibid.: 269). What Ricardo had criticized in the first two editions of Say's *Treatise* becomes clear from a letter to Say of 18 August 1815, in which he observed with regard to Say's *Catéchisme*:

> You have I perceive a little modified the definition of the word *value* as far as it is dependent on utility, but with great diffidence, I observe, that I do not think you have mastered the difficulties which attach to the explanation of that *difficult word*. Utility is certainly the foundation of value, but *the degree of utility can never be the measure by which to estimate value*. A commodity difficult of production will always be more valuable than one which is easily produced although all men should agree that the latter is more useful than the former. A commodity must be useful to have value but the difficulty of its

> production is the true measure of its value. For this reason Iron though more useful is of less value than gold.
>
> (Ricardo, *Works*, vol. VI: 247–8)

In the same letter Ricardo also criticized Say's confounding of value and riches:

> Riches are valuable only as they can procure us enjoyments. That man is most rich, and has most valuables, who can procure in exchange for his commodities, not those things which he himself or the world generally consider as most desireable, because they may possibly be procured at little cost, but those things which are of difficult production, which is always the foundation of great value. It appears to me therefore incorrect to say as you do page 95 that that man is superlatively rich, *although he has few valuables*, who can procure easily or for nothing those things which he wishes to consume.
>
> (Ricardo, *Works*, vol. VI: 248)

Finally, Ricardo commented on a passage in which Say had suggested that an increase of capital could be ascertained by valuing all commodities in the capitalists' inventory at their current prices. As against this Ricardo argued that, 'An increase of capital is to be ascertained only by its power of employing more industry and of adding to the produce of the land and labour of the country' (Ricardo, *Works*, vol. VI: 248–9).

Ricardo's early objections thus concerned three main issues: the theory of value, the distinction between value and riches, and the problem of the measure of value.

3. On differences in scope, method and content

As the early exchange between Say and Ricardo and its reflection in the correspondence of Ricardo with James Mill, Malthus and McCulloch also indicate, their differences of opinion concerned the scope, method and content of economic analysis. As regards scope, Say opted for a Political Economy that was practically useful and this aim, he thought, necessitated the employment of the inductive method (see also Steiner 1996: 25–8; 1998b: 202–6). 'The excellence of this method', we read in the *Treatise*, 'consists in only admitting facts carefully observed, and the consequences rigorously deduced from them' (*T*: xvii). And: 'Political economy, in the same manner as the exact sciences, is composed of a few fundamental principles, and of a great number of corollaries or conclusions, drawn from these principles. It is essential, therefore, that these principles should be strictly deduced from observation' (*T*: xxvi). Say was of the opinion that mathematics had no role to play in the study of economic phenomena and that mathematical calculation was 'the most dangerous of all abstractions' (*T*: xxviii n). Given his concern with practical matters, the time frame of his analysis was often short term.

Ricardo was also interested in establishing principles that could provide guidance to the statesman. However, contrary to Say and notwithstanding his expertise as a highly successful stock jobber, in the theory of value and distribution Ricardo advocated the deductive method of reasoning. In the introduction to the *Treatise* Say criticized him for this:

> It is, perhaps, a well founded objection to Mr. Ricardo, that he sometimes reasons upon abstract principles to which he gives too great a generalization. When once fixed in an hypothesis which cannot be assailed, from its being founded upon observations not called in question, he pushes his reasonings to their remotest consequences, without comparing their results with those of actual experience.
>
> (*T*: xlvii)

In accordance with his deductive bent in the theory of value and distribution, Ricardo did not share Say's view as regards mathematics. This becomes indirectly clear when Ricardo writes about Malthus: 'Another of his great mistakes is I think this; Political Economy he says is not a strict science like the mathematics' (Ricardo, *Works*, vol. VIII: 331). At the same time there is evidence indicating that Ricardo distinguished between different spheres of economic analysis and the ability of the theorist to establish economic laws in them. In his letter to Malthus of 9 October 1820 he specified:

> Political Economy you think is an enquiry into the nature and causes of wealth – I think it should rather be called an enquiry into the laws which determine the division of the produce of industry amongst the classes who concur in its formation. *No law can be laid down respecting quantity, but a tolerably correct one can be laid down respecting proportions.*
>
> (Ricardo, *Works*, vol. VIII: 278)[9]

As regards the determination of value and distribution in a given time and place, Ricardo implied, a law can be formulated. In such a formulation mathematics was of considerable use, as is discernible especially in the chapter 'On value': see, in particular, Ricardo's discussion of the inverse relation between the real wage rate and the rate of profits, his so-called 'fundamental theorem of distribution' (see Blaug [1962]1997:96); and his treatment of fixed capital which shows that he employed the annuity formula in the numerical examples given (see Ricardo, *Works*, vol. I: 54–62). Much of Ricardo's analysis is concerned with analysing the properties of long-period positions of an economic system in conditions of free competition, characterised by a uniform rate of profits and uniform rates of remuneration for each kind of primary factor of production.

Say and Ricardo had somewhat different views of society and its stratification which are reflected in their respective theories. There are passages in Say's writings expressing an essentially harmonious view. However, as we shall see below, he was perfectly aware that the relationship between the different classes of society was conflict-ridden, a fact that found expression in recurrent social unrest. Apparently, he was convinced that Political Economy could help to alleviate, and eventually dissolve, such conflicts of interest. In one place he boldly contended that Political Economy 'satisfactorily proves that the interest[s] of the rich and poor, and of different nations, are not opposed to each other, and that all rivalships are mere folly' (*T*: lix). But his warnings of the selfishness of entrepreneurs and his plea that the state ought to defend the workers against them were more down to earth and reminiscent of Smith's view. In Ricardo, as in Smith before him, social conflicts accounted for a good deal of the thrust of the analysis. The observation that the interests of the different classes of society were not congruent was a common premise of their theoretical edifices and a main explanatory factor of economic and social development. In Ricardo the emphasis was on the conflict of interest between the landed gentry, on the one hand, and the rest of society, on the other, as was reflected, for example, in the controversy about the Corn Laws. He was also concerned, though to a lesser extent, with the conflict between the rising class of industrial, merchant and money capitalists, on the one hand, and workers, on the other.

4. Areas of disagreement between Say and Ricardo

If we now turn to the areas in Political Economy with regard to which Say and Ricardo disagreed in their correspondence and publications, we see that these concerned almost exclusively the following:

(1) the distinction between 'value' and 'riches';
(2) the theory of value, the problem of the measure of value, and the distinction between net and gross revenue; and
(3) the theory of income distribution, especially the explanation of rent and of profits.

There were a few related themes, in particular the impact of machinery on employment and that of agricultural improvements on rents. A careful inspection shows that it was only with regard to the law of markets, later known as 'Say's law', that the two authors were largely in agreement, at least at first sight. Both insisted that acts of saving do not involve a reduction in effective demand for consumption goods, but rather a change from 'unproductive' to 'reproductive consumption'. Hence they concluded that there cannot be a 'general glut' of commodities as was maintained by authors such as Malthus and Simonde de Sismondi. A closer look would reveal, however, significant differences of opinion of the two economists (see Gehrke and Kurz 2001: section VIII). The view that there cannot be a lack of aggregate effective demand was a consequence of the fact that both authors, like the classical economists in general, tended to identify saving and investment. More precisely, they lacked a proper analysis of the interplay of saving and investment.

As regards areas (1)–(3), on which we focus attention, Ricardo's disagreement with Say is all too obvious and not even concealed by his polite and diplomatic ways to refer to this in their correspondence and in print. And, as we have seen, the differences were there right at the beginning of their intellectual encounter and did not go away over time, notwithstanding Say's repeated affirmations that he had absorbed Ricardo's doctrine and had made use of it in the numerous changes between the different editions of the *Treatise*, his magnum opus. While Ricardo took notice of these changes, he felt with an ever increasing astonishment, which was to turn into disenchantment, that the substance of Say's respective arguments, which he thought erroneous or misleading, was basically left untouched. Therefore, his belief in Say's ability to understand his, Ricardo's, doctrine gradually vanished.

Scrutiny shows that the differences of opinion concerned what were then and are today considered to be core fields of Political Economy. Indeed, appearances to the contrary notwithstanding, Ricardo did not endorse the central 'principles' Say advocated, that is, doctrines which the latter had adopted with some adaptations from Smith and which Ricardo had already criticized in Smith. In particular, Ricardo thought that in the theory of value and distribution Say contradicted himself in important respects and that his overall analysis lacked coherence. As to the distinction between net and gross revenue, Ricardo saw Say committing essentially the same error as Smith, an error which derived from the defective theory of value the two authors advocated. According to that theory the price of a commodity equals the added up payments of factor services in its production. This component parts approach to the theory of value misled Smith and Say to contend that all prices would rise or fall as wages rose or fell. The two authors thus missed the constraint binding changes in the distributive variables, given the technical conditions of production, demonstrated by Ricardo. Say emphasized also the importance of utility for prices and argued that the latter were determined by demand and supply. According to Ricardo these propositions were either wrong or vacuous, because the concepts of 'demand' and 'supply' had little or no analytical content. As regards income distribution, Say mixed Smithian ideas such as the one concerning the conflict over wages between master and workmen with his own demand–and–supply approach yielding a compromise which Ricardo found unsound. He criticized Say especially for not having understood the principle of differential rent and, once rent is set aside by focusing attention on marginal (i.e. no-rent) land, that the rate of profits is determined once the real wage rate is known, and that these two distributive variables are inversely related to one another.

All other differences of opinion follow from those rooted in differences in their respective theories of value and distribution. For example, Say very much in the tradition of the physiocrats and Smith maintained that improvements in agriculture would increase rents, whereas Ricardo argued that this was not necessarily the case: it all depended on the particular *form* of improvements under consideration. According to Say the employment of improved machinery could never cause a problem of unemployment. Ricardo in the third edition of the *Principles* showed that there are cases in which the introduction of new machinery was injurious to the labouring classes.

5. Insubstantial modifications: Say's difficulties with Ricardo's theory of value and distribution

Ever since they had first met in 1814 Say felt the need to respond to the objections Ricardo had raised against his doctrines. In the successive revisions of his *Treatise* he explicitly sought to bring his own exposition into conformity with Ricardo's ideas. This process began in 1815, before Ricardo had published his *Principles*,[10] and it continued until Ricardo's death in 1823.

Ricardo reported on Say's reaction to the publication of his *Principles* in a letter to Trower of 23 August 1817:

> Say . . . spoke favourably of my book – was quite sure that *in a few years there would not be a shadow of difference between us*, but he complained that I had made demands too great on the continued exercise of thought on the part of my reader, and had not sufficiently relieved him or assisted him by a few occasional examples, and illustrations, in support of my theory.
>
> (Ricardo, *Works*, vol. VII: 178)

In December 1817 Say informed Ricardo: 'I am still busy correcting my *Traité d'Economie* and I am making much use of your *Principles of Political Economy*' (Ricardo, *Works*, vol. VII: 227).[(1*)] However, instead of a new edition of the *Treatise*, Ricardo was first to receive the French translation of his *Principles* by Constancio, with Say's 'explanatory and critical notes', in December 1818.[11] He commented on them in a letter to Mill of 22 December 1818: 'M Say does not appear to me to have clearly seen the doctrine which I wish to establish' (Ricardo, *Works*, vol. VII: 371). James Mill, in a letter of 24 December 1818, was rather more outspoken:

> I am full of contempt for these notes of Say. . . . *There is not one of your doctrines, that he has seized, or perceives the force of in any degree*. Think of his saying . . . that you have assuredly in the text committed a great error, because in talking of exchangeable value, you have not included profits of stock and rent, as constituent parts. This is to declare, as plainly as words can speak, that *the man knows not in the smallest degree what your book is about*.
>
> (Ricardo, *Works*, vol. VII: 375)[12]

Ricardo's assessment, though expressed less harshly, was substantially the same. In a letter to Mill of 28 December 1818 he said about Say's notes:

> Some of them are ingenious, but *he does not grapple with the real question in dispute, – he makes a shew of answering it, but he completely evades it*. In his note on gross and net revenue [see Say in Ricardo 1819, vol. I: 222–4] – he begs the question; – he first supposes that a part of the revenue received by the labourers is more than their wants require – that is to say is net revenue, and then he says that there is an advantage in increasing the

> gross revenue altho' you do not thereby increase the net revenue. In what I said on that subject I expressly guarded myself, by saying, that Adam Smith had not argued this question on a supposition that by increasing the number of labourers you were increasing the number of human beings susceptible of and enjoying happiness . . . and yet M Say answers my observations by saying that there would be a greater number of human beings enjoying happiness.
>
> (Ricardo, *Works*, vol. VII: 378–9)

Ricardo had contemplated the idea of including a translation of Say's notes in the second edition of his *Principles*, together with his comments on them. But, as he informed Mill, he then decided to drop it and added: 'I think of making no other answer to M Say's observations but that of remarking that *he has left my main position respecting the regulator of rent unanswered*' (Ricardo, *Works*, vol. VII: 379).

In the meantime Say prepared the fourth edition of his *Treatise*.[13] When in October 1819 he sent a copy to Ricardo, he wrote:

> You will see by the corrections I have made, in particular in the first chapters of the second book on the Distribution of Wealth, how useful your criticisms have been for me, since they have obliged me to work again on the most delicate parts of my doctrine. I will consider myself very fortunate if these corrections and several others succeeded in winning you over on the few points where I have had the misfortune not to agree with you.
>
> (Ricardo, *Works*, vol. VIII: 136)[2*]

Ricardo did not consider their differences to be only few and insubstantial. His reaction, in a letter of 11 January 1820, must have disappointed Say:

> Your chapter on value is, I think, greatly improved; but I cannot yet subscribe to all your doctrines on that most difficult part of the science of Political Economy. In that Chapter you appear to have misapprehended a position of mine. I do not say that it is the value of labour which regulates the value of commodities, for that is an opinion I do all in my power to overthrow; but I say that it is the comparative quantity of labour necessary to the production of commodities, which regulates their relative value.
>
> (Ricardo, *Works*, vol. VIII: 149)

Not surprisingly, Ricardo was at a loss to understand how Say could possibly attribute to him the old Smithian view, which Ricardo had long shown to be untenable, that value was regulated by the value of labour, that is, wages, rather than by the quantity of labour 'embodied' in a commodity. To McCulloch Ricardo wrote more frankly, on 23 November 1820:

> I have looked over carefully all the new matter in his fourth edition *without discovering any thing to induce me to alter the opinion which I have given of*

> *the confusion of his ideas respecting value.* Utility, riches, value, according to him are all the same thing. A commodity is more valuable because it is more useful. A man is rich in proportion as he is possessed of value – of utility, and it makes no difference whether commodities are of a low value or of a high value. *Erroneous as I think these views are he has not the merit of uniformly adhering to them*, for he often acknowledges that commodities will fall in value if their cost of production be diminished, altho' they preserve the same utility. The book I think is altogether an able one, but *I am quite convinced that M Say does not see quite through the subject.*
>
> (Ricardo, *Works*, vol. VIII: 298–9)

Say continued to modify his exposition, and when he presented Ricardo with his *Lettres à M. Malthus* in August 1820, he wrote:

> I strongly desire that the explanations I here give of my doctrine of value will satisfy you better than those found in my previous writings. This doctrine seems to me to be suitable for being adopted and further elaborated by you, and I await with impatience the first writings you are going to publish in order to know what you think of it; because I believe to have shown it to be *nothing else but yours only expressed in different words.*
>
> (Ricardo, *Works*, vol. VIII: 280–1)[(3*)]

Ricardo was not of this opinion. In a letter of 4 September 1820 he wrote to Malthus: 'I have seen Say's letters to you . . . I am not convinced by any thing Say says of me – *he does not understand me, and is frequently at variance with himself when value is the subject he treats of*' (Ricardo, *Works*, vol. VIII: 227–8).[14] Malthus for once agreed:

> There are more contradictions in it than those which relate to value, and there are some doctrines, besides those which directly concern me *that appear to me to obscure, rather than to throw light on the general subject.* I cannot agree with him in making no distinction between services and products, in his strange and useless application of the term utility, in his opinions respecting the immateriality of revenues, and in *his mode of reasoning by exclamations* which enable him to stop short when he comes to the stress of the argument.
>
> (Ricardo, *Works*, vol. VIII: 259–60)

Ricardo informed Malthus in a letter of 24 November 1820 that he had written some notes on Say's *Lettres* (which, however, are not extant),

> with which I am by no means pleased. *He is very unjust to me, and evidently does not understand my doctrine;* and for the opinions which we hold in common, he does not give such satisfactory reasons as might I think be advanced.[15] . . . *In Say's works, generally, there is a great mixture of profound*

> *thinking, and of egregious blundering*. What can induce him to persevere in representing utility and value as the same thing?
>
> (Ricardo, *Works*, vol. VIII: 301–2)

And to McCulloch, who had published a review of Prinsep's translation of Say's *Traité* in the *Scotsman*, Ricardo wrote in a letter of 25 April 1821: 'The criticism on Say in the Scotsman is I think very just – *he is certainly very far behind in his knowledge of the present state of the science'* (Ricardo, *Works*, vol. VIII: 374).

When Ricardo presented Say with a copy of the third edition of his *Principles* on 8 May 1821, he pointed out,

> the particular difference which exists between us, respecting the meaning which should be attached to the word 'value'. You use it in the same sense as 'riches' and as 'utility' and it is this part of your valuable work which I am very anxious should have the benefit of your further consideration . . . Allow me also to remark that your work would be much more valuable if you entered more fully into the laws which regulate rent and profit.
>
> (Ricardo, *Works*, vol. VIII: 379–80)

Upon returning from his 'Tour on the Continent' in December 1822 Ricardo reported to Malthus:

> I saw Say several times, but our conversation did not turn much on subjects connected with Political Economy – he never led to those subjects, and I always fancied that he did not much like to talk about them . . . *Neither . . . [Garnier] nor M. Say have succeeded in at all understanding what my opinions are.*
>
> (Ricardo, *Works*, vol. IX: 248–9)

Ricardo gave a similar account in a letter to Trower, and added:

> Speaking to the Duke of Broglie of M Say he observed that he did not appear to him to have the least notion of the doctrines of the New School – *that his notes in the French translation of my book shewed clearly that he did not know what the subject in dispute was.*
>
> (Ricardo, *Works*, vol. IV: 244)

While it is true that Say revised his *Treatise* several times, the modifications he introduced with regard to the central issues that were in dispute between him and Ricardo were insubstantial. A detailed account of these modifications therefore seems dispensable.[16] In the following discussion of these controversial issues we will therefore make use of the English translation of the fourth edition of Say's *Traité* and occasionally draw on the correspondence between the two economists and their other writings.[17]

6. Value and riches

As we noted above, Say's definition of value and riches elicited objections from Ricardo early on. In August 1815 he wrote:

> It appears to me . . . incorrect to say as you do page 95 [of the *Catéchisme*] that that man is superlatively rich, *although he has few valuables*, who can procure easily or for nothing those things which he wishes to consume. He may only wish to consume bread and water and may be able to procure no more. He cannot be so rich as his neighbour who has abundance of valuables which he can exchange for all the luxuries of life, which it [is] his desire to consume. Riches are measured by the quantity of valuables which a man possesses, not by the moderation of his wants.
>
> (Ricardo, *Works*, vol. VI: 248)

Modern readers might be tempted to object that Ricardo's criticism of Say is mistaken, and that there is nothing wrong with saying that a man is 'rich' – *that is*, experiences high 'utility' – when his desires/wants/needs are very limited or modest. If low command over exchange value produces 'bliss' (for such a man), he can well be said to be 'rich' in the above sense although he possesses few valuables. But such an objection would miss Ricardo's point, which is Say's confounding of value and riches. Ricardo made this clear in the final passages of the chapter 'Value and riches' of his *Principles*, where he charged Say with having 'confounded two things which ought always to be kept separate, and which are called by Adam Smith, value in use and value in exchange'. He expounded:

> If by an improved machine I can, with the same quantity of labour, make two pair of stockings instead of one, I in no way impair the *utility* of one pair of stockings, though I diminish their value. If then I had precisely the same quantity of coats, shoes, stockings, and all other things, as before, I should have precisely the same quantity of useful objects, and should therefore be equally rich, if utility were the measure of riches; but I should have a less amount of value, for my stockings would be only half their former value. Utility then is not the measure of exchangeable value.
>
> (Ricardo, *Works*, vol. I: 280 n; emphasis in the original)

In his notes on Ricardo's *Principles* Say responded to Ricardo's criticisms in the chapter on 'Value and riches' in several lengthy notes. To Ricardo's argument that he had made utility the measure of value, and value the measure of utility, Say replied that he indeed considered value to be a measure of utility and that, if two commodities are of the same value, this proves that men derive the same degree of satisfaction from their consumption. He continued:

> I would be very wrong if one could infer from what I have said that when the price of a commodity falls its utility is diminished. The utility of a commodity

> which falls in price approaches the utility of the air, which costs us nothing, although it is extremely useful.
>
> (Say in Ricardo 1819, vol. II: 89)[4*]

It is unclear how Say could consider these statements to be compatible with each other.

Say's response to Ricardo's argument that the confounding of 'riches' and 'value' must lead to contradictions reads as follows:

> The costless action of the natural agents, when it replaces the costly action of men and of capitals, diminishes the value of the product. Since all value is relative, the value of the products cannot fall without increasing the value of the revenues (or of the productive funds from which these revenues are derived). The cheaper the products sell, the richer are the consumers. I have proved elsewhere that the fall of the products resulting from economising in the costs of production does not alter the revenues of the producers.
>
> (Say in Ricardo 1819, vol. II: 92)[5*]

It is not made clear how a fall in the value of commodities, due to the introduction of better methods of production, is compatible with a rise in the 'value of the revenues'. And when Ricardo pointed out that Say, having confounded riches and value, was inconsistent in maintaining that riches are augmented when the value of commodities is reduced because of better methods of production (see Ricardo, *Works*, vol. I: 288), Say replied: 'In the passage cited it is said that *the revenues of society remained the same*; whilst the riches are augmented by all that can be purchased additionally with the same revenue' (Say in Ricardo 1819, vol. II: 97).[6*] Say's 'response' thus consisted in reiterating the statement which had been shown to be inconsistent with his confounding of value and riches. He apparently had not understood Ricardo's argument.

To the sample of inconsistent statements from his *Catéchisme*, by which Ricardo had sought to show him his contradictions, Say responded with a long note in which he introduced the distinction between 'richesses naturelles' and 'richesses sociales'. In the former category he included all things from which utility is derived, including air, sunlight, or the affection of family members, while the latter, with which Political Economy is concerned, comprised only the products of human industry possessed of utility. He then repeated his statement that '*Exchangeable value* and *riches* are synonymes' (Say in Ricardo 1819, vol. II: 99),[7*] and continued:

> Now the main problem is to bring the principles of *Social riches* or Political Economy into a relationship with those of *Natural riches*. If the produce is augmented due to the better use that we make of our land, of our capitals, and of our industry, more utilities (or natural riches) are produced, and at the

> same time the production of social riches appears to be diminished, because the exchangeable value of the product falls. Social riches thus do not follow the same course as natural riches.
>
> (Say in Ricardo 1819, vol. II: 100)[(8*)]

According to Say's view, which appears to be rooted in physiocratic thought, the introduction of new methods of production, and in particular the introduction of machines, is associated with the substitution of 'services productifs', that is, services supplied by productive agents, which are costly, by 'services naturelles', that is, services supplied by nature, which are gratis. 'Richesses naturelles' and 'richesses sociales' may therefore move in different directions. Overlooking this divergence, Say maintained, had prompted Ricardo to advance his unjustified reproach of contradictions in his, Say's, writings. However, the importance of this divergence is far from clear, as Say continued his response with the following statement:

> It remains to identify those who benefit from this augmentation, those who are more rich, not only in terms of natural riches, but also in terms of social riches, in terms of exchangeable values, by this increase in produced utility.
>
> (Say in Ricardo 1819, vol. II: 101–2)[(9*)]

After having first stressed the divergence of 'richesses naturelles' and 'richesses sociales', Say now suddenly asserted that both are augmented simultaneously. According to Say, two cases of an augmentation of riches must be distinguished. The first case is this:

> If, from causes the discussion of which is extraneous to our present argument, the exchangeable value of each bushel of wheat remains constant, in spite of an augmentation in the quantity of wheat produced, the increase in the riches produced goes entirely to the profit of the producers; that is, the proprietors of the funds of capital, the funds of land, and the industrial funds, which generated fivehundred instead of fifty bushels. The revenue derived from these portions of the funds is tenfold.
>
> (Say in Ricardo 1819, vol. II: 102)[(10*)]

No explanation is given how the value of each unit of wheat may remain constant in spite of an augmentation of the quantity produced. Say then contrasted this case with a second one, in which the value of wheat is falling:

> If . . . the exchangeable value of each bushel of wheat has fallen because of the greater quantity produced of it, the profit obtained is still in the proportion of fivehundred to fifty; but this profit is made by the class of consumers, who are richer by what they pay less, that is, by as much as the producers would have had from selling more. Their revenue does not increase tenfold, because they do not spend it entirely on wheat-bread; but the portion of the revenue which

> is ordinarily spent on wheatbread is raised tenfold, and all the portions of the revenue which are raised tenfold, summed up, give a sum that is equal to the value of the product which has increased tenfold, if the price is supposed not to have fallen. In both cases the society thus enjoys an augmentation of values as well as an augmentation of utility.
>
> (Say in Ricardo 1819, vol. II: 102)(11*)

Again, the contradiction pointed out by Ricardo has not been resolved, but merely restated. No wonder, then, that Ricardo did not feel inclined to continue this 'debate'.

Given the unsatisfactory nature of Say's response in his notes, Ricardo saw no reason to withdraw his criticism in the second edition of the *Principles*, despite the changes that Say had made in the third edition of the *Treatise*. And when he rewrote the final part of chapter 20 for the third edition, Ricardo made it clear that no matters of substance were involved: 'M. Say, *notwithstanding the corrections he has made in the fourth and last edition of his work*, "Traité d'Economie Politique," appears to me to have been *singularly unfortunate* in his definition of riches and value' (Ricardo, *Works*, vol. I: 279). The rewriting of the final paragraphs of chapter 20 in the third edition was prompted by the changes made by Say in the fourth edition of his *Treatise*, which made it impossible for Ricardo to retain the extensive citations from the earlier editions. In revising this part, Ricardo now summarized Say's contradictions by confronting inconsistent statements from the fourth edition of the *Treatise* in a series of numbered paragraphs (Ricardo, *Works*, vol. I: 282–3).

In May 1821 Ricardo wrote to Say, informing him that in his new edition he had 'pointed out the particular difference which exists between us, respecting the meaning which should be attached to the word "value". You use it in the same sense as "riches" and as "utility" and it is this part of your valuable work which I am very anxious should have the benefit of your further consideration' (Ricardo, *Works*, vol. VIII: 379). In one of the rewritten passages in chapter 20 Ricardo had asked rhetorically: 'When I give 2000 times more cloth for a pound of gold than I give for a pound of iron, does it prove that I attach 2000 times more utility to gold than I do to iron?' (Ricardo, *Works*, vol. I: 283). To this Say replied in a letter of 19 July 1821:

> No, but if we suppose for a moment that a pound of gold and a pound of iron render a service to man that is perfectly equal in spite of the inequality in their value, then I say that in a pound of iron there are:
>
> 1999 units of natural utility which are a part of riches for which nature does not make us pay, and which do not concern political economy;
>
> and 1 unit of utility created by industry, the capitals and the lands, a utility for which we must pay and which is the only one that contributes to exchangeable riches, the sole object of our investigation.

2000 units of utility altogether, contained in a pound of iron. Whereas in a pound of gold there are:

2000 units of utility, all of which are exchangeable [value] because all of them are the fruits of our industry, our capitals and our lands; utility which is a part not only of our natural riches but also of our *social riches, the only ones with which political economy can be concerned.*

(Ricardo, *Works*, vol. IX: 33–4)(12*)

Ricardo's response was communicated to Say in a letter of 5 March 1822.[18] It is apposite to quote him in full:

> I am happy to observe that the difference between us is much less than I had hitherto considered it. You speak of two different utilities which commodities possess, one, which they derive from nature, without any of the labour of man, the other, which they derive exclusively from his labour. You say that for the first of these, which you call natural utility, nothing valuable can be obtained in exchange, and it is only for that portion of utility which is given to a commodity by labour or industry, for which anything valuable can be obtained... You explain on these principles the case I had put to you of a pound of iron and a pound of gold, which I had supposed had exactly the same utility, though the gold was 2000 times more valuable. If we give 2000 times more for the gold than for the iron, you say, it is because that particular utility of which only Political Economy treats, namely that given by labour, is 2000 times greater than that given to iron, and you add that the iron has 1999 portions of natural utility for which nothing is given; of which the gold has none.
>
> Although I cannot quite approve of the terms used to explain this truth, yet I do now, and always have substantially agreed in the reasoning which proves it, for I have always contended that commodities are valuable in proportion to the quantity of labour bestowed upon them, and when you say that they are valuable in proportion as they are useful, and they are useful in proportion to the quantity of labour or industry bestowed upon them, you are in fact expressing the same opinion in other words.
>
> In your last edition of the 'Catechisme' you say page 2 that the riches of a person are in proportion to the value of the commodities which he possesses, and not in proportion to their quantity: so far you repeat the same opinion, but when your pupil calls upon you to explain what is the measure of the value of things, your [sic] answer that it is the quantity of all other things that the proprietor is enabled to command by their means, if he consents to exchange them. Now in this I think there is a contradiction, for we are told that riches are in proportion to value, and value in proportion to the quantity of things, therefore riches are in proportion to the quantity of things; and yet you say that riches are in proportion to value, and not in proportion to the quantity of things.
>
> (Ricardo, *Works*, vol. IX: 169–70)

Ricardo's letter continues:

> Let us suppose that the same cause, namely, an economical process, which lowers the value of gold one half, lowers at the same time, in the same degree, and by the same means, hats, shoes, cloth and linen. In this state of things a pound of gold will command just as many hats, shoes, cloth, and linen as before any of the economical processes were discovered. I ask is the man equally rich as before who has a pound of gold? *You first answer no, because he has not a commodity of equal value, and you secondly answer yes, because he can command an equal quantity of various other commodities.*
>
> (Ricardo, *Works*, vol. IX: 170)

Touché! This demonstration was Ricardo's final attempt to explain to Say that his concepts of value and riches ended in complete muddle.[19]

7. Theory of value, measure of value, gross and net revenue

According to Say, the utility of a thing 'is the primary source of value' (*T*: 284). He opted for taking the needs and wants of people 'as existing *data*, and reason upon them accordingly' (*T*: 285). Interestingly, Say stressed that only those objects are possessed of a value (in contradistinction to free goods provided by nature, such as air or solar light) which represent utilities necessarily procured by human agency, 'because the very act of production implies an act of mutual exchange, in which the producer has given his personal agency for the product obtained by its exertion' (*T*: 286). Hence, as in Ricardo, the attention focused on produced and reproducible commodities. The producer is said to put up with the productive effort only on the assumption that he receives 'an equivalent' for it.

7.1 Value, its component parts, and utility

Value (or price), Say contended, was governed by 'demand' and 'supply'. He gave these concepts the following analytical meanings. As regards the former, the reference is to 'aggregate demand' for a commodity and it is argued that it depends negatively on the commodity's price. This is due to two effects: first, as the price of the commodity is increased those less well off will gradually have to withdraw from the market: 'the number of its consumers is reduced'; secondly, those who can still afford to buy the product will buy less of it: 'the consumption of each consumer is reduced also' (*T*: 288–9). It seems that Say thought exclusively in terms of the income effect of a change in the price of a commodity; there is at any rate no explicit mentioning of the (relative) price effect. Therefore the passages under consideration must not be interpreted as anticipating the principle of substitution in consumption as developed by marginalist theory.

By 'supply' Say meant the total or aggregate 'supply or amount in circulation', that is, 'the quantity attainable at a given time, and ready for the satisfaction of those who are in want of the specific article' (*T*: 288). He maintained that 'the supply will be more abundant, when the current price is high, and more scanty when that price has declined' (*T*: 290). However, no compelling reason is given why this should be so. At any rate there is no element in Say's discussion resembling the principle of substitution in production as conceptualized by marginalist theory.

Say's reasoning culminated in the proposition that 'the relative intensity of supply and demand . . . is the ground-work of price on every act of exchange'. He stressed: 'Demand and supply are the opposite extremes of the beam, whence depend the scales of dearness and cheapness: the price is the point of equilibrium, where the momentum of the one ceases, and that of the other begins' (*T*: 290). There is a modern ring to this formulation, but there is not yet a sufficiently developed theory behind it. What can at most be said is that Say contributed to shunting the car of economics away from the classical on to a different track which was eventually to lead to marginalist theory.

The link between demand and supply, on the one hand, and cost of production, on the other, Say specified as follows: 'The price paid for every product, at the time of its original attainment or creation, is, the charge of the productive agency exerted, or the cost of its production' (*T*: 298, similarly p. 315). Hence the price of each commodity is composed of, and thus can be resolved into, rents, profits and wages, or rather, as Say preferred to call them, into the '*profit of land*', the '*profit of capital*', and the '*profit of labour*' (*T*: 316–17). With technical progress, cost of production will fall and if, in the short run, the market price remains the same, this will be reflected in a 'larger profit than ordinary in this particular channel'. This above-normal profitability 'is said to naturally attract a larger proportion of productive agency, the exertion of which, by increasing the supply, reduces again the current price to a level with the bare cost of production' (*T*: 298) – and, we may add, brings profitability back to a normal level. Say's argument concerns the 'gravitation' of market prices to their natural levels as contemplated by Smith and the classical English economists (see also Say in Ricardo 1819, vol. I: 79 n; Béraud 1992: 378).[20] The question is whether the new level of profitability equals the old one or is different from it. Say is not clear about this, as his following discussion shows.

The adding-up concept of value is a treacherous ground for the inattentive scholar because he may easily slip into the view that value rises or falls with a rise or fall of each single component. As is well known, Smith in places fell into the trap and so did Say. Thus, like the Scotsman Say was of the opinion that a low (high) wage rate meant low (high) prices. In one place we read:

> In proportion as the value he [the labourer] consumes is small, his ordinary wages may be low, and the product [!] of his labour cheap. If his condition be improved, and his wages raised, either his product becomes dearer to the consumer, or the share of his fellow producers is diminished.
>
> (*T*: 336, similarly p. 339)

As Ricardo was to clarify, a fall (or rise) in the remuneration of any productive factor of necessity involves a rise (or fall) in the remuneration of some other factor, given the technical conditions of production, whereas the variation in the price of a commodity in terms of some standard of value cannot be ascertained a priori, but depends on the technical conditions of production (direct and indirect) of the commodity relative to those of the standard. There is no reason to presume that a lower (higher) real wage generally involves lower (higher) prices of commodities. And it is not true that a higher real wage rate involves 'either' a higher price 'or' a smaller share of some other factor: it always involves the latter.

7.2 Measure of value

This leads directly to the problem of Ricardo's search for an 'invariable measure of value'. Say, like other commentators, had difficulty in understanding the *analytical* significance of this concept. This is not surprising, because without an intimate knowledge of the different steps reflecting Ricardo's consecutive attempts to simplify the problem of distribution and relative prices his concern with an invariable standard was bound to look like chasing a will-o'-the-wisp. According to Sraffa (1951: xxxi–xxxiii), Ricardo proceeded in four steps. The first consisted of eliminating the problem of the rent of land in terms of the theory of differential rent in the *Essay on Profits*, published in 1815 (see Ricardo, *Works*, vol. IV). The second step consisted of trying to get rid of the problem of value in determining the general rate of profits by assuming the 'corn model'. The third step consisted of adopting the labour theory of value. This allowed him to ascertain the values of commodities independently of income distribution and thus helped him to dispel the adding-up doctrine, suggested by Smith and adopted by Say, of price as a sum of wages and profits (and rents). It thereby put into sharp relief the constraint binding changes in the distributive variables. However, as Ricardo became increasingly aware, the labour theory of value could not generally be sustained as a theory of relative prices. This is because with unequal proportions of labour to means of production in different industries and unequal degrees of durability of fixed capital, relative prices would not only depend on the quantities of labour 'embodied' in the various commodities, but also on the level of the rate of profits, and would change with that level: with compound interest the weight of the profit component in prices depends on the rate of profits. Ricardo's search for a measure of value that is 'invariable' with respect to changes in distribution was the final step in his efforts to simplify the theory of distribution.[21]

Say can be expected to have known little about these consecutive attempts and especially about the fact that the concept of a measure that was meant to be invariable with respect to changes in income distribution was essentially a device designed by Ricardo in order to see through the complexities of the dependence of relative prices on the rate of profits. Say objected to the very idea of Ricardo's search for such a measure:

> An invariable measure of value is a pure *chimera*, because one cannot measure values other than in terms of values, that is, by a quantity essentially variable.

> This does not mean that value itself is chimerical; it is no more so than the temperature of bodies, which cannot be fixed beforehand.
>
> (Say in Ricardo 1819, vol. I: 12–13; see also vol. II: 69–70)[(13*)]

This criticism anticipated an objection levelled by Samuel Bailey at Ricardo's concept. As we know today, while Ricardo's idea of a measure that is invariable with regard to changes in the distribution of income can be given a precise expression in well-specified conditions, his overall search was indeed futile (for details, see Kurz and Salvadori 1993).[22]

7.3 Gross and net revenue

Smith was accused of having put forward statements in his discussion of the component parts of value which can be read as confounding gross and net produce. This kind of criticism can certainly be levelled at Say, who stressed vis-à-vis the doctrine of the Physiocrats:

> Whence it appears, that the term *net* product applies only to the individual revenue of each separate producer or [entrepreneur][23] in industry; but that the aggregate of individual revenue, the total revenue of the community, is equal to the *gross* produce of its land, capital, and industry. Which entirely subverts the system of the economists of the last century, who considered nothing but the net produce of the land as forming revenue, and therefore concluded that this net produce was all that the community had to consume, instead of admitting the obvious inference, that the whole of what has been created, may also be consumed by mankind.
>
> (*T*: 318; emphasis in the original)

While Say is justified in criticizing the concept of 'produit net' in the Physiocrats as too narrow, his alternative conceptualization suffers from a confusion with regard to the definition of the net produce. For if the gross produce is defined as the 'total revenue of the community' (or total 'value added'), consisting of wages, profits and rents, then these income components cannot in turn be taken to form the costs of production which must be deducted from the gross produce in order to obtain the net revenue. Ricardo pointed this out in the third edition of the *Principles*:

> Of net produce and gross produce, M. Say speaks as follows: 'The whole value produced is the gross produce; this value, after deducting from it the cost of production, is the net produce.' . . . There can then be no net produce, because the cost of production, according to M. Say, consists of rent, wages, and profits . . . Take a whole from a whole, and nothing remains.
>
> (Ricardo, *Works*, vol. I: 421 n)

8. Theory of income distribution

Say maintained that the problems of value and distribution were of the same nature and therefore had to be dealt with in the same way:

> The causes, which determine the value of things, and which operate in the way described in the preceding chapters, *apply without exception to all things possessed of value . . . amongst others, therefore, to the productive service yielded by industry, capital, and land, in a state of productive activity* . . . [The] relative value [of productive agency], like that of every other commodity, rises in direct ratio to the demand, and inverse ratio to the supply.
>
> (*T*: 314–15)

Therefore, wages, profits and rents are to be explained in terms of demand and supply, where the demand for means of production derives from the demand for products.

8.1 Wages

Much of what Say has to offer on wages he took from Smith, interspersed with a few ideas of his own. These concern the much acclaimed discussion of the specific role of the entrepreneur as opposed to the capitalist in the process of production and the running of a business (*T*: 329–32), and Say's conception of the wages of common labour as a form of profits. As opposed to Smith Say did not reserve the concept of profits to human capital as the result of expensive education and training. He argued: '*A full-grown man is an accumulated capital*; the sum spent in rearing him is indeed consumed, but consumed in a reproductive way, *calculated to yield the product man*' (*T*: 333 n). After this remarkable definition which draws a parallel between the production of commodities and that of men one would expect the investors in this kind of capital to obtain the ordinary rate of return, but this expectation is frustrated: the wages of common labour, Say emphasized, tend to gravitate around an historical and cultural subsistence level, which is taken to be sufficient to maintain also the family of the worker. Say, who again followed Smith closely, provided essentially two reasons in support of this tendency: first, the working of a kind of Malthusian population mechanism which involves a tendency towards an 'excess of population above the means of subsistence' (*T*: 339); secondly, the advantage masters are said to have over workers in the conflict over wages – in this context Say acknowledged the 'conflicting interests of master and workman' (*T*: 338). Hence, the real wage rate of common labour may be taken as given – just as in Smith or Ricardo.

We now come to Say's explanation of profits and of rent. Ricardo's argument, as is well known, typically proceeded in terms of the supposition that there is a quality of land in the economy which is cultivated, but not fully cultivated, and which therefore is not scarce and yields no rent (see Ricardo, *Works*, vol. I: ch. 2). On this quality of land – marginal land – the rate of profit is determined once the real wage rate is known. This was one of Ricardo's analytical devices to see through the complexities of the problem of income distribution and relative prices. Say, as we have seen, in 1815 became acquainted with the *Essay on Profits* which contained already the essence of Ricardo's theory of distribution, and then with the *Principles*, and told Ricardo how much he was impressed with the argument and that he was keen to incorporate it in the *Treatise*. However, when we turn to this work we may begin to understand Ricardo's frustration with the achievements of his admirer. In fact, there is every reason to think that Say had not understood the principle of differential rent and Ricardo's theory of profits. We first turn to the theory of rent.

8.2 Rents

Appearance has it that the mutual difficulties of comprehension of our two authors started at the linguistic level (see Mahieu 1992: 36–7). However, the real causes were deeper and concerned conceptual and analytical issues. In this context it is interesting to note that Say advised Constancio to translate the title of chapter 2 of the *Principles*, 'Of Rent', as 'Du fermage ou Profit des terres' (Ricardo 1819, vol. I: 63), thus re-interpreting Ricardo's concept of rent in terms of his, Say's, own concept of 'profit of land'. This undermined one of the declared aims of Ricardo in this chapter, that is, to distinguish as clearly as possible between the rent of land, on the one hand, and the interest and profit of capital, on the other, and thus to overcome their widespread confounding in the literature (see Ricardo, *Works*, vol. I: 67).[24] Scrutiny shows that in the theory of the rent of land and that of mines, as well as in other fields in dispute between them, we encounter an analytically minded Ricardo, determined to lay down the foundations of the new subject of Political Economy, confronted by a Say incessantly pointing towards 'facts' which he deemed incompatible with the economic principles Ricardo sought to establish. Say's criticism concerned first and foremost Ricardo's doctrine that marginal land (the marginal mine), that is, land (the mine) last cultivated (worked), does not yield a rent to its proprietor. In addition he questioned the possibility of distinguishing with sufficient definiteness between land and capital and thus between rents and profits (see, for example, Say in Ricardo 1819, vol. I: 66–7). In the following we shall first deal with Say's critical notes on Ricardo's theory of rent in the French edition of Ricardo's *Principles* and then turn to the *Treatise*, in which Say presented his alternative conceptualization.

According to Say Ricardo was wrong in assuming that those portions of marginal land (marginal mines) that are cultivated (worked) do not yield a rent to their proprietors. His reasoning is not always very clear but with some effort and goodwill we might perhaps distinguish four objections put forward by him. *First*, he maintained that capital proper and labour required 'la coopération du sol' which in turn would not be granted without a payment – a 'profit foncier' – to the proprietor of the services of land. Hence, in this view rent is the payment to an indispensable factor of production: 'Can it not be said that the proprietors exercise a productive function, because without it there would be no production?' (Say in Ricardo 1819, vol. I: 92 n).(14*),25 *Secondly*, he argued along the lines of Adam Smith that rent is a monopoly price. This is said to be true both with regard to land (see Say in Ricardo 1819, vol. I: 95 n.) and mines. About the owner of a mine he wrote:

> The proprietor . . . has a sort of monopoly which allows him to raise the value of his product above the costs of labour and the interest on the capital that is required to obtain it and bring it to the market. *This monopoly price is reduced by competition, but it cannot, I believe, fall to nothing.*
>
> (Say in Ricardo 1819, vol. I: 112n)(15*)

Unfortunately, Say refrained from telling the reader why competition should be unable to make the rent vanish. In the present context of a discussion of Ricardo's chapter on the rent of mines, that is, exhaustible resources, Say could also have put forward, but did not, an entirely different argument in support of his view that an income has to be paid to the owner of the marginal mine for working it: if he allowed the mine to be exploited without being paid a 'royalty' he would gradually give his asset away without any compensation.[26] Yet, a scrutiny of the relevant passages (see, in particular, Say in Ricardo 1819, vol. I: 112–13 n) shows that there is nothing in Say's reasoning that points in the direction of the concept of royalty.

There is another consideration put forward by Say which, if interpreted favourably, provides some support for his view that the rent of marginal land will generally be positive. This brings us to his *third* objection. To be clear about one possible source of the disagreement between him and Ricardo we need to recall that Ricardo's no-rent-on-marginal-land argument was based on the implicit assumption that landlords have no use for their land other than renting it out to corn producers. Apparently Ricardo saw no harm in setting aside alternative uses of land, given his aim of providing a clear-cut distinction between rent and profit. An important implication of this assumption is that, in modern parlance, the 'reservation price' of the use of land, that is, that price at which the landlord will choose to retain some positive amount of his land, is zero. This is precisely Ricardo's premise with regard to marginal land. Some of Say's objections, who in this regard again followed closely Smith (see also Béraud 1992: 378–9), could perhaps be interpreted as implying that the reservation price of the land service is generally not zero because there are alternative uses of land. He wrote:

> Land is an admirable chemical atelier in which a number of materials and elements combine and collaborate which then leave it in the form of wheat and fruits, from which we obtain our subsistence, of linen, from which we produce our clothes, and of the trees from which we construct our dwellings and ships. . . . It is in this way that the fund of land was able to furnish a tenfold, or a hundredfold quantity of useful products to men.
>
> (Say in Ricardo 1819, vol. I: 82–3 n)(16*)

Say's *fourth* objection was of a similar kind. He argued that whichever plot of land is cultivated is done so because of its characteristic features which distinguish it from all other plots of land available in the economy: 'The land will only be cultivated if the cultivator has been assured of his property; then it is more precious than all the other land of the same quality not yet appropriated' (Say in Ricardo 1819, vol. I: 72 n).[(17*)] However, Say was mistaken in believing that this was a fundamental objection to Ricardo's principle of differential rent. The only difference between Ricardo's original formulation and Say's is that whereas the former assumed that there was a finite number of different qualities of land, the latter may be interpreted as maintaining that the number was infinite.[27] Whether or not marginal land pays a rent and whether or not there is a continuum of different qualities of land, Ricardo's concept of persistent cost differentials in agricultural production and of differential rent based on them is entirely unaffected by Say's criticisms.

In the *Principles* Ricardo contented himself with drawing the reader's attention to the fact that Say obviously had overlooked *intensive* rent: with intensive diminishing returns marginal land may yield a rent to its proprietor: 'By his note to page 182 of the second volume of the French edition [see Ricardo 1819], he [Say] does not appear to be aware that it [the theory of intensive rent] has even been advanced' (Ricardo, *Works*, vol. I: 412 n). Having neglected 'that important doctrine', Say is said to be wrong in assuming 'that he has overturned all the conclusions' which result from his, Ricardo's, theory of rent (Ricardo, *Works*, vol. I: 412 n).[28]

Say's 'realism' and anti-deductivism apparently stood in the way of his coming to grips with the principle of differential rent. This can also be seen in the *Treatise* where Say developed his view against the background of the views of others, especially Destutt de Tracy and Ricardo.[29] He wrote:

> The tenor of their argument is this: the proprietor of land lying waste or fallow having also a capital to dispose of, may, at his pleasure, expend it, either in cultivation, or in some other way. *If he reckons that the cultivation of his land will yield him as large a return as any other investment, he will give it the preference . . .* Well: and what do they infer from this? Why, that cultivation yields no return whatever, beyond the interest of the capital engaged in it; and if so, *what is there left for the profit on the productive powers of the soil? Evidently nothing whatever.*
>
> (*T*: 361–2)

The reader, wondering whether this was meant to be a faithful description of Ricardo's theory of rent, is told by Say: 'I have endeavoured to put the argument in the clearest and most intelligible light'. Then follows the adjunct: 'I have to observe upon it, that it proceeds upon a *partial and imperfect view of the matter*, and upon *a total neglect of the influence of demand in the fixation of value*' (*T*: 362). This criticism is taken to clear the ground for Say's own, that is, 'more complete view of the subject' (ibid.).

Before we turn to the latter we shall briefly comment on the above argument. First, Say focused attention exclusively on *marginal* land. He did not mention once the case of intramarginal, that is, rent-bearing land. He also did not mention Ricardo's distinction between extensive and intensive diminishing returns and extensive and intensive rent. Hence, he did not in the least discuss Ricardo's theory of *differential* rent, let alone put Ricardo's argument 'in the clearest and most intelligible light'. Secondly, we know from Ricardo that if land of the best quality is available in superabundance there can be no rent. However, if the best quality of land is in limited supply, then the total quantity of corn to be brought to the market matters as regards the price of corn and whether a rent will be paid on land of the first (second, third, etc.) quality of land. Therefore, Say's accusation of 'a total neglect of the influence of demand' does not apply to Ricardo's doctrine. Third, despite the obvious shortcomings and indeed quite incomprehensible misinterpretations in his account, Say has glimpsed an important truth with regard to the nature of Ricardo's theory of value and distribution. In a footnote he wrote, specifying a characteristic feature of Ricardo's explanation of all property income, that is, rent, profits and interest: 'According to these writers, *even the interest of capital is not given as the recompense of its concurrence in the business of production*' (*T*: 361n). This is indeed a distinguishing feature of Ricardo's surplus-based approach to the explanation of all shares of income other than wages. Say's claim that 'I have already exposed the fallacy of this opinion' (ibid.) cannot be sustained: simply to contend that profits are the payment for the service of a factor called 'capital' is just that – a contention.[30]

His 'more complete view of the subject' Say introduced in the following terms: 'The productive power of the soil has no value, unless where its products are objects of demand' (*T*: 362). Taking this for granted, he went on to argue that then cultivation will begin, yielding 'the usual rate of interest upon the requisite advances.' He stressed:

> Up to this point, there is no difference between us [i.e. him and Ricardo etc.]. But if any circumstance operate to aggravate the demand beyond this point [?] the value of agricultural product will exceed, and sometimes very greatly exceed, the ordinary rate of interest upon capital; and this excess it is, which constitutes the profit of land, and enables the actual cultivator, when not himself the proprietor, to pay a rent to the proprietor, after having first retained the full interest upon his own advances, and the full recompense of his own industry.
>
> (*T*: 362)

If by 'this point' he meant the amount of product that can be produced using the cost-minimizing method of production to cultivate the entire amount of land of the best quality, then the question is: what is the difference between Say's position and Ricardo's? Ricardo did not deny that if a larger social demand for corn needs to be met, then the price of corn will have to rise. But he did not leave it at that. He indicated by how much the price will have to rise, due to a rise in cost of production, given the technical alternatives and the quantities of the different qualities of land available to cost-minimizing producers. And he showed that the cost differentials between different methods of producing corn used simultaneously hold the key to explaining the level(s) of rent(s) on intramarginal land(s). He also argued that the rate of profits is bound to fall with a rise in the price of corn and the consequent emergence (or rise) of rent(s), given the real wage rate. All this appears to have escaped Say's attention.

In the sequel Say reiterated his view and stressed: 'herein consists the difference between the *profit* and the *rent*: profit is high or low, according to the quantum of the product; rent, according to the quantum of the purchase-money or price' (*T*: 362). By this formulation he may perhaps have meant to appease Ricardo who had insisted, against the adding-up doctrine, that the price of corn is not high because a rent is paid, but a rent is paid because the price of corn is high (Ricardo, *Works*, vol. I: 74). This was a corollary of the principle of differential rent. However, the lack of clarity of Say's above formulation and the rest of his argument in the chapter provide sufficient evidence to maintain that he had not understood that principle. We read, for example, that 'rent is generally fixed at *the highest rate of that profit*' (*T*: 365). This surprising claim is rationalized in terms of the concept of rent as a monopoly price: 'Landed proprietors . . . are enabled to enforce a kind of *monopoly* against the farmers' (ibid.). And: 'Whenever that is the case, the bargain between the land-holder and the tenant must always be greatly in favour of the former' (*T*: 366). This essentially carries over Smith's argument regarding the relative strengths of master and workmen in the conflict over wages to the conflict between landowner and tenant over rent. However, Say was wrong in assuming that some concentration of landed property is incompatible with free competition. And free competition is, of course, perfectly compatible with the existence of rent, as Ricardo's theory of differential rent showed.

8.3 Interest and profits

Say criticized the old scholastic view of usury and the prohibition of taking *interest* as based on a lack of understanding of 'the functions and utility of capital' (*T*: 366) and thus of the function and utility of saving. The interest on a loan of (money) capital is said to be composed of two parts which are not easy to distinguish practically: pure interest and a 'premium of insurance', or risk premium, as an indemnification of the risk the lender incurs (*T*: 344). The former part is said to consist of 'rent paid for the utility and use of capital' (*T*: 348) and to depend on: (1) the size of 'aggregate capital' of a nation, which in turn depends 'on the quantum of previous savings'; and (2) whether there are many or few 'lucrative employments of capital' (*T*: 349). Say enunciated 'the general and eternal law, that the more abundant is the disposable capital, in proportion to the multiplicity of employments, the lower will the interest of borrowed capital fall' (ibid.).

As regards the *profits* of productive capital, Say emphasized the 'extreme difficulty' of distinguishing between 'the profit derivable from the employment of capital', on the one hand, and the 'profit of industry' of the entrepreneur, on the other. Smith and the other classical English economists are accused of having neglected the latter distinction: 'they comprise under the general head of the profit of capital, or stock, as they term it, many items, which evidently belong to the head of the profit of industry' (*T*: 354). We are then told that the rates of profit yielded in different industries depend on 'the relative demand and supply for each mode of employment of capital respectively' (*T*: 356). But what is capital? Say took issue with the view advocated by Smith and others that labour was the first price, the original purchase-money, for all things. He objected that this omits the fact that there is also paid 'the agency and co-operation of the capital employed'. Yet: 'Is not capital itself, they will say, composed of accumulated products – of accumulated labour?' Surprisingly he answered: 'Granted', followed by: 'but [sic!] the value of capital, like that of land, is distinguishable from the value of its productive agency; the value of a field is quite different from that of its annual rent' (*T*: 356). Who has ever disputed this? Of what use are his considerations for an understanding of the factors regulating the ordinary rate of profit? Say appears to have thought that there is a perfect analogy, also reflected in his peculiar terminology, between the 'profit of capital', the 'profit of land' and the 'profit of labour'. He concluded by reiterating his contention that 'the profit of capital, like that of land and the other natural sources, is the *equivalent given for a productive service*, which though distinct from that of human industry, is nevertheless its efficient ally in the production of wealth' (*T*: 357). What is perhaps meant by this 'productive service' is alluded to elsewhere in the *Treatise*, where Say put forward the germs of an explanation of profits in terms of the sacrifices incurred by the saver, his 'forbearance' or, as Nassau W. Senior was to call it, his 'abstinence'. Capital is said to be

> the mere result of *human frugality and forbearance* to exercise the faculty of consuming, which, if fully exerted, would have destroyed products as fast as they were created, and these never could have been the existing property of any one; wherefore, *no one else, but he who has practised this self-denial, can claim the result of it with any show of justice. Frugality is next of kin to the actual creation of products, which confers the most unquestionable of all titles to the property in them.*
>
> (*T*: 293)

Say did not get much beyond the observation that whoever has accumulated capital is entitled to receive profits. And even if his explanation of interest as a compensation of acts of 'self-denial' of the saver were formulated in a more compelling way, it would, of course, be subject to the usual objections put forward against the abstinence theory. In particular, it is not clear in which relation the interest payments obtained by individual saver-investors stand to their individual and thus subjective sentiments of 'forbearance' and 'self-denial', and whether the accumulation of capital does not also generate feelings of pleasure and happiness. Be that as it may, Say's view of interest is in strict contrast to Ricardo's who focused attention on the productive use made of capital and the surplus left over after all necessary costs of production, including the wages of labour, have been deducted from gross outputs.

9. Concluding remarks

As we have seen, at the beginning of their encounter Say acknowledged Ricardo's authority in political economy which is reflected in a submissive tone towards the author of the *Principles*. However, already at the time of his notes to the French edition of that book Say, who orginally had expressed his concern with adapting his doctrine in order to gain Ricardo's approval of it, changed his attitude. After Ricardo's death he openly attacked Ricardo and diminished his achievements. Towards the end of a critical review of McCulloch's 'Discourse on the rise, progress, peculiar objects and importance of Political Economy' in the *Revue Encyclopédique* of 1825 Say wrote about Ricardo: 'I think that his only title to fame is his doctrine of money'. He added: 'Mr McCulloch will perhaps reproach me for not having communicated earlier my views on Ricardo's doctrines.'[(18*)] To excuse himself he mentioned that he did not want to

> cause the slightest affliction to a highly recommendable man, who honoured me with his friendship . . . This is the reason why in the notes which the publishers had asked me to append to the French translation of his book I have touched only cursorily the points on which we disagree. But it will perhaps be seen some day from our correspondence that, *while I avoided to refute him publically, I nonetheless privately fought some battles with him in the interest of truth*.
>
> (Say 1825: 718–19)[(19*)]

Say's more critical stance towards Ricardo is reflected in the fifth edition of his *Traité* (1826), and at one point he also intended to publish his correspondence with Ricardo but then gave up the plan.[31] In his letter to Tooke of 14 May 1825 he explained his change of opinion:

> I have asked Francis Place [the translator] not to consult you with regard to the translation he had carried out of an economic essay and some correspondence between David Ricardo and me . . . I became convinced that the moment was ill-suited for such a publication. I gave up the idea of publishing this piece in England.
>
> (Say 1848: 526)[(20*)]

In his *Cours complet d'économie politique pratique* (1828–9) Say was more outspoken and launched a frontal assault on Ricardo. He admitted that the conversations and correspondence he had with Ricardo, 'have obliged me to work out anew these first principles, and have given me the means to present them with a clarity that would probably never have been reached' (Say 1852, vol. I: 113).[(21*)] However, these improvements did not mean that his position got closer to Ricardo, on the contrary. His major differences with Ricardo concerned the theory of rent (see Say 1852, vol. I: 216–20) and the theory of value. As regards Ricardo's determination of prices in terms of cost of production Say insisted 'that all the productive services are equally suited to all the products' (Say 1852, vol. I: 362).(22*) To the concept of a tendency towards a uniform rate of profits in conditions of free competition he objected: 'This is what I call *metaphysical political economy*. It has no utility whatsoever, because it cannot provide any guidance in practice'(23*) – because there will never be two pieces of land or two firms absolutely equal one to the other. In a footnote he added: 'David Ricardo, in the third edition of his book, appears to be disenchanted that I did not adopt what he considers to be an important doctrine. It is precisely because I do not consider it important that I have not said anything about it. *I only consider important what is useful and applicable'* (Say 1852, vol. II: 68).(24*) And finally, turning to the Ricardian school as a whole, he exclaimed: 'The error of this school is to take each principle too absolutely; and, after having presented it in the form of a theorem, to deduce rigorously consequences which very often do not conform to the facts' (Say 1852, vol. II: 400).(25*)

In one place the author of the *Treatise* wrote about his analysis of the sources of production and of revenue that it leads us 'into the labyrinth of the science of political economy' (*T*: 294). If one had to describe Ricardo's analysis in terms of Say's metaphor, one might say that it was designed to show the reader a way out of that labyrinth.

Acknowledgements

An earlier version of this paper was given at the 'Colloque international Jean-Baptiste Say', Institut des Sciences de l'Homme, Lyon, 26–28 October 2000. We are grateful to the participants of the conference and especially to Pierre Dockès, chairman of the session in which our paper was given, and Joël Ravix, discussant of our paper, for a very lively debate and useful observations. We should also like to thank José Luís Cardoso, Gilbert Faccarello, Geoff Harcourt, Ian Steedman, Philippe Steiner and the referees of *EJHET* for detailed comments and valuable suggestions. English translations are ours; the original French versions of the quoted passages are reproduced below (with a few transformations from ancient to modern French orthography). For suggestions and advice on the translations we should like to thank Astrid Wlach, José Luís Cardoso and, in particular, Gilbert Faccarello. Obviously, the responsibility for the views presented here and any misconceptions that may have remained is entirely ours.

Notes

1 Say had visited Edinburgh and Glasgow in 1814. In the note on his life in his *Oeuvres diverses* we read: 'In Glasgow he was asked to sit down in the chair from which

Adam Smith taught, and it was not without emotion that he told this episode of his journey one day to his audience in the *Conservatoire des Arts et Métiers*' (Say 1848: XI).(26*)

2 Unless otherwise stated, all emphases in quotations were added by us.

3 The latter problem is dealt with in Gehrke and Kurz (2001, section VIII); see also Baumol (1977), Béraud (1992: 474–88) and Steiner (1996: 29 n. 37).

4 However, as Steiner (1996: 22) aptly observed, Say's notes to the French translation of Ricardo's *Principles* published in 1819 marked a rupture in the relationship between the two scholars and showed a Say attacking his declared peer. We shall come back to Say's notes below.

5 For contributions to an assessment of the two authors from a different perspective, see, for example, Béraud (1992), Mahieu (1992: 33–8) and Steiner (1996: 22–35). According to Béraud (ibid.: 507) there have not been many critical studies of Say's contributions to economics.

6 They met again in 1817 and in 1822, on the occasion of Ricardo's visits to Paris.

7 A version of Say's report was published as *De l'Angleterre et des anglais* (1815). In a letter to Say of 24 December 1814 Ricardo wrote: 'The plan for the currency of France which you have sent me to look over differs in no very essential point from that which I recommended to our Bank of England' (Ricardo, *Works*, vol. VI: 165).

8 J.-B. Say wrote of himself: 'I have never been satisfied with my conversation. My second thought is in general better than the first one, and it is unfortunately always the latter which comes about in conversation' – Quoted in *Notice sur J.-B. Say*, prefixed to *Oeuvres diverses* (1848: XV). (27*)

9 Malthus replied on 26 October 1820: 'With regard to your new definition of the objects of Political Economy, I own it appears to me very confined. . . . In the same manner when you reject the consideration of demand and supply in the price of commodities and refer only to the means of supply, you appear to me to look only at half of your subject' (Ricardo, *Works*, vol. VIII: 286). Ricardo's response of 24 November could also have been addressed to Say: 'I do not dispute . . . the influence of demand on the price of corn and on the price of all other things [the reference is obviously to market prices], but supply follows close at its heels, and soon takes the power of regulating prices [the reference is obviously to natural price] in his own hands, and in regulating it he is determined by cost of production. I acknowledge the intervals on which you so exclusively dwell, but still they are only intervals' (ibid.: 302).

10 On 10 September 1815 Say wrote to Ricardo: 'I received these days that interesting little pamphlet [Ricardo's *Essay on Profits*], and I have read it with so much profit that I have made use of it and have cited it in the third edition of my *Traité d'Economie Politique* which I am currently preparing' (Ricardo, *Works*, vol. VI: 270).(28*) In November 1815 James Mill informed Ricardo: 'I have a long letter from our Parisien friend . . . He says he is rectifying his chapters on money to a conformity with your ideas, for the third edition of his book' (ibid.: 321). In July 1817 Say presented Ricardo with a copy of the third edition of his *Treatise*, 'where you will find several corrections, some of which suggested themselves to me from my conversations with you. The following editions will offer some more which I owe to your works. *My theory of value is already much better than the one you have criticized*' (Ricardo, *Works*, vol. VII: 166).(29*)

11 Although the French translation is dated 1819, a copy had reached Ricardo by the middle of December 1818 and Say's notes were discussed in letters between him and Mill of that month (see Ricardo, *Works*, vol. X: 374). In a letter to Ricardo Say explained that he had originally written these notes 'only for my own use. A publisher who had commissioned a translation of the work got knowledge of these notes and pestered me until he had obtained them from me' (Ricardo, *Works*, vol. VIII: 136).(30*)

12 James Mill refers to the following statement in one of Say's notes on Ricardo's chapter 'On value': 'Mr. Ricardo there appears not to have included profits or the interest of capital as a constituent part of the prices of commodities. Consequently, Mr. Ricardo, after Smith, includes in the natural price of commodities neither the interest of capital nor the profits of the land funds which have contributed to their production' (Say in Ricardo 1819, vol. I: 28–9).(31*)

13 In a letter to Pryme, dated Paris, 27 August 1819, Say wrote about the fourth edition: 'It will be more comprehensive, and I hope it will be found more complete and better connected than all the previous ones. The criticisms of Mr. Ricardo have been very useful to me. They have obliged me to elaborate on the doctrine of values as the measure of riches, and to solve, apart from many others, this interesting problem: *How is the low price of products at the origin of the riches of nations?* I have done what I could to make political economy such that there is not any difficulty that cannot be resolved with the help of this fourth edition' (Pryme, 1870: 125–6; emphasis in the original).(32*)

14 He reiterated his assessment in a letter of 9 October 1820 (see Ricardo, *Works*, vol. VIII: 276–7).

15 In one of his notes on John Cazenove's 'A Reply to Mr. Say's Letter to Mr. Malthus' Ricardo observed: 'I am as much dissatisfied as the author with M. Say's defence of the principle which both he and I maintain to be true' (Ricardo, *Works*, vol. X: 410).

16 A summary account of the changes in the successive editions of the *Treatise* is given in Steiner (1998a).

17 As we know from a letter of Say to Prinsep written in May 1821, Say was not very happy with the translation and disliked some of Prinsep's comments on his own doctrines. The translation is indeed not very good, nor are Prinsep's comments, but this does not affect the following rendition of Say's argument.

18 Say had suggested that his letter of 19 July 1821 might be read to the members of the *Political Economy Club*, together with Ricardo's response. Ricardo did so at the next meeting that he attended, on 4 February 1822. At the meeting Say was proposed to be elected as an honorary member and 'The thanks of the Club were voted to both gentlemen for these communications' (Ricardo, *Works*, vol. IX: 172–3 n.).

19 For a different interpretation of the debate, giving some credit to Say, see Steiner (2000: 15–17).

20 The view that in competitive conditions there exists a tendency toward a uniform rate of return on capital (and, more generally, a tendency toward uniform rates of remuneration for each single quality of original factors of production) led the classical economists to distinguish between 'market' or actual values, on the one hand, and 'natural' or normal values, on the other. About the former, these authors maintained, nothing could be said which is of sufficient generality. Therefore, only natural values were considered the legitimate object of scientific inquiry. While Say appears to have accepted the competitive tendency toward uniform rates of remuneration and thus the existence of centres of gravitation of market values, in his later publications he strangely rejected the concept of natural value. In his notes on the French edition of Ricardo's *Principles* he contended: 'The distinction between the natural price and the actual price made by Mr Ricardo, following Adam Smith, appears to me totally chimerical. *In Political Economy there are only actual prices.*' He concluded about Ricardo's argument in chapter 4 of the *Principles:* 'All the rest is hypothetical and of little use in practice' (Say in Ricardo 1819, vol. I: 126–7).(33*) To be clear, only in the actual economy are all prices actual prices, whereas in Political Economy all prices are abstract prices. As a scientific subject, Political Economy cannot do without some concept of normalcy and thus some level of abstraction.

21 Originally, Ricardo was in search of a commodity which at all times would be produced with the same amount of labour. In the third edition of the *Principles* he required that

in addition to this property the perfect measure of value would have to exhibit average proportions of labour to means of production.

22 This fact notwithstanding, Ricardo's concern with defining the average conditions of production under which the different commodities of a given economic system are produced played a useful role in his attempt to render clear how relative prices depended on the level of the rate of profits.

23 The translator, C. R. Prinsep, translated 'entrepreneur' as 'adventurer'.

24 In addition, the fact that the two authors argued against the background of different institutional settings in France and the United Kingdom, respectively, could only contribute to aggravating their problems of communication. See, for example, Ricardo's remark that 'M. Say appears to me to have mistaken the nature and effects of the English land-tax' (Ricardo, *Works*, vol. I: 186).

25 In another passage he draws a parallel between 'la faculté productive du sol' and 'la faculté productive du travail' (Say in Ricardo 1819, vol. I: 95 n.).

26 For a discussion of the relationship between the classical theory of rent and Hotelling's rule in dealing with exhaustible resources, see Kurz and Salvadori (2001).

27 For example, in accordance with von Thünen in *Der isolirte Staat* we might consider a plot of (otherwise homogeneous) land in a particular location as a particular quality of land.

28 On Ricardo on intensive rent, see also Béraud (1992: 386).

29 Interestingly, the translator, C. R. Prinsep, in one of his idiosyncratic footnotes wrote with regard to chapter 2 of the *Principles*: 'This chapter of Ricardo is perhaps the least satisfactory and intelligible of his whole work' (*T*: 361n). While this opinion echoed Say's, it was not confirmed by important contemporary and later authors. On the contrary, the theory of (intensive) rent was taken to be the stuff from which a new theory was elaborated – marginal productivity theory – by generalizing the principle of diminishing returns to all 'factors of production' alike. (For the difficulties the attempted generalization encountered, see, for example, Kurz and Salvadori 1995: ch. 14.)

30 In the above it is assumed that the rate of profit is larger than the minimum rate which according to Ricardo is just enough to compensate the 'risk and trouble' incurred by the capitalist.

31 Steiner (2000: 22) notes that Say rewrote parts of his correspondence for this purpose.

Quotations in the original French

(1*) Je m'occupe toujours à corriger mon *Traité d'Economie* et je fais un grand usage de vos *Principles of Political Economy*.

(2*) Vous verrez par les corrections que j'ai faites, notamment dans les premiers chapitres du Livre 2e sur la Distribution des richesses, combien vos critiques m'ont été utiles, puisqu'elles m'ont obligé à remettre sur le métier les parties les plus délicates de ma doctrine. Je m'estimerais bien heureux si ces corrections et quelques autres parviennent à vous ramener sur les points peu nombreux où j'ai eu le malheur de ne pas me rencontrer avec nous.

(3*) Je désire vivement que les explications que je donne ici de ma doctrine des valeurs, vous satisfasse mieux que celles qui se trouve dans mes précéden[t]s écrits. Cette doctrine me semble maintenant digne d'être adoptée et étendue par vous; et j'attendrai avec impatience les premiers écrits que vous publierez pour savoir ce que vous en pensez; car je crois avoir montré *qu'elle n'est autre que la vôtre en d'autres termes*.

(4*) Mais j'aurais eu très-grand tort si l'on pouvait inférer de ce que j'ai dit, que lorsque le prix d'une chose baisse, son utilité diminue. L'utilité d'une chose qui baisse de prix, se rapproche alors de l'utilité de l'air, qui ne nous coûte rien, quoique fort utile.

(5*) L'action gratuite des agents naturels, quand elle remplace l'action onéreuse des hommes et des capitaux, fait baisser la valeur des produits. Comme toute valeur est relative, la valeur des produits ne peut pas baisser sans que la valeur des revenus (ou des fonds productifs qui donnent ces revenus) n'augmente. Les consommateurs sont d'autant plus riches que les produits sont à meilleur marché. J'ai prouvé ailleurs que la baisse des produits provenant d'une économie dans les frais de production, n'altérait en rien les revenus des producteurs.

(6*) Il est dit dans le passage cité que *les revenus de la société sont restés les mêmes;* car pour les richesses, elles sont augmentées de tout ce qu'on peut acheter de plus avec le même revenu.

(7*) *Valeur échangeable* et *richesse* sont . . . synonymes.

(8*) Maintenant la grande difficulté est de faire concorder les lois de la *Richesse sociale* ou de l'Économie politique, avec celles de la Richesse naturelle. Lorsqu'un produit se multiplie par le meilleur emploi que nous faisons de nos terres, de nos capitaux, et de notre industrie, il y a plus d'utilité (soit de *richesse naturelle*) produite, et en même temps la production de la richesse sociale semble être moindre, puisque la valeur échangeable du produit diminue. La richesse sociale ne suit donc pas la même marche que la richesse naturelle.

(9*) Il reste à connaître quels sont ceux qui profitent de cette augmentation, ceux qui sont plus riches, non seulement en richesses naturelles, mais en richesses sociales, en valeurs échangeables, de tout cet accroissement d'utilité produite.

(10*) Si par des causes dont la discussion est étrangère à l'object de notre spéculation présente, la valeur échangeable de chaque boisseau de blé se soutient, malgré l'augmentation survenue dans la quantité de blé produite, alors l'augmentation de richesse produite est entièrement au profit des producteurs; c'est-à-dire, des propriétaires du fonds capital, du fonds territorial, et du fonds industriel, dont il est sorti cinq cents boisseaux au lieu de cinquante. Le revenu provenant de ces portions de fonds a décuplé.

(11*) Si . . . la valeur échangeable de chaque boisseau de blé a baissé en raison de la plus grande quantité qui en a été produite, le profit obtenu est bien toujours dans la proportion des cinq cents à cinquante; mais ce profit est fait par la classe des consommateurs, lesquels sont aussi riches de ce qu'ils payent de moins, que les producteurs l'auraient été de ce qu'ils auraient vendu de plus. Leur revenu n'a pas décuplé, parce qu'ils ne l'emploient pas tout entier en froment; mais la portion de revenu qu'ils avaient coutume d'employer en froment, a décuplé; et toutes ces portions de revenu ainsi décuplées, se monteraient, si elles étaient réunies, à une somme égale à la valeur décuplée du produit, en supposant qu'il n'eût pas baissé de prix. Dans les deux cas, la société a donc joui d'une augmentation de valeurs comme d'une augmentation d'utilité.

(12*) Non; mais en supposant pour un moment qu'une livre d'or et une livre de fer rendent à l'homme un service parfaitement égal malgré l'inégalité de leur valeur, je dis qu'il y dans une livre de fer:

1999 degrés d'utilité naturelle faisant partie des richesses que la nature ne nous fait pas payer, et qui ne concernent pas l'Economie politique;

et 1 degré d'utilité crée par l'industrie, les capitaux et les terres, utilité que nous payons et qui est la seule qui fasse partie des richesses échangeables, unique objet de nos recherches.

2000 degrés d'utilité en tout, residan[t]s dans une livre de fer. Tandis que dans une livre d'or il y a:

2000 degrés d'utilité tout entière échangeable parce qu'elle est tout entière le fruit de notre industrie, de nos capitaux et de nos terres; utilité qui fait partie, non de nos richesses naturelles, mais de nos *richesses sociales, les seules dont l'Economie politique puisse s'occuper.*

(13*) Une mesure invariable des valeurs, est une pure *chimère*, parce qu'on ne peut mesurer les valeurs que par des valeurs, c'est-à-dire par une quantité essentiellement variable. Il n'en résulte pas que la valeur soit chimérique; elle ne l'est pas plus que la chaleur des corps, qui ne peut pas se fixer davantage.

(14*) Ne peut-on pas dire que [les] propriétaires exercent une fonction productive, puisque sans elle la production n'aurait pas lieu?

(15*) Le propriétaire . . . exerce une espèce de monopole qui lui permet de soutenir la valeur de son produit au-delà des frais de main-d' œuvre, et des intérêts de capitaux nécessaires pour le terminer et le mener sur le marché. *Ce prix-monopole baissé par la concurrence, mais ne saurait, je crois, tomber à rien.*

(16*) La terre est un atelier chimique admirable où se combinent et s'élaborent une foule de matériaux et d'éléments qui en sortent sous la forme de froment, de fruits, propres à notre subsistance, de lin dont nous tissons nos vêtements, d'arbres dont nous construisons nos demeures et nos navires. . . . C'est ainsi qu'un fonds de terre a pu fournir une quantité décuple, centuple, de produits utiles à l'homme.

(17*) Le terrain ne sera cultivé qu'autant qu'on en aura assuré la proprieté au cultivateur; dès lors il a quelque chose de plus précieux que tout autre terrain de même qualité [sic], non encore approprié.

(18*) Je pense que son seul titre de gloire est à sa doctrine des monnaies . . . M. McCulloch me reprochera peut-être de n'avoir pas fait connaître plus tôt ma façon de penser à l'égard des doctrines de Ricardo.

(19*) . . . causer la moindre affliction à un homme aussi recommendable, qui m'honorait de son amitié . . . Aussi n'ai-je touché que très-légèrement dans les notes que les libraires m'ont sollicité d'ajouter à la traduction française de son livre, les points sur lequels nous différions; mais, on verra peut-être quelque jour, par notre correspondance, que, *si j'ai évité de le combattre sous les yeux du public, je soutenais néanmoins à huis clos contre lui, quelques combats dans l'intérêt de la vérité.*

(20*) J'avais prié Francis Place, non de vous consulter sur la traduction qu'il avait entreprise d'un Essay économique et d'une petite correspondance entre David Ricardo et moi . . . Je me suis convaincu que le moment était fort peu propre à une semblable publication. J'ai renoncé à faire paraître ce morceau en Angleterre.

(21*) . . . en m'obligeant à travailler de nouveau ces premiers principes, m'ont fourni les moyens de les présenter avec plus de clarté peut-être qu'on ne l'a jamais fait.

(22*) Il faudrait que tous les services productifs fussent également propres à tous les produits.

(23*) Voilà ce que j'appelle de *l'économie politique métaphysique*. Elle n'a aucune utilité, parce qu'elle ne peut fournir aucune direction dans la pratique.

(24*) David Ricardo dans la 3e édition de son livre, a l'air d'être fâché que je ne me suis pas arrêté sur ce qu'il appelle une importante doctrine. C'est précisément parce que je ne la crois pas importante que je n'en ai rien dit. *Rien ne me parait important que ce qui est utile et applicable.*

(25*) Le tort de cette école est de considérer chaque principe trop absolument; et, après l'avoir énoncé sous la forme d'un théorème, d'en tirer des conséquences rigoureuses, qui, très souvent, ne cadrent pas avec les faits.

(26*) A Glasgow on lui avait demandé de s'asseoir dans la chaire où professait Adam Smith, et ce n'est pas sans èmotion qu'il racontait un jour à ses auditeurs du Conservatoire des Arts et Métiers, cet épisode de son voyage.

(27*) Je n'ai presque jamais été content de ma conversation. Ma seconde pensée est en général meilleure que la première, et malheureusement c'est toujours celle-ci qui se produit dans la conversation.

(28*) J'ai bien reçu dans le tem[p]s cet intéressant opuscule [Ricardo's *Essay on Profits*], et je l'ai lu avec tant de fruit que je l'ai mis à contribution et l'ai cité dans la troisième èdition que je prépare de mon *Traité d'Economie politique.*

(29*) . . . où vous trouverez plusieurs corrections dont quelques-unes m'ont été suggérées par mes conversations avec vous. Les éditions suivantes en offriront bien d'autres encore que je devrai à vos ouvrages. *Ma théorie des valeurs vaut déja mieux que celle que vous avez critiquée.*

(30*) . . . uniquement pour mon usage . . . Un libraire qui f[ai]sait traduire l'ouvrage, a eu connaissance de ces notes et m'a persécuté jusqu'à ce qu'il les ait obtenues de moi.

(31*) M. Ricardo parait n'avoir pas compris là-dedans les pro. ts ou l'intérêt des capitaux comme partie constituante du prix des choses. . . . Par suite M. Ricardo ne comprend point, dans ce qu'il nomme, d'après Smith, le prix naturel des choses, ni l'intérêt du capital, ni les pro. ts du fonds de terre qui ont concouru à leur production.

(32*) Elle sera plus ample et j'espère qu'on la trouvera plus complète et mieux liée que toutes les précédentes. Les critiques de M. Ricardo m'ont été fort utiles. Elles m'ont obligé à approfondir la doctrine des valeurs comme mesure des richesses, et à résoudre, parmi beaucoup d'autres cette importante question: Comment le bas prix des produits fait-il la Richesses des Nations? J'ai fait mon possible, pour que l'Economie politique ne présentât aucune dif. culté qui ne pût être résolue à l'aide de cette 4e Edition.

(33*) La distinction entre le prix naturel et le prix courant que M. Ricardo admet après Smith, paraît être tout-à-fait chimérique. Il n'y a que des prix couran[t]s en Économie politique. . . . Tout le reste est hypothétique et de peu d'usage dans la pratique.

References

Baumol, W. J. [1977] (1999). Say's (at least) eight laws, or what Say and James Mill may really have meant, *Economica* 1977, reprinted in ed. M. Blaug, *Pioneers in Economics*, 15, *Jean Baptiste Say*. Aldershot: Edward Elgar, 106–122.

Béraud, A. (1992). Ricardo, Malthus, Say et les controverses de la 'seconde génération', eds A. Béraud and G. Faccarello. *Nouvelle Histoire de la Pensée Economique*, 1: 365–508.

Blaug, M. [1962] (1997). *Economic Theory in Retrospect*. 5th edn. Cambridge: Cambridge University Press.

Gehrke, C. and Kurz, H. D. (2001). Say and Ricardo, ed. A. Tiran, *Colloque International Jean-Baptiste Say*, Lyon: Presses Universitaires de France.

Kurz, H. D. and Salvadori, N. (1993). The 'Standard Commodity' and Ricardo's search for an 'invariable measure of value', eds M. Baranzini and G. C. Harcourt, *The Dynamics of the Wealth of Nations. Growth, Distribution and Structural Change. Essays in Honour of Luigi Pasinetti*. New York: St Martin's Press, 95–123.

Kurz, H. D. and Salvadori, N. (1995). *Theory of Production. A Long-Period Analysis*. Cambridge: Cambridge University Press.

Kurz, H. D. and Salvadori, N. (2001). Classical economics and the problem of exhaustible resources. *Metroeconomica*, 52 (2): 282–96.

Mahieu, F.-R. (1992). Présentation, in Ricardo (1992), 17–41.

Marx, K. [1867] (1954). *Capital*, vol. I. Moscow: Foreign Languages Publishing House. English translation of *Das Kapital*, vol. I, Hamburg: Meissner.

Pryme, G. (1870). *Autobiographic Recollection of George Pryme, Esq. M.A., sometime Fellow of Trinity College, Professor of Pol. Ec. in the University of Cambridge, & M.P. for the Borough*, ed. by his daughter. Cambridge: Deighton, Bell.

Ricardo, D. (1819). *Des Principes de l'Économie politique, et de l'impôt*, traduit de l'anglais par F. S. Constancio, avec des notes explicatives et critiques, par M. Jean-Baptiste Say. Paris: Aillaud.

Ricardo, D. (1951–73). *The Works and Correspondence of David Ricardo*, ed. P. Sraffa with the collaboration of M. H. Dobb, 11 vols. Cambridge: Cambridge University Press.

Ricardo, D. (1992). *Des principes de l'économie politique et de l'împot*, translated by Cécile Soudan, introduced by François-Régis Mahieu. Paris: Flammarion.

Say, J.-B. (1815). *Catéchisme d'économie politique*. Paris: Crapelet.

Say, J.-B. (1820). *Lettres à M. Malthus, sur différents sujets d'économie politique, notamment sur la cause de la stagnation générale du commerce*. Paris: Bossange.

Say, J.-B. (1825). Examen critique du discours de M. MacCulloch sur l'économie politique, review of J.R. McCulloch: Discourse on the rise, progress, peculiar objects and importance of Political Economy. *Revue Encyclopédique*, 27: 694–719. Reprinted in Say (1848): 261–79.

Say, J.-B. (1848). *Oeuvres diverses de J.-B. Say*. Paris: Guillaumin.

Say, J.-B. [1828–9] (1852). *Cours complet d'économie politique pratique*, 3rd ed. Paris: Guillaumin, vols X and XI of the *Collection des Principaux Economistes*; in the text referred to as vols I and II.

Say, J.-B. [1821] (1967). *Letters to Mr. Malthus on Several Subjects of Political Economy. And on the Cause of the Stagnation of Commerce. To Which is Added: A Catechism of Political Economy or Familiar Conversations on the Manner in which Wealth is Produced, Distributed and Consumed in Society*, translated by John Richter. London: Sherwood, Neely & Jones. Reprint 1967, New York: A.M. Kelley.

Say, J.-B. [1821] (1971). *A Treatise on Political Economy*, translation by C. R. Prinsep of the fourth edition (1819) of *Traité d'économie politique*. Philadelphia: Claxton, Remsen and Haffelfinger. Reprint 1971, New York: A.M. Kelley.

Say, J.-B. (1996). *Cours d'économie politique* et autres essais, ed. and introduced P. Steiner. Paris: Flammarion.

Sraffa, P. (1951). Introduction, in Vol. I of Ricardo, D. (1951–73) *The Works and Correspondence of David Ricardo*, ed. P. Sraffa with the collaboration of M. H. Dobb, 11 vols. Cambridge: Cambridge University Press.

Steiner, P. (1996). Introduction, in Say (1996), 7–35.

Steiner, P. (1998a). The structure of Say's economic writings. *The European Journal of the History of Economic Thought*, 5: 227–49.

Steiner, P. (1998b). J.-B. Say: the entrepreneur, the free-trade doctrine and the theory of income distribution, ed. G. Faccarello. *Studies in the History of French Political Economy: From Bodin to Walras*. London: Routledge, 196–228.

Steiner, P. (2000). La theorie de la production de J.-B. Say, Paper presented at the 'Colloque international Jean-Baptiste Say', Lyon, 26–28 October 2000.

3 Ricardo on agricultural improvements*

A note

Christian Gehrke, Heinz D. Kurz and Neri Salvadori

1. Introduction

Ricardo's discussion of different forms of technical progress and their implications for the distribution of the product between workers, capitalists and landlords in Chapter 2 of the *Principles* (Ricardo, [1817] 1951) attracted the attention of major economists, including John Stuart Mill, Marx, Marshall and Wicksell. However, the numerical examples he put forward to illustrate what we may, for short, call 'land saving' and 'capital (*alias* labour) saving' technical progress generally met with fierce criticism. According to Edwin Cannan, Ricardo 'is absolutely and almost obviously wrong' with regard to the second kind of improvements and his reasoning is said to end 'in complete and hopeless failure' ([1893] 1967, pp. 259–60). Essentially the same criticism was reiterated some fifty years later by Harry G. Johnson who called Ricardo's second numerical example 'erroneous' (Johnson, 1948, p. 792).[1]

In this note we shall argue that Ricardo was not wrong in any substantive sense. He could only be criticized for having changed the definition of rent, which implied a change as regards the timing of its payment from *post* to *ante factum*, when proceeding from one numerical example to the next; alas, without explicitly noting, nor perhaps even noticing, the implication. We shall begin, in Section II, with a summary account of Ricardo's argument. Section III then provides an interpretation of Ricardo's two numerical examples in which each of them emerges as fully correct.

2. Two kinds of agricultural improvements

In Chapter 2 of the *Principles* Ricardo elaborated the concept of differential rent and then pointed out 'the effects of the natural progress of wealth and population on rent, in a country in which the land is of variously productive powers' (1951, p. 78), on the assumption that there is no technical progress. It is only in a second

* Reprinted with permission from *Scottish Journal of Political Economy*, Vol. 50, No. 3, 2003.

step that he addressed the problem of the impact of improvements in agriculture on distribution. He wrote:

> But improvements in agriculture are of two kinds: those which increase the productive powers of the land, and those which enable us, by improving our machinery, to obtain its produce with less labour. They both lead to a fall in the price of raw produce; they both affect rent, but they do not affect it equally. (*Ibid.*, p. 80)

He thus distinguished between what may be called 'land saving' and 'capital saving' progress. Both kinds are invariably characterised by what he considered to be 'the essential quality of an improvement', that is, 'to diminish the quantity of labour before required to produce a commodity' (*ibid.*).

Land saving improvements

Ricardo mentioned as examples of the land saving kind a more skilful rotation of crops and a better choice of manure, and concluded: 'These improvements absolutely enable us to obtain the same produce from a smaller quantity of land' (*ibid.*). He illustrated this kind of improvement in terms of the following numerical example:

> If, for example, the successive portions of capital yielded 100, 90, 80, 70; whilst I employed four portions, my rent would be 60, or the difference between

70 and 100 = 30		100
70 and 90 = 20		90
70 and 80 = 10	whilst the produce	80
60	would be 340	70
		340

> and while I employed these portions, the rent would remain the same, although the produce of each should have an equal augmentation. If, instead of 100, 90, 80, 70, the produce should be increased to 125, 115, 105, 95, the rent would still be 60, or the difference between

95 and 125 = 30		125
95 and 115 = 20	whilst the produce	115
95 and 105 = 10	would be increased	105
60	to 440	95
		440

> But with such an increase of produce, without an increase of demand, there could be no motive for employing so much capital on the land; one portion

> would be withdrawn, and consequently the last portion of capital would yield 105 instead of 95, and rent would fall to 30, or the difference between

105 and 125 = 20	whilst the produce will be	125
105 and 115 = 10	still adequate to the wants	115
	of the population, for it would be 345 quarters, or	105
30		345

> the demand being only for 340 quarters.
>
> (*Ibid*., pp. 81–2)

The example is skilfully constructed and has been approved of by most commentators. The third portion of capital, which is the marginal portion in the post-improvement situation, will not be fully needed in order to match effectual demand, which is taken to be unaltered.[2] What matters *here* according to Ricardo is the preservation of the *differences* between the different amounts of *output*, reckoned in terms of corn, generated by the *same* amounts of *capital*, irrespective of how the latter is measured.

Capital saving improvements

About capital saving improvements Ricardo wrote:

> But there are improvements which may lower the relative value of produce without lowering the *corn rent*, though they will lower the *money rent of land*. Such improvements do not increase the productive powers of the land; but they enable us to obtain its produce with less labour. They are rather directed to the formation of the capital applied to the land, than to the cultivation of the land itself. . . . Less capital, which is the same thing as less labour, will be employed on the land; but to obtain the same produce, less land cannot be cultivated.

He continued:

> Whether improvements of this kind, however, affect *corn rent*, must depend on the question, whether the difference between the produce obtained by the employment of different portions of capital be increased, stationary, or diminished. If four portions of capital, 50, 60, 70, 80, be employed on the land, giving each the same results, and any improvement in the formation of such capital should enable me to withdraw 5 from each, so that they should be 45, 55, 65, and 75, no alteration would take place in the *corn rent*; but if the improvements were such as to enable me to make the whole saving on that portion of capital, which is least productively employed, *corn rent* would immediately fall, *because the difference between the capital most productive, and the capital least productive, would be diminished; and it is this difference which constitutes rent.*
>
> (*Ibid*., pp. 82–3; emphases added)

Apparently, with the emphasis on corn rent Ricardo in this example reckoned capital in terms of corn. Let us call the four different portions of capital considered capitals 1, 2, 3 and 4, respectively, where the employments are ranked in decreasing order of productivity. Capital 4 is obviously that portion of capital which does not pay a rent to the owner of land. The message Ricardo intended to convey in terms of the above numerical example is plain and simple: rent is a *differential* rent; both before and after the improvement capital 1 pays a corn rent of 30 $(= 80 - 50 = 75 - 45)$, capital 2 of 20 $(= 80 - 60 = 75 - 55)$, and capital 3 of 10 $(= 80 - 70 = 75 - 65)$. Total output is the same before and after the improvement and so is total corn rent which amounts to 60 $(= 30 + 20 + 10)$, whereas total capital reckoned in terms of corn has fallen from 260 $(= 80+70+60+50)$ to 240 $(= 75+65+55+45)$. What matters *now* according to Ricardo is the preservation of the *differences* between the different amounts of *capital*, reckoned in terms of corn, needed to generate the *same* amounts of *output*.

3. Interpreting the two examples

It needs to be clarified that each of the two examples can be interpreted in such a way that it emerges as a fully correct illustration of the respective case under consideration. However, the two interpretations are based on different definitions of rent which involve different assumptions as regards the timing of the payment of rent. In fact, in order to be coherent, in the first example one has to assume that rent is paid *post factum*, whereas in the second example it has to be taken as paid *ante factum*. A simple mathematical formulation can render this clear.

If equal amounts of capital K are employed and obtain decreasing amounts of product $X_j (j = 1, 2, \ldots, n;\ X_1 > X_2 > \ldots > X_n)$ (reflecting the scarcity of the land(s)), and if the corresponding rents Q_j are paid *post factum*, then the following equations must hold

$$(1 + r)K + Q_j = X_j. \qquad j = 1, 2, \ldots, n$$

With the marginal portion of capital n paying no rent, $Q_n = 0$, and therefore:

$$(1 + r)K = X_n$$

$$r = \frac{X_n}{K} - 1$$

$$Q_j = X_j - X_n,$$

exactly as in Ricardo's first example.

In contradistinction, if additional amounts of product of equal size X are obtained by increasing amounts of capital K_j $(j = 1, 2, \ldots, n;\ K_1 < K_2 < \ldots < K_n)$ (again reflecting the scarcity of land(s)), and if the corresponding rents Q_j are paid *ante factum*, then the following equations must hold:

$$(1+r)K_j + (1+r)Q_j = X. \qquad j = 1, 2, \ldots, n$$

With $Q_n = 0$, then:

$$(1+r)K_n = X$$

$$r = \frac{X}{K_n} - 1$$

$$Q_j = K_n - K_j,$$

exactly as in Ricardo's second example.

Of course, the reader generally expects an author to be consistent and not to change some basic definition in the course of the development of an argument. Therefore, it should come as no surprise that most critics interpreted both numerical examples in terms of the definition of rent Ricardo put forward at the beginning of the Chapter 'On Rent'. He stressed: 'rent is *always* the *difference between the produce* obtained by the employment of two equal quantities of capital and labour' (Ricardo, 1951, p. 71; emphases added). This definition implies that rent is paid *post factum*. Contrary to his claim, Ricardo did not, however, 'always' define rent in this way, for in his second numerical example he explicitly took it as being constituted by 'the *difference between the capital* most productive, and the capital least productive' (*ibid.*, pp. 82–3; emphasis added) – a definition which implies *ante factum* payment of rent.

We can only speculate why Ricardo in the second example did not employ his usual definition of rent. Perhaps he was not conscious of the fact that the two definitions are not equivalent. Perhaps he was fascinated by the idea of a symmetry between differences in inputs (capital) producing the same output, on the one hand, and differences in outputs (product) produced by the same inputs, on the other, as the basis of differential rent. Perhaps he thought that changing the definition of rent was not all that important and could be justified in terms of the simplicity of the second example. As he pointed out in the context of some other numerical examples:

> In all these calculations I have been desirous only to elucidate the principle, and it is scarcely necessary to observe, that *my whole basis is assumed at random, and merely for the purpose of exemplification*. The results though different in degree, would have been the same in principle, however accurately I might have stated the [details]. My object has been to simplify the subject....
> (1951, pp. 121–22; emphasis added)

Be that as it may, while Ricardo's change of the definition of rent is unfortunate, this does not imply that his analysis is useless or even wrong, as some of his critics maintained. The fact that Ricardo was able to provide a satisfactory illustration of the case of land saving improvements in which rent is paid *post factum* may suggest that an example can also easily be constructed on the same premiss in the case of capital saving improvements. Indeed, a simple modification of his first example does the job. In that example, the 'portion of capital' Ricardo speaks of is not further specified, say, in terms of a given amount of corn (or money). Let us then assume that a 'portion of capital' equals 50 units of corn before the improvement and 45 units after the improvement, taking all other magnitudes mentioned in the example relating to the pre-improvement situation as unchanged. Hence the improvement increases the rate of profits, which is always determined with regard to the employment of that portion of capital that pays no rent to the owner of land, from 2/5 to 5/9. At the same time the improvement leaves total corn rent unchanged, as required by Ricardo, and decreases 'money' rent (that is, the rent in terms of the labour bestowed on it) as a consequence of the reduction of the price of corn in terms of labour by ten per cent.[3]

We may conclude by saying that Edwin Cannan's criticism cited at the beginning of this note, while not without some justification, is certainly 'over the top' and cannot be sustained.

Acknowledgements

The authors would like to express their gratitude to Mark Blaug, Denis O'Brien, Pierangelo Garegnani and Ian Steedman for valuable comments on a related paper by two of the present authors. The useful remarks of two anonymous referees are gratefully acknowledged. All remaining misconceptions are, of course, entirely the responsibility of the authors.

Notes

1 Cannan's criticism of Ricardo's second example was also shared by Mark Blaug ([1967] 1997, p. 113), Denis O'Brien (1975, pp. 128–9) and Paul A. Samuelson (1977, p. 521).

2 John Stuart Mill in his numerical illustration of land saving improvements (see Mill, [1848] 1987, pp. 717–18) by inadvertence constructed an example in which the post-improvement marginal land is fully employed. In this case competition amongst landlords need not suffice to make the rent on this quality of land vanish: it is possible that the marginal land yields its proprietors a positive rent (although this is not necessarily the case). Ricardo avoided the trap into which Mill fell.

3 Ricardo considered gold (money) to be an invariable measure of value that is always produced by means of the same quantity of (direct and indirect) labour per ounce. A reduction in the amount of labour needed to produce a bushel of corn on marginal land therefore implied a proportional reduction in the money price of corn.

References

Blaug, M. ([1967] 1997). *Economic Theory in Retrospect.* 5th edn. Cambridge and New York: Cambridge University Press.

Cannan, E. ([1893] 1967). *A History of the Theories of Production and Distribution in English Political Economy from 1776–1848*. London: P.S. King. Reprint 1967, New York: Augustus M. Kelley.

Johnson, H. G. (1948). An error in Ricardo's exposition of his theory of rent. *Quarterly Journal of Economics*, 62, pp. 792–3.

Mill, J. S. ([1848] 1987). *Principles of Political Economy*, first ed. 1848; new ed. by W. J. Ashley 1909. London, New York: Longmans, Green & Company. Reprint 1987, Fairfield, NJ: Augustus M. Kelley.

O'Brien, D. (1975). *The Classical Economists*. Oxford: Oxford University Press.

Ricardo, D. ([1817] 1951). *On the Principles of Political Economy and Taxation*. Vol. I *of The Works Correspondence of David Ricardo*, edited by P. Sraffa with the collaboration of M. H. Dobb. Cambridge: Cambridge University Press.

Samuelson, P. A. (1977). Correcting the Ricardo error spotted in Harry Johnson's maiden paper. *Quarterly Journal of Economics*, 91, pp. 519–30.

4 One theory or two?*

Walras's critique of Ricardo

Heinz D. Kurz and Neri Salvadori

There are essentially two views about the development of economic theory. According to the one that nowadays appears to be almost universally accepted, the history of economic theory is a one-way avenue leading from primitive conceptualizations of the demand and supply approach to all sorts of economic phenomena to ever more sophisticated ones, merely leaving behind errors of reasoning and unnecessarily restrictive assumptions. According to the alternative view, the history of our subject is not characterized by a linear development. A theory that once dominated the discussion rather tends to get abandoned for a variety of reasons, some of which are internal to that theory and concern its scope and coherence, while others are external to it and concern its ability to explain the facts. A theory may be replaced by fundamentally different ones: a theory may be "submerged and forgotten" at some stage, as one commentator remarked perceptively; it need not, but may, come back at a later stage, especially when new formulations of the theory succeed in overcoming the difficulties encountered by its earlier versions.

In this essay we will attempt to support the discontinuity thesis by considering an important episode in the history of our subject: the abandonment of the classical approach to the theory of value and distribution for what is now known as the neoclassical approach. More specifically, we shall deal with Léon Walras's "Exposition and Refutation of the English Theory," by which Walras meant the theory of the classical economists, paying special attention to David Ricardo's contribution, in lessons 38–40 of part 7 of Walras's *Elements of Pure Economics* ([1874–77] 1954). To the best of our knowledge these lessons have never received the attention they deserve. Holding an early variant of the Whig point of view, the strategy of Walras's criticism was obvious. Three objections were leveled at the classical authors: (1) Walras accused them of having committed "fundamental errors"; (2) to the extent to which their argument can be said to have been correct, he took it to cover but special cases of a more general analysis; and, closely related to the second objection, (3) Ricardo and his followers were criticized for failing to develop, and indeed failing to see the very possibility of developing, "a unified general theory to determine the prices of all productive services in the same way" (416).[1]

* Reprinted with permission from *History of Political Economy*, 34:2, 2002.

Such a unified general theory, Walras contended, had been elaborated by himself by generalizing the principle of "scarcity," which the classical economists had limited to natural resources, to *all* goods and factors of production alike.[2]

In this article we shall scrutinize Walras's objections. In particular, we shall ask whether Ricardo's analysis can at best be interpreted as a special case of Walras's own analysis, as the Lausanne economist maintained. Is there only one theory, or are there two? We shall see that while some of Walras's criticisms are correct, his main premise cannot be sustained: there *is* a distinct classical approach to the theory of value and distribution that is fundamentally different from Walras's neoclassical one. This fact, as we will show, is reflected in some remarkable differences between what Ricardo wrote as opposed to what Walras interpreted him to have written.[3] Moreover, since Walras based his criticism on a reconstruction of Ricardo's argument, we must closely inspect that reconstruction and compare it with more recent ones. We shall in particular refer to the reformulations of Ricardo's rent theory by Nicholas Kaldor (1955–56), Paul A. Samuelson (1959), and Luigi Pasinetti (1960), and especially to Piero Sraffa's interpretation of the classical economists and Ricardo (Sraffa 1951, 1960), and ask whether the difficulties and contradictions of Walras's interpretation are avoided in the available alternative ones.[4]

The composition of the main part of the essay follows closely the structure of Walras's criticism of the classical economists. Section 1 sets the stage by providing a summary of what we consider to be some of the main differences between the classical approach and the Walrasian variant of the neoclassical approach to the long-period theory of value and distribution. This provides the foil against which our argument is developed. Section 2 deals with lesson 38, which is devoted to the classical theory of value. The subject of lesson 39, Ricardo's theory of rent, will be discussed in section 3. Finally, section 4 turns to Walras's disquisition on the classical theory of wages and interest in lesson 40. Section 5 contains some concluding remarks.[5]

1. Classical vs. neoclassical theories of value and distribution

Following Sraffa, the working hypothesis of this article is that Ricardo advocated an approach to the theory of value and distribution that differs fundamentally from the neoclassical approach and thus also Walras's.[6] The difference becomes clear from a reconstruction of the sets of data, or independent variables, from which the two theories typically begin their reasoning. Notwithstanding several differences between different authors, in the interpretation under consideration the classical economists and Ricardo can be said to have approached the problem of value and distribution in a given place and time on the basis of the following givens:

(R1) the set of technical alternatives available to cost-minimizing producers;
(R2) the size and composition of the social product, reflecting the needs and wants of the different classes of society and the requirements of reproduction and capital accumulation;

(R3) the ruling real wage rate for common labor; and
(R4) the quantities of the different qualities of land available and the known stocks of depletable resources, such as mineral deposits.

Scrutiny shows that the data from which Walras typically started in his fully developed general equilibrium analysis are, on the contrary:

(W1) the set of technical alternatives available to cost-minimizing producers;
(W2) the preferences of consumers; and
(W3) the initial endowments of the economy with all productive resources, including "capital goods proper," and the distribution of property rights among individual agents.

A crucial difference between the two authors appears to be methodological. In the theory of value and distribution, Ricardo, like the physiocrats and the other classical economists, referred to data and magnitudes that can, in principle, be observed, measured, or calculated. These authors refrained from having recourse to any nonobservable, nonmeasurable, or noncalculable magnitudes, or concepts that they considered metaphysical, in determining the general rate of profit and relative prices. What the classical economists treated as data or independent variables in the theory of value and distribution, they regarded as unknowns or dependent variables in other parts of their analyses, in particular in their analysis of capital accumulation and technical and social change. Thus, when determining the rate of profit and relative prices in given conditions, they assumed the size and composition of the social product to be given, whereas when discussing socioeconomic development and structural change, the latter were naturally treated as variables. Ricardo and the other classical authors studied the long-run impact of socioeconomic development and structural change on income distribution and relative prices essentially through comparisons of successive long-period positions of the economy, conceived of as centers of gravitation of the respective "market" levels of prices and dependent distributive variables. Economic change was analyzed in terms of changes in the sets of data (R1)–(R4). For example, when, in a "progressive" state of affairs, the total amount of corn to be produced rose, other things being equal, then datum (R2) changed, with the possible consequence that extensive or intensive diminishing returns might have made themselves felt and led to the emergence of differential rents. In this case, with the real wage rate constant, the general rate of profit was bound to fall.

Another crucial feature that distinguishes the Ricardian approach to the theory of value and distribution from the Walrasian one is that in the former the wage rate is considered an independent variable. Closely related to this is the fact that in Ricardo, but not in Walras, there are no initial endowments of capital goods. Therefore, in Ricardo the rate of profit is not explained in terms of the relative "scarcity" of a factor "capital." It is this *asymmetric* treatment of the distributive variables, with profits as a dependent residual, that indicates an important difference between classical and neoclassical theory.[7]

As we have argued elsewhere (see Kurz and Salvadori 1995, 439–41), Walras up to the fourth edition of the *Elements* thought that a uniform "rate of net income," his term for the rate of profit, and thus a long-period equilibrium could be determined starting from a definition of the economy's endowment of capital in terms of quantities of physically specified capital goods. However, by the time of the fourth edition he became aware of the fact that this was not generally true; see the newly inserted section 267 of lesson 28 (308). Hence, the physical capital stock inherited by the economy will in general be incompatible with an "equilibrium" as originally conceptualized by Walras. In these circumstances only the existence of a sort of "temporary equilibrium" could be established, or, in the words of one of the referees of our essay, an equilibrium at a given point in time. We also agree with the referee that this eventually involved the development of a time framework different from the classical economists' frame.[8] Here it suffices to note that in Walras's criticism of Ricardo the distinct time conceptualization played no role: he accepted the long-period framework encountered in Ricardo.[9]

We want to show in the following that the above distinction between two kinds of theories of value and distribution in terms of the different sets of data from which they start makes perfect sense. This view is implicitly corroborated by some earlier neoclassical economists, especially Walras, who had difficulties in coming to grips with the analytical structure of the classical theory of value and distribution. These authors were inclined to interpret the latter as a special case of their own theory. There is an obvious way of deciding this claim. If the classical theory were a special case, it would start from the *same* set of data (W1)–(W3) but impose special restrictions on this set. Yet the neoclassical critics of classical theory, most notably Walras, were not able to demonstrate this. Somehow they themselves appeared to have felt that the special-case interpretation was not fully compatible with the evidence under discussion. As we shall see, this is reflected in the different kind of criticism, put forward, inter alia, by William Stanley Jevons and Walras, that the classical authors attempted to determine two unknowns from a single equation, meaning that they attempted to determine both the rate of profit and total output in terms of a single equation. This accusation of under-determinacy is clearly at odds with the special-case interpretation. As will be shown, given the different analytical structure of the classical theory, there is no problem of underdeterminacy. Raised by the neoclassical critics, the alleged problem of underdeterminacy may rather be interpreted as indicating that there are two different theories of value and not just one.

2. Walras on the Ricardian theory of value

Walras introduced lesson 38 with a compliment to the classical authors: "The efforts of the English School to develop a theory of rent, wages and interest were far more sustained and thorough than those of the various French schools that came into existence after the Physiocrats" (398). Next he recalled the Ricardian distinction between (1) "commodities, the value of which is determined by their scarcity alone," because no "labour can increase the quantity of such goods, and therefore their value . . . varies with the varying wealth and inclinations of those who are desirous to possess them"; and (2) commodities that "are procured by labour . . . and . . . may be multiplied, not in one country alone, but in many, almost without any assignable limit, if we are disposed to bestow the labour necessary to obtain them" (Ricardo 1951–73, 1:12; henceforth *Works*.). In addition he quoted a statement by John Stuart Mill, who had contended with regard to commodities of the second class that "there need be no limit to the multiplication of the products" (Mill [1848] 1909, 444).

Two "fundamental errors"

Walras saw "two fundamental errors which must be refuted" (399). First, "there are no products that can be multiplied without limit" because "all things constituting social wealth consist of land or personal faculties or the products of the services of land and personal faculties." However, "land exists in limited quantities only. If that is also true of human faculties, how can products be multiplied without limit?" (399). Second, there is no "value of costs of production, which, having itself been determined, determines in turn the selling prices of products." The causality is rather said to be "the other way round" (399).

As to the first "fundamental error," Ricardo cannot be accused of having committed it: he spoke explicitly of commodities that "may be multiplied, not in one country alone, but in many, *almost* without any assignable limit." A proper target of Walras's criticism was Mill's statement, not Ricardo's. Ricardo was well aware of the fact that the quantities of the (reproducible) commodities effectually demanded generally have an impact on prices (and income distribution). The whole point of his theory of rent was indeed the dependence of the cost and thus the price of corn on the quantity of corn produced. In a letter to Thomas Malthus dated 9 October 1820 Ricardo wrote: "You say demand and supply regulates value—this, I think, is saying nothing. . . . it is supply which regulates value—and supply is itself controlled by comparative cost of production" (*Works*, 8:279).[10] Demand may affect prices in the long run only insofar as it affects data (R1)–(R4), especially (R2).

In Ricardo's view, demand and supply regulate the "market" prices of commodities, whereas the normal or "natural" prices are the prices that obtain in a cost-minimizing system of production, given data (R1)–(R4). It also deserves to be noted that the case on which Ricardo focused attention is one in which the impact of the scarcity of land on relative prices is somewhat concealed: his theory of rent focused mainly on the case of extensive diminishing returns, and thus extensive rent, which—as regards prices, wages, and profits—allowed him to concentrate on the technical conditions of production on marginal land. Ricardo was also aware of, and discussed, the case of intensive diminishing returns, and thus intensive rent. However, when analyzing the relationship between wages and profits, the problem that concerned him most, he set aside the problem of rent. He justified this premise as follows: "By getting rid of rent, . . . the distribution between capitalist and labourer becomes a much more simple consideration" (*Works*, 8:194). We may add that his approach could also derive some justification from the finding in the modern theory of production that even in the case of intensive diminishing returns there is a fictitious technique that can be obtained from the data of the problem, in which land does not appear (see Guichard 1982).

As to the second "fundamental error," it should be stressed that Ricardo took only the real wage rate as given and determined the general rate of profit and the rents of land endogenously. Walras failed to see that Ricardo advocated a genuinely different theory. Apparently, it did not even occur to Walras that there could be a theory that is fundamentally different from, and not just a special (and incoherently formulated) version of, his demand and supply theory. This explains why he found nothing wrong with assessing the contribution of the classical economists in terms of his own theory. We will come back to this in section 4 below.

Three categories of products

As we have seen, one of Walras's main criticisms concerned the particular causality the classical economists were assumed to entertain, which is said to have run from the prices of the "productive services" to the prices of the products.[11] If it could instead be shown that in the real world the reverse causality prevails, as Walras contended, then his own theory, based, as it were, on utility and the principle of the relative scarcity of goods, could be claimed to be not only more rigorous, but also more relevant than Ricardo's. Yet, in an attempt to distance himself from Ricardo, Walras let himself be carried away and actually contradicted one of his main tenets, namely, that both kinds of prices are determined *simultaneously* and *symmetrically* in terms of the demand for and the supply of the respective products and services.

Walras devoted four more sections (sections 345–348) to a discussion of the issue under consideration and distinguished three classes of products. The first class of products is the one on which all agree: "the case of productive services which have passed out of existence [after having been used], for example, Ricardo's 'rare statues and pictures, scarce books and wines'" (400). He expounded: "The value of such products, as both Ricardo and Mill admit, is the result of the law of offer and demand alone" (400). The second class concerns products produced by some "specific productive services" (400). This set includes Ricardo's example of "wines of a peculiar quality, which can be made only from grapes grown on a particular soil, of which there is a very limited quantity." Also with respect to this class there is not much difference of opinion, analytically (cf. 401). However, in Walras's view this set is much larger than the classical economists were inclined to think: "Had Ricardo and Mill been a little more methodical in their classification, they would have given examples of personal services which are no less specific than the land-services they mentioned, like the personal services of living artists, singers, eminent doctors and great surgeons" (401). It appears to have escaped Walras's attention that in Smith we find several references to the concept of "talent" and the remuneration paid for it, and that Ricardo was in agreement with Smith except whenever he explicitly said otherwise (see his preface to the *Principles*).[12] What is intriguing is that Walras in this context mentioned "personal services" together with "land-services," but interestingly did *not* mention the services of "capital goods proper" among those that can be the source of some "specific productive service" and yield its owner a scarcity rent. In fact, setting aside different "insurance premiums" reflecting different risks, in the long run the self-seeking behavior of producers will result in proportions of the quantities of the different capital goods proper such that a uniform "rate of net income" obtains. Hence, implicitly Walras showed some awareness that "proper capital" cannot be dealt with in the same way as the primary factors of production, land and labor.[13] Yet he missed the opportunity to clarify this aspect of his doctrine by way of contrast with Ricardo's.

Section 347 is devoted to a third class of products: those produced by "unspecialised productive services," which "have competition to fear." Echoing Ricardo's view, he added that this, "admittedly, is the most frequent case" (401). In this case,

> a rise in the prices of unspecialised services will attract to production other similar services which exist in more or less large quantities. If the prices of the products [of unspecialized services] rise, the prices of the productive services will also rise, *but only temporarily;* for these will increase in quantity and hence the quantity of their products will also increase. The end result will be a *slight rise* in the price of both productive services in general and of products in general.
>
> (401–2; emphases added)

The first part of the passage just quoted taken alone might be interpreted as indicating a general agreement between Walras and Ricardo: an increase in the output of a commodity that is produced by unspecialized services may increase the price of that commodity and of the services used in its production *only temporarily*; that is, in the long run these changes will be annihilated. However, with no further explanation Walras surprisingly continued that the "end result" would be a "slight" rise in both kinds of prices. Why? The only possible interpretation of this conclusion we can think of would have to be in terms of unspecialized services of land and labor, whose available amounts are both given, constant, and scarce. That is, there is a change in data (R1)–(R4): a change in the size or composition of the social product has occurred, and this change is such as to affect the extensive or the intensive margin of some qualities of land. Walras seems to believe that any change must have this effect. Now, in Ricardo we certainly encounter the assumption that the quantities of the different qualities of land are given and (almost) constant, and, depending on the levels of production of the various commodities, some of these qualities of land may be scarce. Yet, as we have already seen, Ricardo, whose main concern was the relationship between the wages of labor and the profits of capital, was keen "to get rid of rent" by focusing attention on (nonintensively cultivated) marginal land. That is, although a change in the levels of production of commodities that are (directly or indirectly) produced by means of unspecialized qualities of land may, in principle, affect which quality of land is marginal, and thus will affect costs of production, prices, the rate of profit, and the rents paid to the proprietors of intramarginal lands, in many cases such a change will not have this effect, and in other cases the effect will be small. In these cases it is possible to analyze the relationship between prices, profits, and wages by abstracting from these possible effects.

As regards common labor, according to Ricardo there is no presumption that in the long run it may also be considered a scarce factor of production. (Things may obviously be different with regard to certain special talents.) According to the classical authors from Smith to Ricardo, the required size of the common workforce is essentially generated alongside the accumulation process. In other words, the size of the workforce is taken to be compatible with data (R1)–(R4). Therefore, while due to an abundance or a "scarcity of hands," to use Ricardo's expression, in the short run wages may fall below or rise above their normal or "natural" level, in the long run a sufficient amount of labor will be forthcoming and make actual wages follow the trend of their historically and socially determined normal level, which must not be mistaken to imply a constant real wage rate.

Interestingly, in Walras we encounter a point of view that, according to M. Morishima (1977, 5), resembles that of Ricardo. In his analysis of "economic progress" (as opposed to "technical progress")—that is, an accumulation of capital and a growth of population with an unchanging set of technical alternatives—in lesson 36, Walras arrived at the following conclusion: "*In a progressive economy, the price of labour (wages) remaining substantially unchanged, the price of land-services (rent) will rise appreciably and the rate of net income will fall appreciably*" (390–91; emphasis in the original). Note in particular that according to Walras in the long run any tendency of the wage rate to rise as capital accumulates and the demand for labor increases is effectively offset by an expansion of the supply of labor. Walras assumed in fact that "population . . . does increase, for such an increase is implicit in our definition of progress; and thus additional labour, naturally proportional [!] to the additional future output, is assured" (386). This makes Walras's above objection to Ricardo's long-period theory that not only land, but also human faculties, exist in limited quantities (399) all the more puzzling. In fact, had Ricardo known Walras's aforementioned statement, he might have received it with a certain satisfaction: at least it did not in any obvious way contradict his assumption of a *given* real wage rate when dealing with the problem of value and distribution in a given place and time, and indeed went much farther than he, Ricardo, ever deemed it sensible, by postulating the long-term constancy of the real wage rate.

In section 348 Walras summarized his argument why, "in reality, there is no absolute antithesis between the two cases distinguished by Ricardo and Mill" (402). This necessitated in his view an explanation of *all* prices, including the prices of the productive services, indiscriminately in terms of demand and supply.

The differences between Walras and Ricardo thus concern first and foremost the scope and content of the theory of value and distribution. Both authors were interested in investigating the *long-period* properties of an economic system, characterized by a uniform rate of interest (profit) and uniform rates of remuneration of all primary factors of production (but see our remarks above in section 1). However, the data with which they attempted to achieve this aim differ significantly. These differences reflect both differences in scope and content. Ricardo was mainly concerned with that class of commodities whose long-period prices can be determined in terms of their conditions of production and the state of income distribution, that is, the level of the real wage rate(s). Correspondingly, he based his explanation as much as possible on observable magnitudes, that is, magnitudes that can be counted, weighed, or measured—in short, "objective" factors. Walras, on the other hand, felt prompted to attribute great importance to the class of commodities in whose price determination demand, rather than cost, plays a crucial role—hence, his emphasis on the role of "utility," that is, a nonobservable magnitude. However, since Walras contended that his analysis was generally superior to Ricardo's and therefore also superior with regard to the case of commodities that are producible and reproducible, albeit perhaps at rising unit cost, we shall in the following deal only with this case. This brings us to Walras's criticism of Ricardo's theory of extensive and intensive rent (see *Works*, vol. 1, chap. 2).

3. Walras on the Ricardian theory of rent

Lesson 39 was devoted to an "exposition and refutation" of the Ricardian theory of rent. Walras stressed that this is "a mathematical theory which must be expressed and discussed mathematically" (405). Sections 352–353 are devoted to a geometrical exposition in which each (incremental) investment involves an *amount* of £1,000 (which may be considered the unit of account in money terms in which the analysis is conducted). Walras objected that in Ricardo's presentation of extensive rent (see *Works*, 1:70–71) it is not clear what is meant by "equal amounts of capital and labour": "Ricardo does not state expressly in what terms these employments of capital are evaluated or what their value is; but in the second part he explicitly supposes that they are evaluated in terms of money ["*numéraire*"] and that their value is £1,000 each" (405).[14] In section 354 Walras then criticized Ricardo for proceeding in terms of increments of capital worth £1,000, when he (Ricardo) should have instead argued in terms of infinitesimals and should have supposed "that every time the capital used is increased by an infinitely small quantity, the rate of yield must decrease by an infinitely small quantity" (408). Walras illustrated his argument geometrically and then, in section 355, complemented it by an algebraic formulation.

We shall begin by comparing Walras's reconstruction of Ricardo's theory of rent with Kaldor's more recent and influential interpretation (Kaldor 1955–56). There are three main differences. First, in his diagrammatic illustrations Walras put "capital employed" on the horizontal axis,[15] whereas Kaldor put "labor." In the literature subsequent to Kaldor we find also the expression "labor-cum-capital" to indicate that while the unit of measurement is a unit of labor, the measure refers to total capital advanced, which includes not only the labor paid the given real wage, but also the "seed capital" used by one worker. Second, Walras drew a diagram for each quality of land, whereas Kaldor drew a single diagram for the whole corn sector (where "corn" is taken to represent a whole "complex of agricultural products"). Third, the curves drawn by Walras represent the derivative (or the increment) of "the excess *per hectare* of the total number of units of product over the number of units necessary for the payment of wages [on each kind of land, respectively]" (409), whereas the curve drawn by Kaldor gives the marginal productivity of labor (reflecting the amount of capital employed). Let us consider these three differences in turn.

As regards the first difference, recall Ricardo's first two consecutive attempts to simplify the problem of distribution (see Sraffa 1951). His initial step consisted of getting rid of rent in terms of the theory of extensive rent in the *Essay on Profits* (see *Works*, vol. 4); this allowed Ricardo to focus attention on marginal (in the sense of no-rent) land. In Sraffa's interpretation (Sraffa 1951, xxxi), the second step consisted of trying to get rid of the problem of value by assuming the so-called corn model. The assumptions underlying this model are as follows:

1 There is only one type of agricultural product, called "corn."
2 Corn is the only wage-good.
3 Capital in agriculture consists entirely of the wage-bill, that is, corn is produced by labor and land only.

In this case the rate of profit in corn production can be ascertained directly as a ratio of two quantities of corn—that of the surplus product to that of the wage-bill advanced—without any need of having recourse to prices. With corn entering (directly or indirectly) the production of all other commodities (as the only wage-good and possibly also as an input), the prices of those commodities would have to adjust such that the same competitive rate of return could be earned in their production.

As can be shown, in an economy satisfying assumptions 1–3 it is not difficult to construct production functions and plot marginal productivity of capital schedules for each quality of land. It is even possible to construct a production function and the corresponding marginal productivity of capital schedule for agriculture as a whole, even if land is diversified in quality.[16] However, in the case in which corn enters into the production of corn not only as a wage-good but also, as it is natural to assume, as a means of production (seed), it is no longer possible to plot the conventional marginal productivity schedules or to construct an aggregate production function for agriculture as a whole, unless one is willing to replace assumption 3 by the following assumption:

4 Capital consists of seed corn and wages, and the seed corn input is strictly proportional to the labor input.[17]

Hence, both Walras's and Kaldor's constructions are correct if and only if either of the following sets of highly restrictive assumptions apply: 1, 2, and 3; or 1, 2, and 4.[18]

The second difference mentioned above is thus also dealt with. Once it is clear that a presentation in terms of the marginal productivity of capital is admissible only when there is a single commodity ("corn") and corn inputs are proportional to labor inputs, it is indeed possible to work in terms of a single curve representing agricultural (corn) production in the economy as a whole.[19]

The third difference reflects Walras's deviation from or, as George Stigler (1941) argued some time ago, misunderstanding of, Ricardo's treatment of the wages of labor.[20] In Ricardo wages are included in the capital advanced at the beginning of the uniform period of production; that is, they were taken to be paid *ante factum*: they form an integral part of the dose of capital-cum-labor. Walras reckoned wages instead as a part of the net product; that is, he took them to be paid *post factum*. This fact is relevant also because, for Ricardo, wages are an important part of the capital advanced by the capitalist: wage-goods, and especially corn, are "necessaries" both from the point of view of the single worker and from the point of view of the productive system as a whole. Below we shall see that, strangely enough, in Walras's interpretation of Ricardo's theory of rent corn does not enter directly (seed) or indirectly into its own production. Therefore Walras's reasoning cannot have been based on either of the two sets of assumptions specified above. The "capital" employed in corn production in Walras's argument cannot be corn, but must be some other commodity or bundle of commodities. Alas, this is left in the dark, so that it remains unclear on which foundation his "rigorous formulation" of the English theory of rent (411) rests.

Walras's formalization of classical rent theory

Walras's algebraic argument can be summarized as follows. Let h_i be the excess product per hectare of land of quality i over the payment of wages, x_i the "amount of capital" in terms of the *numeraire* (and exclusive of the wages of labor) employed per hectare on land of that quality, and t the "rate of interest charges expressed in terms of [physical] units of product" (409). Then the rent per hectare of land of quality i, r_i, is given by

$$r_i = h_i - x_i t, \quad (i = 1, 2, \ldots, s), \tag{1}$$

where s is the number of the different qualities of land available, each of which is in given supply n_i, and where h_i is assumed to depend exclusively on x_i, that is,

$$h_i = F_i(x_i). \quad (i = 1, 2, \ldots, s). \tag{2}$$

Walras stressed that in (long-period) equilibrium each quality of cultivated land must earn the same physical return per unit of capital employed, t. In the case in which qualities 1 to m are cultivated ($m \leq s$), we have

$$t = F_1'(x_1) = F_2'(x_2) = \cdots = F_m'(x_m). \tag{3}$$

Counting the number of equations and unknowns in (1)–(3), Walras observed that there are only $3m$ equations but $3m + 1$ unknowns: the unknowns are $r_1, \ldots, r_m; h_1, \ldots, h_m; x_1, \ldots, x_m$; and t. Hence there is a degree of freedom. How did Ricardo close the system? Walras's answer was as follows:

> Another equation is needed. We can, *without deviating in any way from a faithful interpretation of Ricardo's theory*, write the following equation, which is analogous to those given in sections 242 and 248:
>
> $$n_1x_1 + n_2x_2 + n_3x_3 + \cdots = X. \tag{4}$$
>
> According to Ricardo, it seems that in every economy there is a certain amount of capital. . . . *At any given moment, the amount of capital is determinate.* Let us call such a determinate amount X, and let us distribute it among the different kinds of land in such a way that the rate of yield is the same on all lands.
>
> (410; emphases added)

Walras thus interpreted Ricardo as closing the system in terms of a given "quantity" of social capital.

From what has been said above it follows that this interpretation cannot be sustained. First, with heterogeneous capital goods, it is not clear what a given "quantity" of capital in terms of the *numeraire* is supposed to mean, independently of relative prices. Walras's suggested closure only makes sense if there is a single capital good, a case that both Ricardo and Walras relegated to the realm of fiction and to which they attributed at most a heuristic value in economic analysis. Moreover, to take X as given is by no means necessitated by the desire to get a determinate system. This becomes clear when we take a closer look at the exact role played by Walras's above closure. In order to be able to determine the rents of land and the rate of profit, given the real wage rate, what we need to specify is the *amount* of total corn production (see (R2)). This can be done in several ways. In a model in which corn is the only capital good, there is no harm in fixing total corn production in terms of the amount of corn capital employed in the growing of corn. This is indeed the assumption needed in order for Walras's reasoning to make sense. In this case equation (4) would provide the required information. However, there are more direct, and less ambiguous, ways to specify the size of corn production, one of which is, of course, giving the overall level of corn output. Alternatively, the level of corn output exclusive of the wage-bill could be given, and so on. The latter alternative would imply an equation like

$$n_1h_1 + n_2h_2 + n_3h_3 + \cdots = H, \tag{4$'$}$$

where H is the excess product of corn over the payment of wages. Clearly, equation (4′) would do the job as equally well as equation (4) and, in addition, it may be contended, is more faithful to Ricardo.

The dubious assumption of a given "quantity of capital"

The fact that Walras's interpretation is inconclusive follows also from a critical scrutiny of his claim that equation (4) is "analogous" to the equation given in sections 242 and 248. While the two are formally similar, *logically* they are very different. In contradistinction to equation (4), the allegedly "analogous" equation in sections 242 and 248 is not just an equation fixing the total amount of corn produced, but an *equilibrium* equation in which E (which plays the role played by X above) is the "algebraic sum of the individual excesses of income over consumption" (275). E is therefore not a given, but a magnitude to be determined endogenously: it has the role of relating investment to saving and of rendering the two equal to one another. In short, it refers to a savings-investment equilibrium. The reference is not to a given endowment of capital, but to "new capital goods" (281).

Going back to lesson 39, Walras then proceeded to determine t for a given X by first solving equations (3) for given values of t, which gave him the x_i's corresponding to the different values of t, or $x_i = \phi_i(t)$. He stressed: "The lands for which $F'(0) < t$ will not be cultivated; only those for which $F'(0) > t$ will be brought under cultivation" (410–11). Replacing the x_i's by the $\phi_i(t)$'s in equation (4) provided him with one equation for the only unknown t. Alternatively, it is easily checked that replacing the h_i's by the $F_i(\phi_i(t))$'s in equation (4′) gives once again one equation for the only unknown t. Once t is determined, the other variables can be ascertained. Walras concluded: "Thus in the final analysis rent depends on the capital of a country, and is determined without regard to wages, interest or the prices of products. This is the essence of the English theory of rent" (411).

This conclusion can be criticized both externally, that is, with a view to Ricardo's theory, and internally, that is, with a view to the consistency of Walras's argument. The external criticism is, of course, that Ricardo took the levels of normal output instead of the "capital of a country" as the independent variable. This involved considering the size and composition of social capital as an endogenous variable that is taken to be fully adjusted to the other data, such that a uniform rate of profit on and normal levels of utilization of capital obtain. As regards the internal criticism, assume first that the wage rate happens to be at another level. This would change equations (2) and a fortiori the rate of interest. Second, as we have seen, the only cases in which Walras's exposition would be correct are those in which there is only a single commodity (corn) that either does not enter into its own production, apart from the wages paid to workers, or, if it does, enters into them in proportion to labor. In this case it is trivially true that the prices of products do not appear in the equations. In cases with more than one commodity this is obviously no longer true. Since, as we shall see, in Walras's interpretation of Ricardo's rent theory there are at least two commodities to be taken into consideration in the production of corn, namely corn (output) and a capital good proper that is different from corn, the problem of relative prices cannot be avoided.

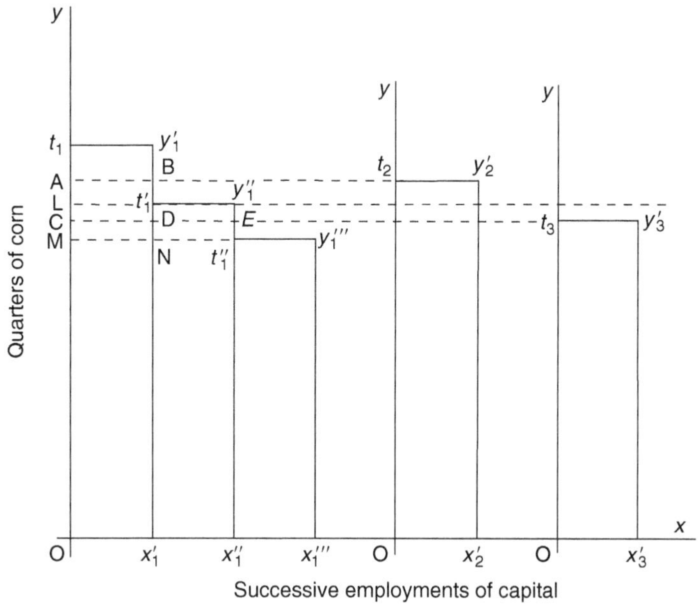

Figure 4.1 Marginal productivity of successive does of capital.

The need for reasoning in terms of infinitesimals

Walras introduced section 356 in the following terms: "The need for restating Ricardo's reasoning in terms of infinitesimals is so imperative that a number of authors have succumbed to it even though they continued to use ordinary language. Hence the rigorous formulation which we have just given to this reasoning is the *true formulation of the English theory of rent*" (411; emphasis added).[21] This formulation is then taken to point out "defects in exposition and deduction resulting from the cruder modes of expression which were used by Ricardo and Mill" (411). Walras maintained that

> Mill's first theorem, which is in essence based on the assumption that the worst land yields no rent, is intrinsically erroneous and formally contradicts the second theorem.... It is only necessary to inspect Fig. 33 [our figure 4.2] to perceive at once that the worst lands under cultivation do, in general, yield a rent, except in the unusual case of a discontinuous productivity curve which cuts the horizontal line (representing the rate of production) only at its starting-point.
>
> (411)

As a matter of fact, we do not need an argument "in terms of infinitesimals" to see that when there is intensive rent the "worst land" may yield a rent. For this

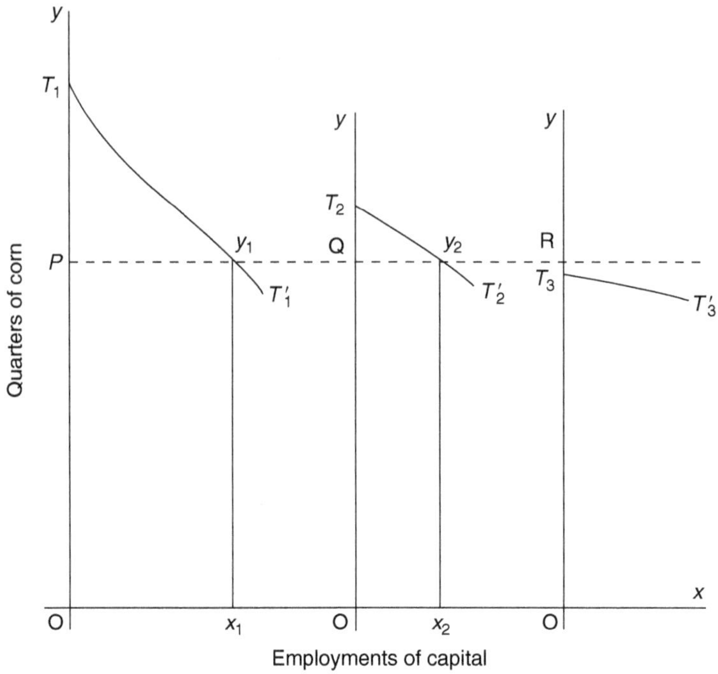

Figure 4.2 Marginal productivity of capital (infinitesimal case).

purpose compare Walras's figures 32 and 33 (our figures 4.1 and 4.2). Walras emphasized the fact that when $t = OP$ in figure 33, land 3 is not cultivated, and land 2 is the "worst land" but nevertheless gets a rent that is equal to the area QT_2y_2. However, if we look at figure 32, we see that when $t = OL$, once again land 3 is not cultivated, and once again land 2 is the "worst land" but nevertheless once again gets a rent that is equal to the rectangle below the segment t_2y_2' and above the straight line $Lt_1'y_1''$. Hence it is not an analysis in terms of infinitesimals that matters in this context, as Walras maintained, but the coexistence of intensive and extensive rent.

Walras's criticism and the modern classical theory of rent

The last sections of lesson 29 (sections 357–362) are devoted to what Walras considered his main criticisms of the Ricardian theory of rent. Before we address these sections it is useful to complete our discussion of Ricardo's consecutive attempts to simplify the theory of value and distribution. In the above we have already mentioned his first two steps – (1) getting rid of rent by focusing on marginal land; and (2) getting rid of the problem of value in terms of the corn model. This discussion turned out to be helpful in understanding the singularly restrictive assumptions implied in order for a Walras, Kaldor, Pasinetti, or Samuelson to be justified in drawing marginal productivity of capital schedules and production functions.

Against Ricardo's basic principle, derived from the corn model, that "it is the profits of the farmer that regulate the profits of all other trades" (*Works*, 6:104), Malthus objected that there is no industry in which the product is exactly of the same kind as the capital advanced (*Works*, 6:17–18). Ricardo did, of course, not dispute this, and, in a third step, in the *Principles* attempted to cope with the problem of heterogeneous goods in terms of a theory of value according to which the exchange values of commodities are regulated by the quantities of labor needed directly and indirectly in their production. Yet, Ricardo soon realized that what was to become known as the "labor theory of value" cannot generally be sustained because of differences in the proportions in which direct labor and means of production are employed in different industries. According to Sraffa (1951, xxxii–xxxiii, xl–xli), the search for an "invariable measure of value" may be considered the fourth and final step in Ricardo's efforts to grope his way toward a coherent theory of value and distribution.

Today we are possessed of an analytical scheme capable of dealing with the intricacies in the theory of distribution and relative prices the classical economists failed to master satisfactorily. Thus, in the modern formulation of this theory the strong assumptions adopted by Ricardo are abandoned (see, for instance, Kurz and Salvadori 1995, chap. 10, and the literature referred to there). We shall now briefly investigate sections 357–362 of Walras's *Elements* against the background of modern classical analysis.

Walras was keen to establish the following price equation:

$$p_b = b_t p_t + b_p p_p + b_{p'} p_{p'} + b_{p''} p_{p''} + \cdots + b_k p_k + b_{k'} p_{k'} + b_{k''} p_{k''} + \cdots , \tag{5}$$

where p_b is the price of the product (b is the abbreviation of the French word for corn, *blé*), the b's are technical coefficients of production, p_t is the rate of rent in terms of the *numeraire*, the p_p's are the prices of "personal services" (i.e., wages), and the p_k's are the prices of "capital services" (i.e., interest charges). The b's are variables,[22] because there is a choice of technique, and all the p's need to be determined by the theory. It is interesting to note that this equation is precisely one of the equations one encounters in the modern theory of rent of classical derivation (see, for instance, the weak inequalities (10.8e) in Kurz and Salvadori 1995, 298),[23] and therefore equation (5) cannot be a source of disagreement between us and Walras. The real disagreement between Walras on the one hand and us (following Ricardo) on the other concerns once again the substance of the theory as it is reflected in the data from which to start: in the model referred to there is no equation or inequality relating to the available "quantity of capital" (or that of labor); instead, one of the distributive variables (the real wage rate or, alternatively, as in our formalization, the rate of profit) is considered as given. As we have seen, Walras advocated a different approach. We now return to lesson 39.

Walras's misunderstandings of Ricardo's theory of rent

In section 352 Walras remarked that in the quoted passage on extensive rent "Ricardo does not state expressly in what terms these employments of capital are evaluated or what their value is; but in the second part he explicitly supposes that they are evaluated in terms of money [*"numéraire"*] and that their value is £1,000 each" (405). In his formalization of Ricardo's theory Walras instead measured the outputs h_i, the rates of rent r_i, and "the rate of interest charges expressed in terms of [physical] units of product" t in terms of product. He therefore felt the need to come back to this issue, especially because it was at the center of his criticism. In section 357 he restated equation (1) when all variables are expressed in terms of the *numeraire* (the i's are dropped for the sake of simplicity):

$$\frac{p_t}{p_b} = h - x\frac{i}{p_b}$$

where i is here "the rate of net income in terms of numeraire"[24] and therefore $r = p_t/p_b$ and $t = i/p_b$.

In our interpretation, with the doses of £1,000 Ricardo intended to refer to the units of account, that is, units of corn, in terms of which he conducted his analysis; and the fact that these doses are expressed as if they were "in money terms" does not affect the substance of the argument. Walras, on the contrary, inferred the following from the fact that they were expressed in money (i.e., the *numeraire*): "Since each application always amounts to £1,000, it follows that the prices of the capital goods in question are determinate and constant" (414). Here Walras is confronted with elements of his interpretation and "correction" of the classical analysis that contradict each other. As we have argued above, the construction of production function(s) followed by Walras (and several other commentators, including, for example, Kaldor) is possible if and only if the assumptions of the corn model hold, that is, if and only if the agricultural sector produces only *one* commodity that is either not used in production or is used in strict proportion to the amount of labor employed and no other produced commodity is used in production. On the contrary, Walras first introduced a production function for each quality of land and insisted on measuring the nonland input in money, and then used this fact to argue that relative prices need to be constant. This interpretation comes as a surprise also because Ricardo was very clear about the fact that in general (i.e., setting aside the case of the corn model) the concept of capital is a difficult one. In a letter to J. R. McCulloch, Ricardo wrote: "I would ask what means you have of ascertaining the equal value of capitals?... These capitals are not the same in kind—what will employ one set of workmen, is not precisely the same as will employ another set" (*Works*, 9:359–60; see also his letter to Torrens, *Works*, 4:393–94). Walras continued: "This hypothesis [of the constancy of input prices] has important consequences" (414). In his opinion "it led Ricardo to base the existence, the origin and the growth of rent on the increasing dearness of products. Indeed, in his view, cost of production determines selling price" (414). How is it possible for the price of the corn output to rise, while the price of corn as an input remains the same? Walras overlooked that corn is needed both as seed and as food for workers: he missed the important aspect of circular flow of production in Ricardo.

Finally, Walras's main argument, which was to show that the price of corn is bound to rise, is totally untenable. He first argued that (note that h in the above formula equals $1/b_t$ in the following one)

$$p_b = b_t(p_t + xi) = \frac{p_t}{r} = \frac{i}{t},$$

then he added: "if we ignore variations in i, this last ratio will increase indefinitely as t decreases, which is the basis of the theory" (415). How can one ignore variations in i? How is it possible that an increase in the price of corn, *given* the prices of the capital items and *given* i, could be said to be "the basis of the theory" of the English economists? Walras summarized as follows:

> Thus, the English theory can only determine the price of land-services and demonstrate its residual character on the twofold assumption that the prices of personal capital, the prices of capital goods proper and the rate of net income are predetermined and constant, and that, therefore, the prices of the services of personal capital and capital goods proper are also predetermined and constant.
>
> (415)

Unfortunately, he refrained from substantiating his surprising claim in terms of some evidence from Ricardo's *Principles*. In fact, no such evidence can be provided. In Ricardo the falling tendency of the rate of interest is inextricably intertwined with the theory of rent. To assume that the rents of land go up, but the rate of profit stays constant, misses the whole point of Ricardo's theory of distribution. It is astonishing how Walras could go so much astray. He continued:

> We may ask . . . why the English School determines rent by the quantities of labour and capital-services employed, rather than wages and interest by the quantities of land-services employed; or why this school does not try to formulate a unified general theory to determine the prices of all productive services in the same way.
>
> (416)

This is indeed the crucial question: Is it possible in a long-period framework of the analysis to generalize the principle of rent to an explanation of all kinds of income in the same way and thus interpret the wages of labor as well as the profits of capital as scarcity prices of the respective factors of production, labor and capital? Walras thought that this was indeed possible. In his concluding words of lesson 39,

> Thus, all that remains of Ricardo's theory after a rigorous critical analysis is that rent is not a component part, but a result, of the price of products. But the same thing can be said of wages and interest. Hence, rent, wages, interest, the prices of products, and the coefficients of production are all unknowns within the same problem; they must always be determined together and not independently of one another.
>
> (418)

The crucial question is: How can this be accomplished? In terms of which approach and using which data can the technique adopted, the distributive variables, and relative prices be consistently determined? Walras and neoclassical economists in general assume that the supplies of labor and capital *must* be among the givens also in a long-period framework. Classical economists argue on the contrary that in the long period either the wage rate or the rate of profit must be treated as an independent variable, because the "capital endowment" cannot be considered a datum in long-period analysis. As has been analytically well established since the debate on capital theory in the 1960s and early 1970s, the intuition of the old classical economists was perfectly sound.[25]

4. Walras on the Ricardian theory of wages and profits

In lesson 40 Walras dealt with the classical theory of wages and profits. The lesson is almost exclusively devoted to a criticism of John Stuart Mill and especially his wage-fund doctrine. These parts need not concern us here. There is only one section that is somewhat related to Ricardo's way of thinking and that deserves to be commented upon. We quote section 368 in full:

> Let P be the aggregate price received for the products of an enterprise; let S, I and F be respectively the wages, interest charges and rent laid out by the entrepreneurs, in the course of production, to pay for the services of personal faculties, capital and land. Let us recall now that, according to the English School, the selling price of products is determined by their costs of production, that is to say, it is equal to the cost of the productive services employed. Thus we have the equation
>
> $$P = S + I + F, \tag{6}$$
>
> and P is determined for us. It remains only to determine S, I and F. Surely, if it is not the price of the products that determines the price of productive services, but the price of productive services that determines the price of the products, we must be told what determines the price of the services. That is precisely what the English economists try to do. To this end, they construct

> a theory of rent according to which rent is not included in the expenses of production, thus changing the above equation to
>
> $$P = S + I.$$
>
> Having done this, they determine S directly by the theory of wages. Then, finally, they tell us that "the amount of interest or profit is the excess of the aggregate price received for the products over the wages expended on their production," in other words, that it is determined by the equation
>
> $$I = P - S.$$
>
> It is clear now that the English economists are completely baffled by the problem of price determination; for it is impossible for I to determine P at the same time that P determines I. In the language of mathematics one equation cannot be used to determine two unknowns. This objection is raised without any reference to our position on the manner in which the English School eliminates rent before setting out to determine wages.

Before we enter into a discussion of this criticism two observations should be made. First, essentially the same objection was put forward by William Stanley Jevons.[26] Second, the claim that Ricardo tried to determine two unknowns with a single equation is perhaps an expression in these authors that comes closest to admitting that there *is* a distinct classical approach that is fundamentally different from the neoclassical one. It is interesting to notice that both Walras and Jevons interpreted Ricardo as having treated the real wage rate as given in the theory of value and distribution, or rather, in the words of Walras, as having determined it "directly by the theory of wages." In other words, both Jevons and Walras appear to have admitted that Ricardo attempted to determine the rate of profit and relative prices in terms of something like datum (R3). This leaves two unknowns: the rate of interest (profit) and the overall size of the product. Now it is not true that Ricardo was "completely baffled" by the problem of price determination, as Walras contended. It is rather Walras who might be said to have been somewhat baffled by the way Ricardo approached the task: he took the overall size of the product as given (see (R2)). For Walras, to whom economics *was* demand and supply theory, this analytical option did not exist—it was in fact unimaginable to him. He rather took it for granted that the size of the product had to be determined on the basis of the available amounts of productive resources, that is, in terms of datum (W3).

Once this is seen, it becomes clear that the critique of Walras and Jevons misses its target. The critique was explicitly refuted by the Russian mathematical economist Vladimir K. Dmitriev ([1898] 1974), who showed that on the basis of (R1)–(R4) the remaining distributive variable(s) and relative prices can be consistently determined.[27] In the following we shall provide an argument that is logically identical to Dmitriev's but that refers also to other parts of the *Elements*. In this way we intend to throw some additional light on certain aspects of Walras's thought that do not always seem to have been properly understood (see also Kurz and Salvadori 1995, 25–26).

Equation (7) is nothing else than equations (4) in section 203 of the *Elements* (240), which are here presented using matrix notation:

$$\boldsymbol{p} = \boldsymbol{Cq} + \boldsymbol{Ew} + \boldsymbol{Ay},$$

where $\boldsymbol{p}$ is the vector of prices of outputs (Walras assumes that the first element of $\boldsymbol{p}$ equals unity since the first commodity acts as the *numeraire*), $\boldsymbol{C}$ is the matrix of the production coefficients of land inputs of the operated processes, $\boldsymbol{q}$ is the vector of prices of land services (i.e., the rent rates), $\boldsymbol{E}$ is the matrix of the production coefficients of labor inputs of the operated processes, $\boldsymbol{w}$ is the vector of prices of personal services (i.e., the wage rates), $\boldsymbol{A}$ is the matrix of the production coefficients of the inputs of capital goods proper of the operated processes, and $\boldsymbol{y}$ is the vector of prices of the services of capital goods proper.[28] If, following Ricardo, as mentioned by Walras himself, we take account only of the technology used at the margin (either extensive or intensive)[29] and if we assume for simplicity that there is only one quality of labor,[30] we obtain the equation

$$\boldsymbol{p} = w\boldsymbol{l} + \boldsymbol{Ay}. \tag{7}$$

In section 238 (and similarly in section 232) Walras asserted that if P_k is the price of a capital good proper, its depreciation charge and its insurance premium are respectively $\mu_k P_k$ and $\nu_k P_k$.[31] If the mentioned capital good is a circulating one, then $\mu_k = 1$; and if the insurance premium on it is nought, then $\nu_k = 0$. If, on the contrary, $\boldsymbol{M}$ is the diagonal matrix with the exogenously given depreciation charges on the main diagonal and $\boldsymbol{V}$ is the diagonal matrix with the given insurance premiums on the main diagonal, then

$$\boldsymbol{y} = (\boldsymbol{M} + \boldsymbol{V} + i\boldsymbol{I})\boldsymbol{p},$$

where i is the "rate of net income,"[32] and equation (7) becomes

$$\boldsymbol{p} = w\boldsymbol{l} + \boldsymbol{A}(\boldsymbol{M} + \boldsymbol{V} + i\boldsymbol{I})\boldsymbol{p}, \tag{8}$$

which is a system of n equations in $n + 1$ unknowns, since by definition the first element of $\boldsymbol{p}$ equals unity, where n is the number of products, some (or all) of which could be capital goods proper.

Taking (with Ricardo) the real wage rate as given, we get the $n + 1$st equation needed to determine prices *and* distribution. In fact if

$$w = \boldsymbol{b}^T\boldsymbol{p},$$

where $\boldsymbol{b}$ is a given vector defining the real wage rate, and assuming (with Walras) that wages are paid *post factum*, equation (8) becomes

$$\boldsymbol{p} = \boldsymbol{lb}^T\boldsymbol{p} + \boldsymbol{A}(\boldsymbol{M} + \boldsymbol{V} + i\boldsymbol{I})\boldsymbol{p}, \tag{9}$$

and if the elements of $\boldsymbol{b}$ and the elements on the main diagonal of matrices $\boldsymbol{M}$ and $\boldsymbol{V}$ are small enough, then matrix $\boldsymbol{I} - \boldsymbol{l}\boldsymbol{b}^T - \boldsymbol{A}\boldsymbol{M} - \boldsymbol{A}\boldsymbol{V}$ is invertible with a semipositive inverse and from equation (9) we obtain

$$\boldsymbol{p} = i(\boldsymbol{I} - \boldsymbol{l}\boldsymbol{b}^T - \boldsymbol{A}\boldsymbol{M} - \boldsymbol{A}\boldsymbol{V})^{-1}\boldsymbol{A}\boldsymbol{p}.$$

That is, $1/i$ is the Perron-Frobenius eigenvalue of matrix

$$(\boldsymbol{I} - \boldsymbol{l}\boldsymbol{b}^T - \boldsymbol{A}\boldsymbol{M} - \boldsymbol{A}\boldsymbol{V})^{-1}\boldsymbol{A},$$

and $\boldsymbol{p}$ is the corresponding eigenvector whose first element equals unity.[33]

We may thus conclude that Walras's criticism is untenable: Ricardo cannot be accused of having attempted "to determine two unknowns with one equation." Ricardo's system is perfectly determinate. The data or independent variables, (R1)–(R4), from which he started his analysis of the problem of value and distribution suffice to determine the unknowns, or dependent variables, that is, the rate of profit, the rent rates, and prices in terms of the given *numeraire*. No other data, such as utility or demand functions, are needed. In his reading of Ricardo, Walras was misled by the idea that there is only a single kind of theory in economics: demand and supply theory. Assessed in terms of his own theory, Ricardo's was bound to look strange. Had Walras taken a closer look at Ricardo's construction he would have found out that there was no indeterminacy.

5. Concluding remarks

In this article we have scrutinized Walras's criticism, in part 7 of the *Elements*, of the classical theory of value and distribution, paying special attention to Ricardo's contribution. We have shown that Walras succeeded in pointing out some weaknesses and unnecessarily restrictive assumptions in Ricardo's theory of rent and that certain aspects of his interpretation may be said to foreshadow the later ones by Nicholas Kaldor, Luigi Pasinetti, and Paul A. Samuelson. However, Walras does not appear to have been aware of the fact that singularly restrictive assumptions must hold in corn production in order for marginal productivity curves of capital with regard to each quality of land to exist. In particular, the only capital good employed has to be corn, that is, an input identical with the output. That Walras did not assume this becomes clear when we turn to Walras's misinterpretations of Ricardo. First, there are misunderstandings of specific elements of Ricardo's theory. These include Ricardo's treatment of the wages of labor as a part of the capital advanced at the beginning of the period of production; instead Walras considered them as a part of the net product. Then there is a lack of understanding on Walras's part of the circular flow of production in Ricardo and especially of the fact that corn is considered a product that enters into its own production (via the wages of labor and seed capital) and, besides this, also into the production of other commodities. This implies, among other things, that the capital employed in corn production in his attempted formalization of Ricardo's rent theory cannot be physically identical to the product. It follows that Walras was not entitled to draw marginal productivity curves of capital.

More important, Walras failed to see that the classical approach to the theory of value and distribution is fundamentally different from his own demand and supply approach. He treated Ricardo's theory as if it were just an early and rude version of his own elaborate neoclassical general equilibrium theory. This theory attempts to determine quantities, relative prices of goods, and the income distribution in terms of the following data: (W1) technical alternatives; (W2) preferences; and (W3) initial endowments of factors of production, including capital. Ricardo in his theory was said to have started essentially from the same sets of data, but to have imposed unnecessary restrictions on them and in addition to have committed logical blunders. Entirely in line with his perspective of Ricardo, Walras believed to have been faithful to the English economist when "closing" his model of the Ricardian theory of rent in terms of a given "quantity of capital." He missed the fact that the data of the classical theory are different: (R1) technical alternatives; (R2) the size and composition of the social product; (R3) the real wage rate; and (R4) the quantities of land available. He also missed the fact that in terms of these data the dependent variables—the rate of profit, the rent rates, and relative prices—are fully determinate. There is no need to add, and indeed no possibility of adding, some further givens, such as the capital endowment of the economy or utility. Walras's objection that Ricardo tried "to determine two unknowns with one equation"—that is, that his system is underdetermined—has been shown to be untenable.

Walras's attack on Ricardo was meant to clear away the classical theory of value and distribution and establish the superiority of his own—the only and "truly scientific theory of social wealth" (428). To Walras all prices and all distributive variables were to be explained simultaneously and symmetrically in terms of demand and supply. The asymmetric treatment of the distributive variables in the classical authors, who took the real wage rate as given and determined all shares of income other than wages residually, was totally extraneous to his way of thinking. In this regard Walras's interpretation of Ricardo does not differ much from that of other neoclassical authors, such as Jevons. They showed similar difficulties to apprehend and appreciate the distinct character of the classical analysis, which had gradually been "submerged and forgotten since the advent of the marginal method" (Sraffa 1960, v).

Notes

1 In the following all unspecified page references refer to the Jaffé translation of Walras's *Elements* ([1874–77] 1954).
2 For a succinct discussion of the structure of Walras's mature comprehensive model, see Walker 1996, chap. 8.
3 In this paper we are not concerned with Walras's criticism of John Stuart Mill. Apart from a few side remarks we shall therefore set aside this aspect of his discussion. This

appears to be justified by the fact that in important respects Mill parted company with Ricardo's doctrine and anticipated later marginalism; on this, see Kurz 2002.

4 For a comprehensive discussion of the classical approach to the theory of value and distribution, see Kurz and Salvadori 1995, 1998a, 1998b.

5 There is a striking similarity between the criticisms leveled at the classical theory of value and distribution, and especially the theory of rent, by Walras and Philip Wicksteed (1894). As is well known, Walras came close to accusing Wicksteed of plagiarism (see pp. 490–92). On this, see Jaffé 1964.

6 For a detailed discussion of the differences between the two kinds of theories, see, for example, Kurz and Salvadori 1995, chap. 1, and Kurz and Salvadori 1998b, chap. 1.

7 As one referee aptly remarked, these differences in the logical structure of the two theories reflect differences in the views of how the economy works. In particular, in the classical authors the wage rate is not the price that clears the labor market. A discussion of this aspect is beyond the scope of this paper (see, therefore, the relevant entries in Kurz and Salvadori 1998a and Kurz and Salvadori 1995, chap. 15). Here it suffices to recall that the logical structure of the classical approach to the theory of value and distribution does not necessitate taking the real wage rate as given, as in (R3). Having recourse to such a premise only makes sense if the latter is well defined in terms of socially and historically specified quantities of necessaries in the support of workers and their families, as was assumed by authors from Adam Smith to Ricardo. In conditions in which workers participate in the surplus, the commodity content of wages can no longer be ascertained independently of the distribution of income and relative prices. In these circumstances the rate of profits instead of the real wage rate could be treated as an independent variable (see Sraffa 1960, 33) because, as a ratio, it has a significance that is independent of relative prices. It should perhaps also be mentioned that, in the context of economic growth, treating the real wage rate as a datum is logically equivalent to introducing something like a technology that produces labor. This idea can be shown to underlay the so-called new growth theories in the form of an accumulable factor dubbed "human capital"; for this interpretation, see Kurz and Salvadori 1998a, chap. 4.

8 While the beginnings of the development of such a different framework can indeed be traced back to Walras, a proper concept of "temporary equilibrium" was only provided by John Richard Hicks.

9 In the following we shall therefore set aside Walras's concerns with temporary equilibria.

10 See also Ricardo's letter to Malthus of 24 November of the same year: "I shall not dispute another proposition in your letter[:] 'No wealth['] you say 'can exist unless the demand, or the estimation in which the commodity is held exceeds the cost of production.' I have never disputed this. I do not dispute either the influence of demand on the price of corn and on the price of all other things, but supply follows close at its heels, and soon takes the power of regulating price in his own hands, and in regulating it he is determined by cost of production. I acknowledge the intervals on which you so exclusively dwell, but still they are only intervals" (*Works*, 8:302).

11 As we have just seen this is not fully correct, because all distributive variables other than wages are treated as unknowns, to be determined together with relative product prices.

12 For a discussion of the classical theory of wage differentials, see Kurz and Salvadori 1995, chap. 11.

13 The need to differentiate is also expressed in Walras's distinction between land and personal faculties, which are said to be "natural wealth," and capital goods proper (and "income goods," i.e., consumption goods), which are said to be "artificial wealth" (399). Artificial wealth can be created and its size and composition adjusted as required by the circumstances.

14 Obviously Walras was right to chastise Ricardo for assuming increments of capital in terms of money. However, in some of the more recent literature on Ricardo the "£1, 000"

mentioned by Ricardo is interpreted just as the unit of account in terms of which the analysis is carried out, taking it for granted that the sum represents a certain amount of corn. We shall come back to this below.

15 Actually, these are the words used in figure 31 (406), whereas in figure 32 (407) [our figure 1; see below] Walras used "successive employments of capital" and in figure 33 (409) [our figure 2] "employments of capital." But these changes do not appear to indicate any change in substance.

16 For a demonstration, see Freni 1991, whose results on this point are reported by Kurz and Salvadori (1992, 230–35). This shows that Morishima's claim to the contrary (see Morishima 1989, 103) cannot be sustained. Obviously, the function need not be continuously differentiable.

17 If neither assumption 3 nor assumption 4 holds, then neither a production function for each quality of land nor a production function for the whole economy can be built up. G. Freni (1991) has provided an example (the reader unable to read Italian can consult Kurz and Salvadori 1995, 313) in which there is only one quality of land (so that there is no question of the existence of a production function for each quality of land or for the agricultural sector as a whole), one product (corn), and one quality of labor, and corn does enter into the production of itself but not in proportion to labor inputs (i.e., seed capital is not proportional to the wage-bill). In this example, for a given rate of profit (interest), a given amount of land, and a given amount of corn to be produced over and above the amount required as an input, there are three possible solutions.

18 The same applies to the construction by Samuelson (1959) and the one by Pasinetti (1960), which is an extension of Kaldor's.

19 Interestingly enough, Walras had an "imperative need" (411) for restating Ricardo's reasoning in terms of infinitesimals with respect to amounts of capital and amounts of product, but not in terms of qualities of land, which are finite in number in his exposition. An exposition in terms of one curve allows also "infinitesimal" differences among qualities of land, which, as a consequence, can be uncountably infinite in number.

20 Stigler (1941, 251) wrote: "We may note that Walras does not understand the true nature of the English dose of capital-and-labour. He subtracts labour costs from the product, whereas in the classical theory the composite dose of capital-and-labour was treated as a unit (and fundamentally, as a dose of *capital*)."

21 Similarly, Wicksteed 1894, 48.

22 Actually Walras assumed that the b_p's and the b_k's are not only variable but "decreasing functions of" b_t (413). This is of course not generally true: it is very well possible that a larger output per hectare is obtained by using less (or even none) of some input(s) and more of some other input(s) or some positive amount of some input(s) not used at all at the smaller level of production.

23 A proper comparison would require too much space. Here it must suffice to note that the formalism is different from the one used by Walras and that instead of variable b's a number of alternative processes are considered, one for each set of feasible b's; for each process there is a weak inequality (involving prices, rents, wage rate, and rate of profit) that needs to be satisfied, which for an operated process needs to be satisfied as an equation.

24 The definition of the rate of net income i is given in section 233 (pp. 268–69) and from it we see immediately that i is a pure number. Nevertheless, when referring to the rate of net income, Walras insisted to add: "in terms of numeraire."

25 See, for example, Garegnani 1990 and Kurz and Salvadori 1995, chap. 14.

26 Jevons ([1871] 1911, 268–69) wrote: "Another part of the current doctrines of Economics determines the rate of profit of capitalists in a very simple manner. The whole produce of industry must be divided into the portions paid as rent, taxes, profits and wages. We may exclude taxes as exceptional, and not very important. Rent also may be

eliminated, for it is essentially variable, and is reduced to zero in the case of the poorest land cultivated. We thus arrive at the simple equation—Produce = profit + wages.

"A plain result also is drawn from the formula; for we are told that if wages rise profits must fall, and *vice versâ*. But such a doctrine is radically fallacious; *it involves the attempt to determine two unknown quantities from one equation*. I grant that if the produce be a fixed amount, then if wages rise profits must fall, and *vice versâ*. Something might perhaps be made of this doctrine if Ricardo's theory of a natural rate of wages, that which is just sufficient to support the labourer, held true. But I altogether question the existence of any such rate" (emphasis in the original).

27 A few years before Dmitriev, Knut Wicksell had defended Ricardo against his critics. In Wicksell's view, "the way in which Ricardo develops his argument . . . is a model of strictly logical reasoning about a subject which seems, at first glance, to admit of so little precision" ([1893] 1954, 34); and "Ricardo's theory of value is, one finds, developed with a high degree of consistency and strictness" (40). He added: "Since, according to Ricardo, wages represent a magnitude fixed from the beginning, and since—as he later shows—the level of rent is also determined by independent causes, the cause of capital profit is already settled. It is neither possible nor necessary to explain capital profit in other ways, if the other assumptions are sound" (36–37). Therefore, in Wicksell's view, Ricardo's system was not underdetermined. (This does not mean, of course, that Wicksell agreed with the content of Ricardo's theory; on Wicksell's theory of distribution, see Kurz 2000.)

28 In accordance with Walras, rents and wages are taken to be paid at the end of the uniform period of production.

29 For the intensive margin we have to follow the procedure provided by J.-P. Guichard (1982).

30 Heterogeneous labor can easily be introduced into the picture; see Kurz and Salvadori 1995, chap. 11.

31 It deserves to be noted that depreciation charges cannot be assumed to be given, as was done by Walras. A proper treatment of fixed capital shows that depreciation charges depend on income distribution; see, for example, Kurz and Salvadori 1995, chaps. 7 and 9. Also this type of complication could easily be introduced into the picture.

32 Walras stressed that in equilibrium the rate of net income "is the same for all capital goods" (269; see also secs. 238 and 249); see also Walker 1996, 214.

33 In this simple exposition we have assumed the existence of a single "technique," that is, the existence of a single triplet $(\boldsymbol{A}, \boldsymbol{M}, \boldsymbol{V})$. If there were alternative techniques, the analysis would be more complex, but it is possible to prove that for each alternative a rate of net income i can be determined, and that in conditions of free competition the alternative will be chosen that yields the highest i. (For the exposition of a slightly different model, see Kurz and Salvadori 1995, chap. 5.)

References

Dmitriev, V. K. [1898] 1974. The Theory of Value of David Ricardo: An Attempt at a Rigorous Analysis. In *Economic Essays on Value, Competition, and Utility*, edited by D. M. Nuti and translated by D. Fry. Cambridge: Cambridge University Press.

Freni, G. 1991. Capitale tecnico nei modelli dinamici ricardiani. *Studi Economici* 44:141–59.

Garegnani, P. 1990. Quantity of Capital. In *Capital Theory*, edited by J. Eatwell, M. Milgate, and P. Newman, 1–78. London: Macmillan.

Guichard, J.-P. 1982. La rente différentielle intensive, expression d'un processus d'intensification de cultures. In *Etudes d'économie classique et néoricardienne*, edited by R. Arena, C. Berthomieu, M.-A. Ferreri, J.-P. Guichard, G. Hountondji, A. Maricic, J. T. Ravix, P.-M. Romani, and D. Torre, 115–38. Paris: PUF.

Jaffé, W. 1964. New Light on an Old Quarrel: Barone's Unpublished Review of Wicksteed's "Essay on the Coordination of the Laws of Distribution" and Related Documents. *Cahiers Vilfredo Pareto* 3:61–102.

Jevons, W. S. [1871] 1911. *The Theory of Political Economy*. 4th ed. London: Macmillan.

Kaldor, N. 1955–56. Alternative Theories of Distribution. *Review of Economic Studies* 23:83–100.

Kurz, H. D. 2000. Wicksell and the Problem of the "Missing" Equation. *HOPE* 32.4:765–88.

——. 2002. Surplus, Abstinenz und Lohnfonds: John Stuart Mill zur Theorie der Einkommensverteilung. In *John Stuart Mill*, edited by E. Streissler, 251–78. Berlin: Duncker und Humblot.

Kurz, H. D. and N. Salvadori. 1992. Morishima on Ricardo: A Review Article. *Cambridge Journal of Economics* 16:227–47.

——. 1995. *Theory of Production: A Long-Period Analysis*. Cambridge: Cambridge University Press.

——. 1998a. *The Elgar Companion to Classical Economics*. 2 vols. Cheltenham, U.K.: Edward Elgar.

——. 1998b. *Understanding "Classical" Economics: Studies in Long-Period Theory*. London: Routledge.

Mill, J. S. [1848] 1909. *Principles of Political Economy*. London: Longmans, Green and Co.

Morishima, M. 1977. *Walras's Economics: A Pure Theory of Capital and Money*. Cambridge: Cambridge University Press.

——. 1989. *Ricardo's Economics: A General Equilibrium Theory of Distribution and Growth*. Cambridge: Cambridge University Press.

Pasinetti, L. L. 1960. A Mathematical Formulation of the Ricardian System. *Review of Economic Studies* 27:78–98.

Ricardo, D. 1951–73. *The Works and Correspondence of David Ricardo*. 11 vols. Edited by Piero Sraffa with the collaboration of M. H. Dobb. Cambridge: Cambridge University Press. In the chapter referred to as *Works*.

Samuelson, P. A. 1959. A Modern Treatment of the Ricardian Economy: I. The Pricing of Goods and of Labor and Land Services. *Quarterly Journal of Economics* 73:1–35.

Sraffa, P. 1951. Introduction to *The Works and Correspondence of David Ricardo*. Cambridge: Cambridge University Press.

——. 1960. *Production of Commodities by Means of Commodities: Prelude to a Critique of Economic Theory*. Cambridge: Cambridge University Press.

Stigler, G. J. 1941. *Production and Distribution Theories*. New York: Macmillan.

Walker, D. 1996. *Walras's Market Models*. Cambridge: Cambridge University Press.

Walras, L. [1874–77] 1954. *Elements of Pure Economics*. Translated by W. Jaffé. London: Allen and Unwin.

Wicksell, K. [1893] 1954. *Value, Capital, and Rent*. Translated by S. H. Frowein. London: Allen and Unwin.

Wicksteed, P. H. 1894. *An Essay on the Co-ordination of the Laws of Distribution*. London: Macmillan.

5 Is Ricardian extensive rent a Nash equilibrium?*

Neri Salvadori

1. Introduction

The Ricardian extensive theory of rent is well known and does not require an introduction. The chapter 'On Rent' in Ricardo's *Principles* is certainly the *locus classicus* of the Ricardian theory of rent. More recently the issue has been investigated by Samuelson (1959), Sraffa (1960, pp. 74–8) and Quadrio Curzio (1967, 1980); see also Kurz and Salvadori (1995, pp. 277–320) and the literature referred to there. Following Ricardo and the other Classical authors, none of the modern contributors give a role to the distribution of land ownership among landlords. In this chapter, on the contrary, I will argue that if the demand for agricultural commodities and the distribution of marginal land ownership is such that demand can be satisfied only if the owner of the largest plot of that land rents out at least part of his or her land, then a positive rent on marginal land is possible (if landlords behave in a strategic way). This chapter is not devoted to a complete analysis of the case under consideration. In this respect I will fully explore only two cases: that in which each owner has the same amount of marginal land and that in which there are just two owners.

The other sections are as follows. Section 2 provides a summary account of a simple model of Ricardian extensive rent in order to introduce the language used in the following sections. Section 3 shows with a simple example in which the marginal land is equally distributed among a finite number of landlords that there are cases in which the equilibrium predicted by the Ricardian extensive theory of rent is not a Nash equilibrium, that no Nash equilibrium in pure strategies exists whereas there is one in mixed strategies. Section 4 shows exactly the same thing when marginal land is not equally distributed and there are only two owners of marginal land. Sections 5 raises some doubts on the relevance of the results presented when interpreted as a criticism of Ricardo; it suggests that a deeper analysis of Ricardo's ideas on the attitudes of landlords would be needed. Section 6 provides some concluding remarks.

* Reprinted with permission from *Money, Credit and the Role of the State: Essays in Honour of Augusto Graciani*, ed. Richard Arena and Neri Salvadori (Aldershot etc.: Ashgate, 2004), pp. 349–360.

2. Ricardian extensive rent theory

In this section I will give a presentation of extensive rent in the simplest case, that is when a commodity is produced by labour and land. The aim is just to introduce the language that will be used in the rest of the chapter. Thus the reader familiar with the literature on rent referred to by Kurz and Salvadori (1995, pp. 305–311) can skip this section. Many of the assumptions used in this section are totally dispensable for the argument developed in the following sections.

Consider an economy which produces only 'corn'. At the beginning of the production period labourers cultivate the land and at its end they harvest the crop. There is no commodity input in the production, i.e. there are no produced means of production. Corn is the only means of subsistence to support the population. Cultivation of the land does not alter the quality of the land. Labour is of uniform quality. There is no use of land other than employing it in corn production. As a consequence, the *reservation price* of the use of land is zero.[1] By contrast, the reservation price of labour in terms of corn is positive, even if it is not specified. Production is taken to be a time-consuming process. The length of the production period is assumed to be uniform across all available processes of production; that period is here called a 'year'. Wages and rents will be paid to workers and landlords respectively at the end of the year. The production technology can be represented, in abstract terms, as a set of processes. Returns to scale with regard to each process are assumed to be constant. There are n different qualities of land, named $1, 2, \ldots, n$, and for each quality of land there is exactly one process producing corn. Each process can be described as follows:

$$t \text{ acres of land } i \oplus l_i \text{ hours of labour} \rightarrow 1 \text{ bushel of corn}$$

or, for short,

$$t_i \oplus l_i \rightarrow 1$$

Table 5.1 provides the list of the existing processes. Obviously the existing qualities of land (and corresponding processes) can be numbered in such a way that $l_1 \leq l_2 \leq \cdots \leq l_n$. Let us first assume that $l_1 < l_2 < \cdots < l_n$. The case in which $l_i = l_{i+1}$, some i, will be considered later. Let G be the amount of corn produced and let T_i be the existing amount of land of quality i. If land i is cultivated, the following equation must be satisfied:

$$t_i q_i + w l_i = 1$$

where q_i is the rent per acre (or rate of rent) of land of quality i and w is the (*post factum*) wage rate.[2] Obviously $w > 0$ and $q_j \geq 0$. Moreover, it is assumed that no process can yield a surplus. Otherwise all farmer-capitalists would prefer to operate the surplus yielding process. Therefore it is assumed that:

$$t_j q_j + w l_j \geq 1 \quad (j = 1, 2, \ldots, n)$$

Table 5.1 The processes of production

Processes	*Land inputs*				*Labour*		*Corn*
	1	*2*	...	*n*			
(1)	t_1	—	...	—	l_1	→	1
(2)	—	t_2	...	—	l_2	→	1
...	...	...	...	...	...	→	...
(*n*)	—	—	...	t_n	l_n	→	1

If none of the qualities of land is scarce, competition amongst landlords drives the rent for each quality of land down to zero. As Ricardo wrote:

> On the first settling of a country, in which there is an abundance of rich and fertile land, a very small proportion of which is required to be cultivated for the support of the actual population, or indeed can be cultivated with the capital which the population can command, there will be no rent; *for no one would pay for the use of land, when there was an abundant quantity not yet appropriated,*[3] *and, therefore, at the disposal of whosoever might choose to cultivate it.*
>
> (*Works* I, p. 69, emphasis added)

Also in the subsequent paragraph Ricardo insists that in these circumstances the rent must be nought.

> On the common principles of supply and demand, no rent could be paid for such land, for the reason stated why nothing is given for the use of air and water, or for any other of the gifts of nature which exist in boundless quantity. With a given quantity of materials, and with the assistance of the pressure of the atmosphere, and the elasticity of steam, engines may perform work, and abridge human labour to a very great extent; but no charge is made for the use of these natural aids, because they are inexhaustible, and at every man's disposal. In the same manner the brewer, the distiller, the dyer, make incessant use of the air and water for the production of their commodities; but as the supply is boundless, they bear no price.
>
> (*ibid.*)

In such a situation with land of quality i being cultivated the wage rate w must satisfy the equation:

$$wl_i = 1$$

As a consequence $w = 1/l_i$. If $i \neq 1$, then a surplus can be generated by operating process (1) since by assumption $l_1 < l_2$. Hence, if landlords get nothing from renting their land, then only land 1 can be cultivated since all farmers would want to employ land 1. Since in this circumstance land 1 is not scarce, G must be lower than T_1/t_1, which is the maximum amount of corn producible on land of quality 1. As we have established, in this case all rent rates must equal zero and

$$w = w_1 := \frac{1}{l_1}$$

A positive rent on land 1 needs to be paid when land 2 is taken into cultivation.

> When in the progress of society, land of the second degree of fertility is taken into cultivation, rent immediately commences on that of the first quality, and the amount of that rent will depend on the difference in the quality of these two portions of land.
>
> (*ibid.*)

This is the case in which $T_1/t_1 < G < T_1/t_1 + T_2/t_2$. Corn cannot be produced by using land of the first quality alone: if demand is to be met, a process $(i) \neq (1)$ must be operated. Apart from process (1), process (2) is the cheapest. If both processes (1) and (2) are operated, then

$$t_1q_1 + wl_1 = 1, \quad t_2q_2 + wl_2 = 1$$

Since $G < T_1/t_1 + T_2/t_2$ at least part of the land of quality 1 or of quality 2 remains uncultivated. Land 1 is fully used, and $q_2 = 0$. In fact, if land 1 were not fully used, then competition amongst landlords would push q_1 down. Of necessity only lands 1 and 2 are cultivated. In fact if land $i \neq 1, 2$ is cultivated, then the tenant will get a lower amount of corn than that he or she can get on land 2. This is enough to determine the wage rate and the rates of rent:

$$w = w_2 := \frac{1}{l_2}, \quad q_1 = q_{12} := \frac{l_2 - l_1}{t_1 l_2}, \quad q_k = 0 \quad (k = 2, 3, \ldots, n)$$

In the present case land of quality 2 is what is called *marginal* land, that is, the quality of land which is cultivated, but not fully used. (Conversely, those qualities of land which are fully used are called *intra-marginal*.) In the formula above q_{12} is the rent rate paid to the owners of land 1 on the assumption that land 2 is marginal.

In general, if $\sum_{h=1}^{i-1} T_h/t_h < G < \sum_{h=1}^{i} T_h/t_h$, the same argument proves that lands $1, 2, \ldots, i-1$ are fully used; land i is used, but only partially, and the wage rate and rates of rent are determined as follows:

$$w = w_i := \frac{1}{l_i}, \quad q_h = q_{hi} := \frac{l_i - l_h}{t_h l_i} \quad (h = 1, 2, \ldots, i)$$

$$q_k = 0 \quad (k = i, i+1, \ldots, n)$$

There remain two special cases to be analysed. The first refers to a constellation where several processes employ the same amount of labour per unit of product, that is *the case in which two or more lands may be marginal at the same time.* In order to simplify the exposition, let us assume that $l_1 < l_2 < \cdots < l_i = l_{i+1} < l_{i+2} < \cdots < l_n$. In this case, if $\sum_{h=1}^{i-1} T_h/t_h < G < \sum_{h=1}^{i+1} T_h/t_h$, then both lands i and $i+1$ may be cultivated and therefore they are both marginal. The remainder of the analysis is unchanged.

The other special case is the one in which $G = \sum_{h=1}^{i} T_h/t_h$, that is *the case in which the marginal land is fully utilised.* In this case Ricardian extensive rent theory recognises that competition amongst landlords who own the marginal land need not be enough to push the respective rent rate down to zero. The marginal land may yield its proprietors a positive rent (though this is not necessarily the case according to the mentioned theory). The number of processes operated *falls short* of the sum of the number of commodities produced (in our case: one) plus the number of the qualities of land paying a rent: thus prices, rents and the wage rate cannot be fully determined and they may assume any level within a closed and bounded range:

$$w_{i+1} \leq w \leq w_i, \quad 0 \leq q_i = \frac{1 - wl_i}{t_i} \leq q_{i,i+1}$$

$$q_{hi} \leq q_h = \frac{1 - wl_h}{t_h} \leq q_{h,i+1} \quad (h = 1, 2, \ldots, i-1)$$

$$q_k = 0 \quad (k = i+1, \ldots, n)$$

Hence we can conclude by asserting that if the quantity of produced corn is not greater than $\sum_{h-1}^{n} T_h/t_h$, then there is a positive wage rate and there are nonnegative rates of rent such that the economy can produce that quantity of corn. Further, '[i]t is only [...] because land of an inferior quality [...] is called into cultivation, that rent is ever paid for the use of [land]' (*ibid.*).

3. The distribution of marginal land ownership: the case of equal distribution of marginal land

In the exposition of the previous section no attention was paid to the distribution of land ownership. A simple example can raise some doubt as to the validity of the argument. Assume that the amount of land 1, T_1, is owned by s landlords and each of them owns T_1/s units of it. Further, assume that $(s-1)T_1/st_1 < G < T_1/t_1$. The Ricardian extensive rent theory predicts that the rent rate q_1 equals 0. But this cannot be a Nash equilibrium. If all landlords but one charge a zero rent and one landlord charges a rent equal to q_{12} this ingenious landlord will be able to get a positive rent and he or she will be able to rent out the positive amount $Gt_1 - (s-1)T_1/s$ of his or her land.

No Nash equilibrium exists in pure strategies. Indeed, if not all landlords rent out their land at the same rate, all landlords who rent out their land at a rate lower than the maximum would get more if they were to rent out their land at a higher rate, provided it is still lower than the highest. If all landlords rent out their land at the same rate which is lower than $q_{12}[sGt_1 - (s-1)T_1]/Gt_1$, at least one of them would get more by renting out his or her land at the rate q_{12}. Finally, if all landlords were to rent out their land at the same rate greater than $q_{12}[sGt_1 - (s-1)T_1]/T_1$, at least one would get more by renting out his or her land at a slightly lower rate in order to rent out the whole amount of owned land instead of only part of it.

A Nash equilibrium in mixed strategies can easily be found. It is clear that no landlord can charge a rate higher than $q_M := q_{12}$, otherwise the tenants would prefer to rent land of quality 2. On the other hand no landlord is willing to charge a rate lower than

$$q_m := \frac{sGt_1 - (s-1)T_1}{T_1} q_M$$

otherwise it would be convenient to rent out the amount $Gt_1 - (s-1)T_1/s$ of land at rate q_M. Let $F_j(q)(j = 1, 2, \ldots, s)$ be the probability that all landlords but landlord j charge a rate lower than q; landlord j is indifferent among the rates in the range $[q_m, q_M]$ at which to rent out his or her land if $F_j(q)$ is such that

$$\begin{aligned} q_m \frac{T_1}{s} &= q_M \left[Gt_1 - (s-1)\frac{T_1}{s} \right] \\ &= q \left[Gt_1 - (s-1)\frac{T_1}{s} \right] F_j(q) + q\frac{T_1}{s}[1 - F_j(q)] \end{aligned}$$

that is

$$F_j(q) = F(q) := \frac{T_1(q - q_m)}{(T_1 - Gt_1)sq}$$

It is immediately recognised that

$$F(q_m) = 0, \quad F(q_M) = 1$$

Finally if $f_j(q)(j = 1, 2, \ldots, s)$ is the probability that landlord j charges a rate lower than q, then

$$F_j(q) = \prod_{h \neq j} f_h(q)$$

and, as a consequence of the perfect symmetry among the landlords, then

$$f_j(q) = f(q) := \sqrt[s-1]{F(q)}$$

It is also possible to calculate the average rate of rent q_{1a}. Since each landlord gets a payoff of $q_M[sGt_1 - (s-1)T_1]/s$, the s landlords get altogether $q_M[sGt_1 - (s-1)T_1]$ for the use of the amount Gt_1 of land 1. Then

$$q_{1a} = q_M \frac{sGt_1 - (s-1)T_1}{Gt_1} = q_m \frac{T_1}{Gt_1}$$

Hence

$$w = \frac{1 - t_1 q_{1a}}{l_1}$$

When $q_{1a} = 0$ (that is $G = (s-1)T_1/st_1$), $w = 1/l_1$, whereas when $q_{1a} = q_M = q_{12}$ (that is $G = T_1/t_1$), $w = 1/l_2$.

Assume now that the amount of land i, T_i, is owned by s landlords and each of them owns T_i/s amount of land. Further, assume that

$$\sum_{h=1}^{i-1} \frac{T_h}{t_h} + \frac{(s-1)T_i}{st_i} < G < \sum_{h=1}^{i} \frac{T_h}{t_h}$$

Following the previously stated argument it is possible to show that the solution predicted by the Ricardian theory of extensive rent is not a Nash equilibrium, that no Nash equilibrium in pure strategies exists and that a Nash equilibrium in mixed strategies exists and the average rent on land i is

$$q_{1a} = q_{i,i+1} \frac{sG^* t_i - (s-1)T_i}{G^* t_i}$$

where

$$G^* = G - \sum_{h=1}^{i-1} \frac{T_h}{t_h}$$

Then the wage rate and the rent rates of all lands are determined:

$$w = \frac{1 - t_i q_{ia}}{l_i}, \quad q_h = \frac{1 - w l_h}{t_h} \quad (h = 1, 2, \ldots, i-1)$$

$$q_k = 0 \quad (k = i+1, \ldots, n)$$

4. Marginal land ownership distribution: The case of two landlords

In the previous section it was assumed that the marginal land was equally distributed among s landlords. In this section I wish to consider the case in which marginal land is not equally distributed, but where there are only two owners of marginal land.

Assume that the amount of land i, T_i, is owned by two landlords, landlord j owns the amount $T_{ij} (j = 1, 2)$ of land i, and $T_{i1} > T_{i2}$. Further, assume that:

$$\sum_{h=1}^{i-1} \frac{T_h}{t_h} + \frac{T_{i2}}{t_i} < G < \sum_{h=1}^{i} \frac{T_h}{t_h}$$

Following the previously stated argument it is possible to show that the solution predicted by the Ricardian theory of extensive rent is not a Nash equilibrium and that no Nash equilibrium in pure strategies exists.

Let us define

$$G^* := G - \sum_{h=1}^{i-1} \frac{T_h}{t_h}, \quad G^{**} := \min\left(G^*, \frac{T_{i1}}{t_i}\right)$$

It is clear that no landlord can charge a rent rate higher than $q_M := q_{i,i+1}$, otherwise the tenants would prefer to rent land of quality $i+1$. On the other hand landlord 1 is not willing to charge a rent rate lower than

$$q_m := \frac{G^* t_i - T_{i2}}{G^{**} t_i} q_M$$

otherwise it would be convenient to rent out the amount $G^* t_i - T_{i2}$ of land at rate q_M. Hence, landlord 2 is also not interested in renting out his or her land at a rate lower than q_m, provided that the probability of landlord 1 renting out his or her land at rate q_m is nought. Let $f_j(q)(j = 1, 2)$ be the probability that landlord j charges a rate lower than q; then landlord 1 is indifferent among the rates in the range (q_m, q_M) at which to rent out his or her land if $f_2(q)$ is such that

$$q_m G^{**} t_i = q_M(G^* t_i - T_{i2}) = q(G^* t_i - T_{i2}) f_2(q) + q G^{**} t_i [1 - f_2(q)]$$

that is

$$f_2(q) = \frac{G^{**} t_i (q - q_m)}{(G^{**} t_i + T_{i2} - G^* t_i) q}$$

It is immediately recognised that

$$f_2(q_m) = 0, \quad f_2(q_M) = 1$$

Similarly, landlord 2 is indifferent among the rates in the range (q_m, q_M) at which to rent out his or her land if $f_1(q)$ is such that

$$H = q(G^* - G^{**}) t_i f_1(q) + q T_{i2} [1 - f_1(q)]$$

that is

$$f_1(q) = \frac{T_{i2} q - H}{(G^{**} t_i + T_{i2} - G^* t_i) q}$$

where H is the expected payoff of landlord 2. Obviously $0 \leq f_1(q) \leq 1$ for each q in $[q_m, q_M]$ if and only if[4]

$$(G^* - G^{**}) t_i q_M \leq H \leq T_{i2} q_m$$

If $H < T_{i2}q_m$, then landlord 2 could get a larger payoff by charging a rent equal to

$$\bar{q} := \frac{H + T_{i2}q_m}{2T_{i2}} < q_m$$

Then $H = T_{i2}q_m$ and

$$f_1(q) = \frac{T_{i2}(q - q_m)}{(G^{**}t_i + T_{i2} - G^{*}t_i)q}$$

It is immediately recognised that

$$f_1(q_m) = 0, \quad f_1(q_M) = \frac{T_{i2}}{G^{**}t_i} < 1$$

This means that landlord 1 rents out his or her land at rate q_M with probability $1 - T_{i2}/G^{**}t_i$, which is positive. As a consequence the support of the set of the strategies of landlord 2 is the range open on the right $[q_m, q_M)$. On the contrary, the support of the set of the strategies of landlord 1 is the closed range $[q_m, q_M]$.

The average rate of rent q_{1a} is determined by the ratio of the sum of the two expected payoffs to the cultivated land:

$$q_{1a} = q_m \frac{G^{**}t_i + T_{i2}}{G^{*}t_i} = \left(1 + \frac{T_{i2}}{G^{**}t_i}\right)\left(1 - \frac{T_{i2}}{G^{*}t_i}\right) q_M$$

Then the wage rate and the other rent rates are determined as at the end of the previous section.

5. Reasons to ignore the fact that distribution of properties may affect rent rates

It could be interesting to investigate whether there are good reasons to ignore the fact that the distribution of landed property may affect rent rates. At the moment I can see only two circumstances which would work in this direction.

First, if each landlord had just a small amount of land, then the strategic behaviour of landlords would explain such a small part of the formation of rent that it could be ignored. This reason is not very close to the idea of society that Ricardo had in mind. The landlords were mainly aristocrats, the monarchy, and the clergy. The idea of a world of small landowners was certainly not in Ricardo's thoughts.

Second, we can assume that landlords – precisely because they are mainly aristocrats, the monarchy, and the clergy – do not behave strategically since rent-seeking or profit-seeking was not part of the behavioural code of these social classes. Both extensive and intensive rent can be explained on the assumption that the tenants are profit-seeking and the landlords just get what is offered to them (in the long run only the tenants offering the highest rent rate would survive). However, this contrast with the attitude of Ricardo towards the *Wealth of Nations* and the fact that Book III of *The Wealth of Nations* abounds with arguments concerning the rent-seeking attitude of landlords; see for instance:

> Farms were enlarged, and the occupiers of land, notwithstanding the complaints of depopulation, reduced to the number necessary for cultivating it, according to the imperfect state of cultivation and improvement in those times. By the removal of the unnecessary mouths, and by exacting from the farmer the full value of the farm, a greater surplus, or what is the same thing, the price of a greater surplus, was obtained for the proprietor, ... [the proprietor] was desirous to raise his rents above what his lands, in the actual state of their improvement, could afford. His tenants could agree to this upon one condition only, that they should be secured in their possession, for such a term of years as might give them time to recover with profit whatever they should lay out in the further improvement of the land. . . . and hence the origin of long leases.
> (*WN*, III.iv.13)

6. Concluding remarks

The analysis of classical themes on the basis of game theory has a well-established tradition. I recall the analysis of competition à la Bertrand. Modern literature has shown that the result obtained by Bertrand requires that each duopolist has enough productive capacity to satisfy the whole demand. When this condition is not met, there are different outcomes.

In this chapter I showed that a similar story can be told with respect to the Ricardian theory of extensive rent. The determination of rents yielded by intra-marginal lands is analogous to the case in which two firms compete à la Bertrand, but the capacity available to each firm is severely constrained: each capacity is lower than or equal to the quantity which is the best reaction in the assumption that the other firm produces a quantity equal to its capacity. The determination of rents yielded by the marginal lands when the owner of the largest plot of marginal land does not need to rent out at least part of his or her land is analogous to the case in which two firms compete à la Bertrand and their capacities are higher than the quantity demanded when price equals zero and so the typical Bertrand outcome is obtained. These two results are also those predicted by the Ricardian theory of extensive rent. But if the owner of the largest plot of marginal land needs to rent out at least part of his or her land, then the Ricardian theory of extensive rent predicts exactly the same outcome. This chapter showed that such a prediction is not a Nash equilibrium and investigated two special cases: that in which marginal land is equally distributed among a finite number of landlords and that in which this is not so, but where there are only two landlords owning the marginal land. In both special cases a Nash equilibrium in mixed strategies was found. This is analogous to the case in which two firms compete à la Bertrand, but their capacities are between the two cases mentioned above.[5]

One of the main differences between the Ricardian theory of extensive rent and the argument proposed here is that the Ricardian theory predicts that if the output increases continuously, prices (including the wage and rent rates) change spasmodically, whereas if distribution of land property is taken into consideration, then if output increases continuously, prices are either constant or change continuously but not necessarily smoothly.

Acknowledgements

Section 2 of this chapter draws freely on still unpublished fruits of a most pleasant collaboration with Heinz Kurz. I should like to thank Antonio D'Agata, Massimo De Francesco, Giuseppe Freni, Heinz Kurz, and Pier Mario Pacini for useful conversations on previous drafts of the other sections.

Notes

1 An alternative use of the land – for example, a landowner retaining a part of his/her land for country walks or hunting – would run counter to the assumption that there is only a single commodity produced in the economy.
2 The use of a post factum wage rate in a framework in which there are no material inputs apart for the use of land avoids the concepts of 'capital' and 'profit'. Alternatively, also in order to be close to the spirit of the Ricardian presentation, we can assume that there is a given real ante factum wage rate $\bar{w} \leq 1/l_n$ and that the rate of profit r is determined by the equation $w = \bar{w}(1+r)$ once the post factum wage rate is determined. In this way a fall in the post factum wage rate turns out to be a fall in the rate of profit.
3 The reference to uncultivated land as 'non-appropriated land' could be considered a sign of a doubt of Ricardo about the issues developed in this chapter. However this doubt is not investigated at all by him.
4 It is easily verified that $(G^* - G^{**})t_i q_M < T_{i2} q_m$ since $G^{**} t_i - T_{i2} > 0$ and $G^{**} t_i + T_{i2} > G^* t_i$.
5 These results concerning firms have been known since Kreps and Scheinkman (1983). In their paper they present a two-stage oligopoly game where in the first stage there is simultaneous setting of production capacities and, in the second, after capacity levels have been made public, there is production and price competition à la Bertrand. The unique outcome equilibrium is the Cournot equilibrium. Unlike capacity, the amounts of land cannot be modified by man: 'Rent is that portion of the produce of the earth, which is paid to the landlord for the use of the original and indestructible powers of the soil' (*Works* I, p. 67). Nevertheless, a two-stage model can be built. In the first stage the distribution of property rights on land among landlords can be established. I do not exclude that the Ricardo theory of extensive rent could be totally vindicated by proving that the outcome of the first stage cannot be that in which the owner of the largest plot of marginal land needs to rent out at least part of his or her land.

References

Kreps, D. and J. Scheinkman (1983), 'Quantity precommitment and Bertrand competition yield Cournot outcomes', *Bell Journal of Economics*, **44**, pp. 326–37.
Kurz, H.D. and N. Salvadori (1995), *Theory of Production. A Long-period Analysis*, Cambridge, Melbourne and New York: Cambridge University Press.
Quadrio Curzio, A. (1967), *Rendita e distribuzione in un modello economico plurisettoriale*, Milano: Giuffrè.

Quadrio Curzio, A. (1980), 'Rent, income distribution, and orders of efficiency and rentability', in L. Pasinetti (ed.), *Essays on the Theory of Joint Production*, London: Macmillan, pp. 218–40.

Ricardo, D. (1951 ssq.). *The Works and Correspondence of David Ricardo*, 11 volumes, edited by P. Sraffa in collaboration with M.H. Dobb, Cambridge: Cambridge University Press. In the text referred to as *Works*, volume number and page number.

Samuelson, P.A. (1959), 'A Modern treatment of the Ricardian economy: I. The pricing of goods and of labor and land services; II. Capital and interest aspects of the pricing process', *Quarterly Journal of Economics*, **73**, pp. 1–35 and pp. 217–31.

Schumpeter, J.A. (1954), *History of Economic Analysis*, New York: Oxford University Press.

Smith, A. (1976), *An Inquiry into the Nature and Causes of the Wealth of Nations*, 1st edn 1776, Vol. II of *The Glasgow Edition of the Works and Correspondence of Adam Smith*, edited by R.H. Campbell, A.S. Skinner and W.B. Todd, Oxford: Oxford University Press. In the text quoted as *WN*, book number, chapter number, section number, paragraph number.

Sraffa, P. (1960), *Production of Commodities by Means of Commodities. Prelude to a Critique of Economic Theory*, Cambridge: Cambridge University Press.

Part II

Sraffa's contributions

6 Keynes and Sraffa's 'Difficulties with J. H. Hollander'*

A note on the history of the RES edition of *The Works and Correspondence of David Ricardo*

Christian Gehrke and Heinz D. Kurz

1. Introduction

It is well known that the realization of the famous editorial project of the Royal Economic Society (RES) to publish *The Works and Correspondence of David Ricardo* (Ricardo, *Works* 1951–73) was delayed for a considerable time. One of the main reasons for delay was the discovery of Ricardo's letters to James Mill in 1943. This forced the editor, Piero Sraffa, to alter the project radically and to postpone completion of the edition (see Sraffa's 'General Preface' in Ricardo, *Works* I: ix–x).[1] Another reason was Sraffa's difficulties in composing the introductions. In this paper we deal with yet another obstacle which up till now is largely unknown. This concerns the role a then leading authority on Ricardo – Jacob Harry Hollander (1871–1940), professor of economics at the Johns Hopkins University, Baltimore, and President of the American Economic Association in 1921 – played in the early phase of the project. Hollander effectively obstructed the progress of the edition for a considerable time. How and why he did so requires an intricate story to be unravelled.

Our paper uses hitherto unpublished material, especially from Piero Sraffa's Papers, Trinity College, Cambridge, John Maynard Keynes's Papers, King's College, Cambridge, and Jacob Harry Hollander's Papers.[2] The latter are kept in the Milton S. Eisenhower Library (Special Collections) of the Johns Hopkins University at Baltimore (USA). However, it should be pointed out that, curiously, there are no letters from Keynes or Sraffa in Hollander's correspondence. Moreover, with respect to Hollander's correspondence with Frank Ricardo, a great-grandson of David Ricardo, only the part relating to the years prior to 1930 has been preserved. It is not clear when and by whom these parts of Hollander's correspondence were removed.[3] Since in these cases we do not have access to the originals, all citations refer to the copies or drafts of letters kept by the senders.[4]

* Reprinted with permission from *Euro. J. History of Economic Thought*, 9:4, 2002.

2. 'The "Big" Ricardo': the RES editorial project and the transfer of editorship

The formal decision to prepare a definitive edition of Ricardo's *Works* was taken at the meeting of the RES Council on 17 December 1925 (see LSE: RES/2/1/2).[5] At the meeting of 11 March 1926 it was decided to entrust Professor T. E. Gregory of the LSE with the editorship. Gregory had been involved over the past couple of years, together with Hollander, in preparing an edition of Ricardo's notes on Malthus's *Principles*. In a letter dated 14 June 1926 Gregory informed Hollander that he was now in charge of 'the "Big" Ricardo'; Hollander replied on 28 June: 'you will feel at liberty to command me in any way in the matter of the Ricardo' (H: MS 59, Box 4).

Gregory, alas, made hardly any progress during the following years and soon showed signs of wanting to resign (see, e.g., K: RES/1/1/164–5 and S: D3/11/62: 52). Who should be invited to take over the task? While we are not aware of any evidence that his name was brought up, it might be thought that Hollander was an ideal candidate. A leading authority on David Ricardo, he had variously edited and published books and articles dealing with Ricardo (see, in particular, Hollander, 1895, 1904, 1910). However the Council, which met on 13 February 1930 to decide the transfer of editorship, might have had good reasons for not approaching him.[6] First, the Council seems to have been keen to entrust a British economist or at least an economist working in Britain with the task as a precondition of a close collaboration with the RES. Second, it had not escaped the attention of the members of the Council that Hollander and Gregory had taken nine years to publish Ricardo's *Notes* (Hollander and Gregory 1928). More importantly, the edition had not been well received: the June issue of 1929 of the *Economic Journal* carried a review by Bonar pointing out a number of annoying editorial slips and printer's errors; and in the November issue of *Economica* of the same year Cannan published a devastating review article which concluded that: 'the printed text is often nonsense if read with all the bracketed matter included, and equally nonsense if the bracketed matter is all excluded' (Cannan 1929: 359). As regards Sraffa, things were different. Several influential members of the Council held him in high esteem as a scholar and expert in the field of classical economics and monetary theory. Gregory, Foxwell, and Cannan had known him as a research student at the LSE in the summer of 1921 and in the academic year 1921–2, and they appreciated his meticulosity and outstanding intellectual power. In 1923 Foxwell had written a highly favourable letter of recommendation on Sraffa's behalf (see Naldi 2000: 27). Edgeworth had admired Sraffa for his 1925 paper (Sraffa 1925). It was hardly a surprise therefore when Keynes was requested to invite Sraffa to take over the editorship (see LSE: RES/2/1/2).[7] Soon afterwards Sraffa appears to have accepted the invitation and embarked on the project. In the early phase he was assisted by Keynes, who supplied him with letters of introduction and helped him with the drafting of letters.

Keynes and Sraffa informed David Ricardo's descendants and a number of scholars and book collectors about the project (see S: D3/11/65: 42). On 17 March

1930 Sraffa wrote to Keynes: 'As regards Hollander, it will perhaps be better to write [to] him only after having ascertained from Gregory about the copyright of the Notes on Malthus' (S: D3/11/65: 40; the original letter is available in K: L/S/42). The next day Keynes wrote to Gregory:

> Sraffa is now *tackling the Ricardo job like a maniac;* so it is becoming necessary to make various practical arrangements. We should like to include the notes on Malthus in some shape or form. Could you advise me what steps we ought to take about this if we are not to get into trouble with you or Hollander or your publishers?
>
> (S: D3/11/62: 51)[8]

Gregory replied on 19 March 1930, making detailed and constructive suggestions for the edition (see S: D3/11/62: 38–46). Sraffa answered the day after and had several appointments with him in May.[9] Sraffa was keen to devote all his time and energy to the project: on 5 June 1930 he applied for leave of absence in the following Michaelmas term (S: B9/1: 15).[10]

Before we provide an account of the collaboration between Hollander, on the one hand, and Keynes and Sraffa on the other, we recall how this collaboration was reflected in what Sraffa put in print about the American scholar in the Ricardo edition.

3. Sraffa in print on Hollander

In the 'General Preface' of Ricardo's *Works* Sraffa makes acknowledgment 'for valuable assistance, advice and information, to the late Dr James Bonar, Professor Jacob Viner, Professor F. A. Hayek, Professor George O'Brien, the late Professor Edwin Cannan, Sir Theodore Gregory, Mr Nicholas Kaldor and Dr R. Mattioli' (*Works* I: xi). Interestingly, Hollander's name is missing. The latter is only mentioned in the following context: 'A bundle of similar papers, which had become separated from the main body, was found earlier by Mr Frank Ricardo and these were published by Professor J. H. Hollander while the present edition was in preparation, so that it was possible to include them as well' (ibid.: viii). This remark should be seen in connection with the special thanks Sraffa expresses to Frank Ricardo 'for his fruitful search for manuscripts, for making available those in his possession and *for much trouble taken in securing others'* (ibid.: xi; emphasis added). The following sections make clear what Sraffa probably meant by the discreet hint in the italicised part of the quotation.

Like Cannan and Bonar, Sraffa did not think highly of the Hollander–Gregory edition of the *Notes on Malthus*. In Volume II of the RES edition Sraffa pointed out: 'The method adopted in the present edition follows Ricardo's hint (when he "supposed" himself "about publishing a new edition" of Malthus's work): namely, of giving Malthus's text at the top and Ricardo's Notes at the bottom. This also conforms to Professor Cannan's idea, when he criticised the Hollander–Gregory edition' *(Works* II: xvi). A few pages later he stressed that the volume had been printed, for Malthus's text, from the first edition of 1820, and, for Ricardo's Notes, from a copy of the Hollander–Gregory edition – purged of 'the errors which abound in that edition and often distort the sense' (ibid.: xviii).

In Sraffa's 'Addenda to the Memoir' (of Moses Ricardo) in Volume X of the RES edition a number of errors in Hollander's biographical essay (Hollander 1910) regarding the date of birth of Abraham Ricardo and his move to England (see *Works* X: 18–21) and the date of birth of David Ricardo (ibid.: 29) are corrected. In 'Appendix A. Bibliography of Ricardo's Works' in Volume X Hollander's 1932 edition of Ricardo's *Minor Papers* is described as follows: 'This volume contains an oddly assorted collection of papers, notes and jottings, as well as a few letters, from that bundle of the Ricardo Papers . . . [which became] separated from the main body and [was] found with the Notes on Malthus in 1919' (*Works* X: 374). And in 'Appendix B. A Survey of Ricardo Manuscripts' Sraffa noted, after providing a brief description of some Ricardo manuscripts containing excerpts from and summaries of the writings of other economists, which he decided not to include in the RES edition: 'The summaries described in this and the preceding paragraph were printed *in extenso* in Ricardo's *Minor Papers*' (*Works* X: 391n; emphasis in the original).

4. Contact with Ricardo's descendants and with Hollander

In his capacity as Secretary of the RES, Keynes first contacted Colonel Henry G. Ricardo at Gatcombe Park, David Ricardo's former residence, who forwarded Keynes's letter to his cousin Frank Ricardo at Bromesberrow Place (Christchurch, Hants). In a letter dated 20 March 1930 Frank Ricardo wrote to Colonel Ricardo:

> Many thanks for sending me enclosure. I agree with you: why in the world do they want to republish all the works again?
>
> I thought – indeed I know – that *Professor Hollander (America) has 'squeezed all the juice' out of the matter.* It was to him that I handed that manuscript which I came across and he has now published it in company with Prof. Gregory of the London School of Economics. *Hollander promised to let me have it back, but he hasn't done so yet.*
>
> *I found a lot more letters of D.R. when clearing out Bromesberrow but they do not contain any MSS.* I have them here.
>
> (S: D3/11/71: 58)

Sraffa, who via Keynes had been invited to visit Gatcombe Park, went there on 28 March. From Gatcombe he informed Keynes about the additional material which had recently been found at Bromesberrow Place, and asked him to write immediately to Frank Ricardo (LSE: RES/2/1/2). To Keynes's letter of 2 April 1930 (S: D3/11/71: 59) Frank Ricardo replied on 6 April:

> I shall be glad to assist in any way I can in the project of the Royal Economic Society of publishing the works of David Ricardo. . . .
>
> As to the manuscript of 'Notes on Malthus' this is still with Professor Hollander: he promised to return it to me & I was then going to put it in the care of some Library or Museum. I note however that you will be communicating with Prof. Hollander and I entirely agree to your including the manuscript in your proposed publication. . . .
>
> I have a box (recently recovered from a lumber room) containing a very considerable number of letters & other papers which originally belonged to D. Ricardo. Some (pamphlets etc.) have marginal notes in his handwriting, others are letters to him of a purely domestic nature, and there are three files (all as I found them) containing respectively letters from Mill, McCulloch, Trower and Malthus – all to David Ricardo. Lastly I have a few letters of his to Maria Edgeworth & of hers to him: these deal chiefly with the Potato Crop and Ireland.
>
> If any of the above are of any use to your Society in their coming Publication I am quite ready to lend them.
>
> (S: D3/11/71: 57)

Keynes replied immediately, asking Frank Ricardo to kindly send the box to King's College where he and Sraffa could examine its contents (S: D3/11/71: 47), and informed Sraffa about the details of Frank Ricardo's find. In replying to this news Sraffa wrote to Keynes (from Milan):

> *The letters from Mill must be the most important thing that could have been found* – even more than Ricardo's own letters to Mill; these would no doubt contain better economics, but we have plenty of that; *what was really wanted was detailed evidence of Mill's influence on R., which must be nearly equivalent to the formation of R's mind.* Incidentally, they may give us some clue for finding the whereabouts of the other side of the correspondence.
>
> (K: RES/1/1/180)

The day after he had written for the first time to Frank Ricardo, Keynes informed Hollander

> that the Council of the Royal Economic Society have decided to publish a *complete edition* of the Works of Ricardo. . . . The editorship was originally to have been given to Professor Gregory. But as he was unable to find the time we have now entrusted it to Mr Piero Sraffa, University Lecturer at Cambridge. Though an Italian citizen [!], he is specially qualified for the work by his knowledge and interest in Ricardian subjects.

> He is, however, *most anxious that we should from the outset have your benevolent approval of our project . . . There is one particular matter in which we shall be grateful for your help. It is, of course, vital for us that the collection should be as complete as we can make it. We are therefore proposing, if we can, to include all extant letters of any importance, and there are also the Notes to Malthus. . . .*
>
> I suppose there is no hope of you visiting England in the near future? It would be a great advantage to us if we could have your personal advice by word of mouth.
>
> (S: D3/11/63: 71(i))

Hollander responded to Keynes:

> At the outset let me say that *I shall be happy to extend any possible aid in connection with the projected edition of the works of Ricardo*, and I beg that you will indicate this to the Council of the Royal Economic Society, if it be proper, and to Mr. Piero Sraffa. . . . You will be glad to know that I am to be in London from about June 25 to July 4. . . . [I] t would be a great pleasure to see something of you and to meet Sraffa.
>
> (S: D3/11/63: 71(ii))

By May Frank Ricardo sent Keynes 'the letters etc. relating to David Ricardo' he had recently found (S: D3/11/71: 53). Keynes reported on Sraffa's reaction when the latter had had the chance to consult the documents: 'Piero was [at] a pitch of excitement and stayed up all night, until six o'clock next morning, reading them' (K: letter to Lydia Keynes, 1 June 1930). A few days later, in a letter of 6 June in reply to one from Sraffa of 3 June (see S: D3/11/71: 54), Frank Ricardo invited Sraffa to Bromesberrow Place:

> I am glad to hear that some, at all events, of the D. Ricardo correspondence is proving of interest.
>
> It is curious – and unfortunate – that *it all appears to break off in 1821.* I do not think I can lay my hand on any more, but when you come here you can see for yourself as, I need hardly say, I have thrown nothing away. I shall be glad for you to glance through the remainder so as to make sure of no omissions.
>
> (S: D3/11/71: 50)

According to Sraffa's diary he went to see Frank Ricardo in Christchurch on 18 June 1930. Among his papers Sraffa kept a handwritten memo: 'Frank Ricardo gives me letter to Hollander, letter 18.6.30 giving him full authority to hand over to me MS of Notes on Malthus' (S: D3/11/71: 44). The question of the missing correspondence of the final years of David Ricardo's life could not be settled on that occasion and, as we shall see, it required more time to finally answer it.

Frank Ricardo made a thorough search at his solicitors on Sraffa's behalf, and then another one in early July, but, as he informed Sraffa in a letter of 3 July, he did 'not have much success' and the only letters he found 'are all of 1820' (S: D3/11/71: 43).

Towards the end of June 1930 Hollander arrived in London. Keynes arranged a lunch with him and Sraffa. In his diary Sraffa noted that on the occasion of the meeting on 1 July he and Keynes were handed over the Notes on Malthus from Hollander. The meeting appears to have been to Sraffa's full satisfaction, because he was given renewed assurance of Hollander's support for the RES project. Sraffa wrote to Keynes: 'Ever so many thanks for the lunch on Tuesday – I enjoyed it immensely' (K: L/S/54). There is no hint that at the meeting Hollander disclosed that he was in the possession of further 'Ricardiana'.

5. 'In Hollander's hands'

Sraffa did not give up the idea of tracing the missing pieces of correspondence. He asked Frank Ricardo to search anew Bromesberrow Place. While a few more items were found, the missing late letters were not among them. In a letter to Sraffa of 16 October 1930 Frank Ricardo speculated that 'the correspondence in question would probably have found its way to the Office of the Solicitors who were concerned with the Probate of his Will. Do you know who they were?' (S: D3/11/71: 42). In December Sraffa gave Frank Ricardo the names and addresses of the successors of David Ricardo's solicitors in order to contact them (see S: D3/11/71: 49). In addition, an announcement of the RES editorial project was placed in the December issue of the *Economic Journal* of 1930 in which the members of the Society were asked to give 'what help they can in tracking down any of Ricardo's letters which have not yet been traced by the Editor'. Similar announcements were also placed in various newspapers.

Together with a letter dated 29 November 1930, in which he inquired about a letter from Ricardo to Say that had recently been sold by the Parisian bookseller Manier, Sraffa sent Hollander a newspaper cutting on the Ricardo edition. Hollander responded on 9 January 1931, disclosing some facts which must have taken Sraffa by surprise and shattered his confidence in Hollander's willingness to cooperate:

> I have a few unpublished Ricardo letters, but like the Manier item *they are of little economic interest.* I am using them, wholly or in part in my opus, and *there-after* you are entirely at liberty to reprint them.
>
> As you will see from the enclosed, the Johns Hopkins Press is about to issue the letters of McCulloch to Ricardo – to which I have thought of adding a few letters of James Mill to Ricardo. In the clipping sent me, as in the paragraph in the current Journal, I notice that you have some, presumably additional letters, of McCulloch and of Mill. *I am wondering whether you would let me have copies of these for inclusion in the Johns Hopkins reprint.*

> If I might have these promptly I could hold up the printers to ensure insertion. Thereafter it would be possible for you to include the entire series in your edition.
>
> (S: D3/11/63: 67)

The enclosure was presumably a pre-publication announcement of the Fourth Series of 'Reprints of Economic Tracts' (see Sraffa's library, item 8112), in which the Johns Hopkins Press invited subscription to a reprint of four tracts: '(1) Letters of John Ramsay McCulloch to David Ricardo, 1818–1823; (2) Minor Papers on the Bullion Report, 1810. By David Ricardo; (3) Contributions of John Stuart Mill to the *Traveller* (London), in December 1822; (4) *Observations on the Circumstances. . . .* By John Barton. London, 1817' (ibid.). Sraffa drafted two replies to Hollander and asked Keynes for his assistance. On 22 January 1931 he wrote to Keynes:

> It is of course *extraordinarily cheeky* of Hollander to ask [for] copies of our letters in order to publish them in a great hurry, while he refuses to let us have copies of his, until he has published them. *But I doubt that his exhibition of jealousy is a good reason for my following his example.*
>
> *I am therefore, on the whole, inclined to let him have the McC. Letters.* We have seventeen of them, all unpublished. He may have as many, or 25 or 26 at most: in this latter case, we would make his collection complete. The case is quite different as regards Mills [sic] letters. We have fourty-seven [sic], and he says he has only 'a few': very few indeed, probably, as he has not even thought it worth while advertising them in the prospectus of the McCulloch letters, to which they are to be 'added'.
>
> (S: D3/11/65: 62)

The letter Sraffa finally sent, after having consulted with Keynes, is dated 31 January 1931 and reads:

> I am most interested to hear of the proposed Johns Hopkins Press re-prints. I hope they come out as soon as possible; we are now getting seriously to work and it would be a great convenience to have the reprints published before we come to deal with the volume of letters. *As regards the letters which we have got hold of, they are somewhat extensive and ought to be reserved for the main collection.* I hope you will *follow up your own suggestion of including in the reprints the letters which you have from James Mill to Ricardo.*
>
> I wonder if it would be asking too much of you to let me have proofs of the reprint or possibly of the letters, of course, *on the direct understanding that we should not publish them or make any other use of them until your volumes are out.* This would enable me to know how much space to keep for them and also to avoid any other last moment corrections. As regards your own Opus, it will be of great benefit to us if that too were to come out at an early date, so that we could have the benefit of it and of the many facts and items which you have got together since you last delivered yourself on this subject.

> But I expect that this is to hope for too much. Do you think that there is any likelihood of your book being finished in time for us to make reference to it in our edition?
>
> (S: D3/11/63: 64(i–ii))

Hollander was never to answer this letter. In a letter dated 8 September 1931 and sent from Rapallo, Sraffa informed Keynes that Hollander had not replied 'to my (or rather, your) last letter, and his Ricardian pamphlets have not appeared: I fear he is holding them up till our edition has appeared. Could anything be done to speed him up?' (LSE: RES/10/2/1). Keynes reminded Hollander on 22 October 1931:

> You will remember that there was some correspondence between you, Sraffa and myself about the Ricardo letters which you are publishing in your forthcoming reprint of Economic Tracts. The last letter was from Sraffa to yourself on January 31st of this year. Since then we have been hoping to hear something further from you, but unavailingly so far.
>
> As your volume was already announced by the Johns Hopkins Press we have been expecting it before now, but doubtless it is on the point of publication. I shall be very glad if you can let me have proofs of the Ricardo portion at your earliest possible convenience.
>
> You will remember that the Royal Economic Society is undertaking publication of the works and correspondence of Ricardo in 6 volumes, *as far as possible complete. Obviously it is essential that we should include your interesting items.* Our publication will not be ready for some little time yet, but preparations are at a fairly advanced stage, and *it would be a matter of very considerable convenience to be able to know just how much space to allow for the new material which you will be including in your reprint.*
>
> (S: D3/11/63: 62)

By 14 December 1931 still no reply from Hollander had arrived. Sraffa therefore attempted to get the necessary information via Jacob Viner to whom he wrote on that day:

> Professor Hollander has announced, about a year ago, some pamphlets containing unpublished letters to, & papers by, Ricardo. Although Keynes & I have written to him several times since then, we have never obtained a reply. We are anxious to know whether they will be published in time to be included in our edition, & if possible to obtain from him his proofs or an early copy – *though of course we would undertake to publish only after him.*
>
> (PU: Jacob Viner Papers)

Viner replied on 19 January 1932:

> Dear Sraffa: The McCulloch Letters to Ricardo have already been published and are, of course, available. I wrote to the Johns Hopkins Press to ask when

> the Bullion Controversy Papers would be published, but they replied that they could not give me any definite date. Hollander will be in Chicago for a conference at the end of this month, and I will then try to obtain definite information from him. *I hope that he is not playing a dog in the manger game.*
>
> (PU: Jacob Viner Papers)

To Viner's regret Hollander did not turn up at the conference. In the meantime, on 18 December 1931, Keynes had received Hollander's reply dated 7 December:

> Under separate cover I am sending you a set of the final page proof of the McCulloch Letters. The printed tract will be out within the week.
>
> I am now at work upon the 'Minor Papers'. None of them have been printed before, and they will prove of considerable interest. I am including certain relevant letters, unpublished, as well as a few of the 'missing' letters from James Mill. I should have been glad to include the additional Mill letters which I understood are in your possession and had so written to Mr. Sraffa. *To my surprise – for I had supposed that our courtesies were to be reciprocal – he has answered that these 'ought to be reserved for the main collection'.*
>
> I regret this decision; but I must, of course, respect it.
>
> (S: D3/11/63: 63)

To this Keynes sent the following reply, drafted jointly with Sraffa, on 21 December:

> *I think there must be a little misunderstanding in what you say about 'reciprocal courtesies'. We had not asked you – obviously it would not have been reasonable – to let us have your new material in advance of your own publication of it. We only wanted to be able to publish it after you had published it.* But meanwhile it would help the planning of our volumes if we could see the material, or at any rate have some idea how much space it would occupy, and also know the probable date of your publication. *We are only too anxious that you should publish your material yourself; and nothing will make us happier than to know that you are going to do so at an early date.*
>
> Moreover, you have to remember that we are trying to prepare a *definitive edition of Ricardo . . . All we are asking of you is that you should yourself make public the valuable material you have, at the earliest possible date, and meanwhile let us know, quite privately and with a pledge, of course, on our part that we should in no event publish it in advance of yourself, what it amounts to.*
>
> (S: D3/11/63:58(i–ii))[11]

When Keynes and Sraffa eventually had access to Hollander (1931), they learned to their great astonishment from the introduction that the Notes on Malthus he had received from Frank Ricardo were not the only items (ibid.: 5). Apparently Hollander had never disclosed this fact to anybody, not even to his former co-editor

Gregory, who had initially been in charge of 'the "Big" Ricardo'. And as we shall see, even on this occasion he did not provide full information on what he had been given twelve years ago. Among his correspondence with Frank Ricardo Sraffa kept a memo: 'Written to Frank Ricardo 25.1.32 Telling him of Hollander's publication of McC.'s letters, & how he holds up Mill's & Currency papers of R. Told him how he got them (quoted preface). Asked him to request H. to return "at his earliest convenience & after having taken copies of them, all the letters & MS *which you have lent him well over 10 years ago*" ' (S: D3/11/71: 39). At long last, one of the puzzles of the missing correspondence of Ricardo was about to be resolved.

Apparently, Keynes and Sraffa were not very optimistic that Hollander could be made to comply with their demands without further effort. Hence they asked colleagues of Hollander in the United States for their support. On 7 January 1932 Sraffa sent a letter to Professor F. W. Taussig (from Rapallo); in the draft version of it we read:

> I should indeed be most grateful if you would be so good as to attempt to bring about a coordination of work between Dr Hollander & me, in the manner which you suggest. I am rather worried by the thought that there are in the possession of Dr Hollander some Ricardo letters, which he will probably publish himself too late for me to make use of them in the edition of R's Works. . . .
>
> It would be a great boon if it were possible to find an arrangement which were [sic] satisfactory to Dr Hollander, & which enabled me to make use of what are the only extant Ricardo MSS which I have not been permitted to see.
>
> (S: D3/11/73: 5)

In April and May 1932 Sraffa, in collaboration with Keynes, made further attempts to obtain the Ricardo items retained by Hollander. On 26 April 1932 Viner wrote to Sraffa informing him about a letter he had received from Hollander in which the latter gave some indications as to what kind of additional material he had and what he planned to do with it (see S: D3/11/74: 12; see also below, endnote 12). Sraffa replied on 17 May 1932:

> *The news from Hollander sounds like having to wait another ten years: in the circumstances I really do not know how to approach him. . . .*
>
> The position is that if I have not access to the Ricardo papers etc. within the next few months I shall not be able to include them in our edition. The alternative is postponement for an indefinite period, but with the type set this will be impossible. *To appear with a note in the Preface to the effect that certain unpublished manuscripts are known to exist, but Hollander who controls them has not consented to show them to us, would be as awkward to us as to Hollander himself. But is there a way out of this dilemma?*
>
> (S: D3/11/74:13)

6. 'We must not grumble – we *are* getting the MSS'

In a letter dated 29 April 1932, which is not extant, Frank Ricardo appears to have requested the return of the remaining material from Hollander. This is indirectly confirmed by Hollander's answer in a letter dated 13 May 1932:

> I have been much distressed by the contents of your letter of April 29. You and your family have been so courteous to me in the past, that it would have been a gross impropriety had I failed to conform in every particular with your desires as to the return of the Ricardo material. I assure you that there has been no such intention on my part.
>
> Your letter states 'I am writing to repeat my request to you to return the remainder of the letters and documents which I lent you several years ago' – to which I can only reply that no such request has ever been received by me. Had it been, there would have been instant compliance.
>
> When you entrusted the material to me, it was with the assurance that I should retain it for study and publication as long as might be necessary and that thereafter it should be safely restored to you.
>
> After the publication of the 'Notes on Malthus', under Professor Gregory's and my editorship, the MS. (of the 'Notes'), according to your instruction, was delivered to Professor Keynes.
>
> More recently the 'Letters of McCulloch' were issued – a copy is enclosed, which I beg you will accept with my compliments. This part of the MSS. would likewise have been returned *but for my thought that instead of such piecemeal delivery you would prefer to have it returned in one parcel.*
>
> I am now returning by registered letter post the MS. referred to in the preceding paragraph, together with other parts of the material.
>
> There remain [sic] in my possession that part of the material which has been used in the 'Minor Papers on the Currency Question', now in course of publication by the Johns Hopkins Press, as per enclosed announcement. *I hope very much that you will permit me to retain this for a few months longer, in order that page proof may be read against the original MS. Any other procedure adds to the chance of typographical errors, which I should like very much to avoid.* I can assure you that the delay in making this final delivery will be inconsiderable.
>
> (S: D3/11/71: 33)

In a letter dated 17 May 1932 – Hollander's letter just referred to had not yet arrived – Sraffa wrote to Frank Ricardo:

> Many thanks for your very kind letter. I am anxious to know whether you have heard from Professor Hollander; *although I doubt that there will be any enclosures, unless it be only McCulloch's letters, which are published.*
>
> In spite of the assurance we have given to him that we shall not publish anything in his possession before he has published it himself, Hollander has

> refused to let us have copies, and has now indefinitely postponed his own publication. *It is now unfortunately clear that he does not see with sympathy our initiative.* . . .
>
> If the R.E.S. could claim the return of the MSS as a matter of right, no doubt they could approach Hollander more effectively than they have been able to do as a matter of courtesy.
>
> (S: D3/11/71: 38)

Sraffa's doubts were well founded. In his reply dated 22 May 1932 – Hollander's above letter still had not arrived – Frank Ricardo wrote to Piero Sraffa:

> I have had no reply from Professor Hollander.
>
> I cannot recollect what exactly the items are that he retains. . . . At the time of loaning them to Prof. Hollander the matter had not the importance that it now has and I am unable to bear in mind whether there were any McCulloch or other letters: if there were they were very few. . . . There was of course no inkling in those days that the RES was going to publish a Life & Works, but now in view of the fact that they are doing so *the Royal Economic Society has my full authority to tell Professor Hollander that I have lent all the documents, correspondence, etc. connected with D.R. to them for the purpose of this publication and that this loan includes the items still retained by Prof. Hollander.*
>
> (S: D3/11/71: 36)

The next day Frank Ricardo finally received Hollander's letter and immediately forwarded it to Sraffa (S: D3/11/71: 35). However, before Frank Ricardo's letter reached Sraffa, Keynes had sent letters to Professors Wesley Mitchell and Edwin Seligman, in which he accused Hollander of 'continued procrastination and retention of certain Ricardo documents which we need for our edition', with the result of having 'put off publication for years'. In addition he asked them to use their 'influence with Hollander to be reasonable' (see S: D3/11/71: 60 and 61).

On 25 May 1932 Sraffa wrote to Frank Ricardo regarding Hollander's letter:

> Your letter has really brought to us the very best news we could have expected. Thanks to your intervention *the main obstacle to our publication will now be removed*, and you have placed us in a new and deep obligation.
>
> As regards the last paragraph in Hollander's letter – since you are so good as to ask my opinion – I shall state it quite frankly: and *I hope that I shall not give you the impression that we wish in any way to be unfair to Hollander* – much less that we wish you to be -: *for nothing could be more remote from our intentions*.
>
> . . . [A]fter careful consideration, I am convinced that the genuine reason of Hollander's wish to retain the MSS 'a few months longer' cannot be the desire to read the proofs against the original MS.

No doubt you will expect me to state the grounds for this opinion, and you will excuse me, I hope, for doing it somewhat at length. In the first place, the prospectus which Professor Hollander has sent you was issued to the public in January 1931; *it is hard to see how, after seventeen months, some months longer can be required for printing what must be a thin pamphlet*, since it is offered to subscribers at 3/-. *The fact is, that Hollander, after having heard of our anxiety to secure an early publication on his part, so that the way should be open for us, had decided to cancel the announcement, and to postpone indefinitely publication: it is only after having received your letter that he has resorted to the earlier plan*. (In proof of this I may quote a sentence from a letter written by Hollander, on April 26th ult., to a Professor unconnected with our publication, and privately communicated to me: 'Starting with a few unpublished Ricardo items, which I planned to issue as a number of my "Economic Tracts", I have gotten together so much more that it has become necessary to substitute Malthus's "Observations on the Corn Laws" (1814) in the "Tracts", and to prepare to issue the Ricardo material in a separate publication.')[12]

Besides, nowadays *it is absurd to suggest that the actual MS is necessary for proof reading. Exact reproductions can be obtained by photostat in a few hours at a cost of less than 6d per sheet;* which for the 'Minor Papers' would probably amount to little over £1. . . .

Hollander's behaviour in this matter has all along been quite inexplicable to me. When I met him in London in July 1930, I gave him a detailed account of the contents of the box of letters you had found at Bromesberrow; and although I told him about the curious gap in the correspondence for the years 1822–23, and the efforts you were making to recover the missing letters by searching at your solicitors, etc., he did not utter a word about the letters he had had for ten years on loan from you. As it has turned out, the McCulloch letters now published by him go a fairly long way towards filling the gap (not less than seven belong to that period).

Afterwards, he has always refused not only to let us have copies of the MSS (although we had undertaken not to anticipate his publication) but even to let us know how much space we should allow for this new material, so that we might proceed with our arrangements. And now *I fear that the further delay it would inflict on us has something to do with his request to retain the 'Minor Papers' for some months longer.*

(S: D3/11/71: 31–2)

On 28 May 1932 Frank Ricardo received from Hollander a first set of documents, which he forwarded to Sraffa the following day. In the accompanying letter Frank Ricardo expressed his lack of understanding why Hollander would want to retain some of the material (see S: D3/11/71: 26). Sraffa replied in a letter of 1 June 1932, the draft of which reads:

D. Mr R., thanks for your letter & for the parcel (containing 17 letters of McCulloch & a number of miscell. letters & newspapers) which I have received. *Its contents has* [sic] *proved rather disappointing, as Hollander*

> *has retained everything of interest*: that is to say, not only the 'Minor Papers on Bullion', as he says in his letter, but also the letters of Mill, which he certainly has; & presumably some letters of Malthus & Trower, which could hardly be absent in such a miscellaneous lot. – As they are, these documents are welcome, as they enable me to correct a number of misprints in Hollander's published ed. of McC's letters, & supply a few scraps of additional information. – It is very kind of you to be willing to write to Holl. requesting the immediate return of the other papers: *it would be desirable if in your letter you specifically referred to the letters from Mill & others which Holl. has retained without even asking your permission.*
>
> (S: D3/11/71: 29)

On 29 June 1932 Frank Ricardo received a further batch of letters from Hollander plus the latter's assurance that he had had reproductions made for proof-reading and was therefore sending back the originals. Frank Ricardo informed Sraffa on the same day by letter in which he also wrote that Hollander 'agrees that he has far outstepped the period allowed for retaining the papers etc. which I lent him, and consequently he is despatching *at once* all the remaining ones' (S: D3/11/71: 25).

At once? Further batches kept arriving, which prompted Frank Ricardo to write to Sraffa on 23 July 1932:

> I do not know . . . how much nearer we are to the 'final instalment'. But still *we must not grumble – we are getting the MSS* – a fact which not many months ago seemed remote and difficult to bring about. . . . *I have not the least idea what more there is to come. I am therefore in Hollander's hands;* but I am quite sure he will return everything. It will probably be best policy to have him do it in his own way.
>
> (S: D3/11/71: 19–20)

During the following weeks more material arrived which was forwarded to Sraffa. Finally, in October 1932 Frank Ricardo told Sraffa with reference to a letter from Hollander: 'I think I have now handed you everything for your purpose which lay in my power' (S: D3/11/71: 18).[13] This issue was settled; yet the difficulties with Hollander were to continue.

7. Hollander's library at the disposal of scholars – with 'a single exception'

Taussig wrote to Sraffa in November 1932 offering his good services (S: D3/11/73: 7) and then again in February 1933:

> I have communicated with my friend Hollander, and have a letter from him in which the following passages appear:
> 'I have included in the Minor Papers *all of the Ricardo manuscripts and letters in my possession. . . .*'

> As you doubtless know, the volume 'Minor Papers' has been published. *I should judge that there are not in Hollander's possession, as you were led to suppose, Ricardo letters still to be published, such as would deserve a place in your edition of the Works.* At all events, he seems to think that nothing remains for him to do.
>
> (S: D3/11/73: 10–11)

The following weeks showed that Taussig's judgement was wrong. In June Sraffa wrote to Maggs Bros. in London, asking for the name of the purchaser of Ricardo's letter to Barton (which had been advertised in Maggs Bros. Autographs Catalogue No. 352 of Christmas 1916). On 9 August 1933 Maggs Bros. eventually informed him that 'Professor Hollander purchased this letter in 1916' (S: D3/11/67: 49). Sraffa informed Taussig about his find on 12 August 1933:

> In your letter of 23rd Feb. of this year you quoted Professor Hollander as having written to you: 'I have included in the Minor Papers all of the Ricardo manuscripts and letters in my possession'. *I acquiesced at the time, although I was aware of some still unpublished MSS in Prof. Hollander's possession.* In 1930 a Paris bookseller, Manier, had offered in his catalogue an autograph letter of Ricardo, 31/4 pages, dated 16th June 1822 and described as 'très belle lettre', *and he informed me that he had sold it to Prof. Hollander.* I wrote at once to Prof. Hollander, who replied on 9th Jan. 1931 declining to allow me access to this letter until he had published it and he added: 'I have a few unpublished Ricardo letters, but like the Manier item they are of little economic interest'.
>
> Unfortunately the 'Manier letter' is not printed in the 'Minor Papers'. *These include only MSS belonging to Mr Frank Ricardo . . .*
>
> I should not have pressed the matter any further, but for a new fact that has recently come to my knowledge.
>
> I had for some time been aware of the existence of a very long letter, written by Ricardo on the 20th May 1817 to John Barton (. . .) and containing a detailed discussion of his theory of wages and profits. My efforts to trace the owner had been unsuccessful till the other day, when I learned from an absolutely reliable source that the autograph of this unpublished letter is (or was at one time) in the possession of Prof. Hollander. I need not emphasise the importance of this letter. The mere fact that as early as May 1817 (a few weeks after the publication of the 'Principles') Ricardo was corresponding with Barton, is of considerable interest – for Barton was undoubtedly one of the main influences which induced Ricardo to change his views on the effects of machinery and to add the chapter On Machinery in the 1821 edition of the 'Principles'.
>
> I very much fear that it will be impossible for me to obtain access to the Barton letter for the purpose of printing it in the Royal Economic Society's edition. On the other hand, I shall have to mention its existence; and it will

be necessary, however distasteful, for me to justify my failure to include it in an edition which purports to be as complete as possible by stating the circumstances of the case.

(S: D3/11/73: 12–14)

Taussig replied on 26 August 1933:

> I have come to the conclusion that I should not address Hollander again. The tone of the answer to my previous letter did not indicate much promise. . . . I am not at all unwilling to help, and hope I am not mistaken in my belief that I should do more harm than good by 'butting in'.
>
> (S: D3/11/73: 15)

Sraffa sought once more the help of Keynes who, in a letter of 14 September 1933, suggested writing 'an entirely unthreatening letter to Hollander' and made a proposal which Sraffa accepted with small changes. In the letter Sraffa sent by express mail on 17 September 1933 we read:

> I am now getting rather near the publication date of Ricardo, and the Royal Economic Society want to get the edition complete in the case of miscellaneous correspondence, as well as his published works and the major series of correspondence.
>
> I should therefore be most grateful if you could let me have a transcript of Ricardo's letter of May 20, 1817 to John Barton, particularly as the contents of this letter have some bearing on the 'Principles'. I should also like to have a transcript of Ricardo's letter of 16 June 1822 (the Manier letter), and anything else in your possession, even if it seems of minor importance. I had been hoping that these letters would appear in your published volume. Although, however, you have not thought them important enough to print, I should still like to have the opportunity of using them for the Royal Economic Society edition.
>
> (S: D3/11/65: 65 (i))

At proof stage Sraffa asked CUP for a blank page in place of the Barton letter and inserted the following (handwritten) note on this page when proof-reading: 'MS in the possession of Professor J. H. Hollander since 1916, who, it is understood, intends to publish it with a reprint of Barton's . . . ; but in the meantime the text is not available' (D3/11/63: 57a).

After seven weeks without a reply from Hollander, Keynes on 9 November 1933 approached Professor Edwin F. Gay of Harvard University asking him to contact a friend at Johns Hopkins well acquainted with Hollander, who might perhaps be able to help: 'As our latest efforts have drawn completely blank, we should be very grateful if one last effort could be made' (S: D3/11/63: 40). As a result of his effort, Gay received a letter from Hollander, dated 15 December 1933, which he forwarded to Keynes. Hollander wrote to Gay:

> In the first place let me express regret that you have been troubled in the matter at all. All the facts involved in what Keynes described as 'his difficulties with Hollander' are known to Keynes himself.
>
> The circumstances are these: On April 3, 1930, from a clear sky, Keynes apprized me of the intention of the Royal Economic Society to publish a complete edition of the works of Ricardo under the editorship of Mr. Piero Sraffa, and besought my 'benevolent approval' of the project. I promptly wrote Keynes of my disposition to aid him in any practicable way, and thereafter took steps to make available whatever I had contributed to Ricardian literature [!]. In the summer of 1930 I met Keynes and Sraffa in London and renewed this assurance. In the course of this interview [!], however, I realized that the concept of 'benevolent approval' consisted in the main of my making available for their use whatever Ricardiana I might possess, either in the form of prompt publication or supply of manuscript copy.
>
> In the succeeding eighteen months I published the 'Letters to McCulloch' and the 'Minor Papers on the Currency Question'; this under strain of time and effort. There remained certain other materials which were already integrated in the manuscript of prospective contributions.
>
> Of this character are the Manier letter and the Barton letter to which Keynes refers. The first I am using in my critique of Ricardo; the second is a vital part of the reprint of Barton's tract, of which announcement has already been made. *It is an unjust and unreasonable request that I should turn over these letters as well as any other materials in process of use. I have not collected them as personalia but as material, and am using them as such. The most scrupulous standards of scientific cooperation would dictate no other course.*
>
> As against the attitude which I have throughout taken, I might finally contrast Keynes' concept of scientific reciprocity. Upon being advised by Sraffa that he was in possession of various letters of James Mill to Ricardo, I informed him that I was about to publish certain others (of Mill to Ricardo) in the 'Minor Papers', then about to appear, and asked that copies of his might be supplied me for inclusion – the entire series thereafter to be used in the definitive edition. Sraffa refused to do this, explaining under date of January 31, 1931 that they 'ought to be reserved for the main collection'.
>
> Inasmuch as you have been troubled in the matter, it seems necessary to inform you of what has transpired. I am entirely willing that you should communicate this letter.
>
> (S: D3/11/63: 39(i–ii))[14]

On 5 January 1934 Keynes forwarded the letter to Sraffa asking for his observations (S: D3/11/65: 61). Sraffa produced a handwritten note for Keynes, in which he commented on the three points marked in his copy of the letter:

> (1) In the interview no mention was made of any Ricardiana possessed by H: indeed we had no idea that he possessed any. We told him about the letters we had found, and of the curious gaps in the series we had; although, as it turned out later, H. possessed many of the wanted letters, he never uttered a word about them. On this occasion he only handed over to us the MS of the published Notes on Malthus, which Frank Ricardo, to whom it belongs, had previously instructed him to give us.
>
> (2) H. purchased the Barton letter at Xmas 1916: it has been 'in process of use' for 18 years – four pages!
>
> (3) H gives the impression that when he 'was about to publish' certain letters of Mill to R. he 'was advised that he (Sraffa) was in possession' of some others & asked them for publication. The reverse is true. H. heard of the letters & of our intention to publish in the interview of June 1930;[15] he heard it again when both things were published in Keynes' letter to the Econ. Journn. Dec. 1930. Then, on Nov. 29, 1930, I wrote to him asking for the Manier letter & any others that he might have. And only on Jan. 9, 1931, in his reply, did H. intimate that he had some other letters in his possession, said that he intended to publish them, and asked for copies of ours to include in his publication. H's intended publication was only advertised in the QJE of May 1931. – As it turned out, H. had only two letters of Mill, as against our forty seven!
>
> The true story therefore is as follows: H. had two letters of Mill since 1919: he sat tight upon them, never disclosing the secret to anyone (not even to Gregory, his joint-editor of the Notes on Malthus, with the MS of which the Mill letters were found), till January 1931. Only some time after the proposed publication of our collection of letters had been advertised, did he disclose the fact of his possession & did he decide to publish. And in response to our appeal to the public for further letters, instead of letting us have his treasures, he asked us to let him have our 47 Mill letters that he might complete his collection of 2. This we declined to do.
>
> Even so, Hollander delayed publication of his two letters till the beginning of 1933; and even this was done only under pressure of Frank Ricardo, the owner of all the letters, who since early in 1930 had given us permission to publish all the MSS belonging to him.
>
> (S: D3/11/63: 37(i–ii))

Keynes replied to Gay on 24 January 1934:

> It is very good of you to have taken so much trouble in this small matter. If only Hollander will carry out his previous intention of publishing the Barton letter at not too remote a date for us, we shall be reasonably content, but the wretch has already had this document of four pages 'in process of use' for eighteen years, without disclosing it to the public or even confessing to us that he possessed such a document. Beyond this I agree that nothing further

> can be usefully done in this connection. But Hollander's letter so completely misrepresents the position, to the best of my understanding, that I should like to append to this letter two papers giving our view of the matter. The first of these is a letter from me to Hollander of the 21st December, 1931, in which you will see that we have never asked him to allow us to publish any of his material in advance of himself. We have only urged him to expedite his own publication, since it is not fair that he should keep such documents up his sleeve for an indefinite number of years. As regards scientific reciprocity, we have never asked him to let us publish anything before he did, though this is what he has been asking us. We only want him not to take more than ten or twenty years in publishing the few scraps in his possession! The other document which I append is a note written for me by Sraffa which puts, I think, rather a different compexion [sic] on the matter of the Mill letters.
>
> (S: D3/11/63: 36)

On 6 November 1934 Hollander sent Sraffa the galleyproof of the reprint of John Barton's tract, which was about to be issued in the series of 'Economic Tracts' and contained, in the appendix, Ricardo's letter to Barton (see S: D3/11/63: 53). Sraffa thanked Hollander on 12 November 1934, adding: 'I am keenly looking forward to your further publications . . . May we hope to see them in the near future?' (S: D3/11/63: 54).

In the following years Sraffa continued his search for Ricardiana and, not surprisingly, came across various of Hollander's activities as a collector.[16] On 19 August 1937 he wrote to him:

> Mr Keynes has lent me the Catalogue of your Library [see Hollander (1937)] and I have studied it with increasing admiration.
>
> I was, of course, particularly interested in your 'Ricardiana' and above all in the impressive list of your collection of Ricardo autograph letters. May I take this opportunity of venturing to reiterate my request that you should be so good as to let me have copies of the unpublished letters of Ricardo in your possession? I should also be most grateful if you would kindly allow me to have a copy of Say's letter to Ricardo of October 10, 1819, which I suppose was presented to you by Mr Frank Ricardo.[17] . . .
>
> I should be doubly grateful if you would let me have copies of these letters (or, if that is more agreeable to you, if you will make them available by publication as you have done on previous occasions). In the first place, for the sake of making the Royal Economic Society's edition of Ricardo as complete as possible. And, in the second place because it would relieve me from an embarrassing situation: I should like to be able to make my fullest acknowledgements to you, to whom I am, along with every student of Ricardo, under such very great obligations; however, *since the catalogue of your library has been widely circulated, I should of course be under the necessity of stating that such and such letters are in your possession and that my failure to include them in the R.E.S. edition is due to my not having been allowed access to*

> *them*. Such a statement would, inevitably, and to my great regret, bear the appearance of a reserve in my acknowledgements to you; and it would unfortunately be emphasised by the fact that I have to make no such reserve in respect of any of the other owners of Ricardo manuscripts.
>
> (S: D3/11/63: 50(i–ii))

Hollander's reply is dated 6 October 1937:

> *The contents of my Library – books and manuscripts – have been and are at the disposal of scholars*. Many books have from time to time been lent, under the usual restrictions . . . *A single exception exists – a few unpublished letters of Ricardo*. These, acquired over a term of years at considerable labor and expense, have been incorporated in the manuscript of my book, presently to be published, and I am unable to supply copies in advance. Such a conclusion conforms to your own practice. Some years ago when about to reprint letters of McCulloch and Mill to Ricardo I requested copies of those in your possession. You found it impossible to comply with this request on the ground that they must be 'reserved for the main collection'.
>
> Finally may I express my amazement at the tenor of the final paragraph of your letter. We in this country are unaccustomed to the kind of pressure it seeks to exert, and I can only assume that your recourse thereto grows out of unacquaintance with the amenities that prevail among scholars. It cannot, of course, affect in the remotest degree the position set forth above, and I beg to assure you that in the event of your edition appearing with any statement as misleading as that which you suggest, I shall take prompt measures to acquaint the economic profession the world over with the facts in the case.
>
> (S: D3/11/63: 49(i–ii))

Sraffa replied in a letter of 29 October 1937, after having consulted with Keynes (see K: EJ/1/4/205–6) and Kahn (see RFK/13/57/255):

> *You are mistaken in thinking that my object is to secure priority of publication over you*. Far from it, . . . *my aim being to produce, not a first, but as far as can be a definitive edition of Ricardo*.
>
> I feel obliged to disagree with the statement of facts . . . and I should like to be allowed to place a more accurate account on record. I wrote to you on November 29th, 1930, asking you for copies of any Ricardo letters in your possession and informing you that these were required for an edition which had been announced many months before: you replied on January 9th, 1931, when, in a document which I have preserved, you (a) refused to comply with my request; (b) requested that, instead, I should let you have our letters so that they might be published by you in advance of our edition.
>
> As regards the last paragraph of your letter, I do not propose to say anything in my preface, which has not been first approved by the Council of the Royal Economic Society; so that you can rest assured that what appears will not

> merely represent a personal view, but will have the authority of the most responsible scholars in this country.
>
> (S: D3/11/63: 51(i))

There was some further correspondence between Sraffa and Hollander in 1938 concerning, *inter alia*, Barton's address as it was wrongly transcribed by Hollander in his publication of Ricardo's letter to Barton. Sraffa would remind Hollander on 14 December 1938: 'I hope also to hear that your work is nearing publication, so that I may get the benefit of it for the last stages of our edition' (S: D3/11/63: 48).[18] And on 23 January 1939 Sraffa sent a telegram to Hollander asking him to 'kindly cable how soon you will publish Say letter 3970 [of] your library catalogue and word-space we should reserve for printing' (S: D3/11/63: 45). On 26 January 1939 Hollander replied by telegram: 'Sending Photostat Say Letter' (S: D3/11/63: 44); the photostat was indeed sent the following day by Hollander's secretary.

8. Suffering under a new 'embargo'

Jacob H. Hollander died on 9 July 1940, with his *magnum opus* still unpublished.[19] In a letter of 30 July 1942 Sraffa asked Jacob Viner what had happened to Hollander's library (see S: D3/11/74: 25). Viner investigated the situation and on 19 October 1942 was able to send the requested information. According to it the library was in storage as an asset of Hollander's estate and the material was not accessible (S: D3/11/63: 35), information confirmed by Hollander's son, to whom Sraffa had written on 30 October 1947 (see S: D3/11/63: 33–4).

Hence Sraffa had to publish his edition without having been able to fully consult the material in Hollander's library.[20] In 1955 Sraffa apparently made inquiries about the Hollander collection via Maggs Bros. Among his papers he kept a copy of a letter from the Maryland Trust Company to Maggs Bros, dated 26 October 1955, which contains the following statement: 'The Library of the late Dr Hollander, which is now owned by the Trustees for his estate, is for sale'. The estimated value of Hollander's library was given as US $ 50.000 (see S: I 69: 3). Sraffa appears to have toyed with the idea of buying the library himself.

In 1958 the Hollander Collection was acquired by the University of Illinois. In a letter of 22 August 1958 Sraffa contacted that university (see S: D3/11/76: 1) and received a letter from Professor J. F. Bell, dated 18 September 1958. It confirmed

> that we have purchased the Jacob Hollander Library. You may possibly know that it was crated and completely out of circulation for at least fifteen years. . . . I will gladly cooperate with you if you know of anything in the collection that may be of interest or of use.
>
> (S: D3/11/64: 4)[21]

Sraffa replied in a letter of 20 October 1958:

> It is a great pleasure to renew acquaintance on such a happy occasion as the acquisition by the University of Illinois of the Hollander Library. To me

> this is particularly welcome news as *I was one of the sufferers under the 'embargo'*... There are two main things in which I have long been interested in the Hollander collection: First, the Ricardo letters (Nos. 3973 to 3983 in the printed Catalogue).... Secondly, the MS of J. S. Mill's Autobiography (No. 4024 in the Catalogue).... Thirdly, there are besides two letters of minor importance of which I should be glad to have photostats: Malthus to Moses Ricardo, 18 June 1830 (No. 3962), and Adam Smith to George Baird, 7 February 1783 (No. 3936)... If you would be so good as to permit of, and arrange for, all this I should be very much obliged.
>
> (S: D3/11/64: 3)

Sraffa was sent photographic copies of the material requested, except Mill's *Autobiography*, which, as Bell told Sraffa, was in the process of being prepared for publication (see S: D3/11/64: 5).

9. Concluding remarks

Jacob H. Hollander variously expressed his concern that a complete and as perfect as possible edition of Ricardo's works and correspondence be brought out, either by him or some other Ricardo scholars whom he liberally offered his good services and assistance. Alas, the material displayed in this paper shows that he did not mean it: Hollander's attitude towards the RES edition of *The Works and Correspondence of David Ricardo* was decidedly obstructive. To him the preservation of Ricardo's intellectual heritage appears to have counted for little as soon as he was no longer in full control of it. His main claim to distinction was in his bibliophile erudition and antiquarian's collection, and the RES editorial project came as a serious blow to him. Viner's comparison of Hollander to the 'dog in the manger' does not quite fit the story. As Paul Samuelson reminded us,[22] the dog in the stable got no benefit from the hay which he deprived the horse of (and that only the horse did). The dog was a '*gratuitous* sadist'. Not so with Hollander who had to be wary of loss of reputation.

It goes without saying that the case under consideration is not unique. It is just one among several parallel cases in the history of textual scholarship, with the Dead Sea scrolls being perhaps the most famous.

Appendix

The delayed publication of Sraffa's Ricardo edition led to several requests for permission to be allowed access to specific parts of the material prior to publication, which Sraffa generally was most willing to give. However, there are two issues which should be briefly remarked upon for clarification. The first concerns the publication of Ricardo's 'Notes on Bentham's *Sur les prix*'. In a letter of 24 January 1939 Jacob Viner informed Sraffa that

> as Editor of the Journal of Political Economy, I received an offer from Dr. Edmund Silberner of a manuscript for publication, consisting of Ricardo's

> comments on an unpublished manuscript by Bentham, edited by Dumont, the latter bearing the title 'Matériaux d'un traité sur la hausse des prix et les effets de papier-monnaie.' . . . I would like to know what you know about the manuscript, and whether you plan shortly to publish it in Ricardo's works.
> (S: D3/11/74: 20)

To this Sraffa replied on 7 February 1939:

> I am very grateful to you for your kindness in writing to me before taking a decision about Ricardo's notes on Bentham-Dumont. As you will see from the stamp upon the enclosed . . . I have had them in page-proof since 1933! I really hope now that the whole thing (9 vols.) will be published before the end of the year. This is one of the very few entirely unpublished writings of Ricardo that will first appear in our edition, & therefore I should naturally be glad not to be forestalled. I do not know how the question of copyright stands in America, or whether Dr Silberner proposes to get in touch with the Ricardo family. In England of course unpublished MSS are copyright & the Ricardos have given the Royal Econ. Soc. the right to publish all D.R.'s works.
>
> On looking up my files I find that the Bibliothèque publique et universitaire of Geneva, who own the manuscript, have given us permission to publish it.
> (PU: Jacob Viner Papers)

Viner replied on 21 February 1939: 'In the light of what you tell me about the Bentham-Ricardo manuscript, I will certainly not accept it for publication in the Journal of Political Economy' (ibid.). However, as Sraffa notes in Volume III of the RES edition (*Works* III: 266), Ricardo's notes on Bentham were nevertheless published by Silberner in 1940 in the *Revue d'Histoire économique et sociale*.

The second issue concerns Sraffa's own collection of manuscripts and autograph letters. In his search for Ricardiana for the RES edition Sraffa had purchased a few letters himself. When publishing them in the edition he would not refer to them as 'MS in the possession of Mr Piero Sraffa' (as in the case of other owners of manuscripts) but by giving the name of the bookseller (or auction house) and the catalogue number (or auction date) where the respective item had been advertised (or been on sale). Similar information was also given in the case of all those manuscripts which Sraffa had transcribed prior to sale and for which he had to respect the purchasers' desire for anonymity.

Acknowledgements

An earlier version of this paper was presented at a session of the *HES* meeting at the University of British Columbia in Vancouver, 30 June–3 July 2000, and at the *HETSA* meeting at Wesley College, Sydney, 4–7 July 2000. We are grateful to the participants for useful remarks. Special thanks go to Nick Baigent, Giancarlo de Vivo, Gilbert Faccarello, Geoff Harcourt, Arnold Heertje, Sam Hollander, John King, Nerio Naldi, Annalisa Rosselli, Paul A. Samuelson, Ian Steedman, and

Donald Winch for valuable comments and suggestions. We should also like to thank four anonymous referees of the Journal of the *Royal Economic Society*, to which the paper had for obvious reasons originally been submitted, and two referees of *EJHET* for the depth of some of the considerations they gave our paper which were of great use to us in revising it. (The reader intrigued by the query why the paper was not published in the former journal might wish to consult the home page: <http://www.kfunigraz.ac.at/vwlwww/kurz/kurz.html>.) Any remaining errors and misconceptions are, of course, entirely our responsibility.

Notes

1 As Sraffa notes in his General Preface, 'by the summer of 1940, six volumes . . . had been set up in page-proof, while the volume of Speeches and Evidence had reached the state of galley-proofs' (Ricardo, *Works* I: ix).

2 For most helpful assistance in the preparation of this paper we would like to thank the library staffs of the Wren Library at Trinity College, Cambridge (UK), of the Modern Archive Centre in the King's College Library, Cambridge (UK), of the Archives Division in the British Library of Political and Economic Science at the London School of Economics, London (UK), of the Seeley G. Mudd Manuscript Library at Princeton University, Princeton (USA), and of the Milton S. Eisenhower Library, Special Collections Branch, at the Johns Hopkins University, Baltimore (USA). We should like to thank the following people and institutions for granting us permission to quote from the various papers: Pierangelo Garegnani, literary executor of Sraffa's papers and correspondence; John S. Weeren (Seeley G. Mudd Manuscript Library); and Joan Grattan (Milton S. Eisenhower Library). We use the following abbreviations of the mentioned archives: S (Sraffa Papers), K (Keynes Papers), LSE (London School of Economics), PU (Princeton University), and H (Hollander Papers).

3 See the letter dated 27 December 1999 from Mrs Joan Grattan of the Milton S. Eisenhower Library to the authors.

4 For general information on the Jacob H. Hollander archive, see the online guide under gopher: //musicbox.mse.jhu.edu: 70/00/mss/ms059.txt.

5 Present at this meeting: 'Dr. Bonar (in the chair), Prof. Edgeworth, Mr Hoare, Prof. Gregory, Prof. MacGregor, Mr Tawney, Mr Keynes, The Assistant Secretary' (LSE: RES/2/1/2).

6 Present at the meeting: 'The President [i.e., H. S. Foxwell], in the chair, Prof. Cannan, Prof. Gregory, Mr. Higgs, Mr. Hoare, Mr. Keynes, Prof. MacGregor, Asst. Secretary' (LSE: RES/2/1/2).

7 We found no evidence in support of Porta's contention that Keynes was 'lending his own good offices over five years in order to secure the project to his own young man' (Porta 1986: 35).

8 All italics in passages cited from letters and drafts of letters are ours, whereas all underlinings are in the original texts.

9 In Sraffa's diary there are notes for appointments with many other scholars, including Bonar, Foxwell, Higgs, Laski and Robbins, in March, April and May 1930.

10 Sraffa's resignation from his lectureship in May 1931 (see S: B9/1: 13) was motivated by his constructive theoretical work and the strain teaching put on him and was only indirectly related to his editorial work.

11 The draft copy kept by Sraffa contained the following additional paragraph crossed out by Keynes: 'Or do you mean by "reciprocal courtesies" that we should publish your material before you do, and that you should publish our material before we do? That would be amusing, but scarcely practical!' (ibid.)

12 The passage quoted by Sraffa is from a letter of Jacob H. Hollander to Jacob Viner, who communicated it to Sraffa in a letter of 26 April 1932 (see S: D3/11/74: 12).

13 Hollander's edition of Ricardo's *Minor Papers* was published in late 1932 (Hollander 1932). Sraffa's own copy (see Sraffa's Library, item 1024) is heavily annotated, with many corrections indicated on the margin.

14 On 9 January 1934 Hollander sent a copy of his letter to Gay also to Edwin Cannan, adding: 'You will be interested in the enclosed copy . . . in connection with representations which Keynes had made to him – and to others – as to my disposition in the matter of certain Ricardo materials' (LSE: MF Cannan 1033/221).

15 According to Sraffa's diary the meeting took place on 1 July 1930; see above Section 4.

16 There is an interesting letter to Harold Laski, dated 19 August 1937, in which Sraffa wrote: 'You once told me the story of how you tried to get in touch, through Maggs, with the owner of the MS of Mill's Autobiography; and how he replied, in an anonymous letter, that *the whole point of buying such a thing was that no one else should see it.* – I was enormously pleased to-day, in turning over the pages of the Catalogue of Hollander's Library, to discover (p. 317) that he is your man! I have myself, together with Keynes, been struggling with this brute for the last six years . . . ' (S: D3/11/66: 32).

17 As Sraffa later found out, Hollander had in fact purchased this letter in 1917. In his copy of Hollander's *Minor Papers* (see Sraffa's Library, item 1024) Sraffa noted on p. 184: 'N.B. Hollander had since 1917 Say's letter to R. of 10 Oct. 1819 (see my edn VIII, 136) but did not publish it! (1.12.51)'.

18 In July 1938 Sraffa was approached by a Mr McCrimmon who, knowing that Keynes was in bad health and not in Cambridge, asked whether Sraffa could perhaps arrange for him to see Keynes's collection of John Stuart Mill's letters (see S: D3/11/67: 44–5). Sraffa forwarded the request to Keynes who replied from Tilton: *'I am rather inclined to do a Hollander over the enclosed.* I have the excuse that the letters are scattered and locked up in various places, I do not quite know where, not easily accessible so long as I am away. In truth, I have nothing which would be of particular value to him except the correspondence with his wife. This, as you know, I still have the project of using myself. And there is nothing there which would be of any value for a general life which he is probably contemplating, and would only be valuable as the material for a special study. So can you manage to put him off?' (S: D3/11/67: 47). Sraffa wrote accordingly to McCrimmon (see S: D3/11/67: 46).

19 Mrs. Holly Callahan, Assistant Curator of Manuscripts at the Milton S. Eisenhower Library, made a search of the Hollander Papers on behalf of the authors, but 'was unable to find either the manuscript on Ricardo or any mention of the manuscript' (letter to the authors, 5 June 2001).

20 In volumes III to X there are several notes on manuscripts which are described as being 'in the possession of Professor Hollander' (see, in particular, *Works* III: 5n and 406; VII: 155n; VIII: 136n; and X: 81n).

21 On Hollander's economic library, see Bell (1959).

22 See his letter to us dated 26 March 2001.

References

Bell, J. F. (1959). The Jacob H. Hollander Economic Library: the Monument of a Man and his Science. *Current Economic Comment*, 21: 21–28.

Cannan, E. (1929). Review of Hollander and Gregory (1928). *Economica*, November: 358–65.

Hollander, J. H. (ed.) (1895). *Letters of David Ricardo to John Ramsay McCulloch 1816–1823*. Edited, with introduction and annotations by J. H. Hollander. New York: Macmillan and London: Swan, Sonnenschein & Co.

Hollander, J. H. (1904). The Development of Ricardo's Theory of Value. *The Quarterly Journal of Economics*, 18: 455–91.
Hollander, J. H. (1910). *David Ricardo – A Centenary Estimate*. Baltimore: The Johns Hopkins Press.
Hollander, J. H. (1928). Editor's Introduction. In J. H. Hollander and T. E. Gregory (eds), *Notes on Malthus's 'Principles of Political Economy' by David Ricardo*. Baltimore: The Johns Hopkins Press.
Hollander, J. H. (ed.) (1931). *Letters of John Ramsay McCulloch to David Ricardo (1818–1823)*. Baltimore: The Johns Hopkins Press.
Hollander, J. H. (ed.) (1932). *Minor Papers on the Currency Question 1809–1823 by David Ricardo*. Edited with an introduction and notes by Jacob H. Hollander. Baltimore: The Johns Hopkins Press.
Hollander, J. H. (1937). *The Economic Library of Jacob H. Hollander*, privately printed (500 copies). Baltimore. Reprinted as E. A. Marsh (ed.) (1966) *Economic Library of Jacob H. Hollander*. Gale Research.
Hollander, J. H. and Gregory, T. E. (eds) (1928). *Notes on Malthus's Principles of Political Economy' by David Ricardo*. Baltimore: The Johns Hopkins Press.
Naldi, N. (2000). Piero Sraffa's early approach to political economy: from the *gymnasium* to the beginning of his career. In T. Cozzi and R. Marchionatti (eds), *Piero Sraffa's Political Economy*. London: Routledge, pp. 23–40.
Porta, P. L. (1986). How Piero Sraffa took up the editorship of David Ricardo's Works and Correspondence. *History of Economics Society Bulletin* (Nashville, Tenn), VIII, (1): 35–7.
Ricardo, D. (1951–1973). *The Works and Correspondence of David Ricardo*, 11 vols. Edited by P. Sraffa with the collaboration of M. H. Dobb. Cambridge: Cambridge University Press.
Sraffa, P. (1925). Sulle relazioni fra costo e quantità prodotta. *Annali di Economia*, 2: 277–328.

7 "Man from the Moon"

On Sraffa's objectivism*

Heinz D. Kurz and Neri Salvadori

1. "Man from the Moon"

Sraffa took an objectivist perspective. This is epitomized in a document entitled 'Man from the Moon', probably written in the late 1920s or early 1930s.[1] In it he clarified the significance of the equations of production he had begun to develop in the second half of 1927:

> The significance of the equations is simply this: that if a man fell from the moon on the earth, and noted the amount of things consumed in each factory and the amount produced by each factory during a year, he could deduce at which values the commodities must be sold, if the rate of interest must be uniform and the process of production repeated. In short, *the equations show that the conditions of exchange are entirely determined by the conditions of production.*
>
> (D3/12/7: 87; emphasis added)

The "man from the moon" was Sraffa himself, but he was neither the only nor the first observer in history to assume such a point of view of the modern economy. He had been anticipated by others - the 'classical' economists and their precursors.[2] He also saw that the man from the moon's point of view was not the one generally adopted in economics at the time he wrote. On the contrary, the dominant view was Alfred Marshall's who had attempted to explain all economic phenomena in terms of demand and supply schedules, where both schedules were taken to reflect also subjective elements. Indeed, Marshall and the other "marginalist" authors started from the premise that in economic valuations the subjective element was pervasive.

In this paper we deal briefly with how Sraffa rendered precise the classical economists' objectivist point of view. We will focus attention on the first period of Sraffa's (re-)constructive work.[3] The composition of the paper is the following. Section 2 refers to Sraffa's attempt, starting from Marshall's partial analysis, of bringing about an "objectivisation" of economic theory, that is, purging it of unnecessary subjective elements. Section 3 turns to the classical view of production

* Reprinted with permission from *Économies et Sociétés*, 35, 2004.

according to which, in the words of James Mill, "the agents of production are the commodities themselves". The section also specifies Sraffa's view on the question in terms of which quantities economic theory should be elaborated. Section 4 deals with the problem that from an entirely objective point of view the central classical concept of "surplus" tends to vanish and how Sraffa coped with it in terms of an application of the principle of sufficient reason. Section 5 contains some concluding remarks.

2. "Objectivisation"

As a student of economics, Sraffa like almost everyone else in Europe was taught demand and supply analysis. His meticulous critical study of Marshall's *Principles* and the related literature led to two essays in which he dealt a serious blow to the foundations of the partial equilibrium method (Sraffa, 1925 and 1926). However, interestingly, there were (admittedly rare) moments in his early intellectual life in which he tinkered with the idea of reformulating the demand and supply approach after having purged it of its subjective elements (see, for example, D3/12/7: 114). Apparently this idea was based on the observation that Marshall (as well as Pigou) in practice worked often "largely upon objective material", although his explicit assumptions were entirely subjective (see D3/12/9: 92). Sraffa despised the "subjective, moral point of view", which, in his judgement, "has so deeply permeated every element in econ.[omic] theory that hardly anything survives if that is removed. On all [things] we look upon as being 'bad' or 'good'." He went on: "The very notion of 'cost' is so intimately interwoven with 'bad' and that of 'product' with 'good', that by removing the moral element the very distinction is washed out." What was needed was an "objectivisation" (D3/12/7: 46).

Had Sraffa ever seriously entertained the view that such an objectivisation could be effected by starting from Marshall's demand and supply framework, he quickly convinced himself that this was impossible and that another avenue had to be tried out. In this context it is important to notice that although Sraffa's criticism concerned first and foremost Marshall's theory, from an early time onward he also began to question Marshall's interpretation of the classical economists. He soon saw that Marshall's portrayal of Ricardo and his followers as early demand and supply theorists, with the demand side in its infancy, was a travesty of the facts. Still more importantly, Sraffa began to see ever more clearly that the classical economists had sought to elaborate an objectivist approach to the theory of value and distribution. In these circumstances the obvious thing to do was to lay bare the essence of the classical approach from under thick layers of Marshallian interpretation. Here we cannot enter into a detailed discussion of this aspect of Sraffa's work. A few observations must suffice.

3. "The agents of production are the commodities themselves"

Sraffa did not have to search long to find traces in earlier authors of the point of view he endorsed. There was most obviously William Petty who, in his *Political*

Arithmetick, had advocated the " 'physician's' outlook":

> The Method I take to do this [*i.e.* political arithmetic], is not yet very usual; for instead of using only comparative and superlative Words, and intellectual Arguments, I have taken the course (as a Specimen of the Political Arithmetick I have long aimed at) to express my self in Terms of *Number, Weight* or *Measure*; to use only Arguments of Sense, and to consider only such Causes, as have visible Foundations in Nature; leaving those that depend upon the mutable Minds, Opinions, Appetites, and Passions of particular Men, to the Consideration of others: Really professing my self as unable to speak satisfactorily upon those Grounds (if they may be call'd Grounds), as to foretel the cast of a Dye; to play well at Tennis, Billiards, or Bowles, (without long practice,) by virtue of the most elaborate Conceptions that ever have been written *De Projectilibus & Missilibus*, or of the Angles of Incidence and Reflection.
>
> (Petty, 1691, Preface; see also Petty (1986), Works, I, p. 244; similarly in his *Political Anatomy of Ireland*, in *Works*, I, pp. 129–30; and D3/12/4: 3)[4,5]

As Marx was to point out with reference to this passage in his *Critique of Political Economy*, Petty was conscious of founding a new science (see D3/12/4: 3), grounded in what Sraffa was to call the *physical real cost* approach to the theory of value, where the real costs of a commodity consist in the commodities that necessarily have to be destroyed in the course of its production. After Petty, he maintained, the new science was taken up and further developed by the Physiocrats. The concept of physical real cost was clearly spelled out in Quesnay's concept of "valeur vénale" (see D3/12/11: 73). The concept is said to recur in the contributions of Adam Smith, David Ricardo and Robert Torrens. Despite some ambiguities in Smith's argument, Sraffa insisted that "When Smith, etc., said 'natural' he . . . meant that physical, truly natural relation between commodities" implicit in Sraffa's "first equations" of production (D3/12/11: 83).[6] The same is said to apply to Ricardo's concept of "absolute value". In fact, in some of his papers Sraffa used Ricardo's term to characterize the prices emerging from the first equations.

A particularly clear expression of the view under consideration was given by James Mill. In the third edition of his *Elements of Political Economy*, published in 1826, Mill wrote:

> *The agents of production are the commodities themselves* . . . . They are the food of the labourer, the tools and the machinery with which he works, and the raw materials which he works upon.
>
> (Mill, 1826, p. 165, emphasis added; see also Sraffa's excerpts from Mill's book taken at the beginning of the 1930s in D3/12/9: 106–118)

The difference between the older economists' point of view, which Sraffa set out to revive, and the modern one he emphasized in the following note: "This point of view implies replacing the notion that 'commodities are produced by factors of production' with the other that 'commodities are produced by commodities'"; the latter amounted to "replacing the idea that the process of production has a beginning and an end with that that it is a circular one – an idea first introduced by the Tableau économique" (D3/12/17: 2).

In this context it is interesting to draw the attention to two further documents which reflect a remarkable continuity in Sraffa's thinking. The first comes from the second period of Sraffa's constructive work, the second from the third. On 30 July 1942 Sraffa jotted down: "Equations = Tableau Économique" (D3/12/16: 7), thus specifying the intellectual tradition to which he felt his respective work belonged. And when in the second half of the 1950s he began to put together his book, for a while he thought of giving it the title "Outline of an Economic System, or, The Production of Commodities by Commodities" (see D3/12/80), echoing Mill's above formulation.[7]

Two characteristic features of the classical approach deserve to be stressed at this point. The first concerns the treatment of wages, the second the specification of the kind of magnitudes upon which economic theory was to be based.

Sraffa illustrated the difference between the classical and the marginalist concept of the wages of labour in terms of the example of a carrot and a donkey (see D2/4/23 and D3/12/10: 61.ii).[8] In Marshall the carrot has to be shown to the donkey to *induce* it to run, just as the wages are taken to induce the worker to work. In the classical economists on the contrary the carrot has actually to be given to the donkey for eating to keep it alive and *enable* it to run, just as the wage goods are needed to enable the workers to work and "reproduce their race" (Smith), before there is any question of inducement. A *given* real wage rate can indeed be said to be the linchpin of the original classical approach to the theory of value and distribution, because with it and with known technical conditions of production of known quantities of commodities the *surplus product*, the substratum of all non-wage incomes, can be ascertained.[9] The surplus refers to those quantities of the different commodities that were left over after the necessary means of production used up and the means of subsistence in the support of workers have been deducted from the gross outputs produced during a year. Hence in Petty and the other classical economists the "bread" of the worker is considered no less a necessary input in the production process than the raw materials and tools.[10] Sraffa emphasized: "The study of the 'surplus product' is the true object of economics". He added: "This notion is connected with that of 'necessity'; and 'necessity' has only a definite meaning from a given point of view, which must be explicitly stated, & then adhered to consistently" (D3/12/7: 161.1).

This provides already a partial answer to the problem of which magnitudes, according to Sraffa, ought to be taken into consideration in economic theory and which not. In an undated note presumably written in the second half of 1929, Sraffa, with view to Marshall's theory on the one hand and the classical theory on the other, distinguished between three groups of quantities.

> 1) Those which cannot possibly be measured, because they are not defined in terms of the method of measuring them, e.g. marg.[inal] utility and sacrifice. (No definition at all is given for measuring them in the case of

> several individuals: in the case of one individual, they are defined as being proportional to certain quantities, *i.e.* prices, but this is, as Cairnes says, "merely giving a name to the unknown causes of price".) Such quantities must be *excluded altogether*: at the worst, they may be used as a fictitious device for solving problems, but must not appear either in the premises nor in the conclusions.

The second group consists of those quantities on which economic analysis should focus attention. Sraffa expounded:

> 2) At the opposite extreme there are quantities which can be, and in fact are, statistically measured. These quantities have an objective, independent existence at every or some instants of the natural (*i.e.* not interfered with by the experimenter) process of production and distribution; they can therefore be measured physically, with the ordinary instruments for measuring number, weight, time, etc. Such are quantities of various materials used or produced, of lands[,] quantities of labour (?), lengths of periods (?), etc. These are the *only* quantities which must enter as constants in economic theory, *i.e.* which can be assumed to be "known" or "given".[11]

Then there is a third group:

> 3) Finally, there is the class of quantities, which form the basis of Marshall's theory (or, rather, of Pareto's), such as demand & supply curves, marginal productivities, (i.e. rate of growth of total) indifference curves, etc. Here the constant quantities have no names – they are the parameters of curves. The several quantities represented by these curves do not exist at any one moment, nor during any period of the recurrent steady process of production or consumption. They are alternatives, only *one* of which can exist in any one position of equilibrium, all the others being thereby excluded (even the one does not really exist if there is no change, since it is the rate of growth of a quantity, *i.e.* marginal product: it can be inferred from price, but so can marginal utility, which under (1) we have agreed does not exist). Therefore, they cannot be found by merely observing the process or state of things, and measuring the quantities seen. They can only be found out by means of experiments – and these quantities in effect are always defined in terms of such *experiments* (successive doses applied to land; alternatives offered to the consumer; etc.)

Sraffa went on:

> These experiments cannot be carried out (and never have been, as a matter of fact) for various reasons, 1) the practical difficulties, 2) the lack of definition of the conditions to be required, which are always summed up in the absurd "other things being equal".

> But even apart from these difficulties, which might conceivably be overcome, there remains something about these experiments which is very curious: they are generally regarded as acceptable, as if they were calculated to reproduce under controlled conditions, so as to be able to measure them, facts which actually happen "in nature" all the time but cannot directly be pinned down by observation. But the experiments have an entirely different significance: they actually *produce* facts which would otherwise not happen at all; if the experimenter did not step in first to produce them, and then to ascertain them, they would remain in the state of "unknown possibilities", which amounts to the deepest inexistence.
>
> (D3/12/13: 2–3, 5)

The sets of quantities which are taken as given define the classical and the different marginalist approach to the theory of value and distribution, respectively. The former, Sraffa was to stress in his magnum opus, "has been submerged and forgotten since the advent of the 'marginal' method." He added, reflecting upon the considerations summarized under 3) above: "The reason is obvious. The marginal approach requires attention to be focused on change, for without change either in the scale of an industry or in the 'proportions of the factors of production' there can be neither marginal product nor marginal cost." On the contrary, in the classical system, "in which, day after day, production continued unchanged in those respects, the marginal product of a factor (or alternatively the marginal cost of a product) would not merely be hard to find – it just would not be there to be found" (Sraffa, 1960, p. v).

4. An application of the "principle of sufficient reason"

Sraffa identified the following additional characteristic features of the classical approach to the theory of value and distribution.[12] The classical authors based their determination of the rate of profits, the rates of rent of different qualities of land, and relative prices on: (i) the concept of physical real costs of producing the various commodities, where the costs include the necessary wages of labour; (ii) the concept of production as a circular flow; and (iii) the explanation of all shares of property income (rents and profits) in terms of the social surplus product. However, he saw a subtle methodological problem that had to be overcome before he could further pursue the objectivist research programme.[13] It is apposite to quote him at some length. He wrote in August 1931:

> if one attempts to take an entirely objective point of view, the very conception of a surplus melts away. For if we take this natural science point of view, we must start by assuming that for every effect there must be sufficient cause, that the causes are identical with their effects, & that there can be nothing in the effect which was not in the causes: in our case, there can be no product for which there has not been an equivalent cost, and all costs (= expenses) must be necessary to produce it.

> The conception of "necessity" has to be extended to everything that happens, & thus vanishes. Every share distributed must be so for a reason, therefore it is necessary: how can there be a surplus left, unless we assume some sort of indeterminacy? This can be assumed from some subjective standpoint, where something is taken as known & given to him, but something is left unknown & dependent upon his will or his actions. But from a purely objective point of view, all must be [an] object of knowledge, & nothing can be indeterminate.
>
> This is the great difficulty: the surplus is the object of the inquiry, but as soon as it is explained, a cause is found for it, and ceases to be a surplus. This sounds as if the object of the inquiry had been defined as "the unknown", but if the inquiry is successful it becomes known, & the object of the inquiry ceases to exist!

Was there a way out of the impasse? Actually, Sraffa saw in principle two such ways:

> One solution might be this. The science of economics must find a cause, a reason, for every actual fact; thus it justifies the existence of the fact. This science (indeed, every science) is by essence conservative. – But for every thing there are also reasons why it should not exist, so much so that at one time it must die, & indeed some things are going out of existence all the time; or else, simply, there are no more reasons for its existence. Thus there is work for economics in finding out these contradictions (existence against reason) or lack of reason. But these are simply other names for the *failures* of economics! – Thus it would appear that the true economic science can only study the conservative side (aspect) of things; and the revolutionary side is the object of study of the inadequate & contradictory economics. The revolutionary economics can only be completed by practice, which solves the contradictions & changes the facts making them adequate to their reasons.[14]

Yet, he did not adopt this solution; he focused attention rather on the second alternative about which he wrote:

> Another solution however lies in *criticizing the above application of the principle of sufficient reason.*
>
> Any given effect is entirely contained in its causes. (But these causes may contain something else besides that effect; *i.e.* they may have other effects as well).
>
> Any given cause is entirely contained in its effects. (But these effects contain more than it, *i.e.* they have also other causes).
>
> The two above statements cannot be rolled into one, except in the form "all effects are contained in all causes": this is meaningless, & at any rate tautological, for "all effects" would be merely another name for "all causes" (if they meant anything at all).

> *Thus there must be a leak at one end or the other: the "closed system" is in communication with the world.*
>
> *When we have defined our "economic field", there are still outside causes which operate in it; & its effects go beyond the boundary.* This must happen in any concrete case. . . .
>
> *The surplus may be the effect of the outside causes;* & the effects of the distribution of the surplus may lie outside.
>
> (D3/12/7: 161 (3–5); emphases added)

The existence of a surplus is thus explicitly taken to reflect some "outside causes" in operation. What are henceforth studied by Sraffa in terms of the equations of production are (some of) the effects of these causes, not the causes themselves. An echo of this argument can be found in a note of 1942 in which Sraffa defined his aim as follows:

> This paper deals with an extremely elementary problem; so elementary indeed that its solution is generally taken for granted. The problem is that of ascertaining the conditions of equilibrium of a system of prices & the rate of profits, independently of the study of the forces which may bring about such a state of equilibrium. Since a solution of the second problem carries with it a solution of the first, that is the course usually adopted in modern theory. The first problem however is susceptible of a more general treatment, independent of the particular forces assumed for the second; & in view of the unsatisfactory character of the latter, there is advantage in maintaining its independence.
>
> (D3/12/15: 2)[15]

5. Concluding remarks

This paper focuses attention on some aspects of Sraffa's early attempts at re-interpreting the classical economists' approach to the theory of value and distribution. The objectivistic character of the approach is stressed. This is reflected in the kind of quantities that are to be taken into consideration as independent variables in order to determine the dependent variables: relative prices and the rate of profits. As long as workers do not participate in the surplus generated in the economic system, the sought quantities are the real wage rate(s), specified in terms of a vector of amounts of wage goods, and the system of production in use, specified in terms of given output levels and the methods of production employed to produce them. This case is aptly described by James Mill's dictum that "the agents of production are the commodities themselves" (that is, food, tools and materials). In this perspective, the cost of a commodity equals the amounts of the various commodities that have to be destroyed in its production: its physical real cost. The information represented by the independent variables mentioned – real wages and the system of production in use – suffice in order to determine

- relative "absolute" prices in the case in which there is no surplus in terms of what Sraffa called his "first [simultaneous] equations";
- or relative "natural" prices (or "prices of production") and the general rate of profits in the case in which there is a surplus, and this surplus is appropriated according to a uniform rate of profits on the value of the capital invested in the different industries, in terms of what Sraffa called his "second [simultaneous] equations".

It is also argued that by means of an application of the principle of sufficient reason Sraffa in his second equations assumed the existence of a surplus which reflects some "outside causes" in operation. What Sraffa thus studied in terms of his equations of production (and productive consumption) are the effects of these causes, not the causes themselves.

Acknowledgements

We should like to thank Pierangelo Garegnani, literary executor of Sraffa's papers and correspondence, for granting us permission to quote from them. The papers are kept at the Wren Library, Trinity College, Cambridge. References to the papers follow the catalogue prepared by Jonathan Smith, archivist. Unless otherwise stated, all emphases are in the original. Christian Gehrke, Gary Mongiovi, Rodolfo Signorino and Ian Steedman kindly read earlier versions of the manuscript and provided valuable comments and suggestions.

Notes

1 The document is not dated but contained in a folder with material most of which was written (and some even dated) in the first period of Sraffa's constructive work (extending roughly from 1927 to 1931) which was eventually to culminate in the publication of his book (Sraffa, 1960). (The other two periods in which he worked on problems tackled in his later book were roughly 1941–1945 and 1955–1958.)

2 On 30 May 1820 David Ricardo made a speech in Parliament on petitions upon the subject of "agricultural distress", in which he criticized the views of the "agriculturalists" who contended that the corn laws of 1815 were inadequate to protect their business and that stronger measures were required. Thereupon Ricardo was accused by one of his critics to have "argued as if he had dropped from another planet", depicting a "Utopian world" of "perfect liberty of trade" (Ricardo, *Works*, Vol. V, p. 56; on Ricardo's response, see p. 85). In a note Sraffa related his metaphor of the "man from the moon" to this incidence (see D3/11/227: 48). The metaphor was also referred to by Sraffa when resuming the work on his book in 1955 after having finally finished the Ricardo edition (exclusive, of course, of the index) (see D3/12/49: 10).

3 Related issues are dealt with in Kurz (1998, 2003a), Salvadori (2000), and Kurz and Salvadori (2002).

4 Sraffa referred to a paper by Cunningham (1892) in which the latter defended Petty's approach against Marshall's description of "economics as the science of measurable

motives". The former is said to lay "a solid foundation of fact. . . . But when we start from motives, we loose all this advantage. . . . Motives are not obvious and we are likely to be mistaken about them." See D3/12/9: 18.

5 In Sraffa's notes there is also a quotation taken from an essay on Goethe's view of Nature, in which the two authors state that Goethe called his "own way of thinking . . . 'thinking in objects' (gegenständliches Denken) . . . . Any idealistic argument that obscured this objective reference is disliked." (D3/12/9: 46) From an essay titled "The Quantum Theory" (Allen, 1928), Sraffa excerpted the following passage on the physicist Werner Heisenberg: "*Heisenberg put forward the demand that only such quantities as are observable should be represented in the mathematical formulation of atomic theory*. . . . This led to the development of the matrix mechanics, every term in a matrix corresponding to something which is, at least ideally, observable." (Allen, 1928, p. 891; cited in D1/9: 13; emphasis by Sraffa in terms of a straight line in the margin) This is echoed, in summer 1929, in a paper dealing with the problem of fixed capital in which Sraffa referred to the analysis he sought to develop as "atomic analysis" (see D3/12/13: 16(9); see also Kurz 2003). (See also item 3204 of Sraffa's library, p. 35.)

6 The "first equations" deal with an economic system without a surplus (or a deficit), that is, "an extremely simple society which produces just enough to maintain itself" (Sraffa, 1960, p. 3); these equations eventually became Chapter 1 of Sraffa's 1960 book.

7 It is also interesting to note that when Sraffa received the galley-proofs of his book (which had first been corrected inhouse by Cambridge University Press), he would note in his diary on 26 September 1959: "Ricevuta 1a bozza corretta completa di 'P. of C. by C.'" [Received the first corrected complete proofs of "P. of C. by C."]

8 Following Ricardo, Sraffa also analysed the case in which workers participate in the surplus product, thus focusing attention on the share of wages in the social product rather than the real wage rate. (For an early document, written during Michaelmas term 1928, see D3/12/10: 2–3 and 5.) This case led Ricardo to maintain: "The greater the *proportion of the result of labour that is given to the labourer*, the smaller must be the rate of profits, and *vice versa*" (*Works*, Vol. VIII, p. 194; emphasis added). This development of the classical approach which revolves around the concept of the share of wages in the social product will not be dealt with in the present paper.

9 In a manuscript written in 1942, Sraffa expounded that in his first and second equations (the latter refer to a system with a surplus and wages that are at a subsistence level) the "food & sustenance of the workers [are] treated . . . on the same footing as that of horses." He added: "Men however (& in this they are distinguished from horses) kick. The horse (or his physiology) takes a strictly private view of his relation with his food, & does not allow any extraneous consideration to interfere: he is a perfect utilitarian & thus forms the ideal object of study of the marg.[inal] utility economist" (D3/12/16: 18).

10 In one place Sraffa stressed that Petty and the Physiocrats still "had the right notion of cost as 'the loaf of bread'" (D3/12/4: 4).

11 In parenthesis he added: "The 'extensive' theory of rent, and the labour theory of value only assume this kind of knowledge." Interestingly, for a long time Sraffa was of the opinion that intensive rent involved applying the marginalist principle of incremental change and therefore was not amenable to his approach. (He abandoned this opinion only in the 1950s.) This becomes clear in the comment on the third group above. See also D3/12/7: 120–21 and Sraffa's assessment that intensive diminishing returns involve a "dynamic assumption" (D3/12/11: 33).

12 For evidence, see, for example, the references to the literature in footnote 3.

13 For a discussion of how Sraffa arrived at this point and what the following lines were designed to answer, see Kurz (2003b, Section 2).

14 This is reminiscent of Marx's theses on Feuerbach and appears to reflect upon Gramsci's concept of paxis as elaborated in his notebooks from prison.

15 In this context, see also Sraffa's comments on Pareto's theory in D3/12/9: 93 and D3/12/10: 39.

References

Allen H. S. [1928], "The quantum theory", *Nature*, Supplement, N° 3084, December 8, pp. 887–95.

Cunningham W. [1892], "A plea for pure theory", *Economic Review*, 11, pp. 25–41.

Kurz H. D. [1998], "Against the current: Sraffa's unpublished manuscripts and the history of economic thought", *European Journal of the History of Economic Thought*, 5, pp. 437–51.

Kurz H. D. [2003a], "The surplus interpretation of the Classical economists". In J. E. Biddle, J. B. Davis and W. J, Samuels (eds.), *The Blackwell Companion to the History of Economic Thought*, Oxford, Blackwell Publishers, pp. 167–83.

Kurz H. D. [2003b], "Towards an 'atomic analysis' – Sraffa's early studies of the problem of fixed capital", manuscript.

Kurz H. D, Salvadori N. [2002], "Mark Blaug on the 'Sraffian interpretation of the surplus approach" ', *History of Political Economy*, 34, pp. 225–36.

Mill J. [1826], *Elements of Political Economy*, 3rd edn, revised and corrected. London 1826 (1st edn 1821), Baldwin, Chadock, and Joy.

Petty W. [1691], *Political Arithmetick, or A Discourse Concerning* . . . , London, Printed for Robert Clavel at the Peacock and Hen. Morlock at the Phoenix in St Paul's Church-yard. Reprinted in W. Petty, *The Economic Writings of Sir William Petty*, edited by C. H. Hull, vols I and II, originally published in 1899, Cambridge, Cambridge University Press. Reprinted in one volume (1986), New York, Kelley.

Ricardo D. [1951–73]. *The Works and Correspondence of David Ricardo*, 11 volumes, edited by P. Sraffa with the collaboration of M. H. Dobb, Cambridge, Cambriudge University Press; referred to as *Works*, vol. number.

Salvadori N. [2000], "Sraffa on Demand: A Textual Analysis", *in* Kurz H.D. (ed.), *Critical Essays on Piero Sraffa's Legacy in Economics*, Cambridge, Cambridge University Press, pp. 181–97.

Sraffa P. [1925], "Sulle relazioni fra costo e quantità prodotta", *Annali di Economia*, 2, pp. 277–328. An English translation by John Eatwell and Alessandro Roncaglia has been published in L. L. Pasinetti (ed.), *Italian Economic Papers*, Bologna, Il Mulino and Oxford, Oxford University Press, pp. 323–63.

Sraffa P. [1926], "The Laws of Returns under Competitive Conditions", *Economic Journal*, 36, pp. 535–50.

Sraffa P. [1960], *Production of Commodities by Means of Commodities. Prelude to a Critique of Economic Theory*, Cambridge, Cambridge University Press.

8 The agents of production are the commodities themselves*

On the classical theory of production, distribution and value

Heinz D. Kurz

> The agents of production are the commodities themselves. . . . They are the food of the labourer, the tools and the machinery with which he works, and the raw materials which he works upon.
>
> (Mill, [1821] 1826, p. 165)

1. The classical approach

The analysis of the classical economists from William Petty to David Ricardo of the problems of production, distribution and value revolved around the concept of the annual *social surplus*. In the first step, this surplus was typically seen to be exclusively distributed to the propertied classes in the form of rents or profits and used for the purposes of consumption and capital accumulation. In the second step, some authors then discussed workers' participation in the surplus. The surplus refers to those quantities of the different commodities that were left over after the necessary means of production used up and the means of subsistence in the support of workers have been deducted from the gross outputs produced during a year. In this conceptualisation, the necessary real wages of labour were considered no less as indispensable inputs and thus agents of production than raw materials, tools or machines. What became known as the 'surplus interpretation' of the classical economists focuses attention on the mature classical economists' approach to how the surplus is distributed and which system of exchange values of the different commodities can be expected to emerge as the result of the gravitation of 'market' or 'actual' prices to their 'natural' or 'ordinary' levels, or 'prices of production'. In conditions of free competition, that is, the absence of significant barriers to entry and exit from all markets, prices can be taken to oscillate around levels characterized by a *uniform* rate of profits on the value of the capital advanced at the beginning of the uniform production period and a uniform rate of rent for each of the different qualities of land.

The determination of the general rate of profits, the rents of land and the corresponding system of relative prices, given the system of production in

* Reprinted with permission from *Structural Change and Economic Dynamics*, 17, 2006.

use, constitutes the analytical centrepiece of classical political economy. It was designed to lay the foundation of all other economic analysis, including the investigation of capital accumulation and technical progress; of development and growth; of social transformation and structural change; and of taxation and public debt.

Piero Sraffa deserves the credit for having rediscovered and clarified the distinct analytical structure of the classical approach to the theory of production, distribution and value. He, at the same time showed that it cannot be interpreted as an early and somewhat crude version of demand and supply analysis which became prominent with the so-called 'marginalist revolution'. Last but not least, Sraffa reformulated the classical approach by shedding the weaknesses of its earlier versions and elaborating on its strengths. Equipped with Sraffa's reconstructive and interpretive work, as it is available in his published and hitherto unpublished work, we may reconsider the classical authors' contributions. This will lead us to a deeper understanding of what they were after, and why; what they accomplished, and how; why they failed to elaborate a fully satisfactory theory revolving around the concept of social surplus, and for which reason; and finally what was needed in order to accomplish the task. In this paper, we focus on Sraffa's interpretation of the classical authors: we shall draw both on his published works (Sraffa, 1951, 1960) and on his unpublished manuscripts.[1] In a note entitled 'Principio' of November 1927 Sraffa specified the task he had taken on as follows:

> I shall begin by giving a short "estratto" of what I believe is the essence of the classical theories of value, i.e. of those which include W. Petty, Cantillon, Physiocrats, A. Smith, Ricardo and Marx. This is not the theory of any one of them, but an extract of what I think is common to them. I state it of course, not in their own words, but in modern terminology, and it will be useful when we proceed to examine their theories to understand their portata {bearing strength} from the point of view of our present inquiry. It will be a sort of "frame", a machine, into which to fit their own statements in a homogeneous pattern, so as to be able to find what is common in them and what is the difference with the later theories.
>
> (D3/12/4: 12)

The composition of the essay is the following. Section 2 deals with the scope and method of the classical theory of production, distribution and value. Section 3 turns to the central classical concept of production conceived as a circular flow and the related concept of physical real cost. Section 4 addresses briefly the tension that exists in major classical authors between concepts on the one hand and tools to deal with them on the other and how this unresolved tension made them have recourse to devices, such as the labour theory of value, that involved, to use Sraffa's word, a 'corruption' of the approach. Section 5 shows in terms of Sraffa's 'first' equations which relate to a system without surplus that relative prices of commodities can be determined exclusively on the basis of their physical real costs by means of a system of simultaneous equations. Section 6 turns to systems with a surplus and the early classical authors' attempts to ascertain the general rate of profits and some of the difficulties they encountered. Section 7 shows how these difficulties can again be mastered on the basis exclusively of the information about physical real costs in terms of what Sraffa called his 'second' equations. Section 8 addresses the problem of how the approach has to be modified in order to allow for the participation of workers in the surplus product. This leads to Ricardo's concept of proportional wages, or wages conceived as a share, and to attempts to determine the rate of profits independently of prices. It is argued that with his concepts of constant capital and organic composition of capital Marx anticipated, albeit imperfectly, two important propositions of production theory. First, in a strictly circular flow framework the maximum rate of profits is finite. Secondly, the actual rate of profits depends on two magnitudes instead of on only one: it depends not only on the share of wages, as Ricardo had thought, but also on the maximum rate of profits, that is, the inverse of the organic composition, properly defined. Section 9 then shows that Sraffa with his construction of the Standard system and Standard commodity succeeded in demonstrating the correctness of the second proposition. The concluding Section 10 then argues that the classical approach can also deal with the empirically important problems of joint production, fixed capital, jointly utilized machines, capital utilization, and renewable and exhaustible natural resources.

2. Scope and method

The concern of the classical economists was the laws governing the emerging capitalist economy, characterized by the stratification of society into three classes: workers, land owners, and the rising class of capitalists; wage labour as the dominant form of the appropriation of other people's capacity to work; an increasingly sophisticated division of labour within and between firms; the co-ordination of economic activity via a system of interdependent markets in which transactions were mediated through money; and significant technical, organizational and institutional change. In short, they were concerned with an economic system incessantly in motion. How to analyse such a system? The ingenious device of the classical authors to see through the complexities of the modern economy consisted in distinguishing between the 'actual' values of the relevant variables – the distributive rates and prices – and their 'normal' values. The former were taken to reflect all kinds of influences, many of an accidental or temporary nature, about which no general propositions were possible, whereas the latter were conceived of as expressing the persistent, non-accidental and non-temporary factors governing the economic system, which could be systematically studied.

The method of analysis adopted by the classical economists is known as the method of long-period positions of the economy (see Garegnani, 1984). Any such position is the system of production towards which the economy is taken to gravitate as the result of the self-seeking actions of agents, thereby putting into sharp relief the fundamental forces at work. In conditions of free competition, the resulting long-period position is characterized by a uniform rate of profits (subject perhaps to persistent inter-industry differentials reflecting different levels of risk) and uniform rates of remuneration for each particular kind of primary input. Competitive conditions were taken to engender *cost-minimizing systems of production*.

The classical economists proceeded essentially in two steps. In the first step, they isolated the kinds of factors that were seen to determine income distribution and the prices supporting that distribution in a given system of production, that is, in a given place and time. The theory of production, distribution and value was designed to identify in abstracto the dominant factors at work and to analyse their interaction. In the second step, the classical authors then turned to an investigation of the causes which over time affected systematically the factors at work from within the economy and which brought about new systems of production. This was the realm of the classical analysis of capital accumulation, technical change, economic growth and socio-economic development.

It is another characteristic feature of the classical approach to profits, rents and relative prices that these are explained exclusively in terms of magnitudes that can, in principle, be observed, measured or calculated. This *objectivist* orientation of classical economics has received its perhaps strongest expression in a famous proclamation by William Petty, who was arguably its founding father. Keen to assume what he called the "physician's" outlook, Petty in his *Political Arithmetick*, published in 1690, stressed:

> I have taken the course (as a Specimen of the Political Arithmetick I have long aimed at) to express my self in Terms of *Number, Weight* or *Measure*; to use only Arguments of Sense, and to consider only such Causes, as have visible foundations in Nature; leaving those that depend upon the mutable Minds, Opinions, Appetites and Passions of particular Men, to the Consideration of others. . . .
>
> (Petty, 1986, p. 244; emphasis in the original)

Notwithstanding their many differences, classical economists generally shared in one form or another an essentially objectivist outlook on the problem of value and distribution. This becomes clear when we turn to the concept of cost entertained by them.

3. Circular flow and physical real costs

Sraffa singled out especially two interrelated features characterizing the classical theory of production and cost. First, the classical concept of production is essentially that of a circular flow. This idea can be traced back to William Petty and Richard Cantillon and was most effectively expressed by François Quesnay ([1759] 1972) in the *Tableau économique* (see Aspromourgos, 1996). The classical view that commodities are produced by means of commodities is in stark contrast with the view of production as a one-way avenue leading from the services of original factors of production to consumption goods, as it was entertained, among others, by the 'Austrian' economists. Second, the classical economists held essentially a concept of physical real cost. Their starting point can be summarized by paraphrasing a famous dictum of James Mill: Man cannot create matter, man can only decompose and recompose it, change its form and move it. Production involves destruction, and the real cost of a commodity consists in the commodities destroyed in the course of its production.

We encounter the classical view in Petty who reckoned as the costs of a commodity the means of production and the means of subsistence in support of the workers necessary in order to carry out the production. Yet, as Sraffa noted, Petty was probably not the first author to have advocated such a point of view. Traces of it can also be found in the concept of 'just price' in the canonists. After Petty the new science of political economy was taken up and further developed by the Physiocrats, who adopted essentially the same point of view. The concept of physical real cost recurs in the writings of Adam Smith, David Ricardo, James Mill, Robert Torrens, and Karl Marx, to name but some of the leading representatives of the classical approach. The physical real cost approach is clearly discernible in the concept of 'capital', which Ricardo defined as 'the food and clothing consumed by the labourer, the buildings in which he works, the implements with which his labour is assisted' (*Works*, vol. I, p. 52). The perhaps clearest expression of the physical real cost approach has been put forward by James Mill in his *Elements of Political Economy*, first published in 1821. Mill insisted that, in the last instance,

> *The agents of production are the commodities themselves*. . . . They are the food of the labourer, the tools and the machinery with which he works, and the raw materials which he works upon.
>
> (Mill, [1821] 1826, p. 165, emphasis added; see also Sraffa's excerpts in D3/12/9: 106–118)

The concept of agency expressed in this passage differs markedly from that entertained by marginalist economics which rose to dominance around the turn of the nineteenth century, with the Cambridge economist Alfred Marshall as one of its main heralds. At the time the concept of 'psychic cost', reflected in such notions as marginal 'utility' or 'disutility', 'abstinence', 'waiting' or 'opportunity cost', gradually replaced the earlier classical concept of material cost. Marshall in the *Principles* tried to patch over the breach by alluding to the received concept in terms of the notion of 'real cost' of production of a commodity but then specifying its content as 'the exertions of all the different kinds of labour that are directly and indirectly involved in making it; together with the abstinences or rather the waitings required for saving the capital used in making it' (Marshall, [1890] 1970, p. 282).

Sraffa who, in the mid 1920s, in two papers had dealt a serious blow to Marshallian partial equilibrium analysis (Sraffa, 1925, 1926) was convinced that Marshall's interpretation of the classical economists as early demand and supply theorists, with the demand side in its infancy, did not stand up to close scrutiny. At the same time it had to be explained why the classical approach had been abandoned and replaced with a theory which Sraffa considered to be inherently flawed. A main reason for the decline of classical economics, as Sraffa saw it, was that the analytical tools available to the classical authors did not live up to the concepts advocated by them. The main reason for the failure of classical economics was not so much a lack of fecundity, an inability to explain salient features of the modern economic world, but deficiencies in the form in which the theory was presented. The doctrines of the classical economists from Adam Smith to David Ricardo, while essentially sound, suffered from internal contradictions and incoherences. Let us have a brief look at what Sraffa considered to be a mismatch between tools and concepts.

4. Concepts versus tools: the classical economists and the problem of value

The classical economists were convinced that the concept of physical real cost held the key to an explanation of value: the value of a commodity was closely related to the amounts of the means of production and the means of subsistence used up, or destroyed, in producing it. As Sraffa stressed, 'the sort of "costs" which determines values is the collection of material things used up in production' (D3/12/7: 106). In the case in which there is no surplus product in the economic system to be distributed as profits, interest or rent, the value of a commodity is equal to the sum total of the values of the products used up. However, this appears to be arguing in a circle, explaining value with reference to value. So how can the values of heterogeneous commodities be ascertained? The classical economists sought to cope with the problem of the heterogeneity of commodities by invoking an 'ultimate measure of value' in which the value of each and every commodity could be expressed (see Garegnani, 2004). Petty had suggested to take as such an ultimate standard the means of subsistence of workers, 'food'. Each and every commodity, he posited, could ultimately be reduced to a well-specified quantity of food needed directly and indirectly in the support of workers producing the commodity. In this way, all commodities could be made commensurable and their values expressed in terms of the total amounts of food requested in order to feed workers across the different stages of the processing of the commodities under consideration.

Authors such as Ricardo (and Marx) did not follow Petty in this regard. Ricardo rather started from the observation that 'labour' is needed in the production of all commodities and he thus took labour to be the sought measure. As far as value theory is concerned, to him commodities represent first and foremost different amounts of direct and indirect labour 'contained' or 'embodied' in them. This then led to the labour theory of value which in its crude version claims that the exchange ratios of commodities equal the relative amounts of labour bestowed upon them. To Sraffa this implied an aberration from Petty's sound starting point: 'A. Smith and Ricardo and Marx indeed began to corrupt the old idea of cost – from food to labour. But their notion was still near enough to be in many cases equivalent' (D3/12/4: 2). Yet, he added, small errors may grow into larger ones:

> The fatal error of Smith, Ricardo, Marx has been to regard "labour" as a quantity, to be measured in hours or in kilowatts of human energy, and thus

> commensurated to value. . . . All trouble seems to have been caused by *small* initial errors, which have cumulated in deductions (e.g. food of worker = quantity of labour, is *nearly* true). Petty had foreseen the possibility of being misunderstood. . . .
>
> (D3/12/11: 36; similarly D3/12/4: 4)

While quantities of food consumed and of means of production used up can be measured in their own technical units, it is far from clear what is meant by a certain 'quantity of labour' and how it could be measured. Typically, the time dimension of the work performed is considered an important aspect of the sought measure. However, as Sraffa pointed out with reference to Petty and the Physiocrats, in agriculture workers have to be paid even in periods when natural conditions prevent them from performing at all or at least from performing their normal tasks, such as in winter time (see Sraffa's respective observations in D3/12/12: 8). Hence, as far as cost is concerned, what matters are real (i.e. commodity) wages paid during a given period of time, irrespective of whether and which kind of work is performed. The difficulties besetting the concept of labour are aggravated once one takes into consideration the aspects of labour intensity and heterogeneity. These have never been dealt with in a satisfactory way by those who advocated some kind of labour cost-based theory of value.[2]

These and other considerations prompted Sraffa to stay aloof as much as possible from the infamous concept of labour as a quantity. Indeed, during most of the first period of his constructive work (1927–1931) we see him totally avoiding the concept. The following passage, presumably written in the late 1920s, counterposes the physical real cost approach and the labour value-based interpretation of the former. It provides a further reason for Sraffa's critical attitude towards the labour theory of value:

> The difference between the "physical real costs" and the Ricardo-Marxian theory of "labour costs" is that the first does, and the latter does not, include in them the natural resources that are used up in the course of production (such as coal, iron, exaustion {sic} of land) – [Air, water, etc. are not used up: as there is an unlimited supply, no subtraction can be made from ∞]. This {is} fundamental because it does away with "human energy" and such metaphysical things.
>
> (D3/12/42: 33)

And in another document stemming from November 1927 he expounded:

> It is the *whole* process of production that must be called "human labour", and thus causes all product and all values. Marx and Ricardo used "labour" in two different senses: the above, and that of *one* of the factors of production ("hours of labour" or "quantity of labour" has a meaning only in the latter sense). It is by confusing the two senses that they got mixed up and said that value is proportional to quantity of labour (in second sense) whereas they ought

> to have said that it is due to human labour (in first sense: a non measurable quantity, or rather not a quantity at all).
>
> (D3/12/11: 64)[3]

Seen in this way, 'all values are "due" to labour, or to wheat or to any other thing that enters in the production of every {one} of them' (D3/12/10: 71). Yet, even setting aside the problems of labour intensity and heterogeneity, it was not at all clear how the quantities of labour embodied in a commodity could be ascertained. Whilst this was no problem in the case of the Austrian view of production as a one-way avenue leading from original factors of production via a *finite* number of stages to the final product, when 'commodities are produced by commodities . . . the idea that the process of production has a beginning and an end {must be replaced} with that that it is a circular one – an idea first introduced by the Tableau économique' (D3/12/7: 2). Hence the idea that labour values could be somehow known and taken as the basis of a theory of normal prices was far from clear.

In Sraffa's view the source of much of the trouble in which the classical approach got entangled was that its advocates lacked the tool which would have effectively allowed them to tackle the problems they were faced with: the tool of *simultaneous equations* and the mathematics to solve them. As Sraffa stressed in a document written around the turn of 1927, 'the fundamental force is physical real cost' which, however, is 'seen only in general equilibrium' (D3/12/42: 46), where by general equilibrium here he meant the solution of a system of simultaneous equations (see below Section 5).[4] Lacking this tool the earlier economists tried to tackle the problem in roundabout ways, the most prominent being the labour theory of value. However, as we have just seen, the route via labour values was not really a way out of the impasse in which they found themselves: it rather landed them right in that impasse again. Commodities were produced by commodities and there was no way to circumnavigate the simultaneous equations approach.[5]

5. 'First' equations: production for subsistence

What made it so difficult, if not impossible, for the classical authors to see that the theory of value and distribution could be firmly grounded in the concept of physical real cost? Given their primitive tools of analysis, they did not see that the information about the system of production in use, described in terms of the amounts of means of production used up and the quantities of the means of subsistence in support of workers, was all that was needed in order to determine *directly* the rate of profits and relative prices. Solving a set of simultaneous equations of production accomplishes the task in a straightforward manner. This was clarified by Sraffa in the winter of 1927–1928 by means of what he called his 'first' and 'second' equations, relating respectively to systems without and with a surplus and given real (or as Sraffa occasionally wrote: 'inventory') wages. To illustrate the two cases we may for simplicity start from James Mill's above broad classification of commodities in three groups: tools (t), raw materials (m), and the food of the labourer (f). In this section, we deal with the no-surplus economy, or production for subsistence; the following two sections then address the with-surplus case. We provide only a summary account of Sraffa's argument and do not enter into the details and precise chronology of his reasoning.[6]

In the case in which the economy is just able to reproduce what has been used up in the course of production, neither more nor less, that is, the economy is in what Sraffa called a 'self-replacing state', production in the three industries may be tabulated in the following way:

$$\begin{aligned} &T_t \oplus M_t \oplus F_t \rightarrow T \\ &T_m \oplus M_m \oplus F_m \rightarrow M \\ &T_f \oplus M_f \oplus F_m \rightarrow F, \end{aligned} \qquad \text{(Q)}$$

where T_i, M_i and F_i designate the inputs of the three commodities (employed as means of production and means of subsistence) in industry i ($i = t, m, f$), and T, M and F total outputs in the three industries; the symbol '$\oplus$' indicates that all inputs on the left hand side of '$\rightarrow$', representing production, are required to generate the output on its right hand side.[7] Adopting the terminology of the classical authors, Sraffa called these relations 'the methods of production and productive consumption' (Sraffa, 1960, p. 3). In the hypothetical case in which the economy is just viable, that is, able to reproduce itself without any surplus (or deficiency), we have $T = \sum_i T_i, M = \sum_i M_i$, and $F = \sum_i F_i$.

From this schema, we may directly derive the corresponding system of values which Sraffa, with explicit reference to Adam Smith and Ricardo, dubbed 'natural' or 'absolute' values. These are taken to express the idea of physical real cost-based values in an unadulterated way. Denoting the value of one unit of commodity i by p_i ($i = t, m, f$), we have

$$\begin{aligned} &T_t p_t + M_t p_m + F_t p_f = T p_t \\ &T_m p_t + M_m p_m + F_m p_f = M p_m \\ &T_f p_t + M_f p_m + F_f p_f = F p_f \end{aligned}$$

Only two of the three equations are independent of one another and allow one to determine relative prices. Fixing a standard of value whose price is ex definitione equal to unity, provides an additional equation without adding a further unknown. We may then solve the equations for the remaining dependent variables.

A numerical example taken from Sraffa's papers illustrates the important finding that the given socio-technical relations rigidly fix relative values:

$$\begin{aligned} &2p_t + 15p_m + 20p_f = 17p_t, \quad && p_t = 3p_m \\ &5p_t + 7p_m + 4p_f = 28p_m, \quad && p_m = \tfrac{2}{3}p_f \\ &10p_t + 6p_m + 11p_f = 35p_f, \quad && p_f = \tfrac{1}{2}p_t \end{aligned}$$

Hence values emerge as the solution of a system of simultaneous equations. These values depend exclusively on necessities of production. They are the only ones that allow to restore the initial distribution of resources and thus guarantee the unhampered continuation of the process.

Once the problem is approached from a rigorous physical real cost point of view, the question of a 'common measure' of commodities loses much of the appeal it had in the contributions of the earlier authors. Or rather, any valuable thing – whether a single commodity or a basket of commodities – could serve as such a measure. One may also 'reduce' the value of one commodity to a certain amount of another commodity needed directly or indirectly in the production of the former. For example, one might reduce one unit of commodity t to an amount needed of commodity m. Hence one might say that each of the three commodities could serve as a common measure and that, for example, commodities t and f exchange for one another in the proportion 1:2 because commodity t 'contains' or 'embodies' twice as much of the third commodity m as commodity f. The scholastic idea of *tertium comparationes* is here almost driven ad absurdum, because there are infinitely many such common equivalents.

6. Production with a surplus: the classical heritage

We now turn to systems with a surplus - the real concern of the classical authors and Sraffa. The assumption of given real wages paid ante factum and thus belonging to the capital advanced at the beginning of the uniform cycle of production will however be retained throughout this and the next section. In the case of free competition, the surplus is taken to be distributed in terms of a uniform rate of profits on the 'capitals' advanced in the different industries. Before we turn to Sraffa's equations in Section 7, a few remarks on some earlier attempts to determine the general rate of profits are in place.

In the 1820 edition of his *Essay on the External Corn Trade* Torrens put forward the simplest conceptualization possible of the surplus approach to the theory of value and distribution: the *corn-ratio theory of profits*. He laid down as a 'general principle'

> that in whatever proportion the quantity of produce obtained from the soil exceeds the quantity employed in raising it, in that proportion the value of the manufactured goods will exceed the values of the food and material expended in preparing them.
>
> (Torrens, 2000, vol. II, p. 362)

Here the rate of profit in agriculture is determined as a ratio between two given quantities of corn: the surplus corn produced and the corn capital advanced in corn production (seed and corn wages). This rate of profit is then said to determine the price of manufactures which, in competitive conditions, yields the manufacturer the same rate of return on his capital advances as the rate obtained by the farmer.

Torrens expressed his indebtedness to David Ricardo's 'original and profound inquiry into the laws by which the rate of profit is determined' (2000, p. xix). This provides indirect evidence in support of Sraffa's corn-profit interpretation of Ricardo (Sraffa, 1951, pp. xxxi–xxxiii). According to Sraffa, 'The advantage of Ricardo's method of approach is that, at the cost of considerable simplification, it makes possible an understanding of how the rate of profit is determined without the need of a method for reducing to a common standard a heterogeneous collection of commodities' (1951, p. xxxii). It also provides a first confirmation of Ricardo's conviction that 'the great questions of Rent, Wages, and Profits must be explained by the proportions in which the produce is divided . . . '; and that the laws of distribution 'are not essentially connected with the doctrine of value' (*Works*, vol. VIII, p. 194; emphasis added). The emphasis on *proportions* will become clear in the following.

It was, of course, clear to Ricardo and Torrens that, as Malthus had objected, the capital advanced in a single industry is never homogeneous with the industry's product. However, there may be homogeneity between product and capital in *aggregate* terms: the commodity composition of the surplus product may be the same (or at least roughly the same) as the commodity composition of social capital. In this case, the general rate of profits may again be conceived of (at least in a first approximation) in purely physical terms. In all three editions of Ricardo's *Principles*, we encounter a numerical example which satisfies this requirement. In the example of every 100 units produced of three commodities – hats, coats, and quarters of corn – workers are paid 25 (or 22) units of each of them and landlords are also assumed to receive 25 (or 22) units; accordingly, profits consist of 50 (56) units of each commodity (see *Works*, vol. I, p. 50). If capital consists only of the real wages bill, an assumption employed by Ricardo in much of his reasoning on profits and wages, the rate of profits can be determined independently of the problem of the valuation of the different commodities and amounts to $50/25 = 2$ (or $56/22 = 28/11$). Similarly, in his *Essay on the Production of Wealth*, published in 1821, Torrens put forward a circular flow example with two industries, one producing corn, the other suits of clothing, where both industries use both products in the same proportions (and actually in the same absolute amounts) as inputs (see Torrens, 2000, vol. Ill, pp. 372–373). With the social surplus and the social capital consisting of the same commodities in the same proportions, the general rate of profits can be determined without having recourse to the system of relative prices. Moreover, given the exceedingly simple conditions underlying the example, the exchange ratio of the two commodities corresponding to a uniform rate of profits is obvious: since both commodities exhibit the same physical real costs per unit of output, and thus the same amount of capital advanced, a quarter of corn is necessarily exchanged for one suit of clothing.[8]

Torrens was critical of Ricardo's labour value-based theory of value and distribution and advocated instead a capital value-based theory. As regards the determination of the rate of profits, this theory applied in a straightforward manner to the example just discussed. However, physical homogeneity of product (and surplus) and capital cannot be expected to hold in any real economy other than in highly unlikely special circumstances. In his attempt to deal with more general cases he was thus of necessity confronted with the complexity of the relationship between income distribution and relative prices. In yet another attempt to contain this complexity and arrive at a clear-cut and simple determination of the general rate of profits, Torrens resorted to the special assumption we just encountered, namely, that in all lines of production the same capital input proportions apply. Hence the capitals advanced in the different industries can easily be compared with one another. What is more, echoing the physical real cost approach in labour terms, the (circulating) *capitals* (means of production and means of subsistence) used up in the course of production can unambiguously be expressed as quantities *of accumulated labour*. In the preface to the *Essay* Torrens stressed:

> The principle that the *accumulated labour*, or, in other words, *the capital expended on production*, determines the exchangeable value of commodities, while it is derived from an extensive induction from particular cases, affords a *satisfactory solution* of some of the most important phenomena connected with the distribution of wealth. Without this correction or limitation of Mr. Ricardo's theory of value it is impossible to give a clear and unexceptionable demonstration of that gentleman's very original and valuable doctrine respecting the profits of stock.
>
> (Torrens, 2000, vol. III, p. vii; emphasis added)

It is clear that in the conditions specified Torrens's capital-value and Ricardo's labour-value theory amount to the same thing. It is also clear that Torrens's suggestion did not afford a generally 'satisfactory solution', as Torrens was inclined to believe. This became clear at the latest, if not earlier, in the context of the criticism of Marx's so-called 'transformation' of labour values in prices of production (see below, Section 7).

Not fully seeing their way through the complexities of the relation between relative prices and income distribution, given the system of production in use, applies in one way or another to all classical economists.[9] Ricardo, as is well known, struggled with the problem until his death: the manuscript fragments on 'Absolute Value and Exchangeable Value' (see *Works*, vol. IV) document in detail his attempts to come to grips with this problem and his failure to elaborate a fully correct theory. They also contribute to a better understanding of why Ricardo (and other classical economists) were so 'obsessed' with one version or another of the labour theory of value. This theory had allowed them to contain the complexities of the problem under consideration and determine, however provisionally and imperfectly, the general rate of profits. As long as no better theory was available, there was no compelling reason to abandon the labour value-based approach.

Sraffa was convinced that the move away from the 'loaf of bread' towards 'labour' had led into a dead-end and was partly responsible for the decline of the classical approach and its replacement by the marginalist one. This was unfortunate because the classical approach, he maintained, had been abandoned prematurely: what was deficient was the form in which it had been handed down, and not its substance.[10]

7. 'Second' equations: the with-surplus case

Systems with a surplus Sraffa began to analyse in terms of what he called his 'second' equations in November 1927. As early as June 1928 he was able to settle the problem of their solvability with his friend and colleague Frank Plumpton Ramsey (see D3/12/2: 28–9). Ramsey reformulated Sraffa's system of linear homogeneous equations by putting the system in its canonical form and then by setting the determinant of coefficients equal to zero in order to obtain a non-trivial solution (see Kurz and Salvadori, 2001, pp. 196–198). Here a few observations on some of the conceptual and doctrinal aspects involved must suffice.

For illustrative purposes we start again from system (Q), but now we assume that $T \geq \sum_i T_i$, $M \geq \sum_i M_i$, and $F \geq \sum_i F_i$, where at least with regard to one commodity the strict inequality sign holds. The case of a uniform rate of physical surplus across all commodities contemplated by Ricardo and Torrens,

$$\frac{T - \sum_i T_i}{\sum_i T_i} = \frac{M - \sum_i M_i}{\sum_i M_i} = \frac{F - \sum_i F_i}{\sum_i F_i} = r,$$

denotes a very special constellation: in it the general rate of profits, r, equals the uniform material rate of produce. Here we see the rate of profits in the quantities of commodities themselves, as having nothing to do with their values. In general, however, the rates of physical surplus will be different for different commodities. It cannot be even excluded that some of these rates are negative.

'Profits', Ricardo stressed, 'come out of the surplus produce' (*Works*, vol. II, pp. 130–131; similarly vol. I, p. 95). Unequal rates of commodity surplus do not, however, by themselves imply unequal rates of profit across industries. In conditions of free competition the concept of normal prices, or prices of production, implies that the social surplus is divided in such a way between the different employments of capital that a uniform rate of profits obtains. This is reflected by the following system of price equations:

$$\begin{aligned} (T_t p_t + M_t p_m + F_t p_f)(1 + r) &= T p_t \\ (T_m p_t + M_m p_m + F_m p_f)(1 + r) &= M p_m \\ (T_f p_t + M_f p_m + F_f p_f)(1 + r) &= F p_f \end{aligned} \tag{P}$$

Flukes apart, these three equations are independent of one another and can be solved for relative prices and the rate of profits. Alternatively, fixing a standard of value provides a fourth equation and no extra unknown and allows one to solve the system for the dependent variables: the general rate of profits and prices.

The important point to note here is the following. With the real wage rate given and paid at the beginning of the periodical production cycle, the problem of the determination of the rate of profits consists in distributing the surplus product in proportion to the capital advanced in each industry. Obviously, as Sraffa expounded,

> such a proportion between two aggregates of heterogeneous goods (in other words, the rate of profits) cannot be determined before we know the prices

> of the goods. On the other hand, we cannot defer the allotment of the surplus till after the prices are known, for . . . the prices cannot be determined before knowing the rate of profits. *The result is that the distribution of the surplus must be determined through the same mechanism and at the same time as are the prices of commodities.*
>
> (Sraffa, 1960, p. 6; emphasis added)

This passage shows that the idea which underlies Marx's so-called 'transformation' of labour values into prices of production (see Marx, 1959, part II) cannot generally be sustained. Marx had proceeded in two steps, a procedure Ladislaus von Bortkiewicz (1906–1907, essay II, p. 38) dubbed 'successivist' as opposed to 'simultaneous'. In the first step, Marx had assumed that the general rate of profits is determined independently of, and prior to, the determination of prices as the ratio between the labour value of the social surplus and that of social capital, consisting of constant capital (means of production) and variable capital (wages). In the second step, he had then used this rate to calculate prices. Underlying his approach is the hypothesis that while the transformation of values into prices is relevant with regard to each single commodity, it is irrelevant with regard to commodity aggregates, such as the surplus product or the social capital, and the ratio of such aggregates. Yet this is a misconception.

The passage quoted also contains the key to Sraffa's critique of the long-period marginalist concept of capital. This concept crucially hinges on the possibility of defining the 'quantity of capital', whose relative scarcity and thus marginal productivity is taken to determine the rate of profits, independently of that rate. However, according to the logic of Sraffa's above argument the rate of profits and the quantity (i.e. value) of capital can only be determined simultaneously (see Kurz and Salvadori, 1995, Chapter 14).

We may now ask: is a two-step procedure which first ascertains the rate of profits independently of relative prices and only afterwards turns to the determination of the latter in principle impossible, or can a logically unassailable version of it be elaborated? In the next but one section we shall see that this is indeed possible, which confirms Ricardo's supposition that the laws of distribution 'are not essentially connected with the doctrine of value'. Sraffa proposed such a device in the context of an investigation of how the classical approach had to be modified in order to be able to cover the case in which wages, 'besides the ever-present element of subsistence, . . . may include a share of the surplus product' (Sraffa, 1960, p. 9). However, we first have to prepare the ground by dealing briefly with the intricate analytical questions the participation of workers in the surplus raised and which Sraffa tackled in what he called his 'third' equations.

8. 'Third' equations: wages paid out of the product

The classical economists and Marx had already started to study the possibility of workers receiving more in the form of wages than mere sustenance (see, for example, Ricardo, *Works*, vol. I, p. 95). This raised immediately the following interrelated questions:

(i) Which wage concept was congenial to the new situation? Since the kind and quantities of commodities on which wages were spent could no longer be assumed to be given independently of and before relative prices were known, which wage concept should be put in place of the traditional one of real, or inventory, wages?
(ii) Since wages were no longer considered to be entirely paid out of the capital advanced at the beginning of the production period, could the assumption of ante factum payment of wages be retained or should it give way to that of wages paid out of the product, that is, post factum?
(iii) Is it possible to ascertain the level of the rate of profits for given wages independently of relative prices?
(iv) How do the rate of profits and relative prices vary with hypothetical variations in the level of wages, given the system of production in use?

In this section, we focus attention on questions (i)–(iii); for a discussion of question (iv), see Kurz and Salvadori (1995, Chapter 4).

In his papers, Sraffa noted carefully the answers to these questions he encountered in the classical authors and Marx. He credited Ricardo with the proposal that a *share* concept of wages was appropriate in the new situation. More specifically, Ricardo had insisted that what could be taken as a given magnitude in the theory of value and distribution is 'the proportion of the annual labour of the country . . . devoted to the support of the labourers' (Ricardo, *Works*, vol. I, p. 49; see also pp. 274, 275 and 420). Ricardo's labour-based share concept was subsequently adopted by Marx in terms of a given 'rate of surplus value', S/V, that is, the ratio between the portion of the net (labour) value added that goes to capital owners, or surplus value, S, and the portion that goes to workers, or variable capital, V. While Sraffa also adopted a share concept, unlike Ricardo (and Marx) he defined wages as a proportion of the national income evaluated in terms of normal priccs.

The next question was whether national income should be defined inclusive of the sum total of wages, or only inclusive of the surplus part of them, or exclusive of wages. It should come as no surprise that many of the classical (but also of the early neoclassical) authors vacillated a good deal when confronted with the alternatives. Adam Smith, for example, on the one hand insisted that the subsistence part of wages ought to be reckoned as a part and parcel of stock, i.e. capital, yet on the other hand anticipated modern national income accounting by treating total wages as revenue. Marx insisted against Smith and others that the two parts of wages – the subsistence and the surplus part – are fundamentally different in nature and ougth to be treated differently. Yet when it came to the determination of the general rate of profits and prices of production in volume III of *Capital* (Marx, 1959) he decided to continue to treat wages as a whole as variable *capital* advanced at the beginning of the period. In Ricardo we encounter essentially the same procedure.

Hence, when dealing with the problem of value and distribution these authors retained an assumption, which, while perfectly sensible in the case of subsistence wages, loses much of its force in an environment in which workers receive a share of the surplus. While in the first period of his work Sraffa followed Ricardo in this regard, in late 1943, after some careful deliberation, he decided instead to treat wages henceforth as entirely paid out of the net product. As he was to stress in his book: 'We shall . . . refrain from tampering with the traditional wage concept and shall follow the usual practice of treating the whole of the wage as variable' (Sraffa, 1960, p. 10) – where the 'usual practice' referred to alludes, of course, to marginalist theory which considers wages as constituting a net income on a par with profits and rents. Sraffa left no doubt that this decision came at a cost, but confronted with a hard choice he opted in favour of what he deemed to be the less bad alternative.

As regards the third question, Sraffa showed that in basically all classical authors we encounter the view that for a given system of production there is an inverse relationship between the *rate* of profits and (real or proportional) wages. However, this view gets every so often blurred because of analytical inconsistencies and contradictions in these authors. It was Ricardo who first firmly established what became known as his fundamental theorem concerning income distribution, namely, the constraint binding changes in the rate of profits and *proportional* wages: 'The greater the portion of the result of labour that is given to the labourer, the smaller must be the rate of profits, and vice versa' (*Works*, vol. VIII, p. 194). He was, thus, able to dispel the idea, generated by Adam Smith's notion of price as a sum of wages and profits (and rents) (Smith, 1976, WN, I.vi), that the wage and the rate of profits are determined independently of each other. Ricardo even contended that his above proposition was true irrespective of whether the technical conditions of production remained the same or changed. This was understandable, given the fact that in his respective observations he typically assumed social capital to consist only of wages (or to be entirely reducible to wages in a finite number of steps). Consequently, the rate of profits, r, was equal to the ratio of profits, P, to wages, W,

$$r = \frac{P}{W} \tag{R}$$

Obviously, Ricardo's theorem does not carry over to the case of production as a circular flow, since in this case capital can never be fully resolved in wages. However far the reduction is carried, besides the wage terms there will always be a 'commodity term' consisting of residual fractions of means of production.

According to Sraffa, it was Marx who carried the surplus approach a good deal beyond where Ricardo had left it. In particular, Marx is to be credited with establishing, however imperfectly, the inverse relationship between the rate of profits and the *share of wages* (in labour terms) within the circular flow framework of his schemes of reproduction. Since Sraffa's assessment of Marx's achievements is dealt with in some depth in another paper (see Gehrke and Kurz, 2006), a few remarks must suffice. At the beginning of the 1940s Sraffa read, or rather re-read,

Marx's *Capital* and to his surprise learned what in the past he either does not seem to have seen or what had escaped his attention, namely, that Marx had been struggling partly with similar problems and had come up with similar solutions as he himself. While Marx had approved of the concept of proportional wages, he had chastised Ricardo for erroneously identifying the rate of profits with the rate of surplus value consequent upon his identification of social capital with the sum total of wages. Once this very restrictive assumption was abandoned, Marx had insisted, Ricardo's above theorem held no longer true any more: The rate of profits can fall (or rise) even if proportional wages remain constant.

Marx, Sraffa noted approvingly, had introduced two important concepts into political economy which paved the way to a better understanding of some of the properties of the modern economic system: first, constant capital, that is, that part of social capital that consists of the means of production; and, secondly, the 'organic composition of capital'. In his labour-value based reckoning the organic composition is given by C/L, that is the ratio of the labour embodied in constant capital, or 'dead labour', C, and the annual labour (of productive workers) performed in the economy during a year, or 'living labour', L (where $L = V + S$). The former concept expresses the fact that commodities are produced by means of commodities and can never be made to disappear completely. This involves that the rate of profits is bounded from above: whereas in Ricardo vanishing wages would be reflected in a rate of profits that tends to infinity, in Marx there is a finite maximum rate of profits, Π. The maximum rate corresponds to zero wages and is equal to L/C; it is, thus, equal to the inverse of the organic composition of the system as a whole $\Pi = [(V+S)/C]$. The maximum rate of profits Marx assumed to be given and independent of the actual rate of profits and thus independent of relative prices.

We may now express Marx's labour value-based approach in the following way. The rate of profits is given by

$$r = \frac{S}{C+V} = \frac{S/L}{C/L + V/L} = \frac{1-(V/L)}{1/\Pi + (V/L)} = \frac{\Pi(1-\omega)}{1+\Pi\omega} \qquad \text{(M)}$$

The expression shows that the actual rate of profits depends on two magnitudes instead of on only one, as Ricardo had contended: it depends on proportional wages, ω (or the rate of surplus value, $(1-\omega)\omega^{-1}$) and on the maximum rate of profits, Π. The above expression was meant to cover all cases, that is, both the case with a constant technical knowledge and the one with a change of it due to inventions. It describes the distributive core of the system under consideration without reference to the particular kinds of commodities produced and consumed and their respective prices. It was meant to contain the key to an investigation of the 'law of motion' of the modern economy – independent of commodity worlds passed through. Since Marx thought that expression (M) was valid even if instead of labour values prices of production would be used as measuring rods, it could be seen as providing a general confirmation of Ricardo's conviction that the laws of distribution could be established independently of the theory of prices.

The connection with the law of motion is close at hand, because it was essentially on the basis of Eq. (M) that Marx, in volume III of *Capital*, analysed the falling tendency of the rate of profits. Differentiating r partially with respect to Π, we get

$$\frac{\partial r}{\partial \Pi} = \frac{1-\omega}{(1+\Pi\omega)^2} > 0.$$

This expression shows why, according to Sraffa, Marx in his discussion of that tendency focused attention on the long-run development of the organic composition of capital, Π^{-1}. For, with a given (and even with a moderately falling) share of wages, the rate of profits is bound to fall as the organic composition rises (which is equivalent to a fall in the maximum rate of profits). Such a rise was in turn considered to be unavoidable if capital accumulates and there are no new technical inventions. The employment of previously invented methods of production which hitherto could not be employed, because it was not profitable to do so at the then going relative prices and income distribution, could not stop that tendency but only decelerate the speed at which it would occur.

This was, in a nutshell, Marx's major achievement as Sraffa saw it at the beginning of the 1940s. However, while Marx had succeded in an important respect to improve upon Ricardo's contribution, he had not managed to elaborate a fully satisfactory analysis. Expression (M) cannot generally be sustained. This was clear to Sraffa long before he discovered Marx's achievements in the early 1940s. As early as toward the end of the first period of his constructive work, in the years 1929–1931, he had developed and investigated what he called his 'third' equations which were meant to apply to a with-surplus system and given proportional wages. It was only then that Sraffa convinced himself that the concept of labour as a quantity could no longer be bypassed. Since wages, measured in some more or less abstract standard, were typically paid in relation to the number of hours or days or weeks worked, the quantity of labour employed in an industry entered his equations (see D3/12/7: 166 and 159 (1)). However, these magnitudes were only needed for the purpose of offering a basis on which to reckon wages. More precisely, the 'quantites of labour' inserted in the equations reflect not only the number of hours (or days or weeks) worked, but also given wage differentials between different kinds of labour. As Sraffa was to stress in his book: 'We suppose labour to be uniform in quality or, what amounts to the same thing, we assume any differences in quality to have been previously reduced to equivalent differences in quantity so that each unit of labour receives the same wage' (Sraffa, 1960, p. 10). Hence, there is no reason to presume that Sraffa's critical stance towards the concept of 'human energy', of which we have heard in the above, had changed by the time of his third equations. What was new was that the sharing out of the surplus product among different claimants now was an issue, which implied that the cost of production of a commodity could no longer be given exclusively in physical terms, as so many tons of steel and bushels of corn, but included also wages expressed in some more or less abstract standard.

With wages paid out of the product, this then led Sraffa to a system of equations which in our three-sectoral example read

$$(T_t p_t + M_t p_m + F_t p_f)(1+r) + wL_t = Tp_t$$
$$(T_m p_t + M_m p_m + F_m p_f)(1+r) + wL_m = Mp_m$$
$$(T_f p_t + M_f p_m + F_f p_f)(1+r) + wL_f = Fp_f$$

where the input quantities of the various commodities, T_i, M_i and $F_i (i = t, m, f)$, now represent only the means of production used up, and w gives the share of wages in net income (defined inclusive of wages).[11] For a given w (or r) these equations allow one to determine r (or w) and prices. The above equations appear to confirm the impression we got already with regard to Eq. (P) that the rate of profits and prices of production can only be determined simultaneously and not successively. However, the next section shows that (i) with proportional wages and (ii) assuming a particular standpoint from which the economic system is observed by way of choice of a standard of value, the rate of profits can be determined independently of relative prices once the share of wages is given.[12]

9. Looking at the actual economy through the lens of a construction

As early as February 1931 Sraffa, in the context of a discussion of the dependence of the prices of consumption and of capital goods on the rate of interest, had put forward the following idea:

> it may be said that the value of total capital in terms of total goods produced cannot vary {consequent upon a change in the rate of interest}, since the goods are composed exactly in the same proportions as the capitals which have produced them.

He added swiftly that this proposition is of course 'false, but may contain an element of truth' (D3/12/7: 157(3)). Some 12 years later, in a note composed in November 1943, he clarified that the proposition was based on the 'statistical compensation of large numbers' (D3/12/35: 28): whereas with regard to each and every single commodity the value of the commodity relative to the value of the capital goods employed in its production can be expected to change with a change in income distribution, these changes might perhaps be considered to largely compensate one another with regard to the corresponding aggregates. In this case, the value of social capital relative to that of social product would be the same irrespective of the level of the rate of profits (and the corresponding level of the share of wages). In the early 1940s, we encounter Sraffa's proposition again under the name 'My Hypothesis' or simply 'Hypothesis'.

Exploring the 'element of truth' mentioned, Sraffa eventually had to abandon the idea that any actual economic system in a self-replacing state could ever be expected to satisfy the hypothesis. There was no presumption that the value of the net product relative to that of social capital would remain constant irrespective of the level of the actual rate of profits. Marx's expression (M) was valid only for a particular level of this rate, that is, $r = 0$, the case in which the labour theory of value or, as Sraffa at the beginning of the 1940s preferred to say, a 'Value Theory of Labour' holds (see, for example, D3/12/44: 3 and D3/12/46: 24). Evaluated in terms of prices the ratio of the two aggregates – the net product and the means of production – would change with changes in the rate of profits. Since no actual system satisfied the Hypothesis and since prices depended on income distribution, the only remaining possibility was to construct an artificial system which mimicked the crucial property of the Hypothesis without, however, sacrificing any of the characteristic features of the actual system. Hence the construction under consideration had to be derived from the equations describing the actual system. This Sraffa accomplished in late January 1944 in terms of the devices of the 'Standard commodity' and 'Standard system' (see D3/12/36: 61 et seq.).

With wages paid post factum, workers' means of subsistence, or wage goods, no longer form a part of what Sraffa called the set of 'basic' products, that is, commodities needed directly or indirectly in the production of all commodities (Sraffa, 1960, p. 8). This set, as newly defined, formed the basis on which the Standard system could be built up by segregating from the actual system such fractions of the various basic industries 'as will together form a complete miniature system endowed with the property that the various commodities are represented among its aggregate means of production *in the same proportions* as they are among the products' (Sraffa, 1960, p. 19). In this system, the maximum rate of profits, R, can be seen at a glance as the ratio of the net product to the means of production. Further, if the Standard net product is divided between wages and profits, where each share consist always, as the whole does, of Standard commodity, then the rate of profits in the Standard system appears as a ratio between quantities of commodities *irrespective of their prices*, and depends linearly on the share of wages, w:

$$r = R(1 - w) \qquad \text{(S)}$$

Since the actual system consists of the same basic equations as the Standard system, once the wage is given in terms of the Standard commodity, the rate of profits is determined for both systems: 'Particular proportions, such as the Standard ones, may give transparency to a system and render visible what was hidden, but they cannot alter its mathematical properties' (Sraffa, 1960, p. 23).

Setting aside different assumptions as to the payment of wages, Eq. (S) is the coherent version of Eq. (M). It confirms the view that the rate of profits depends on two magnitudes: a socio-technical datum, the maximum rate of profits, R (alias the inverse of the organic composition of capital, alias the inverse of the average period of production, for the system as a whole, each one appropriately defined), and on a distributional datum, the share of wages, w. It also provides a final confirmation of Ricardo's contention as to the relationship between the laws of distribution and the theory of value. For an analysis of the long-run, attention should focus on what happens to R and to w.

10. Joint production, fixed capital and natural resources

Up until now, the discussion was essentially limited to single-product systems of production. Given the empirical importance of joint production, fixed capital and scarce natural resources, the classical approach to the theory of production, distribution and value would be of little use and hence interest, if it were unable to address these phenomena. This was the view expressed by its critics, in particular the first generation of marginalist economists. More precisely, while the classical economists were credited with having put forward, in the theory of rent, a basically correct view of the role of land in production and distribution, they were chastised for having failed to see the possibility of developing 'a *unified general theory* to determine the prices of all productive services *in the same way*' (Walras, 1954, p. 416; emphases added).[13] This 'unified general theory', it was contended, involved generalising the principle of *scarcity*, which the classical economists had limited to natural resources, to all goods and factors of production alike.[14] In addition, it was contended that the classical (labour value-based) approach could not deal adequately with joint production and fixed capital. As Jevons maintained, with joint production the number of processes of production operated will generally fall short of the number of products whose labour values (and prices) have to be ascertained. Hence there is a problem of underdeterminacy: 'it is impossible to divide up the labour and say that so much is expended on producing [commodity] X, and so much on [commodity] Y' (Jevons, 1911, p. 200). Essentially the same objection was put forward by Knut Wicksell with respect to durable capital goods which allow one to produce over a number of years. He argued that it is 'just as absurd to ask how much labour is invested in either one or the other annual use as it is to try to find out what part of pasture goes into wool and what part into mutton' (Wicksell, [1901] 1934, vol. I, p. 260).

The criticism levelled at the classical approach cannot be sustained. First, it has been shown that the principle of scarcity in the explanation of income shares in a long-period framework of the analysis cannot be generalised from land (rents) to labour (wages) and capital (profits), as Walras and other marginalist authors deemed it possible (see Kurz and Salvadori, 1995, Chapter 14, and 2002). The main difficulty consists in specifying the endowment of capital in a way that is both compatible with the long-period framework and meaningful. As was clear to authors such as Wicksell, in order to be consistent with the long-period framework the capital endowment of the economy could not be conceived as a set of given physical quantities of produced means of production, but had to be expressed as a *value* magnitude (in terms of some arbitrary numeraire). The reason for this is that if the capital endowment were to be given in kind only a short-period equilibrium, characterized by differential rates of return on the supply prices of the various capital goods, could be established. However, it is not clear what is the economic meaning of a capital endowment that is specified as a value magnitude: In which sense can such a sum of value be considered a 'factor of production' that is 'scarce' and determine – together with the other endowments, technical alternatives and preferences – the general rate of profits?

As to the objection that the classical approach cannot deal with joint production and fixed capital it suffices to point out the following. With joint production the proportions in which the products are produced need not coincide with those in which they are wanted. This raises the problem of the *disposal* of the overproduced quantities of certain products. We may distinguish between free and costly disposal. Interestingly, Adam Smith anticipated the former case when he wrote: 'The skins of the larger animals were the original materials of cloathing. Among nations of hunters and shepherds, therefore, whose food consists chiefly in the flesh of those animals, every man, by providing himself with food, provides himself with the materials of more cloathing than he can wear'. He concluded that the overproduced hides would be 'thrown away as things of no value' (Smith, WN, I.xi.c.4). Here we encounter, possibly for the first time in the history of economic thought, the 'Rule of Free Goods'. In this case, total cost of production would be imputed exclusively to the commodity that is not overproduced; and there would be no problem to ascertain its 'labour value'. In the more interesting and empirically important case of costly disposal, a production process would be combined with a disposal process, and Jevons and Wicksell's above premise, that the number of processes operated falls short of the number of products whose (labour) values (or prices) have to be ascertained, would no longer hold: two equations would simultaneously determine values. In this case the value of the overproduced product would be negative, and the value of the other product would have to cover both total costs of production and disposal costs.

With a choice of technique, it is possible that the needs and wants of society are exactly met by a judicious combination of several joint production processes, where the number of processes operated equals the number of products produced. According to the classical approach to the problem of joint production the investigation of square systems of production has a genuine significance (see Sraffa, 1960, Chapters VII–IX). However, although there are important cases in which the cost-minimizing system of production has exactly as many processes as commodities, this is not generally true. Nonsquare systems can be analysed in terms of an appropriate transformation of the classical approach which makes it resemble the von Neumann approach to joint production, which is formulated in terms of inequalities. For details, see Kurz and Salvadori (1995, Chapter 8).[15]

The treatment of fixed capital as a joint product 'fits easily into the classical picture' and was in fact introduced by Robert Torrens and then adopted by Ricardo, Malthus and Marx (Sraffa, 1960, p. 94). Afterwards it seems to have fallen into oblivion. It re-emerged only with the works of von Neumann ([1937] 1945) and Sraffa (1960). The approach can also deal with the empirically important problems of capital utilization and the joint utilization of durable means of production or 'systems of machinery' (Marx); for a summary account of recent developments, see Kurz and Salvadori (1995, Chapters 7 and 9).

It has already been stated that classical economics is generally credited with having developed the principles of extensive and intensive diminishing returns with respect to the use of land in production. In the theory of differential rent land is commonly considered a renewable natural resource possessed of 'indestructible powers' (Ricardo, *Works*, vol. I, p. 69), that is, a nondepletable resource. However, the classical approach can also deal with renewable resources that are depletable, such as bird and fish populations or forests. A resource of this kind will actually be depleted if the levels of the periodic removal from its stock are unduly high and thus cannot be made good by the natural growth of the resource.

There have also been attempts to deal with the problem of exhaustible resources, that is, resources that are available in given stocks which can only be run down, but which do not increase (significantly) due to natural growth. These stocks are depleted each time parts of them are removed for productive or consumptive purposes. Typical examples of exhaustible resources are fossil fuels and oil. When stocks are run down, we are confronted with a dynamic problem where the price of the resource cannot generally be taken to remain constant: in order for the owner of a mine to obtain the same rate of profits as the one paid in conditions of free competition in any other business, the price of the resource must increase, where the rate of increase per period equals the ruling rate of profits. This is known as Hotelling's rule. While some of the classical economists showed an awareness of the fact that the prices of such resources would have to rise if no other developments (such as, for example, technical progress in extracting or processing the resource or the discovery of new mines) took place, which tended to thwart such a rise, they did not formulate this rule. They were rather of the opinion that exhaustible resources could be dealt with in terms of the theory of differential rent which was developed with respect to a nonexhaustible resource, land, within a framework of static prices. Here is not the place to enter into a discussion of how the classical authors and those working in their tradition attempted to cope with the intricate problem of exhaustible resources and the royalties obtained by the proprietors of stocks of them. It suffices to draw the reader's attention to a recent symposium devoted to this issue in the journal *Metroeconomica* (2001). In addition, it is perhaps worth quoting a passage taken from Piero Sraffa's hitherto unpublished manuscripts which points out some difficulties besetting dynamic economic theory. The passage reads:

> It is "a fatal mistake" of some economists that they believe that by introducing complicated dynamic assumptions, they get nearer to the true reality; in fact they get further removed for two reasons: a) that the system is much more statical than we believe, and its 'short periods' are very long, b) that the assumptions being too complicated it becomes impossible for the mind to grasp and dominate them - and thus it fails to realise the absurdity of the conclusions.
>
> (Sraffa Papers: D3/12/11 (33))

We may conclude by saying that the classical approach to the theory of production, distribution and value has proved many of its earlier critics wrong who had contended that it was in principle unable to deal with important empirical problems such as joint production and fixed capital. More recently, the effort of those working in the classical tradition has focused on problems such as exhaustible resources, costly disposal of discommodities, capital utilization, the treatment of services, and capital accumulation and economic growth. The future will show what can be accomplished in these respects using the classical approach.

Acknowledgements

This is a substantially revised version of the paper I gave at the workshop 'Reappraising Production Theory: Concepts, Cases, Models' at the Max Planck Institute for Research into Economic Systems, Jena 29 November to 1 December 2001. I am grateful to my discussant, Ian Steedman, for valuable comments and suggestions on the version of the paper presented in Jena. I should also like to thank Tony Aspromourgos, Christian Bidard, John Davis, Giancarlo de Vivo, Pierangelo Garegnani, Christian Gehrke, Geoff Harcourt, Fabio Petri, Neri Salvadori, Ulrich Witt and two anonymous referees for useful comments on a previous draft of this paper. The piece draws on earlier contributions of mine, some of which were written together with Christian Gehrke and Neri Salvadori; see, in particular, Kurz (2003), Gehrke and Kurz (2006) and Kurz and Salvadori (2005).

Notes

1 As it is well known, Sraffa published very little during his lifetime. What is less well known is that he left a huge amount of notes and manuscripts. Many of those which relate directly to our theme were written as early as the late 1920s. A selection from his papers and correspondence is currently being prepared for publication. Sraffa was then in the midst of recovering the classical approach from underneath thick layers of interpretation, a task whose accomplishment can only have benefitted from the fact that in 1930 he was entrusted with the Ricardo edition on behalf of the Royal Economic Society. Sraffa in private conversation is reported to have called his notes and papers an 'iceberg', the tip of which is his published work.

I should like to thank Pierangelo Garegnani, literary executor of Sraffa's papers and correspondence, for granting me permission to quote from them and also for numerous valuable discussions of the issues under consideration. It goes without saying that the views contained in this paper are nevertheless entirely my responsibility and do not implicate any of the other participants in the project of preparing an edition of Sraffa's papers and correspondence I am involved in. References to Sraffa's papers which are kept at Trinity College Library, Cambridge, follow the catalogue prepared by Jonathan Smith, archivist. Unless otherwise stated, all emphases are in the original, where words or passages Sraffa underlined are italicised by me. Sraffa frequently abbreviated 'and' by '+'; I shall use the word instead of the symbol. Since in his texts Sraffa used both round and square brackets, all additions by me will be bracketed by {and}. I am grateful to Jonathan Smith and the staff of Trinity College Library for continuous assistance while working on the Sraffa papers.

2 Sraffa in the late 1920 also studied contemporary contributions to economic history, ethnology and anthropology in order to see what these disciplines had to say on 'primitive' societies, characterised by a small or even negligible surplus product. Was value in such societies closely connected with labour, as economists from Smith via McCulloch to Friedrich Engels had maintained? In Büchner (1901) Sraffa read that 'labour among primitive peoples is something very ill-defined' (see D3/12/9: 50); in Eldridge (1923, pp. 21, 22 and 42) that 'in India waiting is a rule', that 'time is immaterial where price is

concerned', and that 'not labor-saving but material-saving devices of modern industry have the greatest vogue in China' (see D3/12/10: 18); and he noted that Hoyt (1926) provides 'striking examples' of a 'failure to accord value to time and labour even when exchange is well developed' (D3/12/9: 42).

3 In this context, it is perhaps interesting to note that in his copy of the French edition of Marx's *Theorien über den Mehrwert* – the eight volumes of the *Histoire des doctrines économiques* (Marx, 1924–1925) – which he read in the summer of 1927 Sraffa noted carefully all passages in which Marx distanced himself explicitly from an approach that proceeds exclusively in terms of commodities or 'use values'. Right at the beginning of the *Histoire*, in volume I, Marx took issue with Petty who had singled out food, not labour, as the measure of value. In the margin Sraffa placed a wrinkled line along the passage in which Marx contended that any such physical input 'n'est pas la mesure immanente des valeurs' (Marx, 1924–1925, vol. I, p. 3, fn). And then again, on the fly-leaf at the end of volume VI, we find in Sraffa's own index the entry 'Marx against physical costs 122' (Marx, 1924–1925, vol. VI).

4 It had not escaped Sraffa's attention that Vilfredo Pareto (and, following him, also Francis Y. Edgeworth) had criticised earlier authors for treating as givens what had to be considered as unknowns in the theory of value: Pareto's focus were especially the wage fund theory, the labour theory of value, cost of production theories and the Austrian theory. Sraffa had carefully studied several of Pareto's contributions at an early time which is reflected in many annotations in copies of these works in his library and in several references to Pareto in his early papers; see, in particular, Pareto (1901, 1902a,b, 1906).

5 As Sraffa noticed in the second period of his constructive work, which for the main part extended roughly from 1942 to 1946, in special circumstances the quantity of labour embodied can be seen at a glance. This is the case in Marx's scheme of simple reproduction where the total quantity of labour employed in both departments – department I producing means of production and department II means of consumption – is equal to the labour value of the net product consisting only of consumption goods. Marx's scheme can be said to foreshadow the concept of 'sub-system' or vertically integrated sector. See Sraffa (1960, Appendix A) and Pasinetti (1973).

6 See, therefore, Garegnani (2004) and Kurz and Salvadori (2005).

7 The notation above is not the one Sraffa employed in the late 1920s. At the time he used '$+$' instead of '$\oplus$' and '$=$' instead of '$\rightarrow$'. While he kept the plus sign throughout his work and also in his 1960 book, he replaced the equality sign by an arrow shortly after having resumed his constructive work in 1942 (see D3/12/23: 1).

8 In the debate about whether Ricardo or Torrens or any other classical author had put forward a 'corn model', this possibility has frequently, and surprisingly, been overlooked by some critics of Sraffa's interpretation. In order for a concept of the general rate of profits in purely physical terms to hold there is no need to discern in the classical authors the fiction of a single industry whose product is physically homogeneous with its capital. Corn models are, however, to be found in these authors and were quite widespread, as, for example, the case of Johann Heinrich von Thünen shows; see Kurz, 1999, pp. 154–157. Therefore, the concern with the corn model in the writings of some critics appears to be out of proportion with regard to the importance of that model in the classical authors: helpful as it may have been at an early stage in the conceptual development of the classical approach to the theory of profits, that approach can do very well without the corn model. See also De Vivo (2001).

9 There is a notable exception: the critic of the Physiocratic doctrine, the French engeneer Achille-Nicolas Isnard; see Gilibert (1981) and Kurz and Salvadori (2000, pp. 159–161). However, Isnard's simultaneous equations approach in terms of quantities of commodities consumed productively and quantities produced can be said to have fallen flat on the ground and had hardly any impact on the development of the theory.

10 Conversely, Sraffa was convinced that the alleged coherence of demand and supply analysis was more apparent than real and that the demand and supply schedules had no objective contents: nothing corresponded to them in the real world; see Sraffa (1925, 1926) and his notes written in summer 1927 (D3/12/3).

11 To conceive of wages as a share, $0 \leq w \leq 1$, requires normalising total employment and the net social product as equal to unity.

12 It goes without saying, that once the share of wages is given both the rate of profits and relative prices are fixed. Here we are only interested in the analytical possibility of ascertaining the former without having to go through the system of production equations in the above.

13 For a critical discussion of Walras's view, see Kurz and Salvadori (2002).

14 William S. Jevons (1871, p. 198) saw his own theory as closely related to the received theory of rent: 'The general correctness of the views put forward . . . derives great probability from their close resemblance to the Theory of Rent, as it has been accepted by English writers for nearly a century'. It was indeed the generalisation of the principle of scarcity and of the concept of *intensive* diminishing returns from land and agriculture to all factors of production, including labour and capital, and all spheres of production which constitutes the core of the marginalist doctrine.

15 In this context, it deserves to be stressed that the von Neumann model (von Neumann [1937] 1945) shares crucial features of the classical approach to the theory of production, value and distribution (circular flow, physical real costs, asymmetric treatment of the distributive variables, profits based on social surplus); see Kurz and Salvadori (1995, Chapter 13).

References

Aspromourgos, T., 1996. On the Origins of Classical Economics. Distribution and Value from William Petty to Adam Smith. Routledge, London, New York.

von Bortkiewicz, L., 1906–1907. Wertrechnung und Preisrechnung im Marxschen System. Archiv für Sozialwissenschaft und Sozialpolitik 23 (1906), 1–50 (essay I); 25 (1907), 10–51 (essay II); 445–488 (essay III).

Büchner, C., 1901. Industrial Evolution. New York.

De Vivo, G., 2001. On Torrens's theory of profits. Camb. J. Econom. 25, 697–703.

Eldridge, F.R., 1923. Oriental Trade Methods. Appleton, New York.

Garegnani, P., 1984. Value and distribution in the Classical economists and Marx. Oxford Economic Papers 36, 291–325.

Garegnani, P., 2004. Di una svolta nella posizione teorica nella interpretatzione dei classici in Sraffa nei tardi anni 20. In Atti dei Convegni Lincei 200. Accademia Nazionale dei Lincei, Roma, pp. 159–194.

Gehrke, C., Kurz, H.D., 2006. Sraffa on von Bortkiewicz. Reconstructing the classical theory of value and distribution. History Political Econ., 38:1, 91–149.

Gilibert, G., 1981. Isnard, Cournot, Walras, Leontief. Evoluzione di un modello. Annali della Fondazione Luigi Einaudi 15, 129–153.

Hoyt, E.E., 1926. Primitive Trade. Its Psychology and Economics. Kegan Paul, Trench, Trubner & Co, London.

Jevons, W.S., 1871. The Theory of Political Economy. Macmillan, London, New York.

Jevons, W.S., 1911. The Theory of Political Economy, fourth ed. Macmillan, London, New York.

Kurz, H.D., 1999. From classical rent theory to marginal productivity theory. The works of F.B.W. Hermann and J.H. von Thünen. In: Mongiovi, G., Petri, F. (Eds), Value,

Distribution and Capital, Essays in Honour of Pierangelo Garegnani. Routledge, London, pp. 145–164.
Kurz, H.D., 2003. The surplus interpretation of the classical economists. In: Biddle, J.E., Davis, J.B., Samuels, W.J. (Eds), The Blackwell Companion to the History of Economic Thought. Blackwell Publishers, Malden, MA, Oxford, pp. 167–183.
Kurz, H.D., Salvadori, N., 1995. Theory of Production. A Long-period Analysis. Cambridge, New York, Melbourne (CUP).
Kurz, H.D., Salvadori, N., 2000. 'Classical' roots of input–output analysis: a short account of its long prehistory. Econ. Syst. Res. 12, 153–179.
Kurz, H.D., Salvadori, N., 2001. Sraffa and the mathematicians: Frank Ramsey and Alister Watson. In: Cozzi, T., Marchionatti, R. (Eds.), Piero Sraffa's Political Economy. A Centenary Estimate. Routledge, London, pp. 187–216. Reprinted in: Kurz, H.D., Salvadori, N. Classical economics and modem theory. Studies in long-period analysis. Routledge, London.
Kurz, H.D., Salvadori, N., 2002. One theory or two? Walras's critique of Ricardo. History Political Econ. 34 (2), 365–398.
Kurz, H.D., Salvadori, N., 2005. Representing the production and circulation of commodities in material terms. On Sraffa's objectivism. Rev. Political Econ., 17(3), July, 413–441.
Marshall, A., 1970. Principles of Economics, first ed., 1890; eight ed., 1920. Macmillan, London (reset and reprinted 1947).
Marx, K., 1924–1925. Oeuvres complètes de Karl Marx. Histoire des doctrines économiques. Translated by Molitor, J., eight vols. Alfred Costes, Paris.
Marx, K., 1959. In: Engels F. (Ed.), Capital, vol. III. Progress Publishers, Moscow (English translation of Das Kapital, vol. III (1894). Meissner, Hamburg).
Metroeconomica, 2001. Symposium on Exhaustible Natural Resources and Sraffian Analysis, vol. 52 (3), pp. 239–328 (special issue).
Mill, J., 1826. Elements of Political Economy. First ed., 1821; third ed., 1826. Henry G. Bohn, London.
von Neumann, J., 1945. A model of general economic equilibrium. Rev. Econ. Stud. 13, 1–9 (English translation of German original published in 1937).
Pareto, V., 1901. Le nuove teorie economiche. Giornale degli economisti e annali di economia 23, 235–259.
Pareto, V., 1902a. Les systèmes socialistes, two vols. V. Giard & E. Brière, Paris.
Pareto, V., 1902b. Anwendungen der Mathematik auf Nationalökonomie. Encyklopädie der mathematischen Wissenschaften, vol. I (7). B.G. Teubner, Leipzig, pp. 1094–1120.
Pareto, V., 1906. Manuale di economia politica con una introduzione alla scienza sociale. Societa editrice libreria, Milan.
Pasinetti, L.L., 1973. The notion of vertical integration in economic analysis. Metroeconomica 25, 1–29.
Petty, W., 1986. In: Hull, C.H. (Ed.), The Economic Writings of Sir William Petty, two vols. Originally published in 1899. Cambridge University Press, Cambridge (reprinted in one volume, Kelley, New York).
Quesnay, F., 1972. In: Kuczynski, M., Meek, R.L. (Eds.), Quesnay's Tableau Economique [1759]. Macmillan, London.
Ricardo, D., 1951–1973. In: Sraffa, P., Dobb, M.H. (Eds.), The Works and Correspondence of David Ricardo, 11 vols. Cambridge University Press, Cambridge (in the text referred to as Works, volume number).

Smith, A., 1976. An inquiry into the nature and causes of the wealth of nations. The Glasgow Edition of the Works and Correspondence of Adam Smith. First published in 1776, vol. 2. Oxford University Press, Oxford.

Sraffa, P., 1925. Sulle relazioni fra costo e quantità prodotta (On the relations between cost and quantity produced). Annali di Economia 2, 277–328. In: Pasinetti, L.L. (Ed.), Italian Economic Papers. IL Mulino, Bologna; Oxford University Press, Oxford, pp. 323–363. Reprinted in: Kurz, H.D., Salvadori, N. (Eds.), The Legacy of Piero Sraffa, two vols. Edward Elgar, Cheltenham.

Sraffa, P., 1926. The laws of returns under competitive conditions. Econ. J. 36, 535–550. Reprinted in: Kurz, H.D., Salvadori, N. (Eds.), The Legacy of Piero Sraffa, two vols. Edward Elgar, Cheltenham.

Sraffa, P., 1951. Introduction. In: Ricardo (1951). Works I, xiii–lxii.

Sraffa, P., 1960. Production of Commodities by Means of Commodities. Prelude to a Critique of Economic Theory. Cambridge University Press, Cambridge.

Torrens, R., 2000. In: de Vivo, G. (Ed.), Collected Works of Robert Torrens, eight vols. Thoemmes Press, Bristol.

Walras, L., 1954. Elements of Pure Economics. Translation of the fifth ed. of Walras's Eléments d'économie politique pure (1874–77) by W. Jaffé. Allen & Unwin, London.

Wicksell, K., 1934. Lectures on Political Economy, vol. I. English translation of the Swedish original (1901) by Classen, E., and edited, with an introduction, by Lionel Robbins. George Routledge and Sons, London.

9 On the collaboration between Sraffa and Besicovitch*

The cases of fixed capital and non-basics in joint production

Heinz D. Kurz and Neri Salvadori

1. Introduction

In the Preface of *Production of Commodities by Means of Commodities* Sraffa thanks three mathematicians: "My greatest debt is to A. S. Besicovitch for invaluable mathematical help over many years. I am also indepted for similar help at different periods to the late Mr Frank Ramsey and to Mr Alister Watson" (Sraffa 1960: vi–vii). In the various drafts of the Preface Sraffa composed, he consistently singled out Besicovitch as the mathematician to whom he owed the greatest intellectual debt. This is not surprising since Besicovitch can be said to have taken a crucial part in the development of Sraffa's thought in the second and third phase of his work on the 1960 book. As is well known, Sraffa's work fell broadly in three periods: the first comprised the years from 1927 to 1931, the second the years from 1940–41 to 1948, and the third from 1954 to 1958. In the first period he was helped on a few occasions by Ramsey, whereas Besicovitch and Watson appeared on the stage only in the second period and continued to be of help to him in the third period. In an earlier contribution we dealt with the collaboration between Ramsey and Watson and Sraffa (Kurz-Salvadori 2001). At the time we set aside Besicovitch for the following reason: "Sraffa consulted Besicovitch on virtually all problems of a mathematical nature he was confronted with. There are numerous documents in his unpublished papers reflecting their close collaboration. A proper treatment of it is beyond the scope of this chapter: the material is too huge and complex and ought to be dealt with separately . . . This is a serious limitation of the chapter, which we hope to be able to make good in another work" (*ibid.*: 255).

In this contribution we attempt to accomplish at least partly the task. We select two fields with regard to which Sraffa sought and received Besicovitch's mathematical assistance: the analysis of fixed capital and the distinction between basic and non-basic commodities in the case of joint production. It can be said that with regard to both fields and some other fields we cannot deal with here Besicovitch provided invaluable help to Sraffa. Indeed, it is hardly an exaggeration to maintain that without Besicovitch's assistance and support Sraffa's treatise might never

* Reprinted with permission from Atti dei Convegni Lincei 200, Convegno internazionale Piero Sraffa (Roma, 11–12 Febbraio 2003), Rome: Accademia Nazionale dei Lincei, 2004, pp. 255–301.

have been completed and published. In addition to dealing in some detail with the two issues specified we give various hints as to the rest of the material that witnesses to the close collaboration between the two Cantabrigians. The interested reader is invited to consult also our earlier paper on Sraffa and the mathematicians (Kurz-Salvadori 2001) which contains some useful information on the general themes which will not be repeated here.

The composition of the paper is the following. Section 2 contains a portrait of Abram S. Besicovitch. Section 3 provides a summary account of Sraffa's meetings, discussions and exchange of letters with Besicovitch, our main sources being Sraffa's diaries and his unpublished papers; unfortunately, we could not trace any remaining papers of Besicovitch: they appear to have been destroyed. The main part of the paper consists of Sections 4 and 5. Section 4 deals with the problem of fixed capital. After several unsuccessful attempts to cope with durable instruments of production from a purely 'objectivist' point of view, Sraffa, around the turn of the year 1942–43, eventually adopted the joint-products approach and, assisted by Besicovitch, quickly solved the problem at hand. Section 5 points out that the completion of Sraffa's book was considerably delayed by his discovery in the second half of the 1950s that the distinction between basic and non-basic products needed to be fundamentally revised in joint production. It was Besicovitch who, around the turn of 1957, helped Sraffa out of the impasse. Section 6 contains some concluding remarks.

2. Abram Samoilovitch Besicovitch

Abram S. Besicovitch was born at Berdjansk, on the sea of Azov, on 24 January 1891.[1] He was thus over seven years older than Sraffa. By descent the family belonged to the Karaim people, whose ancestors were the Khazars, once a powerful kingdom between the Volga and the Dnieper. Some of them were converted by the Karaite Jews.

Besicovitch and his several brothers and sisters were born into a not too well off family. But all children were talented and studied at the University of St. Petersburg. Abram from an early age "had shown extraordinary aptitude for solving mathematical problems" (Taylor 1975: 192). He graduated in 1912. One of his teachers was A. A. Markov, and his first paper was on probability theory.

As a branch of the University of St. Petersburg, in 1916 the University of Perm opened. In 1917 Besicovitch became a Professor in the School of Mathematics. During the civil war in 1919 the University was destroyed. In 1920 Besicovitch became Professor in the Pedagogical Institute of Leningrad and Lecturer in the University, where he stayed from 1920 to 1924. Among other things, he taught classes of workers who lacked an educational background to understand the lessons.

When he was offered a Rockefeller Fellowship to work abroad he applied repeatedly for permission to accept this offer, without success. Finally, in 1924, he made plans to leave the country in company with another mathematician, J. D. Tamarkin. He went to Copenhagen where he worked for a year with Harald Bohr, who was developing the theory of almost periodic functions. Besicovitch then visited

Oxford, staying for several months with G. H. Hardy, who was impressed by Besicovitch's analytical power and secured for him a lectureship at the University of Liverpool for 1926–27. Besicovitch moved to Cambridge in 1927 as a University Lecturer becoming also a College Lecturer and in 1930 a Fellow of Trinity College. Sraffa, whom Keynes had brought to King's College, joined Trinity as a Fellow in 1939. It is there that the two dramatis personae of our story in all probability met for the first time. However, there is no evidence that they developed a close intellectual relationship already in the 1930s (cp. Sraffa's diaries of that period).[2] It appears to have been only in the 1940s that Sraffa began to consult his elder friend on numerous analytical problems with which he struggled.

There are several indications of their close relationship. For example, we know that the two sought each other's company at the High Table and had similar likes and dislikes with regard to other Fellows of the College. On Sundays they occasionally went for a walk together. They liked to talk about problems of national and especially international politics and Sraffa would approach his elder friend with mathematical puzzles outside his own work that had aroused his curiosity.[3] Besicovitch's concern with "the ills of society and... oppression and suffering wherever it was found" (Taylor 1975: 193) can be expected to have quickly gained him Sraffa's sympathy. When in 1950, on his fifty-ninth birthday, Besicovitch was elected to the Rouse Ball Chair of Mathematics, succeeding the first holder J. E. Littlewood, Sraffa made an exception to his otherwise terse style and noted the event in his diary: "Besicovitch elected prof. (on his birthday.[)]" He also noted when on 2 November 1970, after a period of decaying health, Besicovitch died. Similarly, when Sraffa in mid-December 1955 had to undergo an operation because of a hernia and spent several weeks in the Evelyn Nursing Home, Besicovitch visited him twice.[4]

3. Sraffa's Collaboration with Besicovitch: a brief overview

The intellectual relation between Sraffa and Besicovitch was special in several respects and does not compare with that between Sraffa and the other two mathematicians he consulted, Ramsey and Watson. The breadth and depth of their cooperation was indeed remarkable. Both scholars were possessed of exceptional intellectual gifts and showed generous sympathy for one another. Both enjoyed their collaboration and mutually benefited from each other, with the benefits Sraffa received being more clearly discernible. It is also worth mentioning that Sraffa showed repeatedly signs of disenchantment with his own work and in May 1958 even contemplated the possibility of not publishing his book, the manuscript of which he had finished on 29 January of that year. We have reason to assume that his doubts were effectively dispelled by Besicovitch, because on 31 May we find the following entry in Sraffa's diary: "Besicovitch insiste che io pubblichi [...] il fatto che ho potuto prevedere risultati matematici interessanti mostra che c'è qualcosa nella teoria" [Besicovitch insists that I publish; the fact that I was able to forsee interesting mathematical results shows that there must be something in the theory]. This note is also interesting because it puts in a nutshell the essence of the collaboration between the two scholars. It was indeed Sraffa's remarkable analytical intuition and logic which allowed him to *"forsee interesting mathematical results"*, and it was Besicovitch who assisted Sraffa in completing the necessary proofs. We shall encounter below in Sections 4 and 5 examples of their intensive collaboration. To be clear, Sraffa retained full control over the course of his argument and responsibility for the results obtained.

In his *Cambridge Pocket Diaries* Sraffa used to note his appointments and the meetings he attended. The diaries provide a useful skeleton of his activities over time. They also provide useful information about the meetings and collaboration with Besicovitch which receives confirmation from, and conversely provides confirmation of, the material, and especially its dating, contained in his unpublished papers. In view of the large number of reported meetings of Sraffa and Besicovitch it would take too much space to provide detailed evidence. (For a summary account, see Kurz-Salvadori 2001: 256–259.) In fact, in certain periods the two met almost every day and on some days even more than once, or exchanged letters via their letter boxes in College. Here a few observations of a more general character must suffice.

First, probably due to the large number of meetings, occasionally one succeeding the other within a short period of time, and their close neighbourhood in Trinity College, Sraffa apparently did not record his meetings with Besicovitch with the same accuracy as he did with regard to his other 'mathematical friends', especially Watson. Due to Ramsey's premature passing away there were only a few meetings with him, and Watson did not live in Trinity College and not even in Cambridge, and whenever he visited Sraffa letters concerning organisational matters had to be exchanged or phone calls made, which typically left traces in Sraffa's diaries in terms of arrival and departure times, etc. With Besicovitch things were much easier. Sraffa could contact him basically whenever he wanted without much ado, e.g. at lunch or dinner at the College's High Table. Secondly, it was easy to communicate with Besicovitch in written form via their College letter boxes, and we are in fact possessed of a fair number of manuscripts that circulated between the two. In such cases Sraffa would typically send Besicovitch a set of questions or propositions on one or several sheets of paper, leaving space for Besicovitch's answers or comments. Besicovitch would then fill in the empty space, add queries, provide proofs, etc. This would be followed by Sraffa translating Besicovitch's responses into his own language and formalism, asking for clarification in cases in which he was not sure what Besicovitch had meant or he thought that the answer was incomplete, and rephrasing his question or proposition in cases in which he felt that Besicovitch had not properly understood his intention or, in rare cases, expressing doubts as to the correctness of Besicovitch's answer. Several of the documents which gradually developed over a shorter or longer period of time therefore carry the handwritings of both scholars and reflect in detail the chronology of their exchanges. Third, there are a few instances in which Besicovitch felt unable to answer Sraffa's question, a fact he would openly admit. In such cases he would seek the assistance of some other mathematicians, such as Peter Swinnerton-Dyer or John Arthur Todd.[5]

Checking the numerous references to and notes, letters etc. by Besicovitch in Sraffa's papers, the following picture emerges as regards the main topics discussed between the two. Their attention focused first and foremost on

- the treatment of fixed capital and the determination of depreciation quotas;
- the existence and uniqueness of the rate of profits and relative prices, given the real wage rate (or the share of wages in national income), in single production;
- the existence and uniqueness of the rate of profits and relative prices, given the share of wages in national income, in joint production;
- the construction and uniqueness of the standard system and the discussion of its properties in systems with single- and multiple-product processes of production;
- the reduction of prices to dated quantities of labour in single and joint production;
- the dependence of relative prices and one of the distributive variables (wages or, alternatively, the rate of profits) on the level of the other distributive variable, that is, in the terminology used by Sraffa in his notes, but not in the published book, the problem of the 'gradient';
- the distinction between basic and non-basic commodities in joint production.

In the following sections we deal only with two of these problems: we begin with fixed capital and then turn to the distinction between basics and non-basics in joint production.

4. Fixed capital

It is perhaps useful to begin by recalling briefly the contents of Chapter X of *Production of Commodities* – the terminal point, so to speak, of Sraffa's thoughts on fixed capital (Sraffa 1960). The following historical reconstruction can then be seen against the background of the final solution to the problem under consideration. Chapter X consists of 12 sections: §§73–78 introduce fixed capital as a kind of joint product (§§73–74) and compare this approach with the annuity method (§§75–78); §§79–84 show which tools or concepts elaborated for single production (the 'reduction' to dated quantities of labour; the construction of the Standard commodity) do not apply to fixed capital; in this second part §§80–82 are devoted to the analysis of the development of the book-value of a machine when $r = 0$ (§§80–81) and when $r > 0$ (§82). §83 then summarizes and illustrates the argument with respect to an entire group of machines that are in a self-replacing state. Here, the analysis is explicitly confined to the special case of constant efficiency. This implies that the respective argument need not be related to Sraffa's whole construction and, as we shall see, was indeed developed long before the contours of the latter had become sufficiently clear. This is evidenced, for example, by the fact that diagrams similar to Fig. 6 in §83 are to be found from an early time onwards in Sraffa's papers (see, for example, D3/12/20: 12)[6] reflecting his study of books such as Baily (1808) and Pradella (1915).

In the following we first summarize Sraffa's work on fixed capital in the first period of his constructive work.[7] This sets the stage for the following discussion by showing where Sraffa stood when, in the 1940s, he was able to interest Besicovitch to collaborate with him. It should be added that there is no evidence that in the late 1920s or early 1930s Sraffa had consulted with any mathematician on the problem under consideration.

4.1 The state of Sraffa's analysis at the beginning of the 1940s

The problem of fixed capital was on Sraffa's agenda right from the beginning of his constructive work. Shortly after he had developed his first systems of equations without and with a social surplus in November 1927[8] he noted: "The difficulty now is that at the beginning of the year much more has been advanced than is contained in the product: that is, those things that have been present in the process of production but have put no physical part of themselves into the product, i.e. fixed capital" (D3/12/11: 99). He then tried to fit fixed capital into the equations, keeping strictly to his concern with "the objective ground of value" (D3/12/7: 27). This implied that relative prices and the distribution of the product had to be explained exclusively in terms of quantities that can, at least in principle, be observed, counted and measured.

Fixed capital introduces a complication into the theory of value and distribution that had already bothered the classical economists. While the circulating part of capital contributes entirely, at the cost of its bodily existence, to the annual output, that is, "disappears" from the scene, the contribution of the durable part is less obvious and the idea of a material transmigration into the product appears to lose any foundation: at the end of a production cycle a (partly worn out) machine is still there without much sign of physical degradation. How to assess that part of the "physical real cost" of a commodity which is due to the utilization of fixed capital in its production? Is "depreciation" not intrinsically a *value* concept, and does this not involve the danger of a vicious circle, explaining values in terms of values?

The idea that guided Sraffa's thoughts in the late 1920s was to focus attention not on single items of fixed capital but on groups of such items characterised by a balanced age composition and to reduce such groups to circulating or working capital, on the one hand, and land (or perennial capital), on the other: whereas the former enters into the product in its entirety, the latter does not enter into it at all. He maintained: "These two categories are exhaustive: *tertium non datur*" (D3/12/5: 13). The circulating part of social capital, together with the output levels, was then taken by Sraffa as the basis in terms of which the social surplus was to be assessed and interest paid, whereas the land-like part was taken to play no role in these respects. Suppose there are 100 looms with a balanced age composition, each loom lasting ten years. Then there are 10 looms that are ten years old, 10 that are nine years old . . . , and 10 that are brand-new. Now Sraffa insisted that only the 10 new looms constitute circulating capital, while the others constitute land.

He expounded:

> The 10 new machines are entirely, in every particle, 100% working capital; they disappear from the world during one period of production, without leaving trace of themselves, except 10 entirely worn out machines which are no more machines but rubbish to be thrown away. The 90 old machines, of average age $4\frac{1}{2}$ years, are 100% fixed capital; not a bit of them is consumed, or worn out in production. They are there at the end of the year, in the exact state in which they were at the beginning, with exactly the same age composition and the same expectation of life – they have not grown any older, although a year has lapsed. As it were, they have been *mere spectators in production, they have "contributed" nothing, they have "transfused no part of themselves" into the produce.*
>
> (D3/12/5: 13; emphasis added)

He added: "The old machines are, to all effects, 'land', viz. 'undestructible' but not original" *(ibidem).*

Interestingly, the joint-products approach to fixed capital that Sraffa was to adopt in the 1960 book he had encountered already in the 1920s, but at the time had rejected it. In a note written in the winter of 1927–28 as a response to a passage in the posthumous second edition of Malthus's *Principles of Political Economy*[9] quoted by Marx in Volume I of *Capital* (1954: 205n.), Sraffa commented:

> This passage is quoted, with approval by Marx Cap. I, 91, and his context shows that he adopts the same point of view (see also Hist., VI, 110.[10] "la partie non consommée du capital fixe est comptée dans le produit"). Marx allowed therefore himself to be misled by Malthus! But since he says that "sous le nom de capital constant avancé . . . nous ne comprenons donc jamais que la valeur des moyens consommés dans le cours de la production" (Cap. I, 91) his conclusions may not be affected by it.
>
> (D3/12/10: 52)

Sraffa then thought that the joint-products method, by blurring the concept of surplus, also blurred the concept of physical real costs. At the same time he was aware that his method of splitting fixed capital up into a circulating and an everlasting, land-like, part had the drawback of not allowing one to determine the depreciation quotas and annuities as a part and parcel of the selfsame theory. Instead, one had to have recourse to formulas offered in handbooks of financial mathematics, which, however, dealt only with the case of constant efficiency of the fixed capital item.[11]

4.2 The beginning of Sraffa's collaboration with Besicovitch

Sraffa resumed his constructive work immediately after his release from the internment camp on the Isle of Man in October 1940. His collaboration with Besicovitch seems to begin in summer 1942 which is evidenced by a document titled "*15.8.42 dopo [after] Besic*". There must have been meetings with the mathematician in August and September of that year which, however, are not noted in Sraffa's diary. The collaboration between the two scholars typically proceeded in the following way. Sraffa would begin an argument or calculation, Besicovitch would then add to it or correct it, followed by Sraffa who would carry the argument farther, and so on. There are several documents dating from August 1942 analysing the prices of used machines in relation with the price of the new machine when efficiency is constant. In some of these documents we encounter remarks or, more often, calculations in Besicovitch's hand. The documents are not particularly interesting. For instance, D3/12/20: 30–31 contains a discussion of the function

$$w = \frac{\rho}{e^{\rho} - 1}$$

which is clearly the amount that needs to be continuously invested in order to have a principal equal to unity after one year when the instantaneous rate of interest (the power of interest) equals ρ.

There are two types of models which Sraffa and Besicovitch developed in those days. One type has two sectors (machines and bread), with machines whose duration is n years produced in a unidirectional (i.e. "Austrian") process with unassisted labour, and bread produced with labour and machines.[12] The other model is called the 'port model' which was probably inspired by Wicksell's famous discussion of the maturing of wine in the *Lectures* (see Wicksell 1934: 172–184): a capital good is produced during n years and then used only once to produce a finished good. Sraffa was interested in the relationship between the value of the final product (which is generally set equal to unity), the price of the single machine, and the price of the stock of capital, that is, the price of the group of machines which are required, with capital kept intact by one new machine being introduced every year.

The kind of analysis Sraffa was involved in at the time, and his scepticism as to its applicability to fixed capital goods proper, such as machines, are well reflected in the following passage:

> This model is much more suited to Port than to machines: assume that a merchant buys each year the new vintage of port at cost w: he sells every year $\frac{1}{n}$ of each vintage in stock, each at a price of $\frac{w}{n}(1+r)^{\cdots(\text{age})}$. The value of product is the proceeds of any year, the value of capital is the value of his stock.
>
> The trouble when applied to machinery is that, when r rises, there is nothing to prevent any old machine becoming more valuable than a new one: this is OK for port, but absurd for machines.
>
> A remedy is to introduce constant capital (C), & to assume that C is at least as large as is required to prevent the maximum of r (i.e. when $w = 0$) to exceed the limit where the n machines are worth more than n *new* machines. Very artificial.
>
> (D3/12/20: 44)

4.3 First attempts at reducing fixed capital to circulating

Manuscripts concerning fixed capital written in September 1942 are contained in folder D3/12/21. The models are now considerably more advanced than those of summer and seem to be partly influenced by a book by Kent on commercial arithmetic (see the excerpts from it in D3/12/21: 11). Sraffa was keen to reach full clarity about what the problems were and how they could be tackled. He no longer followed the idea that had guided him during the first period of his constructive work, that is, of reducing fixed capital to circulating on the one hand and land on the other. As we have seen, this left an important part of the problem – the determination of the depreciation of aging machines – unanswered. The revised perspective, and the stage of maturity of his thoughts, are well expressed in a paper of seven pages composed in October 1942 titled "Fixed Capital Equivalent Circulating" (D3/12/27: 46). The problems are stated with great lucidity, but the last step toward the joint-products method is still missing. It is apposite to quote large parts of the paper:

> The difference between Circulating and Fixed Capital is this. A piece of circulating capital (such as a lump of raw material or fuel, or a day's labour), after a transit of a definite duration in the process of production, comes out all at one moment and transfers all its value to a piece of product ready for sale. A piece of fixed capital (such as a building, or a machine, or a working animal) on the other hand gives out its value over a period of time, to a whole series of pieces of product which are successively turned out ready for sale.
>
> When $r = 0$, & commodities exchange at their Values,[13] the matter is clear. A machine which lasts n years (without repairs and with equal efficiency) transfers to the product of each year of its life $\frac{1}{n}$th of its original value. It is at once apparent that the machine can be regarded as equivalent to n pieces of circulating capital, each being equal in value to $\frac{1}{n}$ th of the machine, but each having a different period of rotation; one piece having a period of one year, one of 2 years, etc., and one of n years.
>
> But when there is a rate of profit, the matter becomes confused. Then, the owner of the machine must still receive a uniform annual payment in respect of the machine (for profit & depreciation together); for if he did not, & the payment of successive years were different, the products of the machine would have different prices according as they were produced by an old or a young machine. And yet, since the book-value of the machine falls with age, the profit must fall, & depreciation increase. And this difference in annual depreciation (or what part of the original cost is transferred to the product) will vary with the rate of profit. . . .
>
> The difficulty arises from this: for circulating capital, at the same moment that its value passes into the product, in most cases, also the material substance which is the bearer of that value, either passes into the product (raw material) or anyway passes out of the process of production (e.g. fuel). On the other hand, for fixed capital, the transfer of value from, e.g., the machine to

> the product, appears as a purely abstract process, which takes place without any corresponding transfer of material substance: that value is passed is undoubted, for the machine decreases in value while the product increases, but the machine remains complete in all its parts, with its efficiency unimpaired for the time being, & ready to resume operation in the next year.
>
> We must first notice that when the rate of profit rises a piece of circ. cap. adds more to the price of the product, in the shape of additional profit upon itself. But that is not all: the circ. cap. itself changes in prices (rises or falls) and this is an additional source of change (+ or −) in the addition to the price of the product.
>
> The same happens for fixed cap. While the annual capital charge *increases* with r, the price of the new machine also changes, & thus the charge is changed. But the machine has one more degree of freedom than the circ. cap. While the latter must multiply every part of its value by $(1 + r)$, as that is the only profit factor which it has, the machine has a whole range of choice. For it must multiply the part of its own price which it transfers to the product of the first year of its own life, by $(1 + r)$; the part transferred to the product of the second year by $(1 + r)^2$; etc.; and the part transferred to the product of its last year by $(1 + r)^n$.
>
> But this process of transfer is purely abstract: if the machine transferred to the product of each particular year a particular part of itself (e.g. the pistons to that of the first year, the cylinders to that of the second etc.), there would be no option: it would have to transfer the value of the particular part in the particular year. But nothing of the kind happens: the transfer is purely abstract; & while the machine is bound to transfer parts equal in magnitude of value each year, it is free to choose *which* particular part it will transfer in any one year. For these parts of value though equal in magnitude, need not be equal in kind: the machine has been produced by a certain quantity of commodities and by a certain quantity of labour, & accordingly it derives its value in part from the former and in part from the latter.

And later in the text:

> Why do we want to reduce Fixed Cap. to Circulating Capital? Because we must prove that *the only quantities whose knowledge is required to determine prices are the Capital Inputs; while the Capital Stock is not required, & anyhow is only a derived quantity, derived from the inputs.*
>
> (D3/12/47: 46(1–5); the last emphasis is ours.)

On 11 November 1942, Sraffa specified a number of assumptions whose implications he wanted to investigate:

> We shall assume that a fixed capital 1) lasts for a given number of years, 2) during which it operates with equal efficiency and 3) without need of maintenance, repairs, or replacement of parts.

1) It is clear that fixed capitals will die a natural death at different ages, just as men do. We assume that they all live to the average age, as given in their mortality tables.

2) The fall in efficiency can be dealt with since it can be reduced to one of these two cases (or a suitable mixture of the two): the fixed capital can become less productive because a) it produces the same amount by using more labour, or fuel, or materials, and b) it produces less quantity by using the same labour etc. The annual price of the fixed capital can be adjusted by deducting from it, in case a) the price of the additional labour etc., and in case b) the price of the lost product [both of course appearing in the equations as unknowns, to be determined by the general solution].

3) Consider a motor-lorry that lasts 10 years, but requires new tires [*sic*] every year, and a new engine after 5 years. We regard the tires [*sic*] as a fixed capital that lasts a year, the engine as another fixed capital that lasts 5 years, and the rest of the lorry, without tires [*sic*] or engine, as a fixed capital that lasts ten years: thus segregated, each of the items lasts its own lifetime without need of replacement.

(D3/12/27: 38)

A few days later, on 17 November, Besicovitch calculated the book-values of the aging machine (D3/12/27: 6). Sraffa had asked:

How to divide p_m into n parts $x_1, x_2, \ldots, x_n$ such that $x_0 = x_1(1+r) = x_2(1+r)^2 = \cdots = x_n(1+r)^n$ and also $x_1 + x_2 + \cdots + x_n = p_m$ [?]

Clearly, p_m is the price of the new machine; $x_t(1+r)^t$ is the the annual charge on the machine during year t (which, whatever is t, must be the same since the efficiency is constant, otherwise the price of the product would depend on the age of the machine which is used to produce it), x_t is the abstract portion of the machine which is transferred to the product during the t-th year of its utilization. Obviously the price of the t year old machine, p_{mt}, can be determined as

$$p_{mt} = \left[p_m - \sum_{h=1}^{t} x_h \right] (1+r)^t$$

With the problem well stated, Besicovitch had no difficulty in finding the solution. In the same document we read in his hand:

$$x_n = x_n$$

$$x_{n-1} = x_n(1+r)$$

$$x_{n-2} = x_n(1+r)^2$$

....

$$x_1 = x_n(1+r)^{n-1}$$

$$x_1 + \cdots + x_n = x_n \frac{(1+r)^n - 1}{r} = p_m$$

$$x_n = \frac{rp_m}{(1+r)^n - 1}$$

(D3/12/27 : 6)

Despite the fact that the problem was solved, Sraffa was not yet satisfied. A few days later, on 4 December 1942, he wrote a short piece titled "Fixed into Circ.[ulating] – *Objective basis*". We quote it in full:

> (After division of original price into proportional parts which pass into the product in successive years).
>
> It may now be asked, can the matter be left at that? Certainly not. For it is against the object of the present treatment which is to represent the production & circulation of commodities in material terms (i.e. quantities of labour, of commodities & periods of time) *independent of* the distribution of the product, i.e. of the rate of profit.
>
> This can be seen at once if we try to apply Reduction. How much labour, & of what period enters into a commodity. The answer would be, it *depends* on r. If we thus make the quantity of labour entering a commodity depend on r, we are falling straight into the B[öhm-]B[awerk]-Wicksell blunder of making the period of production depend on the rate of interest. We also open the way to another danger; there is nothing to stop that method being applied to the Reduction of wages (as being composed of a quantity of commodities that varies with r) and even to profits. Which would reduce the whole scheme to nonsense.
>
> Therefore it is necessary to make the transformation of Fix.[ed] into Circ.[ulating] in terms, *not* of proportionate parts varying with r, but of actual quantities of labour and commodities, of such magnitudes & of such periods that they will *happen* to vary in price (& not in quantity) as those proportionate parts.
>
> (The trouble of this division into actual quantities of labour & commodities is that it is so arbitrary, & does not correspond to any real events (even if it is possible to do it in *every* case, i.e. for all compositions of capital).)
>
> To this objection against the "abstract" division, as making the *quantities* of labour & commodities *dependent* on r it might be replied: this is true only if we take an isolated machine (individual point of view): but if we take a complete group of machines (social point of view) it is no longer true.
>
> (D3/12/27: 11–12)

Obviously, if the one year old machine is conceived as a different commodity from the new machine or any other of its vintages, the objectivistic claim is met. The example of fixed capital demonstrates neatly two things. First, Sraffa would not allow his epistemological and philosophical preoccupations eclipse his quest for analytical rigour. Secondly, he would not be satisfied with a rigorous but empty solution. He would not give in until a solution was found that met with both concerns.

In the same period Sraffa wanted also to understand better how his method compared with that of the accountant as it is known from textbooks in commercial arithmetic. The latter method he had already studied in the late 1920s. There is a paper of some fifteen pages on this issue written between 2 and 6 December 1942 (D3/12/27: 21–35). Besicovitch does not seem to have been directly involved. We encounter a Sraffa who is now sure that the questions he had raised were right on target:

> There are innumerable schemes of dividing the fixed annuity of Fixed Cap. between replacement of capital and profit. *All* these schemes are equally correct if they satisfy the requirements:
>
> 1) That the total paid in each successive year is constant.
> 2) That the total paid for replacement of capital at any time is equal (*without* the addition of any interest) to the original cost of the asset.
>
> (D3/12/27: 33)

4.4 The joint-products approach

A few days later, on 10 December, Sraffa adopted for good the joint products approach to fixed capital. He specified:

> If in the production of a commodity there enters a fixed capital (e.g. a machine) which has a working life of m years, then we divide the industry that produces it, into m sections each of which uses machines of only one of the m possible ages, and for each section we set up an equation. On the l.h.s. there will be the materials etc., as well as a number of machines of, say, i years' age, and on the right hand side the quantity of commodity produced by the section, plus a number of machines of $i + 1$ years' age: except for the section using $m - 1$ years old machines, which on the r.h.s. will have only the commodity, and no machines – or at most the scrap, the price of which must already be determined elsewhere as a raw material / in other branches of production which produce it & use it as a r.[aw] m.[aterial].
>
> We thus have, for each commodity produced by a fixed capital, in addition to the single original equation, $m - 1$ new equations, and on the other hand the prices of $m - 1$ age-groups of machines to be determined: apart from the equation of the industry that produces the machine, to which corresponds its price when new.
>
> If the machines have a fixed term of life, at the end of which they are discarded, each section will employ the same number of them. But if, as is in general the case (& necessarily so if the f.c. consists of working animals etc.), they are worn out gradually each section will employ the number which, according to the mortality tables of the f.c. in question, are required to maintain

the population stationary when the number used in the section which employs new machines are added (or born) every year.

The machines of different ages may have differing efficiency, & also require varying quantities of labour & materials for their maintenance & repair: these differences will be shown in the equations of the respective sections, in varying quantities appearing on the l.h.s. & in differences in the product.

Calling the fixed capital f, and the quantity of it used new in the production of commodity A, F_a, its price p_f: the number of machines 1 year old ${}_1F_a$, and their price p_{f1} etc., denoting the machines of ages $1, 2, \ldots, m-1$ years and the sections using them respectively by the suffixes $1, 2, \ldots, m-1$ we write the equations for commodity A[14]

$$(A_{a1}p_a + \cdots + F_a p_f + K_{a1}p_k + L_{a1}w)(1+r) = A_1 p_a + {}_1F_a p_{f1}$$

$$(A_{a2}p_a + \cdots + {}_1F_a p_{f1} + K_{a2}p_k + L_{a2}w)(1+r) = A_2 p_a + {}_2F_a p_{f2}$$

$$\cdots\cdots\cdots\cdots\cdots\cdots\cdots\cdots\cdots\cdots\cdots\cdots\cdots\cdots\cdots\cdots$$

$$(A_{am-1}p_a + \cdots + {}_{m-1}F_a p_{fm-1} + K_{am}p_k + L_{am}w)(1+r) = A_m p_a$$

If we assume that the machines have a fixed term of life, during each year of which their efficiency & maintenance are constant & the scrap value nought, we can verify that their prices at various ages which are the solutions of the equations agree with the book-values ascribed to them by the "natural" plan of depreciation which is recommended for those conditions.

(D3/12/30: 5–8 and 10)

On the following day Sraffa continued the manuscript dealing now with the problem of whether the 'Reduction method' was applicable to the case under consideration. His conclusion was negative: He saw 'that the products of Fix. Cap. are inextricably mixed up as joint products [here they appear as products of "successive years" of the same machine] & there is no sense (not merely no possibility) in allotting fractions of cost (of capitals) to different parts of them. Each atom of Fix. Cap. appears to go into the whole series of products: there is no way (indep. of r, of course) of dividing them up' (D3/12/30: 13).[15] In the remaining days of December 1942 he investigated the solvability of the above equations and whether in the case of constant efficiency the accountant's method gives the same result as the joint-products method.

On 27 July 1943 Sraffa returned to the problem of fixed capital in order to finalise his respective argument: the reference is to a paper titled "Two methods of reckoning fixed: 'Malthus's' and 'Accountant's'" (D3/12/34: 12). He stressed that the former regards "old machines as part of annual product" (*ibid.*) and that both methods "conform to the rule of equal annual decay" (*ibid.*), which is the rule stated in the document of 6 December 1942. Sraffa had finally managed to solve the problem of fixed capital in terms of "Malthus's method" which in the late 1920s he had rejected as inadequate. The method made its way into the published book where it is dealt with in §§73–74. However, in Appendix D, References to the

Literature, the method is now traced back to Robert Torrens, from whom Ricardo, Malthus and Marx appear to have borrowed it. There Sraffa provides evidence that Torrens (1818: 336; 1821: 28) had anticipated the idea and therefore deserved to be credited with it.

The comparison between the two methods in §§75–78 culminates in the proof that the two are equivalent in a single case only, that is the only case in which the accountant's method applies: that of constant efficiency throughout the life of a machine. This equivalence is proved in §76. The proof was found with the help of Besicovitch. On 20 and 21 August 1943 Sraffa and Besicovitch wrote a piece titled "*Fixed Capital – The Two Methods (Deducing one from the other)*" (D3/12/34: 1–2). The document starts in Sraffa's hand:

> As we have two methods for dealing with Fixed Capital ((a) the Accountant's method and [(]b) M[althus]'s method of treating aged machines as products) which give identical results, they must be deducible from one another.
>
> a) If we call M a new machine;
> n the duration of the machine;
> Ap_a the product of one machine;
> $B_a p_b + C_a p_c$ materials and $L_a w$ labour.[16]
>
> Assuming constant efficiency of a machine at all ages (which implies, equal consumption of materials & labour & equal product) we have, for the complete set of n machines
>
> $$(A_m p_a + \cdots + L_m w)(1+r) = Mp_m \text{ cost of a new machine}$$
>
> $$(*) \quad n\left\{(B_a p_b + C_a p_c + \cdots + L_a w)(1+r) + Mp_m\left(\frac{r(1+r)^n}{(1+r)^n - 1}\right)\right\} = nAp_a$$
>
> which is the Accountant's equation for commodity A.
>
> b) With the same notation, we have
>
> $$(A_m p_a + \cdots + L_m w)(1+r) = Mp_m$$
>
> $$(\mathrm{I}) \begin{cases} (B_a p_b + \cdots + L_a w + Mp_m)(1+r) = Ap_a + M_1 p_{m_1} \\ (B_a p_b + \cdots + L_a w + M_1 p_{m_1})(1+r) = Ap_a + M_2 p_{m_2} \\ \cdots\cdots\cdots\cdots \\ (B_a p_b + \cdots + L_a w + M_{n-1} p_{m_{n-1}})(1+r) = Ap_a \end{cases}$$
>
> (assuming scrapvalue = 0)

On the same sheet there are some calculations by Besicovitch that are crossed out. The second sheet is mainly in Besicovitch's hand, except the date (one day later: 21 December) and the first line which are in Sraffa's hand:

> Multiply the equation (I) respectively by $(1+r)^{n-1}$, $(1+r)^{n-2}, \cdots, 1$ and add them:
>
> $$(B_a p_b + \cdots + L_a w)(1+r)\frac{(1+r)^n - 1}{r} + M p_m (1+r)^n$$
> $$= A p_a \frac{(1+r)^n - 1}{r}$$
>
> Multiply this = ion by $\frac{r}{(1+r)^n - 1}$ and we arrive at the = ion (*).

This brings the collaboration between Sraffa and Besicovitch on fixed capital to a close.[17] We may conclude by saying that in all relevant material respects Chapter X of the 1960 book was ready for publication in late summer 1943.

5. Basics, non-basics, and joint production

In the Preface to his book, Sraffa (1960, p. vi) reminded us that "Whilst the central propositions had taken shape in the late 1920's, particular points, such as the Standard commodity, joint products and fixed capital, were worked out in the 'thirties and early 'forties". He added:

> In the period since 1955, while these pages were being put together out of a mass of old notes, little was added, apart from filling gaps which had become apparent in the process (such as the adapting of the distinction between 'basics' and 'non-basics' to the case of joint production).
>
> (*Ibid.*)

This section tries to reconstruct Besicovitch's part in this process of "adapting". In order to be able to do so we first consider the structure of the whole book and the role of the distinction between basics and non-basics in the case of single production. Then follows a brief exposition of the general solution of the problem provided by Sraffa in the book. Next we turn to the state of Sraffa's analysis before Besicovitch offered to help him with the intricate problem. Only after these preliminaries can we begin to reconstruct the collaboration of the two scholars in the second half of 1957 on the basic-non basic distinction in the case of joint production.

5.1 The structure of Sraffa's book and the distinction between basics and non-basics

Readers might find it somewhat puzzling that the centre-piece of Part I of the book is devoted to the existence and uniqueness of the Standard commodity. As we have argued elsewhere (Kurz-Salvadori, 1993), this concept constitutes the corner-stone of the (not always complete, but always completable) proofs contained in the book. When readers turn to Part II they see that essentially the same structure underlies also the treatment of the issues dealt with here: joint production, fixed capital, and land. Sraffa asks whether, and under what circumstances, the concepts and the analysis elaborated for systems with single production do, or do not, carry over to systems with joint production. He shows that the tools used and the results derived in the case of single production cannot generally be used or derived also in the case of multiple-product industries. It is hardly an exaggeration to say that in this respect the argument is much more concerned with clarifying why a generalization is *not* possible than with providing the elements of a potential generalization. This underlying structure is to be recalled when we reconstruct the steps taken by Sraffa in order to adapt the distinction between 'basics' and 'non-basics' to the case of joint production.

In single production commodity j enters *directly* into the production of commodity i if and only if

$$a_{ij} > 0.$$

Commodity j enters *indirectly* into the production of commodity i if and only if $a_{ij} = 0$ and there is a sequence $i_1, i_2, \cdots, i_z$ of indices such that

$$a_{ii_1} a_{i_1 i_2} \ldots a_{i_z j} > 0.$$

And a *basic commodity* (or, for short, a *basic*) is a commodity which enters directly or indirectly into the production of all commodities. The distinction between basic and non-basic commodities in single production is important because basics exhibit various properties which non-basics do not. Among these is the property that whereas all basics enter into the Standard commodity, none of the non-basics does. This fact is not so obvious, since in general several composite commodities can be built up which satisfy the initial definition of the Standard commodity, but only the one involving all basics and no non-basic determines a maximum rate of profits at which the prices of basics are positive. Sraffa followed the expository strategy of "removing 'manually' all the non-basic equations and dealing with a system composed exclusively of basic commodities" (D3/12/44: 5).[18] However, in the case of joint production this strategy does not seem to be feasible due to the fact that non-basics may be produced jointly with basics. The way out of this impasse was to look for a set of "multipliers" which, when applied to the various processes, would purge non-basics from the system.

The generally applicable distinction between basics and non-basics is provided in §60:

> In a system of k productive processes and k commodities (no matter whether produced singly or jointly) we say that a commodity or more generally a group of n linked commodities (where n must be smaller than k and may be equal to 1) are *non-basic* if of the k rows (formed by the $2n$ quantities in which they

appear in each processs) not more than n rows are independent, the others being linear combinations of these.

Let $\mathbf{A}$ designate the input matrix and $\mathbf{B}$ the output matrix,

$$\mathbf{A} = \begin{bmatrix} \mathbf{A}_{11} & \mathbf{A}_{12} \\ \mathbf{A}_{21} & \mathbf{A}_{22} \end{bmatrix}, \quad \mathbf{B} = \begin{bmatrix} \mathbf{B}_{11} & \mathbf{B}_{12} \\ \mathbf{B}_{21} & \mathbf{B}_{22} \end{bmatrix}$$

respectively, where $\mathbf{A}$ and $\mathbf{B}$ are $k \times k$ and $\mathbf{A}_{22}$ and $\mathbf{B}_{22}$ are $n \times n$ matrices, then the rank definition of non-basics implies that there is a $(k - n) \times n$ matrix $\mathbf{T}$ such that $\mathbf{A}_{12} = \mathbf{TA}_{22}$ and $\mathbf{B}_{12} = \mathbf{TB}_{22}$. Hence, by multiplying the equation

$$\mathbf{Bp} = (1 + R)\mathbf{Ap} \tag{1}$$

by the matrix

$$\mathbf{M} = \begin{bmatrix} \mathbf{I} & -\mathbf{T} \\ \mathbf{0} & \mathbf{I} \end{bmatrix}$$

we obtain that the maximum rate of profits R and the prices of the first $k - n$ commodities can be determined by the equation

$$(\mathbf{B}_{11} - \mathbf{TB}_{21})\mathbf{p}_1 = (1 + R)(\mathbf{A}_{11} - \mathbf{TA}_{21})\mathbf{p}_1.$$

This is the procedure described by Sraffa, without using matrices, in §§61–63 and justified in Appendix C. Consequently, as Sraffa observes in §65, if there is a tax (or a subsidy) on the production of a basic, this "will affect all prices" and "the rate of profits that corresponds to a given wage", whereas if there is a tax (or a subsidy) on the production of a non-basic, this "will have no effect beyond the price of the taxed [or subsidized] commodity and those of such other non-basics as may be linked with it". The reason for this is that such a tax has no effect whatsoever on matrix $\mathbf{T}$.

The distinction between basics and non-basics is much less important in the case of joint production than in that of single production. Yet it still performs the role of reducing the number of candidates for the maximum rate of profits and, as a consequence, for the composition of the Standard commodity. The latter can now be defined by the equation

$$\mathbf{q}^T(\mathbf{B}_{11} - \mathbf{TB}_{21}) = (1 + R)\mathbf{q}^T(\mathbf{A}_{11} - \mathbf{TA}_{21}).$$

This is the equivalent of the "removing 'manually' all the non-basic equations and dealing with a system composed exclusively of basic commodities". This procedure is referred to as the "device of the basic system" in Sraffa's book. Finally, Sraffa chooses the smallest R among all the candidates determined in this way since the corresponding Standard product "is the only Standard product in terms of which, at... all the levels of the rate of profits from 0 to its maximum..., it is possible for the prices of commodities to be finite" (1960: 54).[19] This choice Sraffa justifies in Appendix C: he confirms that the "object of the exercise is to identify the particular value of R which is appropriate from the economic standpoint"; argues that the values of R which have been eliminated following this device "have the peculiarity that the corresponding prices of all commodities would be zero (with the exception, for each value of R, of the prices of one non-basic or a group of interconnected non basics)"; and maintains that, as a consequence, if these values of R were not eliminated, then the criterion which identifies the "economically relevant value of R" with the lowest one would be invalid (p. 92).

Let us summarize the exposition strategy. The definitions of basics and non-basics are related to a property of the coefficients of production. Then it is proved that 1) some potential candidates to the "maximum rate of profits" can be ignored since at those rates of profits the prices of basics would be zero and that 2) a tax on a non-basic will not affect the "appropriate" candidates to the "maximum rates of profits" and the corresponding prices of basics. The "maximum rate of profits" is then found as the minimum of such "appropriate" candidates. It is stated, but not proved, that a tax on a basic would affect the maximum rate of profits and all prices. This proof was actually provided by Besicovitch when the book was already so advanced that Sraffa did not attempt to incorporate it into the book. This proof could have dispensed with the abstract definition of basics based on the rank property, but the exposition would not have been less abstract. It would have been possible to carry out the following exposition strategy. Commodity i is defined as basic if the existence of a scalar R and a vector $\mathbf{p}$ satisfying equation (1) and such that a tax on i leaves R unchanged implies that $\mathbf{e}_i^T\mathbf{p} = 0$. Then it is proved that the set of the R's satisfying this property is the same for all basic commodities and therefore at those R's the prices of all basics are zero. The "maximum rate of profits" is then found as the minimum of all the other R's satisfying equation (1).

Before we turn to a historical reconstruction of the path by means of which Sraffa, with the help of Besicovitch, arrived at the above solution, it is perhaps useful to investigate a different formalism, which, as we shall see, was followed by Besicovitch in one of his contributions (see D3/12/92: 22–23). Let us partition matrices $\mathbf{A}$ and $\mathbf{B}$ in the following way

$$\mathbf{A} = [\mathbf{A}_1\ \mathbf{A}_2], \quad \mathbf{B} = [\mathbf{B}_1\ \mathbf{B}_2]$$

where $\mathbf{A}_2$ and $\mathbf{B}_2$ are $k \times n$, then the definition of non basics implies that there is a $k \times n$ matrix $\mathbf{C}$ and two $n \times n$ matrices $\mathbf{T}_1$ and $\mathbf{T}_2$ such that $\mathbf{A}_2 = \mathbf{C}\mathbf{T}_1$ and $\mathbf{B}_2 = \mathbf{C}\mathbf{T}_2$. Hence, equation (1) can be stated as

$$[\mathbf{B}_1 - (1+R)\mathbf{A}_1]\mathbf{p}_1 + \mathbf{C}\boldsymbol{\pi} = \mathbf{0}$$

where $\boldsymbol{\pi} = [\mathbf{T}_2 - (1+R)\mathbf{T}_1]\mathbf{p}_2$. Obviously, there are $k-n$ values of R for which the above equation has a non trivial solution. Since a tax on a non-basic will affect $\mathbf{T}_2$, but not $\mathbf{C}$, it will not affect R, $\mathbf{p}_1$ and $\boldsymbol{\pi}$: it will affect only $\mathbf{p}_2$.[20] Similarly for the q-system: there are $k-n$ values of R for which the equations

$$\mathbf{q}^T[\mathbf{B}_1 - (1+R)\mathbf{A}_1] = \mathbf{0}^T \text{ and } \mathbf{q}^T\mathbf{C} = \mathbf{0}^T$$

have a non trivial solution.[21] Let us remark that in the case of an isolated non-basic, matrices $\mathbf{T}_1$ and $\mathbf{T}_2$ are actually scalars and therefore $\mathbf{q}^T\mathbf{C} = \mathbf{0}^T$ is equivalent to $\mathbf{q}^T\mathbf{B}_2 = \mathbf{0}^T$. But this is not true in the case of a set of several linked non-basics. This remark will turn out to be useful in the following discussion.

5.2 The old definition of basics and non-basics – an "empty shell"

Originally Sraffa intended to devote only a single chapter to the analysis of joint production. This chapter was drafted and then typed in spring 1957. However, shortly afterwards, in late April 1957, Sraffa began to grasp, and then in May to see clearly, that the distinction between basic and non-basics products developed for single production could not be carried over to joint production. The case that highlighted the shortcoming of the old definition was the one in which a commodity, although entering the means of production of all the processes of the system, nevertheless turned out not to be included in the Standard system. Hence the two criteria – "entering directly or indirectly" and "being a part of the Standard commodity" – which in the case of single production coincided, no longer did so in the case of joint production.

Sraffa first had doubts as to the applicability of the former criterion. On 7 June he stressed: "The old definition of B[asic] N[on-]B[asic] ('entering or not') becomes an 'empty shell'" (D3/12/093: 28). The meaning of this is explained in some detail in a note composed on 11 June:

> In the single-products system we called 'basic' those products which directly or indirectly entered the means of production of all commodities, and 'non-basic' those that did not.
>
> This criterion had the advantage of being both simple and precise, but it was clear from the beginning that the real point (although not equally simple to define) is to distinguish the products that play an essential part in the determination of prices and the rate of profits – from those that do not.
>
> With only single-product industries all was well since these two features invariably coincided. But as soon as joint products are admitted /taken into consideration/ the two features are liable to become divorced – of which the first signs were cropping out [*sic*] in some of the examples just considered, involving negative multipliers (§ . . .). As we shall presently see it becomes possible in the presence of j[oint]-p[roduction] under such circumstances for commodities which do not 'enter' the means of production of any other product to acquire a determining role, and on the other hand for commodities which do 'enter' the means of production of all commodities to cease to play any part in determination.
>
> If we retained the old definition we should therefore be left with an empty shell: and in order to preserve the essential basis of the distinction we must find a new criterion.
>
> (D3/12/83: 47)

At first Sraffa thought the problem could be quickly fixed, and after some preparatory work at the beginning of June he drafted already a new paragraph containing a revised definition of the two kinds of products (see D3/12/83: 83–4). Its characteristic feature is that the emphasis is shifted from products to processes and the criterion of a commodity "entering, directly or indirectly", is abandoned. Sraffa rewrote the piece several times, but in mid June became convinced that the problem was much more difficult than he had at first thought and that its implications were far-reaching. There were even moments in which he believed that the distinction had to be wholly abandoned. On 16 June he wrote: "Basic & non-basic products to be jettisoned with joint products" (D3/12/83: 45). However, his intuition seems to have prevented him from following this through. On 24 June he asked himself: "Which is the economically significant Standard system (*R*)?" (D3/12/93: 52). And two days later we read in his diary: "Finito rewriting Joint Products, con Basics". Yet this was not the end of the story. On 7 August Sraffa jotted down in his diary: "Trovato il criterio per escludere a priori i non-basics nel joint products: e quindi identificare la soluzione da scegliere" [I found the criterion to exclude a priori non-basics in joint production: and therefore to identify the solution to be chosen]. Alas, his optimism turned out to be premature. What is important to note, however, is Sraffa's assessment as to the relevance of the distinction: his interest in it was motivated by his conviction that it held the key to the choice of the economically relevant maximum rate of profits and the corresponding Standard commodity. In a note dated 23 August he wrote:

> Questa parte centrale dei J.P. (§53–60) può essere salvata abbandonando completamente la distinzione "basic non-basic" e utilizzando il materiale come segue:
>
> 1) Cancella il pezzetto sulla "soluzione" dopo le equazioni.
> 2) Esempi di negative multipliers
>
> I primi due esempi stanno (omettendo la parola "basic")
> I secondi due ("borderline case" van leggermente modificati. Non parlare di non-basic.
>
> (D3/12/93: 5; see also D3/12/93: 58–59)
>
> [This central part of Joint Products (§53–60) can be preserved by abandoning completely the distinction "basic non basic" and by utilizing the material in the following way:
>
> 1) Delete the small piece on the "solution" after the equations.
> 2) Examples of negative multipliers.
>
> The former two examples stand up (by omitting the word "basic")
> The latter two [examples] ("borderline case"[)] have to be lightly modified. Do not speak of non-basic.]

One of Sraffa's preoccupations was that of finding a non-arbitrary definition. Since, in principle, there are several composite commodities which are candidates for serving as Standard commodity, a definition in terms of 'entering the Standard commodity' would have depended on the Standard commodity chosen – and thus would have been self-referential. Similarly for the definition based on the invariability of prices with respect to a tax (tithe). In a note dated 21 June Sraffa remarked:

> Basics & non-basics: under j.-p. the distinction differs in two separate respects from that made in single products:
>
> 1st. In single-p.[roduction] it was defined *independently* of the solution of the system, and therefore non-basics could be removed before a solution was undertaken. Whereas in j.[oint]-p.[roduction] we failed to find an independent definition and had to fall back on one which depends on the solution obtained, or chosen: accordingly, there may [be] several possible/ alternative/ distinctions between b.[asics] & non-b.[asics] in the same system.
>
> 2dly. In the single-p.[roducts case], since negative multipliers were tacitly ruled out, the only possible way to deal with non-basics remaining was zero multipliers. But in j.[oint] p.[roduction] there is the alternative solution of eliminating *all* basic products by pos.[itive] & neg.[egative] multipliers, leaving alone to compose the Standard system [by] any self-reproducing non-basic.
>
> The general position seems to have landed in a contradiction:
>
> a) which are the basics & which the non-b[asi]cs will depend on the solution for *R* & q[uantitie]s chosen
>
> b) we assume that 'commonsense' or suchlike finds a criterion of choice – but that can be only that basics should be included in the St.[andard] system!
>
> (D3/12/83: 9)

Sraffa's attempts to solve the problem fully on his own were not successful. As he admitted with regard to a definition of basics and non-basics he had elaborated: "I am not sure that it is true & cannot prove it, *not even* to my own satisfaction!" (D3/12/92: 9) He needed the help of his mathematical friend. On 31 August he could note in his diary to his great relief: "Besicovitch offre di aiutarmi nei miei problemi matematici" [Besicovitch offers to help me with my mathematical problems]. However, the problems turned out to be much more intricate and time consuming than he, or Besicovitch, could anticipate at the time. It even turned out that Besicovitch's help was not enough and that the assistance of some further mathematicians was needed in order finally to solve the problems under consideration by the end of October 1957. Further aspects, however, were spelled out only in a letter by Besicovitch to Sraffa dated 25 December.

5.3 "Besicovitch offers to help me"

On the same day on which Besicovitch offered to help (31 August), Sraffa wrote a document titled "ad usum Bes.[icovitch]" (D3/12/92: 7–9) and another one in which he jotted down a number of questions (D3/12/87: 24). The first document reports on the state Sraffa's reasoning had reached by then. It is interesting to note that single-product industries are now called 'simple' and joint-product industries 'complex'. It is appropriate to quote the document in full:

I. Simple industries

$$
\begin{aligned}
&(A_a p_a + \cdots + K_a p_k)(1 + r) + L_a w = A p_a \\
&\cdots\cdots\cdots\cdots\cdots\cdots\cdots\cdots\cdots\cdots\cdots \\
&(A_k p_a + \cdots + K_k p_k)(1 + r) + L_k w = K p_k
\end{aligned}
\tag{1}
$$

to arrange them proportionately:

$$
\begin{aligned}
&(A_a q_a + \cdots + A_k q_k)(1 + R) = A q_a \\
&\cdots\cdots\cdots\cdots\cdots\cdots\cdots\cdots\cdots \\
&(K_a q_a + \cdots + K_k q_k)(1 + R) = K q_k
\end{aligned}
\tag{2}
$$

We can distinguish

a) basic products, which enter, directly or indirectly, all raw materials
b) non-basic products of two sorts:

  α) which are not used at all as raw materials
  β) which are only used in the industry that produces them (e.g. pigs to produce pigs)

In equations (2) non-basics of type (α) would have zero coefficients

query: is this true? → { but those of type (β) would have a non-zero coefficient in *one* of the solutions, where would be $R = \dfrac{\text{addition to pig population}}{\text{initial pig population}}$

However, non-basic equations of both types can be crossed out in (1), so that we exclude zero q's.
There is one all-positive solution, and
q[uery]: is this true? → it corresponds to the *lowest possible* value of R.
We put in the (2) the all-positive values of q's, add them up, and the total (which we call "Standard composite commodity") we take as unit of wages and prices, when we have

$$r = R(1 - w)$$

(D3/12/92: 7)

II. Complex industries

$$
\begin{aligned}
&(A_1 p_a + \cdots + K_1 p_k)(1 + r) + L_1 w = A_{(1)} p_a + \cdots + K_{(1)} p_k \\
&\cdots\cdots\cdots\cdots\cdots\cdots\cdots\cdots\cdots\cdots\cdots\cdots\cdots\cdots\cdots \\
&(A_k p_a + \cdots\cdots)(1 + r) + L_k w = A_{(k)} p_a + \cdots\cdots
\end{aligned}
\tag{3}
$$

(N.B. Several quantities may be zero, so that the Simple industries are a particular case of this)

$$(A_1q_1 + \cdots + A_kq_k)(1 + R) = A_{(1)}q_1 + \cdots + A_{(k)}q_k$$
$$\cdots\cdots\cdots\cdots\cdots\cdots\cdots\cdots\cdots\cdots \qquad (4)$$
$$(K_1q_1 + \cdots\cdots)(1 + R) = K_{(1)}q_1 + \cdots\cdots$$

(N.B. The criterion of "raw materials" fails in general to distinguish between basics and non-basics: examples can be shown of "pig-type raw materials" which are basic, and of products which enter all raw-materials and are non-basic. A new definition is given, which in the simple case coincides.

N.B.2. Def. A tax on a product 'a' is one which diminishes $A_{(1)}, \ldots A_{(k)}$ in the same proportion leaving all other quantities unchanged.

N.B.3. We are now unable in general to exclude a priori the non-basics from the system. The definition is given at the end.)

We want to chose the value of R to which, *if* there is one, the all-positive solution corresponds. It is necessarily the smallest value of R, since the non-basics have not been excluded.

{It can be defined as that value, say R', to which corresponds a composite commodity which, if taken as unit of prices & wages, will give finite prices (i.e.: not 0, not ∞) at all values of r, between 0 and R' inclusive, to all products which are basic relatively to that value of R.[22]

A basic product relatively to any value R' is one that cannot be taxed without affecting R'.

Basic products enter the Standard commodity in positive or negative quantities. Non-basics do not enter it at all.

(D3/12/92: 8)

I think I can prove the above.

A less clumsy definition would be the following, but I am not sure that it is true & cannot prove it, *not even* to my own satisfaction!

A basic product is one which enters in non-zero quantity the composite commodity corresponding to *each* of the possible values of R.

The lowest of the R's which have a composite commodity consisting of the smallest number of commodities (which may be 1) is the one to which correspond all-positive q's, *if* there is one.

Non-basic products may enter either no one, or one, or some, composite commodities, but never those that have the minimum number of non-zero commodities.

(D3/12/92: 9)

The document reveals clearly that Sraffa saw a relationship between two properties:

(a) entering into the Standard commodity; and
(b) affecting all prices and the rate of profits as a consequence of a tax.

So he faced three alternatives from which to choose: he could either

(i) define basics in terms of property (a) and then prove property (b);
(ii) or define basics in terms of property (b) and then prove property (a);
(iii) or define basics in terms of a third property which was yet to be specified and then prove both the first and the second property.

It is around these three alternatives that much of the discussion between him and Besicovitch (and some other mathematicians) revolved. He showed reservations with respect to alternatives (i) and (ii) because they did not seem to be solid enough, depending on the chosen solution of R. This is the reason why with regard to alternative (i) he wrote: "A basic product is one which enters in non-zero quantity the composite commodity corresponding to *each* of the possible values of R", where the emphasized word "each" has exactly the task of eliminating the arbitrariness connected with the chosen R. But the introduction of that "each" requires a further proof. Similarly, with regard to alternative (ii) he wrote: "A basic product relatively to *any value* R' is one that cannot be taxed without affecting R'" (italics added), where once again the reference to "any value R'" has the task of eliminating the arbitrariness connected with the chosen R, but at the same time introduces the need of a proof. The third alternative had yet to be found, but it is clear that it had to be based on elements which did not require the calculation of R or of prices and therefore it would not be subject to the arbitrariness characteristic of the first two alternatives.

Analysing the set of questions that Sraffa registered on the same day (D3/12/87: 24) and a few days later – 1 September: D3/12/87: 20–21; 4 September: D3/12/87: 26; 5 September: D3/12/87: 22; 6 September: D3/ 12/92: 4–5; 8 September: D3/12/92: 25 – we see that these now point mainly in the direction of the third alternative. Let us have a closer look at the issue.

Sraffa's diary bears witness to his impatience and his disappointment with the speed of progress he made. On 1 September we find the sober observation: "4 [o'clock] Besicovitch (pochino! [very little!])"; but on 7 September we read: "Besicovitch risponde a domanda". The sets of questions just mentioned contain in some cases also answers, and those of 6 and 8 September (D3/12/92: 4–5 and 25) contain answers in Besicovitch's hand. We consider here only the latter since we do not know whether the other questions were in fact put forward to Besicovitch. On 6 September Sraffa asked the following questions:

$$\begin{cases} (A_1p_a + B_1p_b + \cdots + K_1p_k)(1+R) = A_{(1)}p_a + B_{(1)}p_b + \cdots + K_{(1)}p_k \\ (A_2p_a + \cdots\cdots\cdots\cdots\cdots\cdots \\ \cdots\cdots\cdots\cdots\cdots\cdots\cdots\cdots\cdots\cdots\cdots\cdots\cdots\cdots \\ (A_kp_a + B_kp_b + \cdots + K_kp_k)(1+R) = A_{(k)}p_a + B_{(k)}p_b + \cdots + K_{(k)}p_k \end{cases} \tag{1}$$

> Making, say, $p_a = 1$.
> Consider commodity 'b'.
> [1] Is it true that:
>
> $$\text{if } = \frac{B_{(1)}}{B_1} = \frac{B_{(2)}}{B_2} \cdots = \frac{B_{(k)}}{B_k} = b, \text{ then } p_b = 0?$$
>
> [2] The same is true if all B's = 0 except two (or more) pairs, e.g.
>
> $$\frac{B_{(2)}}{B_2} = \frac{B_{(3)}}{B_3}$$
>
> [3] But it is not true if all B's = 0 except *one* pair. In this case $0 < p_b < \infty$.
> (D3/12/92: 4)

What is interesting in these questions is the antecedent of the "if" propositions. In all cases the column of inputs and that of outputs relative to commodity 'b' are linearly dependent. Hence we know that commodity 'b' is non-basic in terms of the definition given in the published book and actually constitutes a set of non-basics consisting of one commodity only. The consequents of the three if-propositions on the contrary do not correspond to what we know from the published book. The correct question would have been: Does a change in b leave the prices of all other commodities unchanged?

Besicovitch answered as follows:

> [1] This is not true because you can reduce an arbitrary system of eq[uatio]ns (1) to your particular case by adding the same terms to the right & to the left. In fact you can replace B_1 in the first eq[uatio]n by B'_1 defined by the eq[uatio]n.
>
> $$B_1(1+R) - B_{(1)} = B'_1(1+R-b); \ \&$$
>
> $B_{(1)}$ by B'_1 & the same with all the other B's.
> [2] Not true
> [3] True

Document D3/12/92: 5 provides us with the argument followed by Besicovitch plus a remark by Sraffa. The idea is close at hand that Besicovitch's answer may have prompted Sraffa to reformulate his questions. We read in Besicovitch's hand:

> $$\{A_1(1+R) - A_{(1)}\}p_a + \cdots \{ \quad \}p_k = 0$$
>
> ---
>
> ---
>
> $$B_1(1+R) - B_{(1)} = B'_1\{1+R-b\}$$
>
> $$B_2(\quad) \cdots\cdots = B'_2\{1+R-b\},$$

and in Sraffa's hand:

> That is to say, when we know a possible value of R, say R', we can bring, for *any* commodity g, its quantities on the two sides of *each* equation to the same ratio by adding to the two sides any suitable pairs of quantities G_x and $G_{(x)}$ provided $G_x(1+R) = G_{(x)}$, so that G_x can simply be inserted in the parentheses, and $G_{(x)}$ on the r.h.s.

Hence Besicovitch just put the homogeneous system in its canonical form and remarked that changes in inputs and outputs leave prices unchanged provided the sums in brackets are unchanged. Whether these rather technical observations were of much use to Sraffa in coming up with the right questions we cannot know. However, two days later he asked:

$$\begin{cases} (A_1p_a + B_1p_b + \cdots + K_1p_k)(1+R) = A_{(1)}p_a + B_{(1)}p_b + \cdots + K_{(1)}p_k \\ (A_2p_a + \cdots\cdots\cdots\cdots (\cdots\cdots) = A_{(2)}p_a + \cdots\cdots \\ \cdots\cdots\cdots\cdots\cdots\cdots\cdots\cdots\cdots\cdots \\ (A_kp_a + \cdots\cdots\cdots\cdots)(\cdots\cdots) = A_{(k)}p_a + \cdots\cdots \end{cases} \tag{1}$$

$$\begin{cases} (A_1q_1 + A_2q_2 + \cdots + A_kq_k)(1+R) = A_{(1)}q_1 + \cdots + A_{(k)}q_k \\ (B_1q_1 + \cdots\cdots\cdots\cdots (\cdots\cdots) = B_{(1)}q_1 + \cdots\cdots \\ \cdots\cdots\cdots\cdots\cdots\cdots\cdots\cdots\cdots\cdots \\ (K_1q_1 + \cdots\cdots\cdots\cdots)(\cdots\cdots) = K_{(1)}q_1 + \cdots\cdots \end{cases} \tag{2}$$

We suppose that $\frac{B_{(1)}}{B_1} = \frac{B_{(2)}}{B_2} = \cdots = \frac{B_{(k)}}{B_k} = b$.

1. Is it true that $B_{(1)}q_1 + B_{(2)}q_2 + \cdots + B_{(k)}q_k = 0$ for all possible values of R, except $1 + R = b$?
2. If 1. is true, does it follow that if $B_{(1)}, B_{(2)}, \ldots, B_{(k)}$ are all divided by an arbitrary number (= a tax) the values of R are not affected except $R = b - 1$?
3. Is it also true that (provided *at least two* of the pairs $\frac{B_{(1)}}{B_1}, \frac{B_{(1)}}{B_2} \neq 0$)

this division would (a) change all the values of the p's in (1), but (b) leave unchanged those of the q's in (2)?

(D3/12/92: 25)

Besicovitch crossed out the 'b' above and replaced it with β. Then he provided the following answer to the first question:

> [1] There are k particular values of R for which (1) and (2) are possible, that is not all p's or q's are = 0. Of course if $\beta \neq 1 + R$ for one of those values then $B_{(1)}q_1 + \cdots = 0$ for that value of R.[23]
>
> Thus for any R exc[ept] R being one of the k values and at that $= \beta - 1$ $B_{(1)}q_1 + \cdots = 0$.

With respect to the other two questions he just informed Sraffa that answers would follow. Sraffa, however, added on the sheet:

> [The answer to 2 is Yes]
> [The answer to 3 is (α) No and (β) Yes: both p's and q's *unchanged*] The reason is that a column of the determinant can be divided without affecting values, except for $R = \beta - 1$.

Besicovitch's answer was in letter form and arrived five days later, on 13 September.[24]

> In (2) represent the 2nd eq[uatio]n in the form
>
> $$(B_1 q_1 + \cdots + B_k q_k)(1 + R - \beta) = 0.$$
>
> So long as $\beta \neq 1 + R$ we can drop the factor $(1 + R - \beta)$ & thus β is not in the system of eq[uatio]ns (2). Thus $q_1, \ldots, q_k$ do not vary while β does, except $\beta = 1 + R$. In this case (2) is not sufficient for defining $q_1, \ldots, q_k$ uniquely. There is an infinite system of solutions.
>
> With (1) in the form
>
> $$\{A_1(1+R) - A_{(1)}\}p_a + B_1(1+R-\beta)p_b + \cdots + \{K_1(1+R) - K_{(1)}\}p_k = 0$$
> $$\{A_2 \ldots\ldots\ldots\} \ldots + B_2(1+R-\beta)p_b + \cdots\cdots\cdots\cdots = 0$$
> $$\cdots\cdots\cdots\cdots\cdots\cdots\cdots\cdots\cdots\cdots\cdots\cdots\cdots\cdots$$
> $$\{A_k \ldots\ldots\ldots\ldots\ldots\ldots\ldots\ldots\ldots\ldots\ldots\ldots\ldots$$
>
> Replace in these equ[atio]ns $(1+R-\beta)p_b$ by π_b. We shall get k eq[uatio]ns with respect to $p_a, \pi_b, p_c, \ldots, p_k$, which are independent of β, but $p_b = \frac{\pi_b}{1+R-\beta}$ varies with β. If $\beta = 1 + R$ then $p_a, p_c, \ldots, p_k = 0$ & p_b is arbitrary.
>
> (D3/12/92: 22–23)

Besicovitch's answer provided the general argument only for isolated non-basics, not for groups of linked non-basics. Substantially, it involved the alternative formalism mentioned toward the end of Subsection 5.1 for the general case. Sraffa observed that "The result of Besicovitch is a considerable simplification" (D3/12/87: 19). "The essential feature of non-b[asics] is that a change in their price owing to an improvement (or otherwise) in their methods of production does not affect R or other prices. But since with j[oint]-p[roduction] . . . it is simpler to say that a tax, or bounty, on the production of a non-b[asic] will affect only the price of that non b[asic] & leave the value of R & the rel[ative] prices of other products unchanged" (D3/12/87: 19).[25] The fact that the argument was presented with reference to an isolated non-basic and not to a group of linked non-basics created several problems for Sraffa, who was keen to find a general solution. Three days later, on 16 September, he got close to the example eventually to be found in §59:

> 1st Question
> Suppose $B_{(1)}$ different from 0
> but $B_1, B_2, \ldots, B_k = 0$ and $B_{(2)}, B_{(3)}, \ldots, B_{(k)} = 0$
> suppose also $C_{(1)}$ different from 0
> but $C_{(2)}, C_{(3)}, \ldots, C_{(k)} = 0$
> however $C_1, C_2, \ldots, C_k$ different from 0.
> Question: is $q_1C_1 + q_2C_2 + \cdots [+] q_kC_k = 0$?
> 2^{d} Question
> The same question as above, but cross out the first 2 lines referring to *B*.
>
> (D3/12/92: 2)

Besicovitch answered the first question in the positive and the second in the negative. He added also the calculations needed to obtain the answers:

$$(A_1p_a + B_1p_b + \cdots + K_1p_k)(1+R) = A_{(1)}p_a + \cdots$$

$$\cdots\cdots\cdots\cdots$$

$$(A_2p_a) + \cdots\cdots\cdots$$

$$(A_1q_1 + \cdots + A_kq_k)(1+R) = A_{(1)}q_1 + \cdots + A_{(k)}q_k$$

$$(B_1q_1 + \cdots \quad)(\quad) = \underline{B_{(1)}}q_1 + \cdots$$

$$(C_1q_1 + \cdots \quad)(\quad) = \underline{C_{(1)}}q_1 + \cdots$$

$$0 = B_{(1)}q_1 \quad \therefore \; q_1 = 0$$

$$\therefore \; C_1q_1 + \cdots + C_kq_k = 0$$

Strangely enough, when he dealt with the same example on 1 October, Besicovitch appears to have been possessed of the general answer. Sraffa asked:

> Suppose $A_{(1)} > A_1 > 0; A_2 = \cdots = A_k = A_{(2)} = \cdots = A_{(k)} = 0$
> $\qquad B_{(1)} > B_1 > 0; B_{(2)} = \cdots = B_{(k)}) = 0; B_1 \neq \cdots \neq B_k \neq 0$
> 'b' is non-basic: under *same rule*, or another rule?
>
> (D3/12/92: 12)

Besicovitch added 'yes' and jotted down the columns:

$$\begin{cases} a_{11} & b_{11} & a_{12} & b_{12} \\ 0 & 0 & a_{22} & 0 \end{cases}$$

$$\cdots$$

$$0 \quad 0 \quad a_{k2} \quad 0$$

Then Sraffa wrote alongside the columns the following remarks which were apparently dictated to him by Besicovitch:

> Only the first two lines are independent;
> yes the others are linear combinations of them
> [i.e. of the second]

In a box Sraffa added:

> This is the case of a commodity *b*, used by *all* processes, but produced only by one process which however happens also to be the only one that produces a non-basic *a* [which enters in none, or, in this example, only in itself] Then, *b* is also non-basic.

His insistence on the condition that the *q*-multipliers are such that for a non-basic commodity *C*

$$C_1 q_1 + \cdots + C_k q_k = C_{(1)} q_1 + \cdots + C_{(k)} q_k = 0 \tag{3}$$

shows that Sraffa had not yet fully grasped the third alternative mentioned above. He was still trying to follow a definition of basics and non-basics based on the effect of a tax. At the same time when he tried to formalize such a definition, he listed a number of requirements some of which were not actually required. Equations (3) are clearly among these. If equations (3) hold and all $C_{(j)}$'s are mutiplied by the same scalar, this cannot affect the determination of the q's. But this is not a requirement when a group of linked non-basics is involved, as we have remarked at the end of Subsection 5.1. Sraffa was probably prompted to stick to this definition because in the examples studied – that of the isolated non-basic and that in which two non-basics are so since both are produced jointly by one process only and one of them does not enter directly into the production of any other process – equations (3) are satisfied. Further, as we will see, equations (3) are not only not necessary but also not sufficient in order for a commodity to be non-basic. This was to be proved with the help of another mathematician: John Arthur Todd.

5.4 Bringing in the mathematician John Arthur Todd

On the same day Besicovitch gave up and wrote to Sraffa:

> 1.10.57
> Dear Sraffa
> I have tried to do your problems, but I found myself quite incapable. It is not your fault – you set the problem quite clearly, but it is just that I could not make myself think on this kind of stuff.

I am at my worst on purely formal algebra. The problem may be quite easy. Seeing your plight, I wanted quite sincerely to help you, but I can't. Drazin[26] seems to be an obvious solution.

Yours
ASB

An understandably depressed Sraffa noted in his diary: "Besicovitch non ce la fa" [Besicovitch cannot do it]. Yet, the pending tragedy did not unfold: just one day later we find the relieving message: "Bes. si ri-interessa" [Bes. gets interested again]. And a few days later he had another meeting with Besicovitch. The result of it concerns still the distinction between basics and non-basics, but in single production. In fact there is the following note by Besicovitch:

5.10.57
Dear Sraffa,

If for the production of the comm. A you use directly B, D, F you call them *the parents of A*; the parents of B, D, F are grand-parents of A. a.[nd] s.[o] o[n]. Parents, grand parents, great grand parents a.s.o. are called the ancestors of A. If A is a basic commodity then *the ancestors of A represent all the basic c[ommodi]-ties, & the ancestors of any basic commodity are the same.*

Yours
ASB

(D3/12/92: 40)

For a few days the two friends do not seem to have met. Sraffa had some discussions with another mathematician, Peter Swinnerton-Dyer, and worked with Maurice Dobb on the index of Ricardo's *Works*. Then, on 17 October, he met again with Besicovitch in order to prepare a letter to the mathematician John Arthur Todd, asking for suggestions how to solve the problem. Sraffa noted in his diary: "Besicovitch manda il mio problema a Todd" [Besicovitch sends my problem to Todd]. The letter to Todd is important for our reconstruction since the two friends had no reason to presume that Todd would easily understand what the problem was. To mimimize the risk of not being understood by a mathematician not involved in the preceding discussions, the problem had to be stated in the clearest possible way:

17.10.57
Dear Todd,

I enclose an important problem on linear equations (only [with regard to] $x_1, \ldots, x_k$) It would be very good if you could prove or disprove the desired results

Yours
ASB

$$\left(\sum_{j}^{k} a_{ij}x_j\right)(1+z) = \sum_{j=1}^{k} b_{ij}x_j \qquad i = 1, 2, \ldots, k \tag{*}$$

Only real roots for z are considered
$q_1, \ldots, q_k$ are defined by equations

$$\left(\sum_{i=1}^{k} a_{ij}q_i\right)(1+z) = \sum_{i=1}^{k} b_{ij}q_i \qquad j = 1, 2, \ldots, k$$

$k = m + n$
For all (real) z satisfying $(*)$

$$\sum_{i=1}^{k} b_{ij}q_i \neq 0 \qquad \text{for } j = 1, 2, \ldots, m \tag{1}$$

& for at least one z

$$\sum_{i=1}^{k} b_{ij}q_i = 0 \qquad \text{for } j = m+1, m+2, \ldots, m+n \tag{2}$$

Prove that

(i) for all z, for which (2) is not satisfied, $x_1 = \cdots = x_m = 0$
(ii) if for a certain root z all q_i are positive then this is the smallest real z for which (2) is true
(iii) for any $m < l = m + n$ the system

$$\left(\sum_{j=1}^{k} a_{ij}x_j\right)(1+z) = \sum_{j=1}^{k} b_{ij}x_j + cb_{il}x_l$$

is satisfied by all the values of z for which the system $(*)$ & the equations (2) are satisfied.

(D3/12/92: 19–21)

An understanding of this letter is enhanced by taking into account two further documents: first, a paper written by Sraffa which contains probably the list of questions to be put to Todd; secondly, a letter by Besicovitch to Sraffa. The paper in Sraffa's hand is dated 16 October – the day before the letter to Todd was drafted:

1. We divide the k commodities in two groups: m *basics*, n *non-basics*; $m + n = k$.
2. *Basic* are those like '*g*' which for all real roots of R

$$G_{(1)}q_1 + G_{(2)}q_2 + \cdots + G_{(k)}q_k \neq 0 \tag{*}$$

Non-basic those which for *some* (or all) real roots of R the sum is $= 0$.

3. There is at least one[27] root of R for which $(*)$ is true for the m basic commodities and for no others.

3a. Then, at any *other* real root of R for all basic commodities is $p_g = 0$.

3b. Also, *if* there is an all-positive set of qs, it is the one that corresponds to the smallest of the real roots of R defined in 3.

3c. For any non-basic commodity such as 'i' it is possible to divide by the same arbitrary number all the terms

$$I_{(1)}, I_{(2)}, \ldots, I_{(k)}$$

without affecting any of the roots of R defined in 3.

4. If the above definitions are not inconsistent, it is desired to have a definition of basics and non-basics, equivalent to the above, but expressed independently of R, p's and q's.

(D3/12/92: 33)

This list contains all the points mentioned also in the letter to Todd. In addition there is a point, point 4, indicating the difficulty Sraffa had with his own definition. Besicovitch's letter to Sraffa has the same date as the one to Todd and reads

Dear Sraffa,

Copy p.p. 2 & 3 in order to have your problem formulated precisely, for further needs.

Question 4 is not put, in order of avoiding frightening effect

Yours

ASB

Please put it in our letter box

(D3/12/92: 26)

The letter clarifies why Besicovitch dropped Sraffa's point 4 above. The letter to Todd and the related material document Sraffa's last attempt to follow alternative (i) mentioned in Subsection 5.2. Basics are defined as always entering into the gross product of all possible Standard systems, whereas non-basics may enter into the gross product of some possible Standard systems, but not all. Further, Sraffa wanted to prove that, as in single production, there was one value of R for which only basics entered into the gross product of the Standard system, and for all other values of R the prices of basics were zero. If there was a set of multipliers which were all positive, then this corresponded to the smallest R, as in single production. Finally, there was the property that a tax on a non-basic did not affect the R's.

Todd answered on 22 October. He proved in terms of an example that the definition put forward by Sraffa was not consistent and thus paved the way to the eventual adoption of the third alternative mentioned in Subsection 5.3 above. Interestingly, only one day later Besicovitch provided Sraffa already with the general solution we find in the book. We first reproduce Todd's letter:

> Counter example.
>
> Consider the system $\left[\left(\sum_{j=1}^{k} a_{ij}x_j\right)(1+z) = \sum_{j=1}^{k} b_{ij}x_j\right]$, with $k = 3$.
>
> $$(9x_1 + 9x_2 + 4x_3)(1+z) = 15x_1 + 13x_2 + 6x_3$$
> $$(9x_1 + 11x_2 + 4x_3)(1+z) = 13x_1 + 14x_2 + 5x_3$$
> $$(4x_1 + 4x_2 + 2x_3)(1+z) = 6x_1 + 5x_2 + 3x_3$$
>
> The values of z for which the system has non-trivial solutions are 0, 1, 2.
>
> When $z = 0$, $[-1, 1, 1]$ is a solution
> $z = 1$, $[1, -1, 1]$ "
> $z = 2$, $[1, 0, -2]$ "
>
> Since **a** and **b** are, in this case, symmetric, the solution **q** of the system $(\Sigma a_{ij}q_i)(1+z) = (\Sigma b_{ij}q_i)$ are the same.
> Viz:
>
> for $z = 0$, $\mathbf{q} = [-1, 1, 1]$. And $\Sigma b_{ij}q_i$ takes values 4, 6, 2 for $j = 1, 2, 3$.
> for $z = 1$, $\mathbf{q} = [1, -1, 1]$. & " " " 8, 4, 4 ______
> for $z = 2$, $\mathbf{q} = [1, 0, -2]$. & " " " 3, 3, 0 ______
>
> Therefore
>
> (a) For all relevant z $(z = 0, 1, 2)$ $\Sigma b_{ij}q_i \neq 0$ for $j = 1, 2$.
> (b) For at least one value of z (viz: $z = 2$), $\Sigma b_{ij}q_i = 0$ for $j = 3$, & this holds, in fact, only for $z = 2$.
>
> The conjecture would therefore imply that for $z = 0, 1$ (the values of z for which (P) fails to hold), $x_1 = x_2 = 0$. But this is not the case, the relevant solutions being $[-1, 1, 1]$ & $[1, -1, 1]$
>
> (D3/12/92: 11)

In Todd's example no commodity is non-basic according to the definition given in the published book, but one is according to the definition used by Sraffa on 16 October 1957. But then the other properties, and in particular the one asserting that the prices of basics are zero when nonbasics enter into the gross product of the Standard system, do not hold.

5.5 The final solution of the problem

As was mentioned above, just one day later Besicovitch sent Sraffa a letter supporting the third alternative, that is, the one adopted in the book:

> 23.10.57
> Dear Sraffa,
> Suppose that the commodities 1, 2, 3 are taxed, then consider the columns
>
> $$a_{11},\ b_{11},\ a_{12},\ b_{12},\ a_{13},\ b_{13}$$
> $$a_{21},\ b_{21},\ a_{22},\ b_{22},\ a_{23},\ b_{23}$$
> $$\ldots\ldots\ldots\ldots$$
> $$a_{n1},\ b_{n1},\ \ldots\ldots\ldots\ldots,\ b_{n3}$$
>
> The i-th line is similar or dissimilar to the j-th line according as the [condition]
>
> $$\frac{a_{i1}}{a_{j1}} = \frac{b_{i1}}{b_{j1}} = \cdots = \frac{b_{in}}{b_{jn}}$$
>
> is satisfied or is not.
>
> *Theorem* If there are at most three dissimilar lines then there will be 3 roots of z depending on taxation but not the rest & the prices of the commodities $4, \ldots, n$ remain unaltered.
>
> As a matter of fact there is a more general theorem but its annunciation is a bit more difficult for you.
>
> In fact it is this:
>
> If of all the lines of the columns there are = 3 lines "independent" & the rest are combinations of these.
>
> Yours
> ASB
>
> (D3/12/92: 17–18)

Sraffa was still unconvinced and on 26 October jotted down what he thought he had to do:

1) Spiegare Bes. in mia lingua [Explain to Bes. in my language]
2) Il mio *perchè* di somma zero [My *why* the zero sum]
3) Il mio *id.* di valori infiniti [My *id.* of infinite values]
4) Parallelism of the 3 types [of non basics] in single & multiple [production]

    1) does not enter at all [means of production]
    2) enters only its own
    a) & is produced only by *one* proc.

b) & is produced by more than one (whether jointly or not. *Same* proportion: is the real equivalent; in fact is the real cond. of which single process is only partic. case.
3) 'independence'

The equivalent of "entering [or not] dir. or indir. the m. of p. of all comm." is: for *one*, entering m. of p. & product of various processes so that the ratio of its quantities as input & as output are the same in any process which it enters; for a group of n: when the n enter the . . . so[28]

(D3/12/87: 7)

The explanation Sraffa appears to have given to his mathematical friend on the basis of this *aide mémoire* was important, because Besicovitch in a letter (dated 28 October by Sraffa) proposed what was to become the 'device of a basic system' in the published book:

Dear Sraffa

You have $k = m + n$ equations

$$(a_{i1}z + b_{i1})x_1 + \cdots + (a_{ik}z + b_{ik})x_k = 0 \quad i = 1, 2, \ldots, k. \tag{1}$$

These equations are possible only if

$$\begin{vmatrix} a_{11}z + b_{11}, \ldots\ldots\ldots\ldots \\ \ldots\ldots\ldots\ldots\ldots\ldots\ldots\ldots \\ \ldots\ldots\ldots\ldots a_{kk}z + b_{kk} \end{vmatrix}$$

are equations of k-th degree. Suppose that the matrix formed by the $2m$ columns

$$\begin{vmatrix} a_{11}, & b_{11}, & \ldots, & a_{1m}, & b_{1m} \\ \cdot & \cdot & & \cdot & \cdot \\ \cdot & \cdot & & \cdot & \cdot \\ \cdot & \cdot & & \cdot & \cdot \end{vmatrix}$$

is of rank m. Then we can form an equivalent system

to (1) by taking linear combinations of the equation (1).

$$(a_1z + b_1)x_1 + \cdots + (a_kz + b_k)x_k = 0 \tag{2}$$

in which in the first $2m$ columns all lines after the m-th line consist of zeroes [*sic*].

The eqn in z will be split into two eqns

$$\begin{vmatrix} a'_{11}z + b'_{11} + \ldots\ldots\ldots\ldots a'_{1m}z + b'_{1m} \\ \ldots\ldots\ldots\ldots\ldots\ldots\ldots\ldots\ldots\ldots \\ \ldots\ldots\ldots\ldots\ldots\ldots\ldots\ldots a'_{mm}z + b'_{mm} \end{vmatrix} = 0 \tag{3}$$

&

$$\begin{vmatrix} a'_{m+1,\,m+1}z + b'_{m+1,\,m+1}, \dots\dots\dots\dots, a'_{m+1,\,k}z + b'_{m+1,\,k} \\ \dots\dots\dots\dots\dots\dots\dots\dots\dots\dots\dots\dots \\ \dots\dots\dots\dots\dots\dots\dots\dots\dots\dots\dots b_{kk} \end{vmatrix} = 0 \qquad (4)$$

The self reproducing compound commodities will be of two kinds: m of them will be linear comb[inatio]ns of the com[mo]d[i]ty $C_1, \dots, C_k$, but the n others will be l.[inear] comb[inatio]ns only of $C_{m+1}, \dots, C_{m+n}$. This is exactly what you wanted.

Yours

ASB

For any z of (3) $x_{m+1} = \cdots = x_k = 0$.

(D3/12/92: 14–16)

After this letter, in a document dated 9 November 1957, Sraffa accepted for good: "Non-b. to be defined *exclusively by linear dependence*" (D3/ 12/87: 2), and worked on the presentation of the argument in his style.

Alas, now Besicovitch was not totally satisfied. He had proved an if-proposition and now sought to find an if-and-only-if-proposition. Ironically, in this way he was able to show that Sraffa's original intuition of a definition in terms of a tax was equivalent to the definition in terms of linear dependence. What was missing was the correct formalization of this intuition. The proof of the if-and-only-if-proposition was eventually contained in a letter sent to Sraffa on 25 December 1957. On that day we read in Sraffa's diary: "Besicovitch (prova non-basics in multiple syst.)". However, Sraffa decided to include neither the statement nor the proof of the if-and-only-if-proposition in his book. Here is the letter by Besicovitch:

25.12.1957

Dear Sraffa,

Given a system of $m + n$ equations

$$\sum_{j=1}^{m}(a_{ij}y_j + a'_{ij})x_j + \sum_{j=m+1}^{m+n} a_{ij}x_j = 0 \quad i = 1, 2, \dots, m + n = k$$

which for $y_1 = \cdots = y_m = 0$ is satisfied by $x_1^0, x_2^0, \dots, x_{m+n}^0$ of which not all $x_{m+1}^0, \dots, x_{m+n}^0$ are $= 0$.

A necessary & sufficient condition for the system to be satisfied for any $y_1, \dots, y_m$ & $x_{m+1} = x_{m+1}^0, \dots, x_{m+n} = x_{m+n}^0$ is that the rank of

$$\begin{vmatrix} a_{11}, & , & a'_{11}, & , & a_{12}, & , & a'_{12}, & , & \dots & , & a_{1m} & , & a'_{1m} \\ a_{21} & . & . & . & . & . & . & . & . & . & . & . & . \\ . & . & . & . & . & . & . & . & . & . & . & . & . \\ a_{kl} & . & . & . & . & . & . & . & . & . & . & . & . \end{vmatrix} \qquad (1)$$

be $\leq m$.

The sufficiency c[on]d[itio]n is obvious.

The necessity. Let $x_j^0, j = m+1, \ldots, m+n$ be values of $x_{m+1}, \ldots, x_{m+n}$ satisfying the eqns for all $y_1, \ldots, y_m$. Writing $\sum_{m+1}^{m+n} a_{ij}x_j^0 = b_j$ we conclude that the rank of the matrix

$$\begin{vmatrix} a_{11}y_{11} + a'_{11} & , & \ldots & , & a_{1m}y_m + a'_{1m} & , & b_1 \\ . & & . \; \ldots \; . & & . & , & . \\ a_{k1}y_1 + a'_{k1} & , & \ldots & . & . & , & b_k \end{vmatrix}$$

is $\leq m$ for all $y_1, \ldots, y_m$. Consequently the determinant of each of the matrix formed by any $m+1$ lines of the above matrix is $= 0$, e.g.

$$\begin{vmatrix} a_{11}y_{11} + a'_{11} & , & \ldots & , & a_{1m}y_m + a'_{1m} & , & b_1 \\ . & & . \; \ldots \; . & & . & , & . \\ a_{m+1,\,11}y_1 + a'_{k1} & , & \ldots & . & . & , & b_k \end{vmatrix} = 0$$

Representing this determinant as a polynomial in $y_1, \ldots, y_m$ we conclude that its coefficients are $= 0$ that is the determinant of order $m+1$ formed from (1) by taking one column of each of the two

$$\begin{matrix} a_{1j}, & a'_{1j} & j = 1, \ldots, m & \text{\& the column} & b_1 & \text{is always} = 0 \\ . & . & & & . & \\ . & . & & & . & \\ a_{kj}, & a'_{kj} & j = 1, \ldots, m & & b_k & \end{matrix}$$

If suppose the rank of $\begin{vmatrix} a'_{12} & , & \ldots & , & a'_{1m} & , & b_1 \\ a'_{m2} & , & \ldots & , & a'_{mm} & , & b_m \end{vmatrix}$ is m

Then denoting l_i the i-th line we have

$$l_{m+1} = p_1 l_1 + \cdots + p_m l_m$$

where $p_1, \ldots, p_m$ are constants. If either

$$a'_{m+1,1} \neq p_1 a'_{11} + \cdots + p_m a'_{m1} \text{ or } a_{m+1,1} \neq p_1 a_{11} + \cdots + p_m a_{m1}$$

then either

$$\begin{vmatrix} a'_{11} & a'_{12} & \ldots & a'_{1m} & b_1 \\ . & . & . & . & . \\ a'_{m+1,1} & . & . & . & . \end{vmatrix} \neq 0$$

$$\text{or} \begin{vmatrix} a_{11} & a'_{12} & \ldots & a'_{1m} & b_1 \\ . & . & . & . & . \\ a_{m+1,1} & a'_{m+1,2} & & . & b_{m+1} \end{vmatrix} \neq 0$$

which is impossible. In this way we see that if λ_i is the i-th line of (1)

$$\lambda_{m+1} = p_1\lambda_1 + \cdots + p_m\lambda_m$$

i.e. λ_{m+1} is a linear combination of $\lambda_1, \ldots, \lambda_m$. Similarly so are $\lambda_{m+2}, \ldots, \lambda_{m+n}$.

Yours ASB

All is for given, but possible, value of R.

x_j price untaxed.

$y_j x_j$ price taxed (i.e. if taxed 100% $y_j = 2$)

m are taxable commodities (non-basic)

n are basic

(D3/12/94)

The intricate problem of defining basics and non-basics in systems with joint production had at long last been solved to Sraffa's satisfaction. A month later, on 29 January 1958, we find in Sraffa's diary the exclamation: "Filled last gap in my work (Rent) FINIS".

6. Concluding remarks

The paper deals with the collaboration between Piero Sraffa and Abram Samoilovitch Besicovitch in two fields of interest of Sraffa's while working on *Production of Commodities by Means of Commodities* in the first half of the 1940s and the second half of the 1950s. The first concerns the treatment of fixed capital and the problem of depreciation and the second the distinction between basic and non-basic commodities in the case of joint production. The paper reconstructs the progress of Sraffa's work over time and the kind of problems he faced. Given the mathematical nature of several of these problems and Sraffa's inadequate training in mathematics he had to seek the assistance of mathematicians, especially that of his elder friend Besicovitch who was of 'invaluable help' to him.

In the case of fixed capital a solution was easily found together with Besicovitch in early 1943 once Sraffa had understood that his objectivist approach to the theory of value and distribution necessitated the adoption of the joint-products approach which regards "durable instruments of production as part of the annual intake of a process, . . . while what is left of them at the end of the year will be treated as a portion of the annual joint product of the industry, of which the more conspicuous part consists of the marketable commodity that is the primary object of the process" (Sraffa 1960: 63).

As regards the distinction between basics and nonbasics, things were much more complex. In order to understand the chronology and logic of the path followed by the two scholars requires an intricate story to be unravelled. Originally Sraffa intended to devote only a single chapter to the problem of joint production. Shortly after he had drafted the chapter in spring 1957, he saw that the distinction between the two types of commodities developed for single production did not carry over to joint production. The two criteria – that of "entering directly or indirectly all commodities", on the one hand, and that of "being a part of the Standard commodity", on the other, which coincided in the former case no longer did so in the latter. Sraffa tried hard to get out of the impasse, but did not succeed and eventually turned to Besicovitch for help. Alas, while the two made some progress, Besicovitch had to admit that the problem was too difficult for him – "I am at my worst on purely formal algebra". Hence the two sought the assistance of some further Cambridge mathematicians, especially John Arthur Todd. The problem was finally solved to Sraffa's satisfaction in terms of a definition of non-basics by linear dependence in November 1957. This is the solution we find in Sraffa's 1960 book. Interestingly, Sraffa did not include Besicovitch's formalization of Sraffa's original intuition of defining basics and non-basics in terms of whether a tax on them would, or would not, affect the rate of profits (and relative prices). This formalization Besicovitch elaborated in late December 1957.

It was only after this problem had finally been solved that Sraffa could swiftly complete the manuscript of his book by the end of January 1958.

Acknowledgements

We should like to thank Pierangelo Garegnani, literary executor of Sraffa's papers and correspondence, for granting us permission to quote from them. The papers are kept at the Wren Library, Trinity College, Cambridge. References to the papers follow the catalogue prepared by Jonathan Smith, archivist. Unless otherwise stated, all emphases are in the original. We should also like to thank Ian Steedman for valuable help with the presentation of the argument and the participants at the Conference 'Piero Sraffa' organized by the Accademia Nazionale dei Lincei for useful discussions. Last but not least we owe sincere thanks to Jonathan Smith and the staff of the Wren Library for continuous assistance while carrying out the project. We should like to stress that the views contained in our essay have not been discussed with the other participants in the project of preparing an edition of Sraffa's papers and correspondence we are involved in and therefore do not implicate them.

Notes

1 This section draws heavily on Burkill (1971) and Taylor (1975).
2 Recall that during the 1930s Sraffa was not working on his constructive task.
3 See, for instance, documents D3/12/34: 18, 19, 27.
4 In private conversation with one of us, Georg Kreisel (born 1923), who had studied mathematics at Trinity College and who knew both Besicovitch and Sraffa, pointed out that the two shared similar political views and orientations. (Kreisel is an eminent representative of proof theory and the metamathematics of constructivity; from 1955–57 he was a visitor to the Institute for Advanced Study in Princeton, collaborating with Kurt Gödel, and from 1962 until his retirement in 1985 Professor at Stanford University.)
5 Swinnerton-Dyer (born 1927) was a Research Fellow of Mathematics of Trinity College, 1950–4, and later became a Professor of Mathematics at Cambridge University. Todd (1908–98) was a Lecturer in Mathematics at the University of Cambridge, 1937–60, and a Reader in Geometry; he was a Fellow and then the Master of Downing College.

6 This document was produced in August 1942, but folder D3/12/5, labelled by Sraffa "Notes on looms", includes also several notes on this issue written in winter 1927–28.
7 For a more detailed discussion of this aspect, see Kurz 2003.
8 These systems led eventually to Chapter I and §§ 4–5 of Chapter II of his 1960 book.
9 "If we reckon the value of the fixed capital employed as a part of the advances, we must reckon the remaining value of such capital at the end of the year as a part of the annual returns" (Malthus 1836: 269).
10 The references are to the French editions of *Capital* and of the *Theories of Surplus Value*.
11 References to this kind of literature are already to be found in the late 1920s; see, in particular, Sraffa's excerpts from Baily (1808) in D3/12/7: 146–452.
12 Sraffa, who read German, had studied Knut Wicksell's *Über Wert, Kapital und Rente nach den neueren nationalökonomischen Theorien* (Wicksell 1893). When in 1934 an English translation of Knut Wicksell's *Förelasingar i Nationalekonomi*, originally published in Swedish in 1901, came out in two volumes (Wicksell 1934) Sraffa had also access to the *Lectures*. As is well known, Wicksell's theory of value, production and distribution drew heavily on Eugen von Böhm-Bawerk's Austrian theory. The latter generally assumes unidirectional processes of production of finite length in which the services of one or several original factors of production, labour (and land), via one or several intermediate products (e.g. a machine), eventually mature and result in the output of a consumption good (e.g. bread).
13 Sraffa's reference is obviously to labour values.
14 We corrected some typos in the second equation.
15 He dealt with the problem of Reduction again in January 1943 – see D3/12/33: 83 – but it was clear that the respective method could not be applied in general in the case of fixed capital.
16 Actually in the document we read '$B_a p_b + C_a p_b$ materials and $L_a w$ labour', but the typo is obvious.
17 There appears to be only one later document dealing with fixed capital which refers to Besicovitch (see D3/12/41: 8). It is in his hand and contains some calculations, but does not appear to be of great interest.
18 The reconstruction of how and why Sraffa adopted this procedure and how it was related to his discussions with Alister Watson is investigated in Kurz-Salvadori (2001).
19 This remark requires that the system of production is regular in the sense of Schefold (1976).
20 Obviously, there are also n other values of R such that $\mathbf{p}_1 = 0$ and $\mathbf{p}_2$ is a solution of the equation

$$[\mathbf{T}_2 - (1 + R)\mathbf{T}_1]\mathbf{p}_2 = \mathbf{0}.$$

21 Obviously, there are also n other values of R such that

$$\mathbf{q}^T[\mathbf{B}_1 - (1 + R)\mathbf{A}_1] = \mathbf{0}^T \text{ and } \mathbf{q}^T\mathbf{C} = \mathbf{u}^T$$

where $\mathbf{u}$ is a solution to the equation

$$\mathbf{u}^T[\mathbf{T}_2 - (1 + R)\mathbf{T}_1] = \mathbf{0}^T.$$

22 On the left margin of this passage Sraffa asks: "is this true?".
23 To this sentence Sraffa adds: "and there is always a singular value of R for which this is true".
24 The date on the letter was added by Sraffa.
25 In a footnote appended to the last R he added: "As with single products . . . we disregard the freak solution in which R is equal to the ratio of the non-basic on both sides of each

eq.[uation] which it enters. Also in what follows it is assumed that all such freak values of *R* are ruled out/excluded from cons.[ideration]" (*ibid.*)

26 The reference appears to be to Michael Peter Drazin (born 1929) who was a Fellow of Trinity College from 1952 to 1956. (Jonathan Smith has kindly provided us with this information.) In private correspondence we learned from Professor Drazin, now Emeritus at Purdue University, that at the time when Besicovitch wrote his letter "I had just (less than two weeks earlier) emigrated to the U.S.".

27 Besicovitch added "real".

28 The manuscript breaks off here.

References

Baily F., 1808. *The Doctrine of Interest and Annuities Analytically Investigated and Explained. Together with Several Useful Tables Connected with the Subject*, London: sold by John Richardson, Royal Exchange.

Burkill J. C., 1971. *Abram Samoilovitch Besicovitch. 1891–1970*, in "Biographical Memoirs of Fellows of the Royal Society" 17: 1–16.

Kurz H. D., 2003. *Sraffa's Early Studies of the Problem of Fixed Capital: Towards an 'Atomic Analysis'*, manuscript, Graz.

Kurz H. D., Salvadori N., 1993. *The "Standard commodity" and Ricardo's Search for an "invariable measure of value"*, in M. Baranzini, G. C. Harcourt (eds), *The Dynamics of the Wealth of Nations. Growth, Distribution and Structural Change. Essays in Honour of Luigi Pasinetti*, St. Martin's Press, New York: 95–123.

Kurz H. D., Salvadori N., 2001. *Sraffa and the Mathematicians: Frank Ramsey and Alister Watson*, in T. Cozzi, R. Marchionatti (eds), *Piero Sraffa's Political Economy. A Centenary Estimate*, Routledge, London-New York: 254–284.

Malthus T. R., 1836. *Principles of Political Economy Considered with a View to Their Practical Application*, first ed. 1820, revised and enlarged edition, William Pickering, London.

Marx K., 1954. *Capital*, vol. I, Progress Publishers, Moscow. English translation of *Das Kapital*, vol. I (1867), Meissner, Hamburg.

Pradella P., 1915. *Algebra ed Aritmetica: ad uso dei licei*, G. B. Paravia, Turin.

Schefold B., 1976. *Relative Prices as a Function of the Profit Rate: A Mathematical Note*, Zeitschrift für Nationalökonomie 36: 21–48.

Sraffa P., 1960. *Production of Commodities by Means of Commodities*, Cambridge University Press, Cambridge.

Taylor S. J., 1975. *Abram Samoilovitch Besicovitch*, Bull. London Math. Soc. 7: 191–210.

Torrens R., 1818. *Strictures on Mr. Ricardo's Doctrine Respecting Exchangeable Value*, Edinburgh Magazine, October: 335–338.

Wicksell K., 1893. *Über Wert, Kapital und Rente nach den neueren nationalökonomischen Theorien*, Fischer, Jena. Translated into English as *Value, Capital and Rent*, Allen & Unwin, London 1950.

Wicksell K., [1901] 1934. *Lectures on Political Economy*, vol. I, translation from the Swedish of the third ed. (first edn 1901), George Routledge & Sons, London.

Part III

Linear theory of production

An assessment

10 Von Neumann, the classical economists and Arrow–Debreu*

Some notes

Heinz D. Kurz and Neri Salvadori

1. Introduction

John von Neumann gave his paper on equi-proportionate growth for the first time in the Winter of 1932 at the Mathematical Seminar of Princeton University where he had been offered a professorship in 1931. In 1936 he gave the paper in Karl Menger's Mathematical Colloquium at the University of Vienna. The paper was published for the first time in German in the proceedings of the colloquium, *Ergebnisse eines mathematischen Kolloquiums* (von Neumann, 1937).[1] In 1945, upon the initiative of Nicholas Kaldor who was a friend of von Neumann's, an English translation of the paper was published in the *Review of Economic Studies*, which was then edited by Kaldor, together with a commentary by the Oxford economist David Champernowne (von Neumann, 1945; Champernowne, 1945).

Von Neumann's paper is rightly famous in economics, although it has repeatedly been maintained that from an economic as opposed to a mathematical point of view the paper is not all that interesting. One author even contended that the paper contains "not very good economics" (Koopmans, 1974). We do not agree with this judgement, which assesses the model against the background of a particular point of view, neoclassical analysis, of which von Neumann was critical (see Section 3 below). From another point of view, that of classical analysis, the von Neumann model turns out to be a very important contribution to the theory of "normal" prices, or "prices of production", and income distribution in the tradition of such authors as William Petty, the Physiocrats, the English Classical economists, especially David Ricardo and Robert Torrens, Vladimir K. Dmitriev, Ladislaus von Bortkiewicz and Georg von Charasoff, a tradition which culminated in the work of Piero Sraffa (1960). In this paper we make an attempt to clarify the issues at hand. We do this partly with recourse to previous contributions by us to an interpretation of the von Neumann model (Kurz and Salvadori, 1993; 1995, ch. 13; 2001). However, we add further flesh to our argument and present it more succinctly and, hopefully, also more convincingly.[2]

The composition of the paper is the following. *Section 2* provides a discussion of the analytical structure of the classical approach to the theory of value

* Reprinted with permission from *Acta Oeconomica*, 54(1), 2004.

and distribution and its constitutive substantive elements. The emphasis will be on the classical economists' concern with the properties of the economic system as a whole, conceived of as a system of production, income distribution, and given needs and wants. These properties refer first and foremost to the system of prices supporting a given system of production, and the way in which its surplus product is distributed amongst different groups of society (workers, capitalists and landlords) in conditions of free competition. The properties concern necessary relationships between what are the unknowns or dependent variables of the problem under consideration imposed by the data or independent variables, which determine the former magnitudes. *Section 3* expounds briefly the salient features of the von Neumann model. It is shown that both its long-period method, its analytical structure and its constitutive elements are classical in spirit. The emphasis is on the capacity of the economic system to generate a physical surplus and the distribution of the surplus in terms of a uniform rate of return on capital. Interestingly, in von Neumann's paper the problem of scarcity plays no role whatsoever. *Section 4* turns to the Arrow–Debreu model and specifies its alternative neoclassical, short-period features. Here the problem of scarcity assumes centre stage of the analysis. A main assumption of the model are given initial endowments of the economy of all sorts of physically and temporally specified factors of production: capital goods' services, labour services and the services of natural resources, including land. *Section 5* compares the von Neumann model and neoclassical models; the emphasis will be on the Arrow–Debreu model and especially on one important assumption in each of the two models. These concern von Neumann's premiss that each and every commodity enters and/or exits each and every process of production and the premiss of Arrow–Debreu that each agent possesses an initial endowment that allows him to survive. Interestingly, some interpreters have maintained that the two assumptions are equivalent. It will be shown that they are not, and that they highlight the fact that the two models belong conceptually to two different traditions of economic thought. *Section 6* contains some concluding remarks.

2. Classical theory[3]

The economy experienced by the classical economists from William Petty to David Ricardo typically generated an annual *social surplus* which was distributed amongst the propertied classes in the form of rents or profits, and was used for the purposes of consumption and capital accumulation. The surplus refers to those quantities of the different commodities that were left over after the necessary means of production had been used up and the means of subsistence in the support of workers have been deducted from the gross outputs produced during a year. In this conceptualisation the necessary real wages of labour were considered no less indispensable as inputs, and thus agents of production, than raw materials, tools, or machines. What became known as the "surplus interpretation" of the classical economists focuses attention on the mature classical economists' approach to how the surplus is distributed and which system of exchange values of the different commodities can be expected to emerge as the result of the gravitation of "market" or "actual" prices to their "natural" or "ordinary" levels, or "prices of production". In conditions of *free competition* – that is, in the absence of significant barriers to entry and exit from all markets – prices can be taken to oscillate around levels characterised by a *uniform rate of profits* (or *interest*) on the value of the capital advanced at the beginning of the uniform production period and a uniform rate of rent for each of the different qualities of land.

The determination of the general rate of profits, the rents of land, and the corresponding system of relative prices constitutes the analytical centrepiece of classical political economy. It was designed to lay the foundation of all other economic analysis, including the investigation of capital accumulation and technical progress; of development and growth; of social transformation and structural change; and of taxation and public debt. The pivotal role of the theory of value and distribution can be inferred from the fact that the latter is typically developed right at the beginning of major classical works: think of Adam Smith's *Wealth of Nations* (WN, I, vi–xi), or of David Ricardo's *Principles* (*Works*, I, chs I–VI).

The classical economists were concerned with the laws governing the emerging capitalist economy, characterised by the stratification of society into three classes: workers, land owners, and the rising class of capitalists; wage labour as the dominant form of the appropriation of other people's capacity to work; an increasingly sophisticated division of labour within and among firms; the coordination of economic activity via a system of interdependent markets in which transactions were mediated through money; and significant technical, organisational, and institutional change. In short, they were concerned with an economic system that was incessantly in motion. How should one analyse such a system? The ingenious device of the classical authors for seeing through the complexities of the modern economy consisted in distinguishing between the "actual" values of the relevant variables – the distributive rates and prices – and their "natural", "normal" or "necessary" values. The former were taken to reflect all kinds of influences, many of an accidental or temporary nature, about which no general propositions were possible. The latter were instead seen to express the persistent, non-accidental and non-temporary factors governing the economic system as a whole and guaranteeing its reproduction and possible expansion. Only these could be systematically studied. Accordingly, the attention focused on the determination of the normal rate of profits and normal prices.

The classical economists proceeded essentially in two steps. In the first they isolated the kinds of factors that were seen to determine income distribution and the system of relative prices supporting that distribution in specified conditions, that is, *in a given place and time*. The theory of value and distribution was designed to identify *in abstracto* the dominant factors at work and to analyse their interaction. In a second step, the classical authors then turned to an investigation of the causes that, *over time*, affected the factors at work from within the economic system, i.e. *endogenously*. This involved the classical analysis of capital accumulation, technical and organisational change, economic growth and socio-economic development.

It is another characteristic feature of the classical approach to profits, rents and relative prices that these are explained essentially in terms of magnitudes that can, in principle, be observed, measured or calculated. The *objectivist* orientation of classical economics has received its perhaps strongest expression in a famous proclamation by William Petty, who was arguably its founding father. Keen to assume what he called the "physician's" outlook, Petty in his *Political Arithmetic* (1690) stressed:

> "The Method I take to do this, is not yet very usual; for instead of using only comparative and superlative Words, and intellectual Arguments, I have taken the course (as a Specimen of the Political Arithmetic I have long aimed at) to express my self in Terms of *Number, Weight* or *Measure*; to use only Arguments of Sense, and to consider only such Causes, as have visible foundations in Nature; leaving those that depend upon the mutable Minds, Opinions, Appetites and Passions of particular Men, to the Consideration of others . . . ."
> (Petty, [1899] 1986, p. 244; emphases in the original)

This brings us to the substantive part of the problem under consideration. *Five aspects* are especially worth noting in the context of the present comparative study.

2.1 Production as a circular flow

First, the concept of production the classical economists deemed appropriate to the kind of interdependent economy under investigation was that of a *circular flow*. This idea can be traced back to William Petty and Richard Cantillon and was most effectively expressed by François Quesnay in the *Tableau économique*, which foreshadowed Marx's schemes of reproduction and Leontief's input-output analysis. Actually the classical economists, at least in some of their analyses, advocated the radical view that commodities are in the last instance produced by commodities. Thus, James Mill in his *Elements of Political Economy* insisted that the agents of production are the commodities themselves (Mill, 1826, p. 165), that is, (a) the food of the labourer; (b) the tools and the machinery with which he works; and (c) the raw materials that he works upon.

2.2 Physical real cost

This view led naturally to the concept of *physical real cost*. Man cannot create matter, man can only change its form, decompose and recompose it, and move it. Production involves destruction, and the real cost of a commodity consists in the commodities destroyed in the course of its production.

2.3 Labour

In the writings of the classical economists the size of the work force is seen essentially as generated by the accumulation process itself. In other words, labour power is treated as a kind of producible commodity. It differs from other commodities in that it is not produced in a capitalistic way by a special industry on a par with other industries, but is the result of the interplay between the generative behaviour of the working population and socio-economic conditions. In the simplest conceptualisation possible, labour power is seen to be in infinitely elastic supply at a given real wage rate. Increasing the amount of real wages involves a proportional increase of the work force. In this view the rate of growth of labour supply adjusts to any given rate of growth of labour demand without necessitating a variation in the real wage rate.[4] Labour can thus put no limit to growth because it is "generated" within the growth process itself. The only limit to growth can come from other, non-accumulable factors of production.

2.4 Natural resources, especially land

The classical economists were first and foremost concerned with commodities that can be produced and *reproduced*. This case is best studied by setting aside the only candidate for bringing the concept of *scarcity* into the classical frame of thought, that is, the limited availability of natural resources. Setting aside scarce natural resources and taking the set of methods of production from which cost-minimising producers can choose as given (i.e. setting aside technical improvements), the economy could grow forever. Interestingly, the champion of extensive and intensive diminishing returns and the corresponding concepts of extensive and intensive rent in classical political economy, David Ricardo himself, contemplated this case. In a letter to Malthus dated 18 December 1814 he wrote:

> "Accumulation of capital has a tendency to lower profits. Why? Because every accumulation is attended with increased difficulty in obtaining food, unless it is accompanied with improvements in agriculture; in which case it has no tendency to diminish profits. *If there were no increased difficulty, profits would never fall, because there are no other limits to the profitable production of manufactures but the rise of wages. If with every accumulation of capital we could tack a piece of fresh fertile land to our Island, profits would never fall.*"
>
> (Ricardo, VI, p. 162; emphasis added)

Similarly, in his letter to Malthus of 17 October 1815 he stated that

> "... profits do not *necessarily* fall with the increase of the quantity of capital because the demand for capital is infinite and is governed by the same law as population itself. They are both checked by the rise in the price of food, and the consequent increase in the value of labour. *If there were no such rise, what could prevent population and capital from increasing without limit*?"
>
> (Ricardo, VI, p. 301; first emphasis in the original)

If land of the best quality were abundant (and its ownership sufficiently dispersed), its use would be a *free good*: there could be no rent paid to the landowner

(Ricardo, I, p. 69). From an economic point of view land may therefore be ignored like air or sunlight.

2.5 Fixed capital and joint production

In the classical economists we encounter both a discussion of the role of fixed capital in production and distribution and of joint production. Here the following aspects deserve mentioning. As regards fixed capital, it was Robert Torrens who first suggested to treat what is left of fixed capital at the end of the production period as a kind of joint product. Thereafter the method was generally adopted by Ricardo, Malthus, James Mill and Marx (Sraffa, 1960, pp. 94–95). The fact that joint production proper was ubiquitous did, of course, not escape the attention of the classical authors: cases of wool and mutton, corn and straw, etc., could hardly be overlooked. Adam Smith pointed out that with joint production the proportion in which the products can be produced need not coincide with those in which they are wanted. Hence some products may be overproduced, with the consequence that "the greater part of them would be thrown away as things of no value" (Smith, 1976, I,xi,c.4). Here we encounter, possibly for the first time in the history of economic thought, the application of the *Rule of Free Goods* to products. (As we have seen under (4) that rule was also known to the classical economists as regards natural resources that are in excess supply.)

3. The von Neumann model

Nicholas Kaldor who knew von Neumann from Budapest, their home town, recalls that "One day he expressed an interest in economics and he asked me whether I could suggest a short book which gives a formal mathematical exposition of prevailing economic theory" (Kaldor, 1989, p. viii). Kaldor suggested Knut Wicksell's *Über Wert, Kapital und Rente nach den neueren nationalökonomischen Theorien* (cf. Wicksell, 1893; 1954). "He read it in a very short time and expressed some scepticism of the 'marginalist' approach on the grounds that it gives too much emphasis to substitutability and too little to *the forces which make for mutually conditioned expansion*." According to Kaldor, von Neumann subsequently had a look at the original Walrasian equations (cf. Walras, [1874] 1954): "He told me afterwards that they provide no genuine solution, since the equations can result in negative prices (or quantities) just as well as positive ones" (Kaldor, 1989, p. viii; emphasis added). Thus, while the works of Wicksell and Walras, two foremost marginalist authors, appear to have been a source of inspiration to von Neumann, according to Kaldor's recollection he was not only dissatisfied with the fact that no proper proof of equilibrium was provided but also with the economic substance of the argument put forward.

There is no evidence that John von Neumann was familiar with the writings of the classical economists or those working in that tradition, such as the eminent statistician and economic theorist Ladislaus von Bortkiewicz who was von Neumann's colleague at the University of Berlin during the latter's staying there from 1927 to 1929 as a *Privatdozent*. Von Neumann may have met von Bortkiewicz and talked to him, but we are not aware of any document confirming this. The interesting thing to note here is that despite his reported acquaintance with major contributions of two major marginalist authors, von Neumann would develop a model which determines relative prices, the rate of interest, relative quantities and the rate of growth in a manner which is decidedly different from the marginalist one, passing over both consumer preferences and initial endowments of factors. Instead he would put forward a model which in crucial respects exhibits a close family resemblance with the theory of the classical economists, relying exclusively on magnitudes that can be observed and measured.

Before we demonstrate this, one observation is apposite. As we have argued in some detail in another paper (cf. Kurz and Salvadori, 1993), the proximate starting point of von Neumann's paper was in all probability a paper by Robert Remak, a colleague of John von Neumann at the Berlin Institute of Mathematics. Remak's paper of 1929 was entitled *Kann die Volkswirtschaftslehre eine exakte Wissenschaft werden? (Can Economics Become an Exact Science?)*. Interestingly, similar to von Neumann, Remak was also critical of the received marginalist approach in terms of demand and supply functions and maintained that the behaviour of agents which is at the back of such functions "can be neither experimentally nor theoretically ascertained quantitatively" (Remak, 1929, p. 712). He therefore suggested the concept of "superposed prices" whose determination presupposes nothing but the knowledge of the socio-technical relations of production, that is, the methods of production in use and the needs and wants of producers. The system investigated by Remak is a system of single production (joint production is not considered), and thus is only circulating capital, which produces just enough of each commodity (e.g. corn) to replace what has been productively consumed of it during the year in terms of means of production (e.g., seed corn) and means of sustenance of producers (e.g., corn as a consumption good). We may characterise Remak's model as a simple classical model of production without a surplus, or, using Sraffa's concept, of "production for subsistence" (Sraffa, 1960, ch. I). Remak gave his paper at a meeting of the Berlin Mathematical Society and his ideas were discussed at the Institute of Mathematics in Berlin. There is also reason to presume that von Neumann was familiar with Remak's contribution and was critical of it (Kurz and Salvadori, 1993, pp. 148–149). A comparison of von Neumann's model with that of Remak shows that the former is in every respect more general than the latter, and that whenever Remak drops an idea or poses a question that is beyond the scope of his own model, von Neumann offers a conceptualisation and provides an answer.[5]

In his paper von Neumann assumed that there are n goods which can be produced by m constant returns to scale production processes. The problem was to establish which processes will actually be used and which not, being "unprofitable". Von Neumann (1945) based his analysis on the following assumptions:

(1) "Goods are produced not only from 'natural factors of production', but *in the first place from each other*. These processes of production may be *circular*" (*ibid.*, p. 1; emphases added). In fact, in von Neumann's paper natural factors

of production are either set aside (land) or hidden (labour); see the following two paragraphs. This is reminiscent of the circular flow perspective of the classical economists and especially of James Mill's dictum: "the agents of production are the commodities themselves".

(2) "Consumption of goods takes place only through the processes of production which include necessities of life consumed by workers and employees" (*ibid.*, p. 2). Von Neumann thus takes the real wage rate, consisting of the "necessities of life", to be given and paid at the beginning of the uniform period of production, and therefore like the classical economists reckons real wages among the capital to be advanced *(ibid.)*. In von Neumann's view, as in that of the classical economists, costs are thus essentially *physical real costs*: means of production and means of subsistence.

(3) As regards labour and land he assumed that they cannot limit the growth of the economic system: "the natural factors of production, including labour, can be expanded in unlimited quantities" *(ibid.)*. His assumptions are equivalent to those discussed under (3) and (4) in *Section 2*, where labour is in infinitely elastic supply at a given real wage rate and "with every accumulation of capital we [can] tack a piece of fresh fertile land to our [economy]" as Ricardo put it (Ricardo, VI, p. 162).

(4) The processes of production "can describe the special case where good G_j can be produced only jointly with certain others, viz. its permanent joint products" (Neumann, 1945, p. 2). Hence, both circulating and fixed capital can be dealt with: "wear and tear of capital goods are to be described by introducing different stages of wear as different goods, using a separate P_i [process i] for each of these" *(ibid.)*. This is the joint-products method that we encountered in (5) in the previous section. It effectively reduces fixed capital to circulating.

(5) Since he allowed for universal joint production, von Neumann also had to face the problem of overproduction of some products. In this he had recourse to the Rule of Free Goods we already encountered: "if there is excess production of G_j, G_j becomes a free good and its price $[p_j] = 0$" (*ibid.*, p. 3).

(6) Finally, he assumed "that all income in excess of necessities of life will be reinvested" (*ibid.*, p. 2). According to this assumption interest receivers are "mere investing machines" (Lancaster).

Von Neumann's approach can be summarised as follows. Let **A** and **B** be the $m \times n$ input and output matrices, respectively, where **A** includes the means of subsistence in the support of workers; and let $\mathbf{q}$ be the m-dimensional vector of activity levels and $\mathbf{p}$ the n-dimensional price vector. Let $\alpha = 1+g$ be the expansion factor, where g is the expansion or growth rate; let $\beta = 1+r$ be the interest factor, where r is the rate of interest (or rate of profits). The model is subject to the following axioms.

$$\mathbf{q}^T\mathbf{B} \geqq \alpha\mathbf{q}^T\mathbf{A} \tag{1a}$$

$$\mathbf{Bp} \leqq \beta\mathbf{Ap} \tag{1b}$$

$$\mathbf{q}^T(\mathbf{B} - \alpha\mathbf{A})\mathbf{p} = 0 \tag{1c}$$

$$\mathbf{q}^T(\mathbf{B} - \beta\mathbf{A})\mathbf{p} = 0 \tag{1d}$$

$$\mathbf{q} \geq \mathbf{0} \text{ and } \mathbf{p} \geq \mathbf{0} \tag{1e}$$

Axiom (1a) implies that α times the inputs for a given period are not larger than the outputs of the previous period. Axiom (1b) is the no extra profits condition. Axiom (1c) states the free disposal assumption. Axiom (1d) implies that processes that incur extra costs will not be operated. Finally, (1e) requires that both the intensity and the price vector are semipositive. In order to demonstrate that for any pair of non-negative matrices **A** and **B** there exist solutions for **q** and **p** and for $\alpha, \alpha \geq 0$, and $\beta, \beta \geq 0$, von Neumann in addition assumes:

$$\mathbf{A} + \mathbf{B} > \mathbf{0}, \tag{1f}$$

which implies that every process requires as an input or produces as an output some positive amount of every good.

On the basis of these givens von Neumann demonstrates the existence of a solution. He determines (a) which processes will be operated; (b) at what rate the economic system will grow; (c) what prices will obtain; (d) what the rate of interest will be; and (e) that, of necessity, $\alpha = \beta$, i.e. the growth and the interest factor are equal.

As mentioned above, the stimulation to publish an English version of the paper came from Nicholas Kaldor, then chairman of the editorial committee of *The Review of Economic Studies*. Kaldor arranged also for the translation of the paper and was concerned with rendering the mathematically demanding paper attractive to an audience of economists. A first step in the pursuit of this goal appears to have been the adaptation of the paper's title (cf. Kaldor, 1989, p. x), a literal translation of the original German version of which would have been "On an economic system of equations and a generalisation of Brouwer's Fixed Point Theorem". The second part of the title which reflects von Neumann's assessment that the main achievement of the paper consisted in the generalisation of a mathematical theorem was dropped entirely, and the neutral term "economic system of equations" was replaced by the not so neutral term "model of general economic equilibrium".

The second step consisted in asking David Champernowne, "the most mathematically minded economist I knew, to write an explanatory paper *ad usum delphini*, for the use of the semi-numerates, to appear alongside it in the *Review of Economic Studies*" (*ibid.*, p. x).[6] In a footnote to the introduction of his paper, Champernowne thanks Nicholas Kaldor for help with economic ideas, and Sraffa and Crum for "instruction in subjects discussed in this article" (Champernowne, 1945, p. 10, n. 1). Interestingly, in Champernowne's interpretation von Neumann's model emerges as one characterised by essentially "classical" features. This interpretation is fully confirmed by our investigation of the classical economists from Adam Smith to David Ricardo and those authors working in the "classical" tradition prior to von Neumann. Indeed, there are striking similarities between the contributions of these economists and von Neumann. These concern: (a) the concept of production as a circular flow; (b) the concept of the surplus product which forms the basis of an explanation of all shares of income other than wages; (c) the notion of a uniformly expanding economy in which the rate of expansion is determined endogenously, i.e. a "quasi-stationary system"; (d) the concept of duality of the relationship between relative quantities and the rate of growth on the one hand, and that between relative prices and the rate of interest (rate of profits) on the other; (e) the way in which the choice-of-technique problem is approached and the use of inequalities in it; and (f) the way the Rule of Free Goods is applied to primary factors of production and to products, respectively. Von Neumann applied that rule in fact in the same way as the classical economists did. While he assumed "That the natural factors of production, including labour, can be expanded in unlimited quantities" (von Neumann, 1945, p. 2), this did not make him treat all these factors alike. Rather, he singled out labour as the only factor that is exempt from that rule; all other primary factors, although needed in production, "disappear" from the scene because they are taken to be non-scarce.[7] Labour is assumed to receive an exogenously given wage bundle which is independent of the degree of employment.[8]

The contention that von Neumann's approach has been anticipated in all important aspects by authors working in the "classical" tradition is, of course, not meant to play down the importance of von Neumann's contribution. After all it was he who provided a comprehensive and general formulation of what other authors were able to put forward only partially and with respect to special cases, and it was he who was able to prove the existence of a solution.

4. Neoclassical theory

Neoclassical models, whether short- or long-period ones, are typically characterised as follows. The unknowns or dependent variables of the theory are all prices, including the prices of "factor services", wages, rents and capital rentals or the rate of interest, and all quantities produced of the different commodities and the corresponding allocation of given productive resources. Prices are typically interpreted as indexes of scarcity. In conventional neoclassical theory they are determined simultaneously and *symmetrically* in terms of demand and supply, where the latter are conceived of as functions or correspondences. The data or independent variables from which the theory starts are the following:

(a) the initial endowments of the economy of different kinds of labour, land and capital goods and the distribution of property rights among agents;
(b) consumer preferences; and
(c) the set of available methods of production to produce the various commodities.

In *long-period* versions of neoclassical theory such as those of Eugen von Böhm-Bawerk, Knut Wicksell, John Bates Clark down to Robert M. Solow's growth model, the endowment of capital must be given in terms of a single magnitude, otherwise the solution is overdetermined, and there must be a known relation between such a magnitude and the value of capital since the relative scarcity of the "quantity of capital" is supposed to be reflected in the level of the rate of interest. Many, but not all, authors have given it directly as a *value* magnitude. The physical composition of that "quantity" is then supposed to be a part and parcel of the equilibrium solution of the system. This composition has to fulfil the criteria that a uniform rate of return on the supply price of all capital goods obtains – a criteria which with regard to an arbitrarily given vector of quantities of capital goods would only be satisfied by a fluke, that is, as mentioned, the problem would be overdetermined.

In *short-period* versions of neoclassical theory the capital endowment of the economy is instead given in terms of a vector of physically specified amounts of different capital goods. Léon Walras in the first three editions of his *Eléments*, first published in 1874, thought that even with such a physical specification of social capital he would in competitive conditions be able to determine a uniform rate of interest across all heterogeneous capital goods. However, in the fourth edition he saw that this was not generally the case (Kurz and Salvadori, 1995, pp. 22–26 and 439–441). In this case capital goods had rather to be conceived of totally on a par with different kinds of land which yielded their proprietors a rent, provided they were scarce. The general rate of interest (or profit) has therefore to be replaced by rentals specific to the different kinds of capital goods.

A major motive for breaking away from traditional long-period neoclassical theory and the development of temporary and intertemporal equilibrium models had been the capital theoretic problems the former faced and could not satisfactorily solve.[9] These problems surfaced already in the late 1920s and made Erik Lindahl and later John Richard Hicks abandon the long-period method. The intertemporal equilibrium theory made rapid progress and culminated in the publication of the essay *Existence of an equilibrium for a competitive economy* by Arrow and Debreu (1954) followed by Debreu's *Theory of Value* (1959). The model became known as the "Arrow–Debreu model". The starting point of Arrow–Debreu was Walras's theory. They motivated their analysis in the following way:

> "The investigation of the existence of solutions is of interest both for descriptive and for normative economics. Descriptively, the view that the competitive model is a reasonably accurate description of reality, at least for certain purposes, presupposes that the equations describing the model are consistent with each other. Hence, one check on the empirical usefulness of the model is the prescription of the conditions under which the equations of competitive equilibrium have a solution.
>
> Perhaps as important is the relation between the existence of solutions to a competitive equilibrium and the problems of normative or welfare economics."
>
> (Arrow and Debreu, 1954, p. 265)

They emphasised that in order to study this problem, "it is first necessary to specify more carefully than is generally done the precise assumptions of a competitive economy" (*ibid.*, p. 266). In addition to assumptions (a)–(c) above these include:

(1) "There are a finite number of distinct commodities. . . . For the present purposes, the same commodity at two different locations or two different points of time will be regarded as two different commodities" (*ibid.*, p. 266). This implies a *finite, arbitrarily given time horizon of the model.*
(2) "The commodities, or at least some of them, are produced in *production units* (e.g., firms). The number of production units will be assumed to be a finite number *n*" (*ibid.*, p. 266). Arrow and Debreu added: "the list of production units should include not only actually existing ones but those that might enter the market under suitable price conditions" (pp. 266–267). This is designed to take care of the case of factors that are not transferable in the market. To assume a given and constant number of production units implies that *the analysis is short-run.*
(3) Returns are taken to be non-increasing.
(4) "It is impossible to have any output unless there is some input" (*ibid.*, p. 268).
(5) "The number of *consumption units is m" (ibid.).*
(6) The set of consumption vectors "includes all consumption vectors among which the individual could conceivably choose if there were no budgetary restraints. Impossible combinations of commodities, such as the supplying of several types of labour to a total amount of more than 24 hours a day or the consumption of a bundle of commodities insufficient to maintain life, are regarded as excluded from [the set]" (*ibid.*, p. 269).

The Arrow–Debreu model assumes that there exist current markets for *all* commodities, whatever their physical, temporal (within the given time horizon) or spatial specification. Hence, in the "economy" contemplated all trade for the entire time horizon takes place at the beginning of the first period. If markets were reopened at later dates, then no additional trade would take place. As Arrow and Hahn stressed, the hypothesis that there exists a complete set of markets for current goods "'telescopes' the future into the present" (1971, p. 33). Given a set of prices, each agent chooses a plan for all the elementary periods. An equilibrium for a "private ownership economy" requires that all individual plans are, from the initial date onwards, mutually consistent for all future dates and compatible with given initial endowments.

The original Arrow–Debreu model exhibits several features that are disquieting.[10] A major difficulty concerns the treatment of time.

> "The principal objection to the restriction to a finite number of goods is that it requires a finite horizon and there is no natural way to choose the final period. Moreover, since there will be terminal stocks in the final period there is no natural way to value them without contemplating future periods in which they will be used."
>
> (McKenzie, 1987, p. 507)

What the Arrow–Debreu model in fact assumes is that all economic activity stops at the arbitrarily given terminal instant, that is, resources existing at the end of the time horizon have *zero* value. Due to the recursive structure of the model, all economic activities decided in the initial instant are derived with regard to the final period, since it would make no sense to transfer resources from the last but one period to the last one.[11]

As regards the instant from which the economy is analysed, i.e. the "present instant", the question arises whether there has been no economic activity prior to that date. The answer is in the negative: the economy is not created "now"; it is rather assumed that, for the purpose of analysing the economy's future development, the legacy of the past is *exclusively and completely* reflected in the amounts of resources inherited and the distribution of private ownership of these resources. In particular, it is assumed that there are no commitments carrying over from the past that constrain agents' present decisions. This implies of course that the logic of the model does not extend to the past, because otherwise one would have to admit that at some dates in the past agents entered into contracts referring to dates that are still in the future.

As we have seen, earlier neoclassical authors, most notably Walras, were concerned with the long- and short-run equilibrium relationships between the prices of durable capital goods and the prices of their services, that is, the rates of return on different kinds of capital goods, and whether the short-run relationships gravitate towards some long-run relationship characterised by a uniform rate of return throughout the economy. To this effect Walras proposed an explicit *tâtonnement* procedure which he conjectured converged to long-period equilibrium. These concerns are not present in the Arrow–Debreu model. It is not even considered how the economy is supposed to get into equilibrium. The notion of equilibrium is simply one of simultaneous clearing of all markets; there is no discussion of any adjustment process when defining equilibrium. As Arrow and Debreu stressed: "Neither the uniqueness nor the stability of the competitive solution is investigated in this paper" (Arrow and Debreu, 1954, p. 266; similarly Debreu, 1959). As Currie and Steedman (1990, p. 147) stressed, it makes no sense to think in terms of the "rates of return" in the context of the Arrow–Debreu model. This follows from the assumption that all transactions take place at the present instant. They added:

> "Meaningful asset equilibrium conditions – involving uniformity in appropriately defined rates of return – can be established for models which allow for changes in relative prices over time but *only* for those models with spot markets at each date, since, in such models, ownership of a durable good is a way of transferring wealth over time. In contrast, in the Arrow–Debreu model, the notion of transferring wealth over time has no real meaning."

Obviously, to take the capital endowment as given in kind implies that only "short-period" equilibria can be determined. Because firms prefer more profit to less, the size and composition of the capital stock will rapidly change. Thus, major factors which general equilibrium theory envisages as determining prices and quantities are themselves subject to quick changes. This, in turn, makes it difficult to distinguish them from those accidental and temporary factors, which, at any given moment of time, prevent the economy from settling in a position of equilibrium.

More important, the fast variation in relative prices necessitates the consideration of the influence of future states of the world on the present situation. The assumption that all intertemporal and all contingent markets exist, which has the effect of collapsing the future into the present, can be rejected on grounds of realism and economic reasoning (see, for example, Bliss, 1975, pp. 48 and 61). In addition, there is the following conceptual problem (Schefold, 1985). If in equilibrium some of the capital stocks turn out to be in excess supply, these stocks assume zero prices. This possibility appears to indicate that the expectations entrepreneurs held in the past when deciding to build up the present capital stocks are not realised. Hence, strictly speaking we are faced with a *dis*equilibrium situation because otherwise the wrong stocks could not have accumulated. Therefore, the problem arises how the past or, more exactly, possible discrepancies between expectations and facts influence the future.

5. Von Neumann's model and neoclassical theory

We have seen in *Section 3* above that the von Neumann model is a long-period model: It is concerned with determining the competitive rate of interest and normal prices and accomplishes this task because it does not start from a given vector of endowments of heterogeneous capital goods. It would therefore be quite pointless to compare von Neumann's model with any of the short-period neoclassical models. The differences between the two types are all too obvious.[12] In fact, to the best of our knowledge none of the major neoclassical general equilibrium theorists has maintained that their models belong to the kind of models to which von Neumann contributed. However, in the literature one occasionally encounters sweeping statements as to the "neoclassical" derivation of the model. Von Neumann's contribution is typically considered a contribution to the so-called "Walras–Cassel" model as it was discussed by Karl Schlesinger and Abraham Wald in Menger's Vienna colloquium at the beginning of the 1930s. The original Cassel model however had no capital goods but only scarce natural resources, about which Cassel in a second model then assumed that they are all subject to a uniform increase. This assumption of an exogenously given uniform rate of growth of all productive resources seems to have prompted some observers to closely relate the von Neumann model and the Walras–Cassel tradition. Yet this is misleading for a variety of interconnected reasons.

First, as we have already seen, von Neumann is not at all concerned with the problem of *scarcity*, but only with that of *reproducibility*, whereas in the neoclassical model the problem of scarcity of resources occupies centre stage. There are no initial endowments of reproducible and accumulable inputs (capital goods) in the von Neumann model and all non-accumulable inputs (labour, land, etc.) are taken to adjust to the needs of economic growth (labour) or to be available in abundance. The difference between the two kinds of models can also be seen in the fact that von Neumann determines the (steady-state) rate of growth *endogenously*, whereas Cassel (and later Solow, who, unlike Cassel, in his growth model allowed for a choice of technique) took it as given from outside. *Second*, real wages in von Neumann's model are given from outside, while in neoclassical models they are determined by the model. Interest in the von Neumann model is consequently a residual income whose magnitude reflects the capacity of the system to generate a surplus. Interest in the neoclassical model is instead a scarcity price, just like wages.

After having established that von Neumann's model is classical and not neoclassical in spirit, we conclude by showing that a false analogy has been drawn between von Neumann's assumption (1f) (see *Section 3* above) and a crucial assumption of the Arrow–Debreu model.

Initially, it should be stressed that neither Arrow and Debreu (1954) nor Debreu (1959) asserted that the von Neumann model is connected with theirs.[13] The only references to von Neumann (1945) are technical. In Arrow and Debreu (1954, p. 270, fn. 6) it is asserted that the second half of their *assumption IV.a* (on the same page) "plays the same role as the one made by Professor von Neumann in his study of a dynamic model of production . . . that each commodity enters into every production process either as an input or as an output".[14] And in the Preface to Debreu (1959) it is asserted that "A little earlier J. von Neumann . . . had begun to develop, in different contexts, a mathematical tool which was eventually to play an essential role in that area under the definite form as a fixed point theorem it received from S. Kakutani" (p. ix). Hence the relationship between Arrow and Debreu and Debreu on one side, and von Neumann on the other, is relegated to formal aspects only.

It may be of some interest to identify the formal similarities between the two frameworks. In order to do so, the Arrow–Debreu theorems can be seen as giving sufficient conditions of the existence of vectors $\mathbf{y}_j^*$, $\mathbf{x}_i^*$, $\mathbf{p}^*$ such that

$$\mathbf{y}_j^* \in Y_j \tag{2a}$$

$$\mathbf{y}_j^*\mathbf{p}^* \geqq \mathbf{y}_j\mathbf{p}^* \quad \forall \mathbf{y}_j \in Y_j \tag{2b}$$

$$\mathbf{x}_i^* \in \left\{ \mathbf{x}_i \in X_i | \mathbf{x}_i\mathbf{p}^* \leqq \zeta_i\mathbf{p}^* + \sum_{j=1}^{n} \alpha_{ij}\mathbf{p}^*\mathbf{y}_j^* \right\} \tag{3a}$$

$$\mathbf{x}_i^* \gtrsim \mathbf{x}_i \quad \forall \mathbf{x}_i^* \in \left\{ \mathbf{x}_i \in X_i | \mathbf{x}_i\mathbf{p}^* \leqq \zeta_i\mathbf{p}^* + \sum_{j=1}^{n} \alpha_{ij}\mathbf{p}^*\mathbf{y}_j^* \right\} \tag{3b}$$

$$\mathbf{p}^* \geqq \mathbf{0} \tag{4a}$$

$$\mathbf{e}\mathbf{p}^* = 1 \tag{4b}$$

$$\sum_{i=1} \mathbf{x}_i - \sum_{j=1} \mathbf{y}_j - \sum_{i=1} \zeta_i \leqq \mathbf{0} \tag{5a}$$

$$\mathbf{p}^* \left[\sum_{i=1} \mathbf{x}_i - \sum_{j=1} \mathbf{y}_j - \sum_{i=1} \zeta_i \right] = 0 \tag{5b}$$

where Y_j and X_i are closed and convex sets such that X_i is bounded from below (cf. Arrow and Debreu, 1954, p. 268), Y_j has no semipositive element and satisfies the property that

$$\mathbf{y}_j \in Y_j \Rightarrow -\mathbf{y}_j \notin Y_j$$

(ibid.); the preference ordering $\gtrsim$ is such that a utility function can be built on X_i and such a function is continuous and has a maximum in X_i and is monotonic on each segment connecting two elements of X_i (cf. *ibid.*, p. 269); and the given constants $\boldsymbol{\zeta}_i$ and α_{ij} are such that

$$\exists \mathbf{x}_i \in X_i | \mathbf{x}_i < \boldsymbol{\zeta}_i \tag{6}$$

$$\alpha_{ij} \geqq 0, \quad \sum_i \alpha_{ij} = 1$$

(cf. *ibid.*, p. 270).[15] The constant $\boldsymbol{\zeta}_i$ denotes the initial endowment of agent i and the constant α_{ij} denotes the share that agent i has in firm j. It is easily recognised that conditions (2) correspond to condition 1 stated by Arrow and Debreu (*ibid.*, p. 268): "$\mathbf{y}_j^*$ maximises $\mathbf{p}^*\mathbf{y}_j$, over the set Y_j, for each j". Similarly, conditions (3) correspond to condition 2 stated by Arrow and Debreu (*ibid.*, p. 271): "$\mathbf{x}_j^*$ maximises $u_i(\mathbf{x}_i)$ over the set $\{\mathbf{x}_i \in X_i | \mathbf{x}_i\mathbf{p}^* \leqq \boldsymbol{\zeta}_i\mathbf{p}^* + \sum_{j=1}^n \alpha_{ij}\mathbf{p}^*\mathbf{y}_j^*\}$", and conditions (4) and (5) correspond to properties 3 and 4 stated on the same page. This way of stating the problem of the existence of a competitive equilibrium allows for a comparison with the problem studied by von Neumann.

In the von Neumann model there is no consumption choice and "Consumption of goods takes place only through the processes of production which include necessities of life consumed by workers and employees" (von Neumann, 1945, p. 2). Hence in the von Neumann model there is no analogue of condition (3): it is as if all the $\mathbf{x}_i$'s were set equal to $\mathbf{0}$ and the "necessities of life" were inserted in the $\mathbf{y}_j$'s. Then condition (2) is the analogue of conditions (1b), (1d), and the first of conditions (1e); condition (4) is the analogue of the second of conditions (1e); condition (5) is the analogue of conditions (1a) and (1c), paying attention to the fact that $\mathbf{x}_i = \mathbf{0}$ for each i, and that in von Neumann the $\boldsymbol{\zeta}_i$'s are not given as in Arrow and Debreu, but are endogenously determined in order to maintain a steady state. These formal similarities allow one to use the same topological tool to solve the problem.[16]

As we have seen, Arrow and Debreu assumed that each agent has an initial endowment that suffices to guarentee the agent's survival until the very end of the time horizon of the model even if the agent should not participate in production and exchange, that is, even if the agent would just live on his own endowments (see condition (6) above). Arrow and Debreu argued that this assumption "plays the same role as the one made by Professor von Neumann in his study of a dynamic model of production . . . that each commodity enters into every production process either as an input or as an output". This contention deserves to be carefully scrutinised. We ask, what can be meant by the "same role"? As a matter of fact, both assumptions are used to show that some sets are not empty (cf. Arrow and Debreu, 1954, p. 278 and von Neumann, 1945, p. 4). But the conditions are totally different from other points of view. The condition stated by Arrow and Debreu is a continuity condition of the budget set and may be interpreted as a viability condition of the consuming agent: there is a feasible consumption path for each and every agent such that the agents initial endowments are sufficient for their survival even if they do not enter into any exchange or cooperation with one another, including any production activity. The assumption thus guarantees that the number of agents defining the economy will remain the same over the entire time horizon contemplated. If that number were to change, a new model would have to be formulated any time that happens. (This indicates anew that the Arrow–Debreu model is essentially a short-period model.) On the contrary, the condition stated by von Neumann is a typical simplifying assumption which can be dropped at the cost of some complication – without, however, affecting the model as such. This has been shown by Kemeny, Morgenstern and Thompson (1956).

Despite the mathematical similarities, the two dissimilarities we have mentioned, the one relative to consumption and the other one relative to the endowments are enough to consider the two models as belonging to two different traditions of economic thought.

6. Concluding remarks

In this paper we compared John von Neumann's growth model with the classical economists' approach to the theory of value and distribution on the one hand and to the neoclassical approach on the other. It was shown that von Neumann's model shares all important features of the former in terms of method of analysis, analytical structure and economic content, and differs in important respects from the latter. In particular, like the classical economists, von Neumann does not start from given endowments of the economy of "capital" as the neoclassicists, and unlike the latter takes the real wage rate(s) as given in accordance with the classical authors. His main concern is the problem of reproducibility of the system under consideration, while he sets aside the problem of scarcity. Interest, that is the only share of income other than wages in von Neumann's case, is explained in a full-fledged classical manner in terms of a surplus product, or residual. Other than the models of steady-state growth of Gustav Cassel (and later Robert Solow), von Neumann determines the rate of expansion *endogenously* – reflecting the surplus-creating capacity of the economic system. It is also shown that setting aside some purely formal aspects there are no connections between the von Neumann model and the Arrow–Debreu model. A claim according to which an assumption of the latter plays the "same role" as an assumption of the former is scrutinised and rejected.

Acknowledgements

We would like to thank Nick Baigent, Egbert Dierker, Malte Faber, Christian Gehrke, Ulrich Schwalbe, Ernö Zalai and two referees of *Acta Oeconomica* for useful comments on an earlier draft of this paper. Obviously, the responsibility for what is stated in this paper is entirely ours.

Notes

1 The *Ergebnisse* which were terminated shortly afterwards due to the "Anschluß" of Austria to Nazi Germany have recently been reprinted (Dierker and Sigmund, 1998).
2 The interpretation of the von Neumann model first suggested in our 1993 paper was favourably received in the literature; see, for example, Leonard (1995).
3 Our interpretation of the classical economists draws heavily on Piero Sraffa's findings both in his published work on the matter and in his unpublished papers kept at the Wren Library of Trinity College, Cambridge. Sraffa deserves the credit for having rediscovered the distinct classical approach to the theory of value and distribution and for having reformulated it in a logically coherent and substantively encompassing way.
4 In the more sophisticated conceptualisations underlying the arguments of Smith and Ricardo, higher rates of growth of labour supply presuppose higher levels of the real wage rate. However, the basic logic remains the same: in normal conditions the pace at which capital accumulates regulates the pace at which labour grows (Kurz and Salvadori, 2005).
5 There is evidence that Remak was in contact with von Bortkiewicz; see on this Wittmann (1967).
6 It is interesting to note that in the title of Champernowne's paper (1945) the title of the English version of von Neumann's paper is referred to incompletely: the adjective "general" is left out.
7 Assuming that natural resources are non-scarce is of course not the same thing as assuming that there are no natural resources at all. Von Neumann's model is frequently misinterpreted in the latter sense. In this context it deserves to be noted that von Neumann does not define goods in the same way as Debreu (1959, p. 32): he does not consider a particular plot of land in a particular location as a special good.
8 "At most, one could say that a Rule of Zero 'Excess' Wages is applied because labour is less than fully employed" (Steedman, 1987, p. 419). The interpretation given by Dore of von Neumann's use (or rather non-use) of the Rule of Free Goods is difficult to sustain: according to Dore (1989, p. 83) in the von Neumann model "Cassel's 'principle of scarcity'... is given an extreme binary interpretation whereby a resource has either a positive economic value if it is fully utilized, or its value is zero. Unless every single man and woman is fully employed, the social value of labour is zero; this is indeed extreme. Why did von Neumann resort to this formulation?" The answer to this question is: he did not.
9 In the 1960s and 1970s the problems were at the centre of the debate during the so-called Cambridge controversies in the theory of capital and interest (for a summary account, see, for example, Kurz and Salvadori, 1995, ch. 14). It was shown that the long-period neoclassical model could be only sustained in extremely special conditions.
10 Here we are concerned exclusively with the original Arrow–Debreu model. Suffice it to say that several of its shortcomings have been addressed by subsequent work a discussion of which, however, is beyond the scope of this paper. Yet one aspect which was brought to our attention by Nick Baigent deserves at least to be mentioned. It concerns the fact that one strand of thought developed game-theoretic general equilibrium (cf. the contributions of Shubik, Rubinstein, Wolinsky and others), and given that von Neumann was a founder of game theory, the intriguing question is close at hand how his growth paper relates to his work on game theory.
11 Until a few decades ago the time horizon in intertemporal general equilibrium theory was assumed to be finite and, therefore, arbitrary. The study of intertemporal models

with an infinite time horizon has begun with Bewley (1972). The introduction of an *infinite* horizon turned out to be critical (see also Burgstaller, 1994, pp. 43–48). It pushed the analysis towards steady-state analysis. (It ought to be stressed that the latter is only a special case of long-period analysis and must not be identified with it.) This was clearly spelled out, for instance, by Robert Lucas in a contribution to the theories of endogenous growth. Lucas observed that "for *any* initial capital $K(0) > 0$, the optimal capital-consumption path $(K(t), c(t))$ will converge to the balanced path asymptotically. That is, the balanced path will be a good approximation to any actual path 'most' of the time" and that "this is exactly the reason why the balanced path is interesting to us" (Lucas, 1988, p. 11).

12 For a discussion of some additional aspects of the relationship between von Neumann's model and neoclassical theory, see the paper by Zalai (2004).

13 See, however, Arrow (1989, p. 17), who relates the von Neumann model closely to that of Cassel. Similarly, Weintraub (1985, p. 77), McKenzie (1987, p. 500), Dore, Chakravarty and Goodwin (1989, p. 2) and Punzo (1989; 1991).

14 Assumption IV.a is reported in the following as condition (6). We shall comment on this statement below.

15 In sections 4 and 5 of their paper property (6) is partially weakened.

16 Now we know that this tool is not necessary to solve the von Neumann problem, but it is in order to solve the Arrow–Debreu problem; and this is so exactly because of condition (3).

References

Arrow, K. J. (1989): Von Neumann and the Existence Theorem for General Equilibrium. In: Dore, M., Chakravarty, S. and Goodwin, R. (1989), 15–28.

Arrow, K. J. and Debreu, G. (1954): Existence of an Equilibrium for a Competitive Economy. *Econometrica*, 22: 265–290.

Arrow, K. J. and Hahn, F. H. (1971): *General Competitive Analysis*. San Francisco: Holden-Day.

Bewley, T. F. (1972): Existence of Equilibrium in Economics with Infinitely Many Commodities. *Journal of Economic Theory*, 4: 514–540.

Bliss, C. J. (1975): *Capital Theory and the Distribution of Income*. Amsterdam: North-Holland.

Burgstaller; A. (1994): *Property and Prices. Toward a Unified Theory of Value*. Cambridge: Cambridge University Press.

Champernowne, D. G. (1945): A Note on J. v. Neumann's Article on 'A Model of Economic Equilibrium'. *Review of Economic Studies*, 13: 10–18.

Currie, M. and Steedman, I. (1990): *Wrestling with Time. Problems in Economic Theory*. Manchester: Manchester University Press.

Debreu, G. (1959): *Theory of Value*. New York: Wiley.

Dierker, E. and Sigmund, K. (eds) (1998): *Karl Menger. Ergebnisse eines Mathematischen Kolloquiums*. Vienna and New York: Springer.

Dore, M. (1989): The Legacy of von Neumann. In: Dore, M., Chakravarty, S. and Goodwin, R. (1989), 82–99.

Dore, M., Chakravarty, S. and Goodwin, R. (eds) (1989): *John von Neumann and Modern Economics*. Oxford: Clarendon.

Hahn, F. H. (1982): The Neo-Ricardians. *Cambridge Journal of Economics*. 6: 353–374.

Kaldor, N. (1989): John von Neumann: a Personal Recollection (foreword). In: Dore, M., Chakravarty, S. and Goodwin, R. (1989), vii–xi.

Kemeny, J. G., Morgenstern, O. and Thompson, G. L. (1956): A Generalization of von Neumann's Model of an Expanding Economy. *Econometrica*, 24: 115–135.

Koopmans, T. C. (1974): Contribution to General Discussion on Past and Future of the von Neumann Model. In: Łoś, J. and Łoś, M. W. (eds) (1974), 3–4.

Kurz, H. D. and Salvadori, N. (1993): Von Neumann's Growth Model and the Classical Tradition. *European Journal of the History of Economic Thought*, 1: 129–160.

Kurz, H. D. and Salvadori, N. (1995): *Theory of Production. A Long-Period Analysis*. Cambridge: Cambridge University Press.

Kurz, H. D. and Salvadori, N. (2001): Sraffa and von Neumann. *Review of Political Economy*, 13: 161–180.

Kurz, H. D. and Salvadori, N. (2005): Endogenous Growth in a Stylised Classical Model. In: Stathakis, G. and Vaggi, G. (eds), *Economic Development and Social Change: Historical roots and modern perspectives*. London: Routledge, 106–124.

Leonard, R. J. (1995): From Parlor Games to Social Science: Von Neumann, Morgenstern, and the Creation of Game Theory, 1928–1994. *Journal of Economic Literature*, 33(2): 730–761.

Łoś, J. and Łoś, M. W. (eds) (1974): *Mathematical Models in Economics*. Amsterdam and New York: North-Holland.

Lucas, R. E. (1988): On the Mechanics of Economic Development. *Journal of Monetary Economics*, 22: 3–42.

McKenzie, L. W. (1987): General Equilibrium. In: Eatwell, J., Newman, P. and Milgate, M. (eds): *The New Palgrave. A Dictionary of Economics*. London: Macmillan, vol. 2, 498–512.

Mill, J. (1826): *Elements of Political Economy*. 3rd edition (revised and corrected). London: Baldwin, Chadock, and Joy. (1st edn in 1821.)

Neumann, J. von (1937): Über ein ökonomisches Gleichungssystem und eine Verallgemeinerung des Brouwerschen Fixpunktsatzes. *Ergebnisse eines mathematischen Kolloquiums*, 8: 73–83.

Neumann, J. von (1945): A Model of General Economic Equilibrium. *Review of Economic Studies*, 13: 1–9. English translation of von Neumann (1937).

Petty, W. (1899): *The Economic Writings of Sir William Petty*. (Ed. by C. H. Hull.) Vols I and II. Cambridge: Cambridge University Press. (Reprinted in one volume in 1986, New York: Kelley.)

Punzo, L. F. (1989): Von Neumann and Karl Menger's Mathematical Colloquium. In: Dore, M., Chakravarty, S. and Goodwin, R. (1989), 29–65.

Punzo, L. F. (1991): The School of Mathematical Formalism and the Viennese Circle of Mathematical Economists. *Journal of the History of Economic Thought*, 13: 1–18.

Remak, R. (1929): Kann die Volkswirtschaftslehre eine exakte Wissenschaft werden? *Jahrbücher für Nationalökonomie und Statistik*, 131: 703–735.

Ricardo, D. (1951 ssq.): *The Works and Correspondence of David Ricardo*. (11 volumes, ed. by P. Sraffa, with the collaboration of M. H. Dobb). Cambridge: Cambridge University Press. In the text referred to as *Works*, volume numbers and page numbers.

Schefold, B. (1985): Cambridge Price Theory: Special Model or General Theory of Value? *American Economic Review, Papers and Proceedings*, 75: 140–145.

Smith, A. (1976): *An Inquiry into the Nature and Causes of the Wealth of Nations*. Ist edn in 1776. Vol. II of *The Glasgow Edition of the Works and Correspondence of Adam Smith* (ed. by R. H. Campbell, A. S. Skinner, and W. B. Todd) Oxford: Oxford University Press. In the text quoted as *WN*, book number, chapter number, section number, paragraph number.

Sraffa, P. (1960): *Production of Commodities by Means of Commodities. Prelude to a Critique of Economic Theory*. Cambridge: Cambridge University Press.
Steedman, I. (1987): Free Goods. In: Eatwell, J., Newman, P. and Milgate, M. (eds): *The New Palgrave. A Dictionary of Economics*. London: Macmillan, vol. 2, 419–420.
Walras, L. (1874): *Eléments d'économie politique pure*. Lausanne: Corbaz. 5th and definitive edn Paris: F. Richon, 1924.
Walras, L. (1954): *Elements of Pure Economics*. London: George Allen & Unwin. English translation of the definitive edition of Walras (1874) by W. Jaffé.
Weintraub, E. R. (1985): *General Equilibrium Analysis. Studies in Appraisal*. Cambridge: Cambridge University Press.
Wicksell, K. (1893): *Über Wert, Kapital und Rente nach den neueren nationalökonomischen Theorien*. Jena: Fischer. English translation as Wicksell (1954): *Value, Capital and Rent*. London: George Allen & Unwin. (Reprinted New York 1970: Kelley.)
Wittmann, W. (1967): Die extremale Wirtschaft. Robert Remak – ein Vorläufer der Aktivitätsanalyse. *Jahrbücher für Nationalökonomie und Statistik*, 180: 397–409.
Zalai, E. (2004): The von Neumann Model and the Early Models of General Equilibrium. *Acta Oeconomica*, 54(1): 3–38.

11 Fund–flow versus flow–flow in production theory*

Reflections on Georgescu-Roegen's contribution

Heinz D. Kurz and Neri Salvadori

> The reasonable man adapts himself to the world; the unreasonable one persists in trying to adapt the world to himself. Therefore all progress depends on the unreasonable man.
>
> (G.B. Shaw)

1. Introduction

Nicholas Georgescu-Roegen ended his 1969 Richard T. Ely Lecture on "The Economics of Production" with the observation:

> The economics of production, its elementary nature notwithstanding, is not a domain, where one runs no risk of committing some respectable errors. In fact, the history of every science, including economics, teaches us that the elementary is the hotbed of the errors that count most.
>
> (1970, p. 9)

In Georgescu-Roegen's view neoclassical production theory was just such a "hotbed". He was therefore keen to elaborate an alternative to it. Another author with a critical stance toward neoclassical theory was Piero Sraffa, who had likewise developed an alternative conceptualization starting from the physical real cost approach of the classical economists.[1] Therefore, it is perhaps interesting to see how the contributions of the two authors compare with regard to the critical and the constructive task they set themselves. In this paper, the emphasis will be predominantly on Georgescu-Roegen's approach to the theory of production. We shall examine his works and check his more analytical propositions against the background of Sraffa's analysis. For convenience, we shall take Georgescu-Roegen's 1969 Ely Lecture as a useful point of reference whenever this is possible.[2]

The structure of the paper is as follows; in Section 2, we shall explore the concept of the production function and the criticism leveled at it. Section 3 turns to Georgescu-Roegen's alternative approach to the theory of production,

* Reprinted with permission from *Journal of Economic Behavior & Organisation*, volume 51, 2003.

comparing it with the approach of the classical economists that was revived by John von Neumann and Piero Sraffa. Section 4 counterposes Georgescu-Roegen's distinction between funds and flows, on the one hand, and the distinction between fixed and circulating capital goods, on the other. Section 5 compares the fund–flow approach with what may be called the "flow–flow" approach, in which fixed capital is reduced to circulating capital within a joint-products framework. Section 6 establishes the superiority of the flow–flow approach in terms of a discussion of the important problem of the choice of technique; it is shown that the fund–flow approach may fail to identify the cost-minimizing technique. Section 7 contains some concluding remarks.

2. The production function

In his Ely lecture and elsewhere, Georgescu-Roegen criticized the "analytical imbroglio" of the conventional production function (see also Georgescu-Roegen, 1971, pp. 241–244).[3] He objected that the time factor is often ignored, that stocks and rates of flow tend to get confounded,[4] and that production functions are constructions of economic theorists and not "data" taken from engineers or industrial chemists. This criticism prompted him to some epistemological and methodological considerations. He expressed the view that any analytical representation of a production process is bound to be partial. To require such a representation to be complete in the sense that each and every aspect pertinent to a production process is taken into consideration would amount to taking into account the "seamless absolute whole"—an impossible task. He stressed that "analysis must proceed by some heroic simplifications and totally ignore their ultimate consequences" (1970, p. 2). This does not mean that anything goes. It means that, since not everything can be taken into account, there must be a judicious selection of aspects to be dealt with, which he notes requires "some intimate knowledge of the corresponding phenomenal domain" (p. 3). The theorist cannot avoid specifying the "analytical boundary" of the process of production: without such a boundary, there can be no analysis. The former is the "basic element" of the latter. In this way he claims that "some slits (are) cut into the absolute whole" (p. 2).

The conventional concept of the production function was criticized in the so-called Cambridge controversies in the theory of capital.[5] Contrary to a widespread misconception, the criticism concerned not only Solow-type aggregate production functions, but *all* attempts to represent amounts of heterogeneous capital goods by quantities of a single factor "capital" that is independent of income distribution and relative prices. This concept of capital comes essentially in two versions. The first, contending that a scalar representation of vectors of heterogeneous means of production can be found, had as its most prominent advocate Eugen von Böhm-Bawerk with his concept of the "average period of production". According to the second version the amount of capital employed in the economy as a whole can be conceived of as a *value* magnitude. Variants of this version were put forward, for example, by John Bates Clark and Alfred Marshall. The capital critique of the 1960s and 1970s established clearly that neither version can be sustained.[6]

Surprisingly, Georgescu-Roegen made hardly any attempt to relate his criticism to the one put forward in the Cambridge controversies. The statements that come perhaps closest to mentioning implicitly the latter start from his objection to Marx's concept of "congealed abstract capital". He added, "As a highly abstract simile, the standard form of the Neoclassical production function—as a function of K, the cardinal measure of homogenous 'capital', and H, the cardinal measure of homogenous 'labor'—is not completely useless". This statement could easily be misunderstood, but the one immediately following it produces clarity: "the value of the standard form of the production function as a blueprint of reality is nil. It is absurd therefore to hold on to it in practical applications" (Georgescu-Roegen, 1971, p. 244). The rock on which the neoclassical production function is said to founder is that heterogeneous capital goods "have no common measure".[7] Georgescu-Roegen concludes, "Marginal productivity . . . comes out as an empty word" (Georgescu-Roegen, 1971, p. 244).[8]

3. A different approach

In his 1970 paper, Georgescu-Roegen argued that the analytical boundary consists of two components, one that separates the process from the rest of reality while the other specifies the duration of the process, because a timeless *process* is obviously a *contradictio in adjecto*. It comes as no surprise that he was opposed to the concept of instantaneous production as encountered, for example, in Walras. According to Georgescu-Roegen, the following aspects are crucial. First, "Because of the principle, 'No analytical boundary, no analytical process', analysis must renounce any hope of including in this description the happenings inside an analytical process" (Georgescu-Roegen, 1970, p. 3), once the boundaries of the *elementary* process have been specified. Second, he insisted that another "heroic step" must be taken, which consists of assuming that the number of elements involved is finite and that every element is cardinally measurable. He stressed, "Each element of an analytical process—as we have decided—must be completely homogeneous". This condition, he added, "does not always cover sameness" (Georgescu-Roegen, 1970, p. 4). The reference is to durable instruments of production and workers, both of which are liable to undergo some change during the production process: tools are subject to wear and tear and workers invariably become tired.

In Georgescu-Roegen's view, these two cases "raise a troublesome problem for the economist". This is so because the economist's "commodity fetishism" (Georgescu-Roegen, 1970, p. 4) presumes given qualities of the elements considered in the analysis and is thus incompatible with qualitative change. However, contrary to what the reader might expect, this is not followed by an attack on commodity fetishism. Georgescu-Roegen rather defends his vision of the "economist":

> Our entire analytical edifice would collapse if we were to accept the alternative position that the aim of economic production is to produce not only the usual products but also tired workers and used tools.
>
> (Georgescu-Roegen, 1970, p. 4)

This view is difficult to sustain and, as we shall see, has serious implications for the approach elaborated by Georgescu-Roegen. Also, while some economists do perhaps fit his description, others certainly do not. More important, it is an undoubtable *fact* (which is quite independent from whether it could also be an "aim") that production over any length of time generates tired workers and partly worn-out tools. And facts, it seems, ought to be taken as what they are. In one place Georgescu-Roegen stressed that his concern was "mainly with the problem of valid analytical representation of the *relations among facts*" (Georgescu-Roegen, 1992, p. 130, emphasis added; see also Georgescu-Roegen, 1971, pp. 217–218). Unfortunately, his fund–flow approach does not follow this maxim (see Section 4).

Among the economists who naturally allowed for used tools are John von Neumann and Piero Sraffa with their treatment of fixed capital in a joint-products framework. Accordingly, the production process is subdivided in elementary processes, with a main product exiting from production at the end of each.[9] In addition, there may be a by-product: a new fixed capital good such as a machine that enters the production process is considered as a particular input that, in principle, is not different from circulating capital goods, such as raw materials, while the older machine available at the end of an elementary process is considered as a particular joint output of the process; the older machine then enters as an input in one of the other elementary processes. The young and the old machine are thus treated as different commodities, which involves reducing fixed to circulating capital. This way to deal with fixed capital is able to account for the fact that tools are subject to wear and tear. Moreover, if, as Georgescu-Roegen often emphasized, a machine enters and exits from production, then the subdivision in elementary processes needs to be more detailed: the exit of not only a main product but also a machine from production or the entry of any machine (old or new) into production must signal the end (and the beginning) of an elementary process. In this case, semi-finished products need to be defined as hypothetical commodities since all machines and all semi-finished products exit the elementary process (to enter into other elementary processes), and even if they are not sold and bought, they need to be priced.

Sraffa did not deal with tired workers in the same way as with used machines, but there is no obvious reason why dealing with it could not be done. Perhaps von Neumann had it in mind when constructing his model.[10] In this case, production processes may be considered as producing, among other things, tired workers, whereas separate "recreation processes" could describe a part of the activity within households, with tired workers entering as inputs (jointly with commodity inputs and services) and "fresh workers" exiting as outputs. In the sense used in the literature on the Leontief model,[11] a model with these features would be more closed (less open) than the usual model without such recreation processes and thus without tired workers as outputs of the usual production processes.[12] In other words, one may formulate systems of production showing both how the "factors" produce the commodities and the commodities (plus other inputs) produce the factors (including labor power).

Strangely, Georgescu-Roegen, who otherwise advocated a strictly objectivist-materialist point of view, in this regard chose an "idealistic" way out of what he considered to be an impasse. He contended:

> A new heroic step is needed to eliminate this difficulty. It consists of the familiar, old fiction of a process in which capital is maintained constant. The fiction does raise some analytical issues, for if all tools and all workers are to be maintained at a constant level of efficiency, any production process will have to include most of the enterprises and households in the world.
>
> (Georgescu-Roegen, 1970, p. 4)

What Georgescu-Roegen presumably had in mind when referring to the "familiar, old fiction" is a vertically fully integrated industry which produces a net amount of a particular commodity while also reproducing all the means of production directly and indirectly used up in the production of that net amount. Actually, his concept of vertical integration would have to be still more comprehensive, because it necessitates also the reproduction of the physical and mental state of the workers when they entered the production process. Since what Georgescu-Roegen calls "fund" is but another name for his concept of keeping capital or any other factor of production fully intact, the latter deserves careful scrutiny.

Were Georgescu-Roegen to imply that "maintaining capital constant" involves keeping each and every durable means of production at its "level of efficiency" when brand-new, then the following objections arise: (1) it is doubtful that this requirement is at all technically feasible; if it were, (2) it would make no sense economically, because in most (all?) cases, it would be a wasteful exercise. Georgescu-Roegen appears to have been aware that such an extreme specification of the concept cannot sensibly be sustained. However, was this enough to sound the retreat? For this is what Georgescu-Roegen did when he wrote: "A simple glance at the activity inside a plant or a household suffices to convince us that efforts are constantly directed not toward keeping durable goods physically self-identical (which is quite impossible [sic]), but toward maintaining them in good working condition. And this is all that counts in production" (Georgescu-Roegen, 1970, p. 4).

This specification is rather vague and therefore not very useful. Something more can be said. If we adopt the joint-products approach to fixed capital, the concept of "maintaining capital constant" can be given a clear analytical expression. In fact, it is possible to combine the elementary processes producing a final good (for the sake of simplicity, we set aside the problem of joint production of final goods) in such proportions that the quantities of used machines entering the whole set of processes is exactly equal to the quantities exiting the whole set of processes. It is important to stress that the proportions mentioned depend on the rate of growth of the economic system and change with that rate. In this way, the capital stock is maintained not because each machine is maintained at its original efficiency, but because the physical changes of machines are taken into account in such a way that the set of machines is the same even if each single machine changes its role within the system as a consequence of its wear and tear and some old machines are disposed of and some new machines are introduced.[13]

4. Funds and flows versus fixed and circulating capital

The above considerations led Georgescu-Roegen to the distinction between *funds* and *flows*. A fund is characterized by "economic invariableness", because it enters a production process and (ideally) comes out "without any impairment of its economic efficiency" (Georgescu-Roegen, 1970, p. 5): it is taken to be perfectly "maintained" during the process. Flows on the other hand appear only as inputs or as outputs. Examples of funds are "Ricardian land" possessed of "original and indestructible powers" (L), instruments and tools of production, or "capital equipment" (Georgescu-Roegen, 1970, p. 5) (K), and workers or rather their human capital alias labor power (H). Input flows include raw materials (R), circulating capital goods (I) and inflows "earmarked for maintenance" (M); output flows include products (Q) and waste (W). Georgescu-Roegen stressed that the production process so defined is a "reproducible process"; and that its description is incomplete if it does not contain both categories–funds, or "immutable agents", and flows.

The upshot of his argument is the well-known analytical representation of a reproducible process:

$$[R_0^{\mathrm{T}}(t), I_0^{\mathrm{T}}(t), M_0^{\mathrm{T}}(t), Q_0^{\mathrm{T}}(t), W_0^{\mathrm{T}}(t); L_0^{\mathrm{T}}(t), K_0^{\mathrm{T}}(t), H_0^{\mathrm{T}}(t)]$$

as a point in abstract functional space. The time element is specified: the process has a beginning and an end, and its duration is finite. This description is said to be "a far cry from the notion inherited from Wicksteed, according to which a process is represented by a point in the ordinary (Euclidian) space" (Georgescu-Roegen, 1970, p. 5).

The theorist, initially concerned with providing a complete representation of a process, cannot stop there but "has to decide which elements may be left out because they are economically irrelevant" (Georgescu-Roegen, 1970, p. 5). This selection implies that the description of a process will normally not comply with the laws of physics. Georgescu-Roegen noted this fact in terms of two examples: natural resources that are available in abundance and are thus free goods, and waste products that are subject to free disposal.[14]

The underlying premises make perfect sense when discussing levels of production that are "small" compared with the amounts of the best qualities of natural resources available, on the one hand, and on the other levels of waste generation that are "small" compared with the environment into which the waste is dumped. Even in conditions where these premises no longer hold, there may still be good reasons for setting aside the problems of the scarcity of natural resources and of the costliness of waste disposal when discussing certain problems. This does not mean that one has necessarily fallen victim to the twin fallacy of regarding nature as both a horn of plenty and a bottomless sink. Georgescu-Roegen's warnings that one must not lose sight of the laws of thermodynamics are justified. But a clarification is perhaps useful with regard to his statement that "waste by definition has no value" (Georgescu-Roegen, 1970, p. 5). Obviously, a waste product can only be a joint output of some other output. Moreover, the waste of some process may be a useful input in some other process(es) (e.g. manure): "Where there's muck, there's brass!" The important point is that in general it is impossible to say that a product is "waste" (or a "bad") on the basis of a partial view of the economic system. The character of a joint product—whether it has a positive price or not—is decided only for the system of production and consumption as a whole. Without taking into consideration the overall quantities required (or effectually demanded) of the different products and the methods of production available from which cost-minimizing producers can choose, including the methods to recycle precious materials, this question cannot be answered. If certain amounts of a product cannot be used in consumption or production, then the superfluous quantity of it needs to be eliminated. Such disposal processes are generally not free, but costly. In this case, the waste product under consideration will fetch a *negative* price, because in order to get rid of the product, labor and other kinds of inputs have to be employed. Therefore, waste products will often have a negative value; only in exceptional cases can they be treated as free goods.

Let us now turn briefly to Georgescu-Roegen's distinction between factors I and K. Both consist of produced means of production, or capital goods, many of which will be reproduced. They differ in terms of their longevity: while the former exhaust their powers during the (elementary) production period, which is set by the theorist, the latter survive more than one period and, according to the assumption of perfect maintenance, are indeed conceived of as an everlasting source of productive services. The fund–flow distinction is here equivalent to that between perennial and circulating capital.

At least since the time of the Physiocrats, economists have been aware of the fact that fixed capital introduces a formidable complication into the theory of value: while the circulating part of capital advances contributing entirely to the annual output, in effect "disappears" from the scene, the contribution of the durable part is less obvious and can only be imputed in correspondence to its wear and tear. This imputation problem appears to be also at the bottom of Georgescu-Roegen's fund–flow distinction as applied to produced means of production: "While it is true that the cloth—the inflow element—effectively passes into the coat, the same cannot apply to the needle—a fund element. . . . The point is that the problem of how the contribution of a fund affects the value of the product is not as directly simple as in the case of a flow factor" (1970, p. 5). This cannot be disputed. Yct, again, more can be said.

5. The "fund–flow" and the "flow–flow" approach to fixed capital

While Georgescu-Roegen did not treat fixed capital in terms of the joint-products method, he was certainly familiar with von Neumann's paper on equi-proportionate growth. In fact, he referred to it (see, for example, Georgescu-Roegen, 1966, p. 311, n. 16). However, he provided no reason for not conceiving, for example, of a t-year-old tractor as a joint output of corn produced by means of a t–1 year old tractor. This method allows one to determine the price of each machine at each point in time (where time is taken as a discrete variable) and therefore the time profile of the price (or rather book value) of the aging tractor. Implicit in this is the depreciation pattern of the machine. This method does not presuppose the singularly special case of constant efficiency throughout the tractor's economic life. Moreover, the approach is not restricted to the case of a single fixed capital item utilized in a process, but can also cope with the empirically important case of jointly utilized durable instruments of production (see Kurz and Salvadori, 1995, chapters 7 and 9). Nevertheless, in the literature, one encounters the view that Georgescu-Roegen's approach to the theory of production is superior to alternative approaches, including the one adopted by von Neumann and Sraffa (see, for example, Maneschi and Zamagni, 1997, p. 702, especially n. 7, and Piacentini, 1995, pp. 466–467). In the following, we will critically scrutinize this view.

The von Neumann–Sraffa approach to fixed capital consists in formalizing the old classical idea of treating old machines left at the end of each period as economically different goods from the machines which entered production at the beginning of the period. This approach to the problem of fixed capital may be dubbed "flow–flow". It avoids the bold assumption of the "fund–flow" approach that funds leave the process just as they had entered it.

In the flow–flow approach with joint products, the problem of the choice of technique is dealt with in the following way. In standard notation, the price vector $\boldsymbol{p}$ and the intensity vector $\boldsymbol{x}$ will be determined jointly with the wage rate w by the system:

$$[\boldsymbol{B} - (1+r)\boldsymbol{A}]\boldsymbol{p} \leqq w\boldsymbol{l} \tag{1}$$

$$\boldsymbol{x}^T[\boldsymbol{B} - (1+r)\boldsymbol{A}]\boldsymbol{p} = w\boldsymbol{x}^T\boldsymbol{l} \tag{2}$$

$$\boldsymbol{x}^T[\boldsymbol{B} - (1+g)\boldsymbol{A}] \geqq \boldsymbol{d}^T \tag{3}$$

$$\boldsymbol{x}^T[\boldsymbol{B} - (1+g)\boldsymbol{A}]\boldsymbol{p} = \boldsymbol{d}^T\boldsymbol{p} \tag{4}$$

$$\boldsymbol{p} \geqq \boldsymbol{0},\ \boldsymbol{x} \geqq \boldsymbol{0},\ w \geq 0, \boldsymbol{q}^T\boldsymbol{p} = 1 \tag{5}$$

where $\boldsymbol{A}$ is the material input matrix, $\boldsymbol{l}$ the labor input vector, $\boldsymbol{B}$ the output matrix, $\boldsymbol{d} \geq \boldsymbol{0}$ the consumption vector, r the rate of interest, and g the uniform rate of growth. Inequality (1) implies that no process is able to pay extra profits. Eq. (2) implies, also because of inequalities (5), that if a process is not able to pay the given rate of interest, it is not operated. Inequality (3) implies that the total demand (consumption and gross investment) is satisfied.[15] Eq. (4), also because of inequalities (5), is the Rule of Free Goods: overproduced commodities fetch a zero price. Eq. (5) fixes the numéraire, where $\boldsymbol{q}$ is any given semipositive vector.

The special case in which there is no joint production of finished goods, but there is, of course, the joint production of one finished good and one or several specific old machines, holds if and only if an assumption is made about the conformation of matrices $\boldsymbol{A}$ and $\boldsymbol{B}$.[16] The interested reader can find the whole story in Kurz and Salvadori (1995, chapters 7 and 9). Here, it must suffice to illustrate the issue in terms of an example. If there are five finished goods, four of which (the first, the second, the fourth and the fifth) are produced using fixed capital, for each finished good i, m_i processes to produce it and t_i used machines specific to it are available ($i = 1, 2, \ldots, 5$). The matrices $\boldsymbol{A}$ and $\boldsymbol{B}$ are conformed as in Figs. 11.1 and 11.2, respectively, where grey areas represent nonnegative elements, white areas zero elements, and black areas positive elements.

This is enough to distinguish commodities in "finished goods" and "old machines" and to prove a number of good properties including the one that prices do not depend on the vector of consumed commodities, whereas they may depend on the growth rate when machines are jointly utilized. However, a proper analytical treatment of "depreciation" requires some additional assumptions. It is, in fact, necessary to connect all used machines and some "finished goods", interpreted as

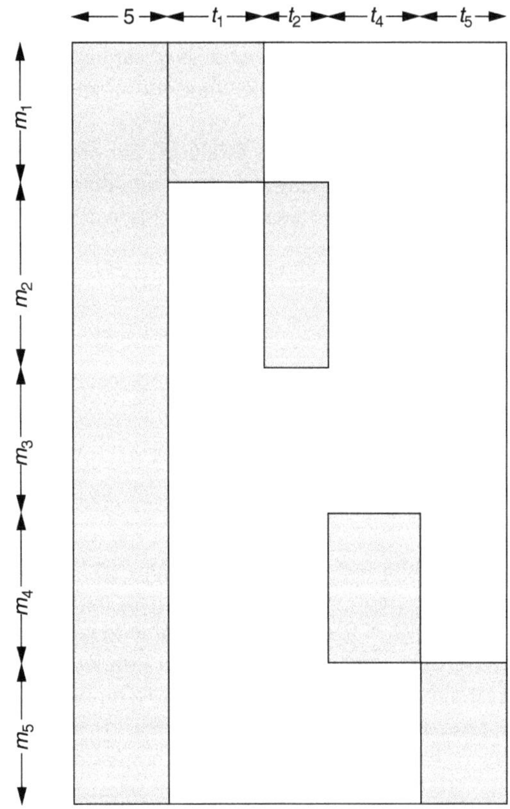

Figure 11.1 Matrix $\boldsymbol{A}$.

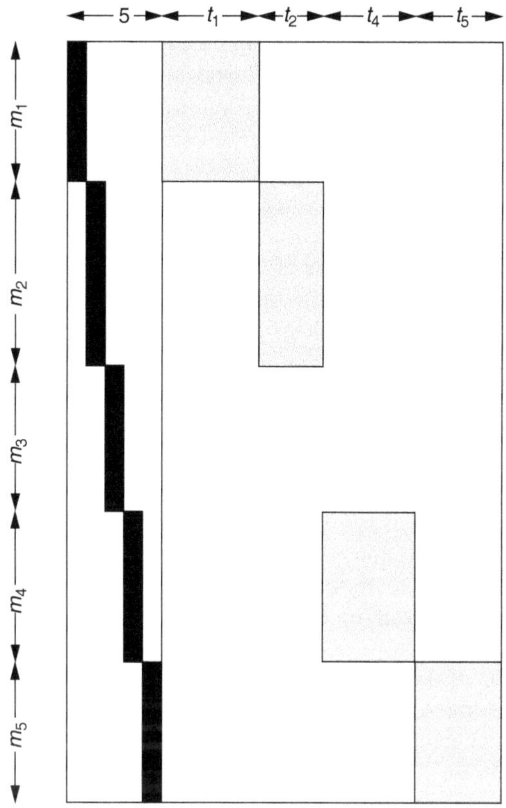

Figure 11.2 Matrix ***B***.

"new machines," among themselves in order to identify them as vintages of some "types of machine" (see Kurz and Salvadori, 1995, pp. 260–261).

The treatment of fixed capital in a joint-products framework, of course, does not do away with Georgescu-Roegen's important distinction between the "*agents* of a process" of production (funds) and its flow elements "which are *used* or *acted upon* by the agents" (1971, p. 230; emphasis in the original). Hence there is no presumption that by analytically reducing fixed capital to circulating, the former becomes substitutable against the elements of circulating capital as conventionally defined. Fund and flow elements are essentially complementary, as Georgescu-Roegen rightly stressed. The corresponding distinction between "finished goods" and "used machines" emphasizes the fact that only some finished goods may be interpreted as material to be transformed, whereas both "new machines" and "'used machines" cannot be so.

In this section, we restrict ourselves to stressing that there are several problems concerning fixed capital which cannot be investigated in terms of a formalism in which fixed capital does not wear out. There is both the choice of the *economic lifetime* of a fixed capital item and the choice of its *pattern of utilization*. The possibility of a machine becoming economically obsolete before the end of its technically feasible lifetime (which may be taken to be infinite) is obviously ruled out in cases of constant or increasing efficiency (setting aside technical progress, of course). With decreasing or changing efficiency, however, premature truncation is advantageous as soon as the price (or book value) of a partly worn out instrument of production becomes negative. Since the price of a machine (whether new or "aged") is equal to the capital value one gets by discounting all future net receipts that may be obtained by further use of it, where the actual rate of interest (profit) is taken as the discount rate, negative prices would indicate "losses". The optimal truncation date of a fixed capital item generally depends on income distribution (the rate of interest). The utilization aspect exhibits both an extensive and an intensive dimension. The former relates to the number of units within a given time period (day, week) during which a durable capital good is actually operated—for example, whether a single- or a double-shift scheme is adopted; the latter relates to the intensity of operation per unit of active time (h) of the item, for example, the speed at which a machine is run.[17] The economic lifetime of a fixed capital good and the pattern of its operation are, of course, not independent of one another.

Let us now see what Georgescu-Roegen had to say about the problem of the utilization of funds. We read, for example:

> I contend, one of the most important aspects of the economics of production is how to minimize these periods of fund idleness, whether we are thinking of man, capital equipment, or land.
>
> (Georgescu-Roegen, 1970, p. 6; see also Georgescu-Roegen, 1971, pp. 247–248)

He added that "the economics of production reduces to two commandments: first, produce by the factory system (i.e. by arrangement in parallel) and, second, let the factory operate around the clock" (Georgescu-Roegen, 1970, p. 8). These are intriguing statements and Georgescu-Roegen himself seems to have felt the need to qualify them. He pointed out that due to seasonal variations, in large parts of husbandry the factory system cannot be adopted. Hence, what can at most be done is to try "to render the idleness of the agents as small as possible in each particular case" (Georgescu-Roegen, 1970, p. 9). He went on to maintain:

> The second commandment is particularly relevant for the underdeveloped economies. In a rich country, it makes perfect sense to operate every factory with one shift, even if the shift be of six or four hours only. In a rich country, there is also no need for night shifts, except whenever technology imposes around-the-clock production. Briefly, in a rich country, leisure is a commodity which people may prefer to higher income.
>
> (Georgescu-Roegen, 1970, p. 9)

The length of the working day is said to be "the simplest and the most direct lever of economic development" (Georgescu-Roegen, 1970, p. 9).

While we do not deny that raising the degree of capital utilization may be a good strategy to accelerate the process of developing an economy, we have reservations with regard to some of Georgescu-Roegen's other propositions. First, in deciding the degree of capital utilization, several factors besides those already mentioned matter. The view that in competitive conditions there is a tendency to utilize expensive fixed capital as much as possible can be traced back far in the history of our subject. John Stuart Mill went so far as to argue that keeping machines working for 24 h "is evidently the only economical mode of employing them" Mill (1848, 1965, p. 131).[18] However, at any given moment of time there may be cultural, institutional, political and economic factors at work that prevent the utilization of capital around the clock. For example, input flows per unit of output and input and output prices are generally not time-invariant; many of these quantities and prices tend to change during the day, month or year. Take the simple case of shift work, where the ordinary wage per hour plus a shift premium has to be paid to workers during the night shift despite the fact that the productivity of labor at night is often smaller than during the day due to the disturbance of man's biorhythm. Such a wage premium and the lower productivity are potential deterrents to adopting a double- or treble-shift system.[19] We are therefore skeptical about the validity of Georgescu-Roegen's contention that if the proper utilization of capital "were realized by miracle overnight, we would discover that we have long since been planning for a world with an immense excess capacity of industrial production" (1970, p. 9). Perhaps, in normal conditions at least, competitive economic systems are not very far away from cost-minimizing degrees of capital utilization.[20]

Secondly, these factors may explain why in industrialized countries plant and equipment are left idle for much of the time quite independently of any potential deficiency of aggregate effective demand. Obsolete machines are no longer used because technical innovations followed by changes in relative prices make it no longer profitable to do so. People's preference for leisure over income, to which Georgescu-Roegen referred, has little to do with the less than full utilization of capital. It is true that leisure may be preferred over real income. Yet this need not be in conflict with an interest in generating a given real income in a cost-minimizing way. It is the behavior of firms, concerned with reducing costs of production, that in specific institutional and economic conditions accounts for a substantial part of observable idleness of plant and equipment.[21] If Georgescu-Roegen was right, then one would expect that the richer a country (in terms of per capita income), the smaller is its (average) degree of utilization of plant and equipment. However, empirically the opposite is true: a growing income per capita and a gradual reduction in average working hours per laborer are accompanied by a persistent upward trend in the overall degree of capital utilization (see, for example, Betancourt and Clague, 1981, and Foss, 1981).

In this section, we have summarized the flow–flow approach to fixed capital. We have shown that with its help certain economic problems can be analysed in a more satisfactory way than by using the fund–flow approach. Since we could not identify any aspect which can be tackled using the latter, but not the former, this is enough to decide in favor of the flow–flow approach. However, the difficulties besetting

Table 11.1 The flow–flow scheme of the numerical example

	Commodity inputs					Labor		Outputs				
	C	New machines	M_1	M_2	N_1			C	New machines	M_1	M_2	N_1
(1)	5	0	0	0	0	1	→	0	1	0	0	0
(2)	5	2	0	0	0	1	→	20	0	1	0	1
(3)	5	0	1	0	1	1	→	30	0	0	1	0
(4)	5	1	0	1	0	1	→	30	0	0	0	1
(5)	5	1	0	0	1	1	→	30	0	1	0	0
(6)	5	1	1	0	0	1	→	30	0	0	1	1
(7)	5	0	0	1	1	1	→	20	0	0	0	0

the conventional fund–flow approach are perhaps not yet sufficiently clear. We shall, therefore, in the next section deal with the important problem of the choice of technique in terms of a simple numerical example in order to show that even in cases in which prima facie the fund–flow approach seems to be equivalent to the flow–flow approach, this need not be the case: the fund–flow approach may be misleading in regard to the problem of identifying the cost-minimizing technique.

6. The problem of the choice of technique: a numerical example

Let us consider a technology which can be described using the flow–flow scheme of Table 11.1. Commodity C is produced by using two machines (M and N) which last 3 and 2 years, respectively. For the sake of simplicity, it is assumed that the new M is indistinguishable from the new N, whereas the two durable instruments of production differ when they are old. Processes (2)–(7) represent all possible arrangements. In process (2), the two new machines are used jointly, and two machines M and N, each one year old, are produced jointly with commodity C. In processes (4), (5), and (6), a new machine is used jointly with one old machine (a 2-year-old M, a 1-year-old N, a 1-year-old M, respectively): the corresponding older machines are found among the outputs (a 1-year-old N, a 1-year-old M, a 2-year-old M and a 1-year-old N, respectively). In processes (3) and (7), only old machines are used; in particular, the 1-year-old N is used jointly with a one or 2-year-old M: the corresponding older machine M is found among the outputs of process (3), whereas process (7) does not include any output of machines. We set aside the problem of scrap, which is equivalent to invoking free disposal. All processes use labor and commodity C as inputs and all processes (2)–(7) produce commodity C.

The same technology can be described using a fund- or stock-flow description. Two new machines plus one unit of labor and five units of commodity C enter the stage. At the end of the year (the beginning of the second year), 15 units of commodity C exit, and one unit of labor enters. At the end of the second year (beginning of the third year), 25 units of commodity C exit, and one new machine and one unit of labor enter. At the end of the third year (the beginning of the fourth year) 25 units of commodity C exit, and one new machine and one unit of labor enter. The same happens at the end of the fourth and the fifth year (the beginning of the fifth and the sixth year). At the end of the sixth year, 20 units of commodity C exit.

The two descriptions seem do the job equally well. But this is not so, as will be shown in a steady-state framework in which the rate of growth, g, is given from outside the system. The six processes of the flow–flow description are unified in one entity in the stock-flow description, hiding that this is actually not the cost-minimizing choice. In a cost-minimizing technique, if there are five commodities (C, the new machine(s), M_1, M_2, N_1) only five processes are operated, unless the other two are linearly dependent processes (see Kurz and Salvadori, 1995, p. 258). In fact, in the flow–flow description processes (2)–(7) do not need to be operated one after the other: they could be operated *side by side*, that is, in parallel. But when this is done, it is immediately observed that instead of operating processes (2) and (7), it is possible to rearrange the same inputs in order to operate processes (4) and (5), thereby obtaining a larger output in terms of corn. The reader must not rush to the conclusion that only processes (1) and (3)–(6) can be operated. In fact, processes (3)–(6) cannot sustain large growth rates, and for high values of g process (2) is required in order to increase the production of 1-year-old machines. When this is the case, process (3) cannot be operated, since it is the largest consumer of 1-year-old machines. Mathematical proofs of these claims can be found in the appendix.

This shows that the fund–flow approach to the problem of fixed capital may be misleading as regards the problem of the choice of the cost-minimizing technique. The flow–flow approach adopted in this paper allows instead for a correct solution. It also deserves to be emphasized again that the problem of the choice of technique cannot generally be answered without taking into consideration the economic environment, in particular, whether the economy is growing and at what rate.

There are other important economic issues that can be properly treated only in terms of a satisfactory analysis of the problem of the choice of technique. Think, for example, of the case of idle land. We set aside the valid reasons given by Georgescu-Roegen (1971, pp. 250–253) for the idleness of workers and land inherent in agriculture due to the seasonal rhythm of each region on earth. As is well-known since the classical economists and especially David Ricardo's contribution to the theory of the rent of land, it may be perfectly sensible from an economic, cost-minimizing point of view not to employ certain qualities of land and instead cultivate some other qualities, some perhaps even intensively.[22] It is not fully clear which concept of "scarcity" Georgescu-Roegen held. Occasionally, one gets the impression that he tended to speak of scarcity whenever a natural resource happens to be available in an absolutely limited amount only. The economic concept of scarcity is different from this physical notion. As Ricardo pointed out with regard to land available in abundant quantity: "no rent could be paid for such land, for the reason stated why nothing is given for the use of air and water, or for any of the gifts of nature which exists in boundless quantity" (Ricardo,

[1817] 1951, p. 69). Hence, what matters from an economic point of view is how the available (known and finite) amount of a natural resource compares with the effectual demand for it.

7. Concluding remarks

The paper discussed Georgescu-Roegen's approach to the theory of production against the background of the approach of the "classical" economists, which has been revived and generalized by John von Neumann and Piero Sraffa. The emphasis is on the treatment of fixed capital and the problem of the choice of technique. It is shown that Georgescu-Roegen's "fund–flow" approach runs into difficulties when facing the latter problem. This is illustrated in terms of a numerical example: the fund–flow approach may give the wrong answer to the problem of the cost-minimizing choice of technique. Essentially, the difficulty is that the fund–flow model, even when it appears to represent the same structure of production as the flow–flow model, makes illegitimate prior assumptions about which of the underlying techniques will be used. In the von Neumann–Sraffa approach fixed capital is dealt with in a joint-products framework, which amounts to reducing fixed to circulating capital. The "flow–flow" approach allows for a correct solution of the choice of technique problem. In addition, the paper comments on the problem of capital utilization.

Appendix A

Let g^* be the unique positive real solution of the equation:

$$g^3 + 3g^2 + 2g - 1 = 0,$$

i.e.

$$g^* = \sqrt[3]{\frac{1}{2} + \frac{1}{6}\sqrt{\frac{23}{3}}} + \sqrt[3]{\frac{1}{2} + \frac{1}{6}\sqrt{\frac{23}{3}}} - 1 \approx 0.32472.$$

Let G be the unique positive real solution of the equation ($G \approx 0.80298$):

$$27 + 14g - 25g^2 - 31g^3 - 13g^4 - 2g^5 = 0$$

and R_1 be the unique positive real solution of the equation ($R_1 \approx 0.859404$):

$$25 + 18r - 19r^2 - 29r^3 - 13r^4 - 2r^5 = 0.$$

The reader can easily check that on the assumption that only commodity C is consumed, if the rate of profit r and the growth rate g are such that $0 \leq r \leq R_1$ and $0 \leq g \leq g^*$, then processes (1)–(7) can be operated with the following intensities:

$$x_1 = \frac{5 + 16g + 19g^2 + 10g^2 + 2g^4}{5(25 + 18g - 19g^2 - 29g^3 - 13g^4 - 2g^5)} C^*$$

$$x_2 = 0$$

$$x_3 = \frac{1 - 2g - 3g^2 - g^3}{5(25 + 18g - 19g^2 - 29g^3 - 13g^4 - 2g^5)} C^*$$

$$x_4 = \frac{2 + g}{5(25 + 18g - 19g^2 - 29g^3 - 13g^4 - 2g^5)} C^*$$

$$x_5 = \frac{(2 + g)(1 + 2g + g^2)}{5(25 + 18g - 19g^2 - 29g^3 - 13g^4 - 2g^5)} C^*$$

$$x_6 = \frac{1 + 5g + 4g^2 + g^3}{5(25 + 18g - 19g^2 - 29g^3 - 13g^4 - 2g^5)} C^*$$

$$x_7 = 0,$$

where C^* is the amount of commodity C available for consumption. Moreover, processes (1) and (3)–(6) determine the following prices, which are such that processes (2) and (7) cannot be operated since at these prices their costs are larger than their proceeds:

$$w = \frac{5(25 + 18r - 19r^2 - 29r^3 - 13r^4 - 2r^5)}{11 + 25r + 24r^2 + 11r^3 + 2r^4}$$

$$p_C = 1$$

$$p_{\mathrm{nm}} = \frac{30(6 + 9r + 5r^2 + r^3)}{11 + 25r + 24r^2 + 11r^3 + 2r^4}$$

$$p_{M1} = \frac{30(4 + 8r + 5r^2 + r^3)}{11 + 25r + 24r^2 + 11r^3 + 2r^4}$$

$$p_{M2} = \frac{30(2 + 5r + 4r^2 + r^3)}{11 + 25r + 24r^2 + 11r^3 + 2r^4}$$

$$p_{N1} = \frac{30(3 + 6r + 4r^2 + r^3)}{11 + 25r + 24r^2 + 11r^3 + 2r^4}.$$

Similarly, if $0 \leq r \leq G$ and $g^* \leq g \leq G$, then processes (1)–(7) can be operated with the following intensities:

$$x_1 = \frac{5 + 16g + 19g^2 + 10g^3 + 2g^4}{5(27 + 14g - 25g^2 - 31g^3 - 13g^4 - 2g^5)} C^*$$

$$x_2 = \frac{-1 + 2g + 3g^2 + g^3}{5(27 + 14g - 25g^2 - 31g^3 - 13g^4 - 2g^5)} C^*$$

$$x_3 = 0$$

$$x_4 = \frac{2 + g}{5(27 + 14g - 25g^2 - 31g^3 - 13g^4 - 2g^5)} C^*$$

$$x_5 = \frac{3 + 3g + g^2}{5(27 + 14g - 25g^2 - 31g^3 - 13g^4 - 2g^5)} C^*$$

$$x_6 = \frac{(1 + g)(2 + g)}{5(27 + 14g - 25g^2 - 31g^3 - 13g^4 - 2g^5)} C^*$$

$$x_7 = 0.$$

Moreover, processes (1) and (2), and (4)–(6) determine the following prices, which are such that processes (3) and (7) cannot be operated since at these prices their costs are larger than their proceeds:

$$w = \frac{5(27 + 14r - 25r^2 - 31r^3 - 13r^4 - 2r^5)}{11 + 25r + 24r^2 + 11r^3 + 2r^4}$$

$$p_C = 1$$

$$p_{\mathrm{nm}} = \frac{10(19 + 25r + 12r^2 + 2r^3)}{11 + 25r + 24r^2 + 11r^3 + 2r^4}$$

$$p_{M1} = \frac{10(20 + 36r + 21r^2 + 4r^3)}{11 + 25r + 24r^2 + 11r^3 + 2r^4}$$

$$p_{M2} = \frac{10(10 + 23r + 7r^2 + 4r^3)}{11 + 25r + 24r^2 + 11r^3 + 2r^4}$$

$$p_{N1} = \frac{10(15 + 27r + 17r^2 + 4r^3)}{11 + 25r + 24r^2 + 11r^3 + 2r^4}.$$

Finally, if $g = g^*$ and $0 \leq r \leq R_1$, only processes (1) and (4)–(6) are operated: prices and the wage rate are not determined, and they may vary in a range.

Acknowledgements

This paper is the result of revising and merging the two papers that one of us gave at the conference "L'Oeuvre Scientifique de Nicholas Georgescu-Roegen" in Strasbourg, 6–7 November 1998. We are grateful to the participants and especially to Rodolphe Dos Santos Ferreira, Mario Morroni, Robin Rowley and Piero Tani for valuable discussions. We would also like to thank Christian Gehrke, Peter Groenewegen and Christian Lager for useful comments on the original papers. Finally, we would like to express our gratitude to two anonymous referees and the editor of the *Journal of Economic Behavior & Organization* for valuable observations and suggestions. The usual caveats apply.

Notes

1 Before Sraffa, John von Neumann (1937, 1945) had put forward in print an approach that shares salient features with the one elaborated by the classical economists; see Kurz and Salvadori (1993). As we know from his unpublished papers kept at Trinity College

Library, Cambridge (UK), Sraffa had developed his first systems of equations of production as early as the second half of 1927 (see Kurz, 1998). Sraffa also assisted David Champernowne when the latter composed his commentary on the English translation of von Neumann's paper for the Review of Economic Studies.

2 For a more detailed exposition of his ideas on production, see Georgescu-Roegen (1971, chapter IX); see also Dos Santos Ferreira (1974).

3 According to Georgescu-Roegen (1970, p. 1), the starting point is Wicksteed (1894, 1992). It should be mentioned, however, that a linear homogeneous production function is present already in Wicksell (1893); see Sandelin (1976).

4 A remarkable exception is Winston (1982).

5 See, for example, Kurz and Salvadori (1995, chapter 14) and Kurz and Salvadori (1998).

6 See also Fisher (1993).

7 This is not quite true: the common measure of goods are their prices. The real problem is that prices depend on income distribution. Therefore, no measure of heterogeneous capital can be found that is independent of the latter.

8 In this context, it is perhaps interesting to note that as early as in a note dated 19 June 1943, Sraffa pointed out that the marginalist authors are precluded from raising objections to the labour theory of value: "For the Marginal Product theory of capital *presupposes, implicitly*, that Hypothesis" (D3/12/34: 33, Sraffa's emphasis; see also D3/12/16: 34). Sraffa was thus clear at an early stage of his investigation that the "parable" of neoclassical theory presupposes the "realism" of the labor theory of value; see Samuelson's (1962) attempt to support the neoclassical theory in terms of the "surrogate production function." The references are to Sraffa's unpublished papers and follow the catalogue prepared by Jonatham Smith, archivist. We should like to thank Pierangelo Garegnani, literary executor of Sraffa's papers, for granting us permission to quote from them.

9 In the case of pure joint production the output consists of several products.

10 "Consumption of goods taken place only through the process of production which includes necessities of life consumed by workers and employees" (Neumann, 1945, p. 2).

11 In the "closed" Leontief model the household sector is treated as if it were an ordinary industry. Thermodynamically, the system is, of course, not closed, because it relies on geothermal and solar energy. In Leontief's economic accounting, these are set aside; that is, they are treated as free goods. Therefore, in this respect the "closed Leotief model" is open!

12 There are other important aspects which will be set aside here; one of them concerns learning by doing and training on the job. This latter aspect is related to the problem of the formation of "human capital," a topic beyond the scope of this paper; see, however, Kurz and Salvadori (1995, chapter 11).

13 This concept is fully compatible with the Smithian notion of the division of labour, which, as Georgescu-Roegen rightly stressed, heralds the factory system, "one of the greatest *economic* inventions in the history of mankind" (1971, p. 248). See also Georgescu-Roegen (1965, Section 4) and Georgescu-Roegen (1971, chapter IX, Sections 9 and 11).

14 See also the following statement: "It is the idea of capital equipment *being kept as a constant fund by the very process in which it participates*. Strictly interpreted, this idea is a fiction. A process by which something would remain indefinitely outside the influence of the Entropy Law is factually absurd. But the merits of the fiction are beyond question" (Georgescu-Roegen, 1971, p. 229; emphasis in the original). However, somewhat later in the same volume Georgescu-Roegen was very critical of the assumption of production as a circular flow as it was advocated by the Physiocrats, the classical economists and Marx. He contended that "no other conception could be further from the correct interpretation of facts" (Georgescu-Roegen, 1971, p. 281).

Here, we cannot enter into a detailed discussion of this problem. It must suffice to remark that the usefulness of an assumption is reflected in the findings one is able to derive with its help. For a treatment of the problem of exhaustible resources in terms of the classical approach to the theory of production, see Kurz and Salvadori (2000, 2001).

15 If $\mathbf{x}$ is the vector of the intensities of operation of the different processes at time t, then $(1+g)\mathbf{x}$ is the vector of the intensities of operation at time $t+1$.

16 The assumption that old machines are specific is generally called "intransferability of old machines" in this literature. Salvadori (1999) proves that, at least in the case in which machines are not jointly used, this assumption can be replaced by the more reasonable one that the efficiency of non-specific (or transferable) old machines does not depend on the sector in which they are used.

17 Georgescu-Roegen was fully aware of these aspects (see, especially, Georgescu-Roegen, 1971, pp. 246–247).

18 The same view was advocated by socialist authors concerned with the problem of their economies catching up in the debate about rapid industrialisation.

19 For a discussion of the problem of capital utilization in a "classical" framework, see Kurz (1990, chapter 5) and Kurz and Salvadori (1995, chapter 7, Section 7).

20 This view would have to be qualified for economies that are characterised by a high degree of concentration, because oligopolies voluntarily tend to keep spare margins of capital utilization in order to deter potential competitors from entering the market.

21 For the reasons given, there is no presumption that the (overall) degree of capital utilization desired by firms equals full utilization. The difference between the latter and the former may be considered "voluntary". Degrees of utilization that fall short of the desired one may (entirely or partly) be traced back to a lack of effective demand.

22 For a treatment of the role of land in production and rent, see, for example, Kurz and Salvadori (1995, chapter 10).

References

Betancourt, R.R., Clague, C.K., 1981. Capital Utilisation. A Theoretical and Empirical Analysis. Cambridge University Press, Cambridge.

Dos Santos Ferreira, R., 1974. Valeur et agrégation dans la problématique de la production, Ph.D. Thesis. Université Louis Pasteur, Strasbourg, France.

Fisher, F. M., 1993. Monz, J. (Ed.), Aggregation. Aggregate Production Functions and Related Topics. MIT Press, Cambridge, MA.

Foss, M.F., 1981. Long-run changes in the workweek of fixed capital. American Economic Review, Papers and Proceedings 71(2), pp. 58–63.

Georgescu-Roegen, N., 1965. Process in farming versus process in manufacturing: a problem of balanced development. In: Papi, U., Nunn, Ch. (Eds), Economic Problems of Agriculture in Industrial Societies. Macmillan, London, pp. 497–528. Reprinted in Georgescu-Roegen, 1976, pp. 71–102.

Georgescu-Roegen, N., 1966. Analytical Economics. Issues and Problems. Harvard University Press, Cambridge, MA.

Georgescu-Roegen, N., 1970. The economics of production. The Richard T. Ely Lecture. American Economic Review 60, 1–9. Reprinted in Georgescu-Roegen, 1976, pp. 61–70.

Georgescu-Roegen, N., 1971. The Entropy Law and the Economic Process. Harvard University Press, Cambridge, MA.

Georgescu-Roegen, N., 1992. Georgescu-Roegen about himself. In: Szenberg, M. (Ed.), Eminent Economists: Their Life Philosophies. Cambridge University Press, Cambridge, pp. 128–160.

Kurz, H.D., 1990. Capital, Distribution and Effective Demand. Basil Blackwell, Oxford.

Kurz, H.D., 1998. Against the current: Sraffa's unpublished manuscripts and the history of economic thought. European Journal of the History of Economic Thought 5, 437–451.

Kurz, H.D., Salvadori, N., 1993. Von Neumann's growth model and the classical tradition. European Journal of the History of Economic Thought 1, 129–160.

Kurz, H.D., Salvadori, N., 1995. Theory of Production. A Long-Period Analysis. Cambridge University Press, Cambridge.

Kurz, H.D., Salvadori, N., 1998. Reverse capital deepening and the numeraire: a note. Review of Political Economy 10, 415–426.

Kurz, H.D., Salvadori, N., 2000. Economic dynamics in a simple model with exhaustible resources and a given real wage rate. Structural Change and Economic Dynamics 11, 167–179.

Kurz, H.D., Salvadori, N., 2001. Classical economics and the problem of exhaustible resources. Metroeconomica 52, 282–296.

Maneschi, A., Zamagni, S., 1997. Nicholas Georgescu-Roegen, 1906–1994. Economic Journal 107, 695–707.

Mill, J.S., 1965. Robson J.M. (Ed.), Principles of Political Economy with Some of Their Applications to Social Philosophy, 1st Edition, 1848. University of Toronto Press, Toronto.

Neumann, J. von, 1945. A model of general economic equilibrium. Review of Economic Studies 13, 1–9 (originally published in German in 1937).

Piacentini, P., 1995. A time-explicit theory of production: analytical and operational suggestions following a fund–flow approach. Structural Change and Economic Dynamics 6, 461–483.

Ricardo, D., 1951. On the Principles of Political Economy and Taxation. In: Sraffa, P. (Ed.), with the Collaboration of M.H. Dobb, The Works and Correspondence of David Ricardo, Vol. I. Cambridge University Press, Cambridge (1st Edition, 1817; 3rd Edition, 1821).

Salvadori, N., 1999. Transferable machines with uniform efficiency paths. In: Mongiovi, G., Petri, F. (Eds), Value, Distribution and Capital. Routledge, London, pp. 297–313.

Samuelson, P.A., 1962. Parable and realism in capital theory: the surrogate production function. Review of Economic Studies 29, 193–206.

Sandelin, B., 1976. On the origin of the Cobb Douglas production function. Economy and History 19, 117–123.

Sraffa, P., 1960. Production of Commodities by Means of Commodities. Cambridge University Press, Cambridge.

Wicksell, K., 1893. Über Wert, Kapital und Rente nach den neueren nationalökonomischen Theorien. Gustav Fischer, Jena.

Wicksteed, P.H., 1992. The Co-ordination of the Laws of Distribution. Edward Elgar, Aldershot (first published in 1894; revised edition with an introduction by Ian Steedman).

Winston, G.C., 1982. The Timing of Economic Activities. Cambridge University Press, Cambridge.

12 Endogenous growth in a multi-sector economy*

Giuseppe Freni, Fausto Gozzi and Neri Salvadori

1. Introduction

There are at least three different approaches to endogenous growth (see Jones and Manuelli, 1997). Two include non-convexities or externalities or both. The third relies on convex models of growth in which, properly interpreted, the two welfare theorems hold (see, e.g., Jones and Manuelli, 1990 and Rebelo, 1991). The models in this last strand of literature are characterized by the fact that production is not limited by primary resources and hence the equilibrium paths can show endogenous growth. For the sake of simplicity we call 'convex' those models whose equilibria satisfy the conditions of the two Fundamental Theorems of Welfare Economics, and subdivide them into 'bounded models' (those whose feasible paths are limited by the availability of natural resources) and 'unbounded models'. In the last fifteen years, models with explicit consumption and a production side in which 'goods are made out of goods alone'[1] have been widely used in the new growth theory, especially in that approach to endogenous growth based on the assumption that all production factors are reproducible (Lucas, 1988; Rebelo, 1991). It could be argued that any mechanism found in the literature to make sustained growth possible has essentially involved the assumption that there is a 'core' of capital goods whose production does not require (either directly or indirectly) non-producible factors. In fact the reduced form of most endogenous growth models is linear or asymptotically linear in the reproducible factors (see for example, Frankel, 1962; Romer, 1986b, 1987, 1990b).[2] Consequently, in the endogenous growth literature, static analysis is mainly centred around the concept of the 'balanced growth path', which, in this context, performs the role played by the stationary state in convex bounded models.

It is common in the literature on growth to study one- or two-sector models. The exceptions are some convex models. Recent contributions to n-sector unbounded growth models have been provided by Dasgupta and Mitra (1988), Dolmas (1996), Kaganovich (1998), Ossella (1999), and Freni et al. (2001, hereafter FGS).

* Reprinted with permission from *The Theory of Economic Growth: A Classical Perspective* ed. Neri Salvadori (Cheltenham: Edward Elgar, 2003), pp. 60–80.

In FGS we studied a multi-sector 'AK model' in continuous time. We provided an existence result for optimal strategies, a set of duality results, and a complete classification of the price-supported steady states of the model. In doing so we used a number of assumptions (for the full list of assumptions used in FGS see Section 3 below). A consequence of combining these assumptions with the lack of primary resources that characterizes the 'AK' model was that for positive rates of growth (low discount rates) the structure of prices in the unique steady state of the model turned out to be invariant with respect to preferences. Hence the independence of the interest rate from preferences that holds in the one-sector 'AK' model carries over to the multi-sector model we studied in FGS. But this result is not confirmed when negative growth rates (i.e. high discount rates) are considered. On the contrary, we envisaged two other regimes, in one of which the prices in the steady state depend dramatically on the discount rate. This proves that the introduction of a multiplicity of sectors entails problems which are not visible in a one-sector model even if stability is not taken into account. However, the multi-sector linear growth model in FGS still has a very simple static structure and predicts that the long-run rate of growth of an economy does not depend on the initial conditions. Thus one could wonder if path dependence can be obtained in a linear endogenous growth framework or whether increasing returns and/or imperfectly competitive markets are required to obtain it. In the present chapter we will discuss removing some of the assumptions made in FGS in order to show that the structure of the steady-state set of the 'AK' model can be considerably enriched. Moreover, we provide several interpretative elements, relevant in dealing with convex unbounded models.

The various building blocks of the model presented in FGS have different origins. In particular, the production side of the model has a clear classical flavour (see Kurz and Salvadori, 1995) and is very close to the production side of the von Neumann model, in which commodities are produced out of each other because '[w]age costs are not considered as such, for laborers are not separately considered any more than are farm animals' (Champernowne, 1945, p. 12). This structure hints at a 'technological' theory of the long-run rate of interest, that 'appears as the natural and optimum rate of organic expansion of the system, and depends on the technical processes of production which are available' (*ibidem*). Nevertheless, the model has also a Ramsey-like preference side in which the optimal behaviour of the representative agent determines the system's saving rate. Since we maintain the hypothesis that the behaviour of the representative agent does not affect the technical conditions of production, our rational agent cannot be a worker, because the real wage is still 'whatever is needed to persuade people to work' (*ibidem*, p. 16). Therefore, it is '[t]he question of consumption by the propertied class' (*ibidem*) that properly arises in the model with an intertemporal utility functional. However, even under this 'representative capitalist' interpretation, the introduction of explicit consumption creates a tension in the model as regards the forces determining the long-run rate of interest.[3] Both considerations of technology-and-cost arbitrage and preferences concur in determining the growth rate, the profit rate and the relative prices that prevail in the long-run equilibrium. Nevertheless, in the model there is some space for the 'classical' opinion that 'even if part of the income from property were spent on consumption, and not saved, the rate of interest would not necessarily be much affected: it might still be *approximately* equal to the greatest expansion rate that *would* have been possible *if* all income from property had been saved' (*ibidem*).

Although the production framework used in FGS is the 'simple linear production model' (Gale, 1960, p. 294) which excludes both joint production and choice of technique, the complete set of results we summarize in the Classification Theorem provided in that paper is novel. The reason is that the study of multi-sector closed linear models of production with explicit consumption has been confined almost exclusively to the discrete-time framework (see McFadden, 1967; Atsumi, 1969 and the more recent literature mentioned above), while we study a continuous-time model. As a consequence, some kinds of complications which in discrete time can be avoided at first (see however Atsumi, 1969, p. 270), arise from the beginning. These complications are generally connected with joint production and decomposability, but in a continuous-time model they can also be connected with the way fixed capital is formalized in order to avoid an infinite number of commodities (depreciation by evaporation).

The chapter is organized as follows. In Section 2 we present the model in a general format whereas in Section 3 we present the results obtained by FGS in a restrictive setting. Section 4 is devoted to a comparison with the von Neumann–Sraffa–Morishima models developed mainly in the 1960s and 1970s. Section 5 clarifies the extensions of the results by FGS which, on the basis of the comparison, are expected to be easily obtained and what should require more effort. It is also devoted to clarifying the differences in the analysis connected with relaxing some assumptions, allowing decomposability of the input matrix, joint production, and multiple consumption goods. Section 6 provides some conclusions.

2. A class of convex multi-sector endogenous growth models in continuous time

The commodity space is finite (n in number) and the technology is stationary. Production consists in combining the productive services from the stocks to generate flows that add to the existing stocks. Decay and consumption, on the other hand, drain away the stocks. The production set is generated by a finite number $m, m \geq 1$, of independent activities (or processes), each of which can be run at any scale of operation. Hence, process $j (j = 1, 2, \ldots, m)$ can be represented by a pair of n-dimensional input–output vectors:

$$\mathbf{a}_j^T \rightarrow \mathbf{b}_j^T,$$

where $\mathbf{a}_j^T \mathbf{e}_i \geq 0$ is the amount of productive services from stock i that process j uses at the unitary level of activation and $\mathbf{b}_j^T \mathbf{e}_i \geq 0$ is the flow of commodity i produced by the same process at the same level of activation. Thus, we can summarize the production processes with a pair of *mxn* non-negative matrices:[4]

$$\mathbf{A} \rightarrow \mathbf{B}.$$

For the sake of simplicity, we assume that the rate of decay of the stocks in production is given by a single constant $\delta_x, \delta_x \geq 0$. Stocks not used in production are 'stored'. Stored commodities decay at the rate δ_z, $\delta_z \geq 0$. To avoid jumps in the stocks we conceptualize 'disposal' as a storage process with $\delta_z \geq \delta_x$. Each stock can be produced and no productive service from primary factors is relevant in the system. The way we handle storage (or disposal) processes implies that we assume that, in addition to the m processes formally included in the technology, free disposal activities for the productive services of the stocks are available.

We give a basic characterization of the technology by means of the following two classical von Neumann-like assumptions (Gale, 1960, p. 311):

[HP1] Each column of matrix **B** is semipositive

This assumption means that all commodities are reproducible and therefore there is no primary factor.

[HP2] Each row of matrix **A** is semipositive

This assumption means that no process can be activated without using (the service of) some commodity as an input. It therefore implies that for each $t \geq 0$ the intensity levels of the production processes are bounded from above by the existing stocks. It is convenient to assume that the system can grow at a positive rate since this case is the most interesting one from an economic point of view:

[HP3] $\exists \mathbf{x} \geq \mathbf{0}, g > 0 : \mathbf{x}^T[\mathbf{B} - (\delta_x + g)\mathbf{A}] \geq \mathbf{d}^T$, where **d** is any non-negative vector proportional to the vector of consumed commodities.

FGS and Gozzi and Freni (2001) concentrate on the case in which there is no joint production in flow outputs. That is:

[FGS1] Each row of matrix **B** has one and only one positive element.

Note that in this case each positive element of **B** can be normalized to 1 without loss of generality. Under Assumption [FGS1] processes can be unambiguously linked to industries. If, moreover, each industry has one production process, then the input/output matrices are square and we will have:

[FGS2] $m = n$(i. e. **A** is square and $\mathbf{B} = \mathbf{I}$)

Another assumption about production we sometime use is:

[FGS3] $\mathbf{x}^T[\mathbf{B} - (\delta_x + g)\mathbf{A}] \geq \mathbf{0}^T, g > -\delta_x, \mathbf{x} \geq \mathbf{0}, \mathbf{x} \neq \mathbf{0} \Rightarrow \mathbf{x}^T\mathbf{B} > \mathbf{0}^T$

It means that the services from each stock enter directly or indirectly into the production of each commodity (see Kurz and Salvadori, 1998c, pp. 95-7). In particular, if Assumptions [FGS1] and [FGS2] hold, [FGS3] is equivalent to the assumption:

[FGS4] The square matrix **A** is indecomposable

As mentioned above, the way disposal is conceptualized implies the assumption:

[HP4] $\delta_z \geq \delta_x$

The discount rate, $\rho \in \Re$, and the instantaneous utility function, u, describe the preference side of the economy because, as is quite common in the new growth theory, we are dealing with a single-consumer economy whose preferences can be represented by a utility functional $U(\mathbf{c}(t))$ with the form:

$$U(\mathbf{c}(t)) = \int_0^{\infty} e^{-\rho t} u(\mathbf{c}(t)) dt,$$

where $u(\cdot)$: $\Re_+^{c_m} \rightarrow \Re \cup \{-\infty\}, 1 \leq c_m \leq n$. Note that if $c_m < n$, then there are $n - c_m$ pure capital goods. Since the production side of the model is linear, the whole model is homogeneous if the preference side is so. We therefore assume that the utility function is the usual iso-elastic one:

[HC1] $u(\cdot) = \dfrac{1}{1-\sigma}[v(\cdot)]^{1-\sigma}$ for $\sigma > 0,\ \sigma \neq 1$,

$u(\cdot) = \log[v(\cdot)]$ for $\sigma = 1$;

[HC2] $v(\cdot) : \Re_+^{c_m} \rightarrow \Re_+$ is increasing, concave and homogeneous of degree one. If $c_m > 1$, then $v(\cdot)$ is strictly concave.[5]

Preferences are fully described by ρ, σ, and function $v(\cdot)$. In the following we will say that $v(\cdot)$ describes the preferences concerning consumption at a given moment in time, whereas ρ and σ describe preferences concerning distribution of consumption (and saving) over time. Note that if $c_m = 1$, the utility function $v(c) := c$ is equivalent to any other. Hence, if[6]

[FGS5] $c_m = 1$,

then parameters ρ and σ completely describe the preference side of the model.

Let **s** be the $n \times 1$ vector of stocks, **x** be the $m \times 1$ intensity vector and c be the $n \times 1$ vector obtained from the consumption vector **c** by adding a zero component for each pure capital good. The evolution of the stocks is given by the following differential equation:

$$\dot{\mathbf{s}}^T = \mathbf{x}^T\mathbf{B} - \delta_x \mathbf{x}^T\mathbf{A} - \delta_z(\mathbf{s}^T - \mathbf{x}^t\mathbf{A}) - \hat{\mathbf{c}}^T$$

with the constraints

$$\mathbf{x}^T\mathbf{A} \le \mathbf{s}^T, \mathbf{x} \ge \mathbf{0}, \ \mathbf{c} \ge \mathbf{0}.$$

The common approach to the analysis of competitive equilibria in the above setting is through the extension of the first and second welfare theorems for finite dimensional economies. This strategy leads to the investigation of the link between the competitive equilibria of the system and the solutions, if there are any, to the problem:

$$\begin{aligned} V(\mathbf{s}^*) &= \sup \int_0^\infty e^{-\rho t} u(\mathbf{c}(t))dt \\ \dot{\mathbf{s}}^T &= \mathbf{x}^T\mathbf{B} - \delta_x \mathbf{x}^T\mathbf{A} - \delta_z(\mathbf{s}^T - \mathbf{x}^T\mathbf{A}) - \hat{\mathbf{c}}^T \qquad \text{(P)} \\ \mathbf{x}^T\mathbf{A} &\le \mathbf{s}^T, \mathbf{x} \ge \mathbf{0}, \mathbf{c} \ge \mathbf{0}, \mathbf{s}(0) = \mathbf{s}^* \ge \mathbf{0} \ \textit{given}. \end{aligned}$$

We will therefore be interested in the existence and characterization of the paths for which the problem (P) has a solution. Moreover, since under the above assumptions (P) is a homogeneous programme, our interest will lie also in the existence and characterization of the special paths that solve (P) and enjoy a steady-state structure. These paths provide the simplest reference point for the analysis of the asymptotic behaviour of non-stationary paths.

In studying the optimal control problem (P), Hamiltonian formalism is often used to introduce the 'price' variables. From an economic point of view, this is a particularly significant procedure because it leads to the introduction of competitive prices. Indeed, what are defined as competitive paths are simply stock-price paths supporting the maximized Hamiltonian (see Cass and Shell, 1976). In our context, since the optimal control problem (P) is autonomous, the discounted Hamiltonian is used. It is given by:

$$H^D(\mathbf{s}, \mathbf{v}) = \max_{\mathbf{c} \ge \mathbf{0}} \left[u(\mathbf{c}) - \hat{\mathbf{c}}^T\mathbf{v} \right] - \delta_z \mathbf{s}^T\mathbf{v} + \max_{\substack{\mathbf{x}^T\mathbf{A} \le \mathbf{s}^T \\ \mathbf{x} \ge \mathbf{0}}} \mathbf{x}^T[\mathbf{B} - (\delta_x - \delta_z)\mathbf{A}]\mathbf{v}.$$

The linear programming problem involved in the definition of $H^D(\mathbf{s}, \mathbf{v})$ requires the existence of a vector $\mathbf{q}^*(\mathbf{s}, \mathbf{v}) \in \Re^n_+$ which is a solution to the dual problem and can be interpreted as the vector of the equilibrium 'rental' rates for the use of the stocks. Hence, if $\mathbf{c}^*(\mathbf{v}), \mathbf{x}^*(\mathbf{s}, \mathbf{v})$ indicate a set of controls solving the max problems involved in the definition of $H^D(\mathbf{s}, \mathbf{v})$, then the set of paths $[\mathbf{s}(t), \mathbf{v}(t), \mathbf{c}^*(\mathbf{v}(t)), \mathbf{x}^*(\mathbf{s}(t), \mathbf{v}(t)), \mathbf{q}^*(\mathbf{s}(t), \mathbf{v}(t))]$, which satisfy appropriate continuity properties and solve

$$\dot{\mathbf{s}} \in \partial H^C_{\mathbf{v}}(\cdot, \cdot) \qquad (1)$$

$$\dot{\mathbf{v}} - \rho \mathbf{v} \in -\partial H^C_{\mathbf{s}}(\cdot, \cdot) \qquad (2)$$

is called a *competitive program*, i.e. a critical point for the problem (P). A transversality condition is then involved in the extension of the first and second welfare theorems to infinite horizon economies. The first welfare theorem, in particular, will state that absolutely continuous competitive paths with non-negative prices that satisfy a suitable transversality condition are optimal. It is well known, however, that a full converse of this result does not hold due to the possibility that absolutely continuity of prices cannot be granted for stock paths hitting the non-negativity boundary. Moreover, prices supporting non-interior stock paths can fail to exist altogether (examples of this phenomenon are provided by FGS, Appendix D).

In closing this section, we should point out that there are some convex endogenous growth models that cannot be reduced at once to the present framework, a few of which are mentioned here. First, models with pure consumption goods and/or non-reproducible resources that are not essential (see e.g. Bose, 1968; Weitzman, 1971; Jones and Manuelli, 1990; Rebelo, 1991). Second, models with adjustment costs (see e.g. Dolmas, 1996; Ladron-de-Guevara, Ortigueira and Santos, 1999). Third, models in which the technology is not polyhedral (e.g. Kaganovich, 1998). Finally, models with an infinite dimensional commodity space (Boldrin and Levine, 2002).

3. Steady states in a 'Simple' multi-sector AK model

In FGS Assumptions [HP1]–[HP3], [FGS1]–[FGS5], [HC1]–[HC2] hold. Moreover, it is also assumed that all commodities are available at time 0 and that the (unique) consumption good enters directly in its own production. That is, if the consumption good is commodity 1,

[FGS6] $\mathbf{s}^* > \mathbf{0}$,

[FGS7] $a_{11} > 0$.

The first of these two assumptions implies that there is an admissible solution to problem (P) with a positive **s** for each $t > 0$. The second assumption guarantees that $\mathbf{s} > \mathbf{0}$ for each $t > 0$ in each optimal solution starting at any $\mathbf{s}^* > \mathbf{0}$. This result is relevant since if $\mathbf{s} > \mathbf{0}$, then **q** is bounded and, therefore, prices **v** cannot jump. FGS first prove that an optimal path exists if and only if

[HE] $\delta\Gamma > \Gamma - \rho$

where $\Gamma = \sup\{g : \exists \mathbf{x} \geq \mathbf{0} : \mathbf{x}^T[\mathbf{B} - (\delta_x + g)\mathbf{A}] \geq \mathbf{e}_1^T\}$ and $\mathbf{e}_1$ is the first unit vector: a vector proportional to the vector of consumed commodities.[7] Under the assumptions maintained by FGS it turns out that $\Gamma = \lambda_{PF}^{-1} - \delta_x$, where λ_{PF} is the Perron–Frobenius eigenvalue of matrix **A**.

The above existence theorem is completed with two theorems concerning the optimality conditions for the problem at hand, that are the extensions to the present framework of standard results holding in smooth-bounded models. In particular it is proved (1) that a competitive program is optimal if the usual condition that the value of the stocks converges to zero holds and (2) that for each optimal solution to problem (P) it is possible to find price and rental paths such that the optimal solution is also a competitive program whose value of the stocks converges to zero. For formal statements and corresponding proofs see the original paper by FGS.

As a step towards the study of the dynamics of the system, FGS analysed the *steady-state optimal solutions* to problem (P), which are defined as optimal solutions $(\mathbf{s}(t), \hat{\mathbf{c}}(t), \hat{\mathbf{x}}(t))$ to problem (P) for which there is a real number g, a real number c_0, and a non-negative vector $\mathbf{x}_0$ such that $\hat{\mathbf{c}}(t) = c_0 e^{gt}\mathbf{e}_1, \hat{\mathbf{x}}(t) = \mathbf{x}_0 e^{gt}$, where $\mathbf{e}_1$ is the first unit vector. The definition of steady-state optimal solutions does not state that the supporting relative prices are constant over time.[8] However, FGS have proved that for each steady-state solution there are a price path and a rental path such that

$$\mathbf{v}(t) = \mathbf{v}(0)e^{-g\sigma t}, \ \mathbf{q}(t) = (\rho + \delta_z - g\sigma)\mathbf{v}(0)e^{-g\sigma t}.$$

We will refer to these prices and rentals as *steady-state price-rental paths*. On the basis of these and other results, FGS reduce the problem of the optimal steady states to the analysis of finding scalars $g \in [\frac{1}{\sigma}(\lambda_{PF}^{-1} - \delta_x - \rho), \lambda_{PF}^{-1} - \delta_x)$ and c_0 and vectors $\mathbf{s}_0, \mathbf{x}_0$, and $\mathbf{v}_0$ such that:

$$\mathbf{e}_1^T \mathbf{v}_0 = c_0^{-\sigma} \tag{3a}$$

$$[\mathbf{I} - (\rho + \delta_x + g\sigma)\mathbf{A}]\mathbf{v}_0 \leq \mathbf{0} \tag{3b}$$

$$\mathbf{x}_0^T[\mathbf{I} - (\rho + \delta_x + g\sigma)\mathbf{A}]\mathbf{v}_0 = \mathbf{0} \tag{3c}$$

$$\mathbf{x}_0^T\mathbf{A} - \mathbf{s}_0^T \leq \mathbf{0} \tag{3d}$$

$$\mathbf{x}_0^T[\mathbf{I} - (g + \delta_x)\mathbf{A}]\mathbf{v}_0 = c_0\mathbf{e}_1^T\mathbf{v}_0 \tag{3e}$$

$$\mathbf{x}_0^T[\mathbf{I} - (g + \delta_x)\mathbf{A}] \geq c_0\mathbf{e}_1^T \quad \text{for } g + \delta_z \geq 0 \tag{3f}$$

$$\mathbf{s}_0^T - \frac{1}{g + \delta_z}\{\mathbf{x}_0^T[\mathbf{I} - (\delta_x - \delta_z)\mathbf{A}] - c_0\mathbf{e}_1^T\} \geq \mathbf{0} \quad \text{for } g + \delta_z < 0 \tag{3g}$$

$$c_0 > 0, \mathbf{v}_0 \geq \mathbf{0}, \mathbf{x}_0 \geq \mathbf{0}. \tag{3h}$$

Optimal steady-state solutions with steady-state support are relevant also since in these states some relevant concepts, such as that of 'real rate of profit' or 'growth rate', can be defined. The literature on growth often refers to steady states in order to convey some macroeconomic insights. Lucas (1988. p. 11), for instance, refers freely to steady-state concepts as 'the rate of growth' or the 'real rate of profit' under the explicit assumption of a fast convergence to the steady state.

As a matter of fact there are profitability concepts which can be used with reference to optimal solutions even if they are not steady states. It is always possible to deal with the 'own rate of return of commodity i' as the rate of profit which can be obtained by an investment measured in commodity i getting a revenue measured in commodity i (see, for instance, Malinvaud, 1953). FGS show that in any optimal solution:[9]

$$r_i(t) = \rho - \frac{\mathbf{e}_j^T\dot{\mathbf{v}}(t)}{\mathbf{e}_j^T\mathbf{v}(t)}$$

where $r_i(t)$ is the own rate of return of commodity i at time t. FGS also proved that in any optimal solution the growth rate of consumption equals the ratio of the difference between the own rate of return of commodity 1 and ρ over σ:

$$\frac{\dot{c}(t)}{c(t)} = \frac{r_1(t) - \rho}{\sigma}. \tag{4}$$

In a steady-state solution supported by steady-state prices all the own rates of return are equal to each other so we can call this common rate the 'real rate of profit r'. Similarly, in a steady-state solution all the intensities of operation of processes as well as consumption grow at the same rate so we can call this common rate the 'growth rate g'. Obviously, in a steady-state:

$$g = \frac{r - \rho}{\sigma}. \tag{5}$$

From equations and inequalities (3) FGS obtained a Classification Theorem, in which three different regimes are envisaged, depending on the values of the parameters involved. The Classification Theorem states a particular relationship between the growth rate g and the rate of profit r. This $r - g$ relationship is drawn in Figure 12.1. In the first regime r is constant and equals $\lambda_{PF}^{-1} - \delta_x$, whereas g varies in the range $(-\delta_x, \lambda_{PF}^{-1} - \delta_x)$. In the second regime g is constant and equals $-\delta_x$, whereas r varies in the range $[\lambda_{PF}^{-1} - \delta_x, a_{11}^{-1} - \delta_x]$. In the third regime r is constant again and equals $a_{11}^{-1} - \delta_x$, whereas g varies in the range $(-\infty, -\delta_x)$. This relationship is not to be confused with another $r - g$ relationship, that is, equation (5). The former depends on technology and on preferences concerning consumption at a given moment in time and does not depend on preferences concerning distribution of consumption over time.[10] The latter, by contrast, depends only on preferences concerning distribution of consumption over time. In a steady-state solution r and g are determined by the intersection between these two $r - g$ relationships.

The interpretation of the Classification Theorem is simple. If $g > -\delta_x$, then all commodities need to be produced and therefore n processes are to be operated. Thus, the n equations relating prices and rate of profit relative to the operated processes (the no arbitrage conditions) determine both the $n - 1$ relative prices and the real rate of profit. In this regime prices are proportional to $\mathbf{v}_{PF} > \mathbf{0}$, that is the right eigenvector of matrix $\mathbf{A}$ corresponding to λ_{PF}. If $g < -\delta_x$, the only process which is relevant is the process producing commodity 1. Since the inputs used by this process are produced jointly by the process itself at a rate larger than the growth rate, all commodities used in the production of commodity 1 except commodity 1 itself have a zero price. In other words, production is reduced to the production of commodity 1 by means of commodity 1 and free goods. Hence, in a similar way to the previous case the equation relating prices and the rate of profit relative to the operated process producing commodity 1 can determine the rate of profit (apart from commodity 1, all commodities which are either produced or stored have a zero price). If $g = -\delta_x$ then once again the only relevant process is that producing commodity 1, and the inputs used by this process are produced jointly by the process itself. Yet this is realized at a rate equal to the growth rate and

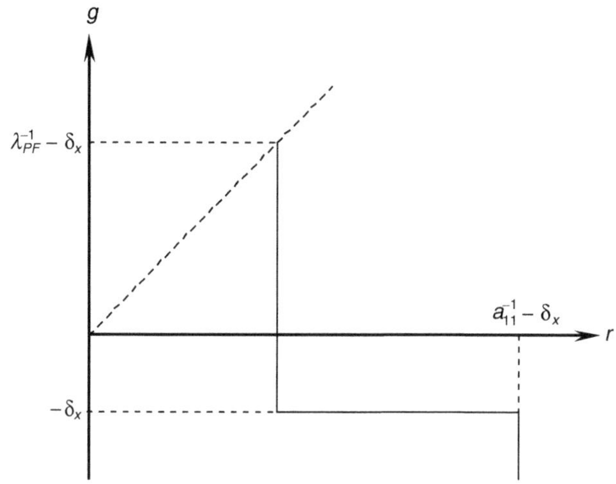

Figure 12.1 The Classification Theorem: Single production and indecomposable matrix **A**.

therefore these commodities (except commodity 1) may have either a positive or a zero price. Those with a positive price cannot be separately produced or stored; their existing stocks can be regarded as stocks of 'renewable' resources for which a growth rate of $-\delta_x$ can be granted in the production of commodity 1.

4. A Comparison with the von Neumann–Sraffa–Morishima models

Let us consider the case of $g + \delta_z \geq 0$, taking account of the fact that in a steady-state equation (4) holds. Let us substitute r for $\rho + g\sigma$ in inequality (3b) and in equation (3c). Let us drop Assumptions [FGS1]–[FGS4] in order to allow for choice of techniques and joint production and, therefore, substitute matrix **B** for **I** in inequalities (3b), (3g), (3h) and in equations (3c) and (3f). Then we obtain from inequalities (3b), (3g), (3i) and equations (3c) and (3f) exactly the model analysed in the von Neumann–Sraffa Morishima literature developed in the 1960s and 1970s, with contributions up to now (Kurz and Salvadori, 1995, summarize the whole approach):

$$[\mathbf{B} - (r + \delta_x)\mathbf{A}]\mathbf{v}_0 \leq \mathbf{0},$$

$$\mathbf{x}_0^T[\mathbf{B} - (r + \delta_x)\mathbf{A}]\mathbf{v}_0 = \mathbf{0}$$

$$\mathbf{x}_0^T[\mathbf{B} - (g + \delta_x)\mathbf{A}] \geq c_0\mathbf{e}_1^T,$$

$$\mathbf{x}_0^T[\mathbf{B} - (g + \delta_x)\mathbf{A}]\mathbf{v}_0 = c_0\mathbf{e}_1^T\mathbf{v}_0$$

$$c_0 > 0, \mathbf{v}_0 \geq \mathbf{0}, \mathbf{x}_0 \geq \mathbf{0}.$$

The main difference consists in the fact that in the literature in question there was almost always at least one primary factor called ‘labour’. In the cases in which no primary factor was taken into consideration, or the wage of labourers was taken to be zero, an extra inequality was mentioned, which in our case it is certainly satisfied since equation (3a) and inequality (3h) hold:

$$\mathbf{x}_0^T \mathbf{B}\mathbf{v}_0 > 0.$$

The first problem to be analysed is the following. The first regime mentioned in the Classification Theorem is mentioned in the von Neumann–Sraffa–Morishima literature. Actually it is ‘the’ result that would have been predicted for an economy with stationary relative prices and a wage rate equal to zero. But what about the other regimes? The literature in question has rarely considered negative growth rates. Could one expect such a difference?

The problem arises since for $g < -\delta_x$ the distinction between single production and joint production is not relevant. This section is devoted to clarifying this point as a contribution to understanding the problems involved in multi-sector models. A graphic exposition in terms of two goods will be sufficient here. Consider a joint production process

$$\mathbf{a} \rightarrow \mathbf{b},$$

and let us represent it in a commodity space in which vectors **a** and **b** and vector $\mathbf{b} - (g + \delta_x)\mathbf{a}$ appear. Figure 12.2 depicts four alternative vectors $\mathbf{b} - (g + \delta_x)\mathbf{a}$, depending on the size of $g : g' < -\delta_x < g'' < g'''$. In Figure 12.3, instead,

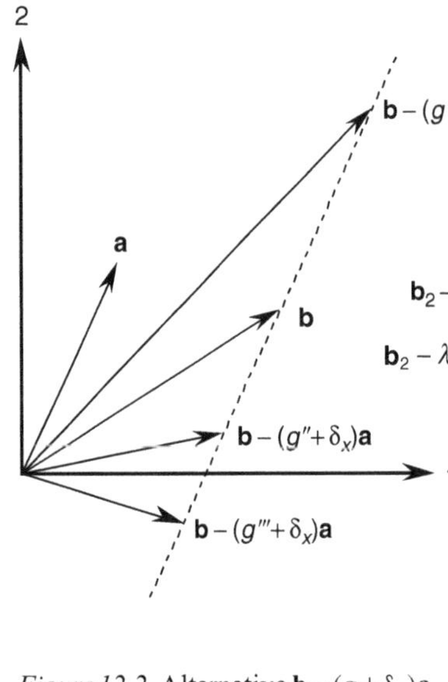

Figure 12.2 Alternative $\mathbf{b}-(g+\delta_x)\mathbf{a}$ vectors.

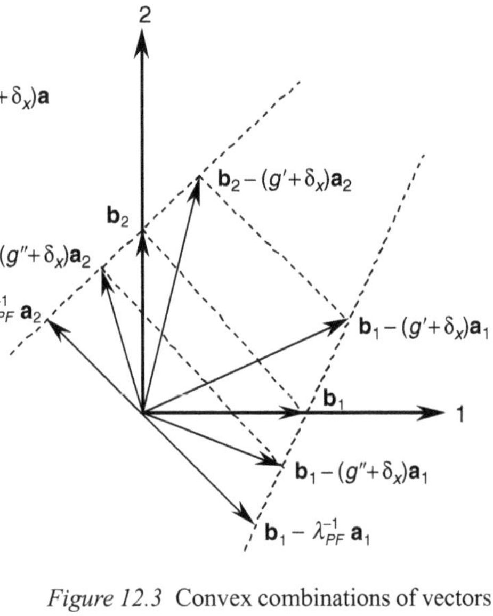

Figure 12.3 Convex combinations of vectors $\mathbf{b}_i - (g + \delta_x)\mathbf{a}_i (i = 1, 2)$.

there are two single production processes, one producing commodity 1 and one producing commodity 2. Also in this case in the figure we have drawn alternative vectors $\mathbf{b}_i - (g + \delta_x)\mathbf{a}_i$. It is immediately recognized that when $g + \delta_x$ is positive, the cone consisting of convex combinations of vectors $\mathbf{b}_i - (g + \delta_x)\mathbf{a}_i (i = 1, 2)$ includes the positive orthant, whereas for negative values of $g + \delta_x$ the same cone is included in the positive orthant. Both processes are needed to produce the consumption vector at the required growth rate only if the consumption vector is *internal* to that cone. Let us focus on the other cases: that in which the consumption vector is *external* to the cone and that in which the consumption vector is *on the boundary* of the cone.

In a two-commodity economy the fact that the consumption vector is external to the above-mentioned cone means that no convex combination of processes can supply an amount of the required consumption without overproduction of a commodity which, as a consequence, has a zero price. Moreover, there is a problem of choice of technique even if the original model contemplated a number of processes equal to the number of commodities: as a matter of fact the model is equivalent to one in which the commodity with a price equal to zero does not exist, whereas the number of processes is unchanged. The same argument is immediately applicable to an n-commodity economy: once again some prices need to be zero, a convex combination of the operated processes meets the components of the consumption vector with a positive price and overproduction of commodities with a zero price.

In a two-commodity economy the fact that the consumption vector is on the boundary of the cone means that there is a convex combination of processes which can supply an amount of the required consumption without the condition that a commodity is overproduced, but this convex combination is actually made up of only one process: no commodity needs to be overproduced, but the no arbitrage conditions determine a number of constraints lower than the number of the prices to be ascertained. Hence we have to study whether the fact that the consumption vector is on the cone boundary is just by chance or whether there are economic forces at work to impose this condition. In the former case prices are undetermined and vary in a range. In the latter case the forces at work have an impact on prices which can be determined. The same argument is immediately applicable to an n-commodity economy: once again the no-arbitrage conditions determine a number of relations among prices lower than that which would be necessary to determine prices. Thus the economic forces which drive the consumption vector to the boundary may determine the further constraints which are able to complete the determination of prices. Otherwise prices are not fully determined and may vary in a range.

With these arguments in mind we can move on to analyse the last two regimes mentioned in the Classification Theorem. The third is clearly a case in which the consumption vector, which in our case is proportional to the first unit vector, is outside the cone: all commodities needed for the production of commodity 1 except commodity 1 itself are overproduced. The second regime mentioned in the Classification Theorem is clearly a case in which the consumption vector is on the boundary of the cone. In this range the no-arbitrage conditions are not able to fully determine prices; then in the long run an increment in ρ pushes down the prices of the inputs of commodity 1 pushing the rate of profit r up in such a way that the increment in ρ is exactly compensated and the growth rate is unchanged. Note that if the growth rate were pushed up, then the no-arbitrage conditions would impose prices proportional to $\mathbf{v}_{PF}$, whereas if it were pushed down, then the no-arbitrage conditions would impose zero prices for all inputs of commodity 1 apart from commodity 1 itself.

5. Generalizations

The arguments developed in the previous section suggest that:

- If there is joint production the second and third regime of the Classification Theorem do not need to be connected with negative growth rates;
- If more than one commodity is consumed (in a single production setting), then:
  - the first regime of the Classification Theorem may also hold for values of the growth rate lower than $-\delta_x$;
  - if the proportion in which commodities are consumed depends on prices, then the second regime may determine a relationship between the rate of profit and the growth rate which may be different from a horizontal segment:
  - if there is continuous substitution in consumption, the third regime of the Classification Theorem may not exist.

Simple examples illustrating the above properties are easily constructed. In the appendices to this chapter we provide such examples. Appendix A presents two examples involving joint production. The first example shows that the second regime of the Classification Theorem and part of the third can actually occur for positive growth rates. The second example shows that the first regime does not need to exist when joint production is involved.

Appendix B presents a number of examples involving two consumption commodities. These examples are related to the value assumed by a parameter. Three possibilities are envisaged. In all of them for high growth rates (i.e. low discount rates) the rate of profit and the prices are determined as in the Classification Theorem studied in FGS. However for low growth rates (i.e. high discount rates), the relationship between prices and quantities and growth and profit rates are very different from what was predicted by the theorem.

In general, the arguments developed in the previous section suggest that many of the results obtained in long-period models of Classical inspiration like those of von Neumann and Sraffa can at least partly be imported in the framework here presented. In particular the problem of choice of technique[11] and that of joint production appear to be easily handled. Similarly, some difficulties recognized in those models should have corresponding difficulties here. In particular we know that dropping Assumption [FGS4], or its general form [FGS3], may lead to difficulties. The analogue of these difficulties in the present framework can be illustrated with an example. In Appendix C we present an example with two commodities: commodity 2 enters directly into the production of both commodities, whereas commodity 1 (which is the only commodity to be consumed) enters directly only into its own production. This simple model is analysed to illustrate the difficulties that a decomposable matrix **A** can generate.[12] In this example, besides the three regimes mentioned in the Classification Theorem, there is a fourth regime, in which commodity 2 behaves like a renewable resource which, if it is left to itself, grows at a rate higher than that of the consumption good. In order to produce commodity 1, producers pick it just as fruits were collected in the Garden of Eden: at no cost. This example can also be used to show what may happen when assumption [HP4] is dropped and, therefore, when storage is not part of the process of disposal but is effected in order to preserve the commodities. This point is clarified at the end of Appendix C.

6. Concluding remarks

This chapter has investigated a number of problems which are absent in any single sector economy, but can be present in a multiple sector economy. This has been done with the help of a generalization of the multi-sector 'AK model' in continuous time which we analysed in a previous paper. This analysis has also shown how this model is connected to the von Neumann–Sraffa–Morishima linear models investigated in the 1960s and 1970s.

Appendix A

Let (P) be the problem

$$V(\mathbf{s}^*) = \sup \int_0^\infty e^{-\rho t} \frac{c^{1-\sigma}}{1-\sigma} dt$$

$$\dot{\mathbf{s}}^T = \mathbf{x}^T\mathbf{B} - \delta_x \mathbf{x}^T\mathbf{A} - \delta_z(\mathbf{s}^T - \mathbf{x}^T\mathbf{A}) - \mathbf{c}^T$$

$$\mathbf{x}^T\mathbf{A} \leq \mathbf{s}^T, \mathbf{x} \geq \mathbf{0}, \mathbf{c} \geq \mathbf{0}, \mathbf{s}(0) = \mathbf{s}^* > \mathbf{0} \textit{ given.}$$

where

$$\mathbf{A} = \begin{bmatrix} 1 & 1 \\ 1 & 0 \end{bmatrix}, \quad \mathbf{B} = \begin{bmatrix} 2 & 1 \\ 1 & 2 \end{bmatrix} \quad \text{and} \quad \mathbf{c} = c \begin{bmatrix} 1 \\ 0 \end{bmatrix}.$$

It is easily checked that the steady-state optimal solutions can be represented in the same three regimes referred to in the Classification Theorem. If $\delta_x < 1$, the second regime of the Classification Theorem and part of the third occur for positive values of the growth rate.

Let (P) be the same problem above, except that the input–output–matrices are now given by

$$\mathbf{A} = \begin{bmatrix} \frac{1}{4} & \frac{1}{2} \\ 0 & \frac{1}{2} \end{bmatrix} \quad \text{and} \quad \mathbf{B} = \begin{bmatrix} 2 & 2 \\ 0 & 1 \end{bmatrix}.$$

It is easily verified that the steady-state optimal solutions can be represented by two of the three regimes referred to in the Classification Theorem. The second process is inefficient with respect to the first process and therefore it is never operated. Hence the first regime of the Classification Theorem cannot exist.

Appendix B

Let (P) be the problem:

$$V(\mathbf{s}^*) = \sup \int_0^\infty e^{-\rho t} \log(c_1^{1-\alpha} c_2^{\alpha}) dt$$

$$\dot{\mathbf{s}} = \mathbf{x} - \mathbf{s} - \mathbf{c}$$

$$\mathbf{x}^{\mathrm{T}} \begin{bmatrix} \frac{1}{8} & \frac{1}{4} \\ \frac{1}{8} & 0 \end{bmatrix} \leq \mathbf{s}^T, \mathbf{x} \geq \mathbf{0}, \mathbf{c} = \begin{bmatrix} c_1 \\ c_2 \end{bmatrix} \geq \mathbf{0}, \mathbf{s}(0) = \mathbf{s}^* \geq \mathbf{0} \textit{ given.}$$

If $\alpha = 0$ or $\alpha = 1$, there is a single consumption commodity. Hence, let $0 < \alpha < 1$. The instantaneous Cobb–Douglas utility function determines consumption share, in value, as constant and depending only on α: along any optimal path:

$$\frac{c_1 v_1}{c_2 v_2} = \frac{1-\alpha}{\alpha}$$

and, as a consequence, both prices and both consumption levels are positive. Hence in a steady-state optimal solution:

$$c_1 = x_1 - (1+g)s_1 > 0, c_2 = x_2 - (1+g)s_2 > 0.$$

Let us partition all possible cases on the basis of operated processes. If both processes are operated, then:

$$r = 3, \frac{v_1}{v_2} = 2, \quad \frac{c_1}{c_2} = \frac{1-\alpha}{2\alpha},$$

$$x_1 = \frac{8(4 - 3\alpha + \alpha g)}{(1-\alpha)(27 - 6g - g^2)} c_1, \quad x_2 = \frac{1 + 6\alpha + g - 2\alpha g}{(1-\alpha)(27 - 6g - g^2)} c_1.$$

There are two critical values for the parameter α : 1/3, and 1/2. For $0 < \alpha < 1/3$ vector $\mathbf{x}$ is positive if and only if $g < [(3\alpha - 4)/\alpha]$ or $[(1+6\alpha)/(2\alpha - 1)] < g < 3$. For $\alpha = 1/3$ vector $\mathbf{x}$ is positive for $g < 3$. For $1/3 < \alpha < 1/2$ vector $\mathbf{x}$ is positive if and only if $g < [(1+6\alpha)/(2\alpha - 1)]$ or $[(3\alpha - 4)/\alpha] < g < 3$. For $1/2 \leq \alpha < 1$

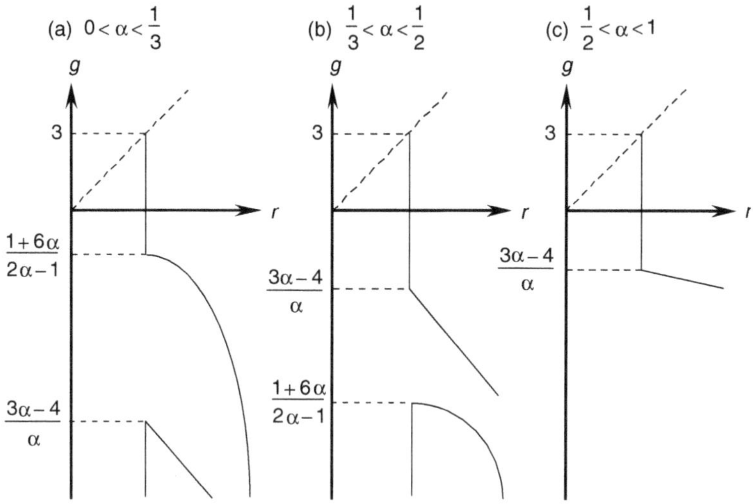

Figure 12.4 Multiple consumption goods.

vector **x** is positive if and only if $[(3\alpha - 4)/\alpha] < g < 3$. If only the first process is operated, then:

$$\frac{v_1}{v_2} = \frac{2(1+r)}{7-r}, \frac{c_1}{c_2} = \frac{g-7}{2(1+g)}, 3 < r < 7 \text{ and } g < -1.$$

Hence $g = [7 + (8\alpha - 1)r]/[(8\alpha - 7) + r]$ and $\alpha < 1/2$. If only the second process is operated, then

$$\frac{v_1}{v_2} = \frac{8}{1+r}, \frac{c_1}{c_2} = -\frac{(1+g)}{8}, r > 3 \text{ and } g \leq -1.$$

Hence $g = -[1 + (1 - \alpha)r]/\alpha$. Figures 12.4 provide the relationship between g and r for values of α in one of the three relevant ranges: $0 < \alpha < 1/3, 1/3 < \alpha < 1/2, 1/2 \leq \alpha < 1$, respectively.

Appendix C

Let (P) be the problem:

$$V(\mathbf{s}^*) = \sup \int_0^\infty e^{-\rho t} \frac{c^{1-\sigma}}{1-\sigma} dt$$
$$\dot{\mathbf{s}}^T = \mathbf{x}^T\mathbf{I} - \delta_x \mathbf{x}^T\mathbf{A} - \delta_z(\mathbf{s}^T - \mathbf{x}^T\mathbf{A}) - \mathbf{c}^T$$
$$\mathbf{x}^T\mathbf{A} \leq \mathbf{s}^T, \mathbf{x} \geq \mathbf{0}, \mathbf{c} \geq \mathbf{0}, \mathbf{s}(0) = \mathbf{s}^* > \mathbf{0} \textit{ given}$$

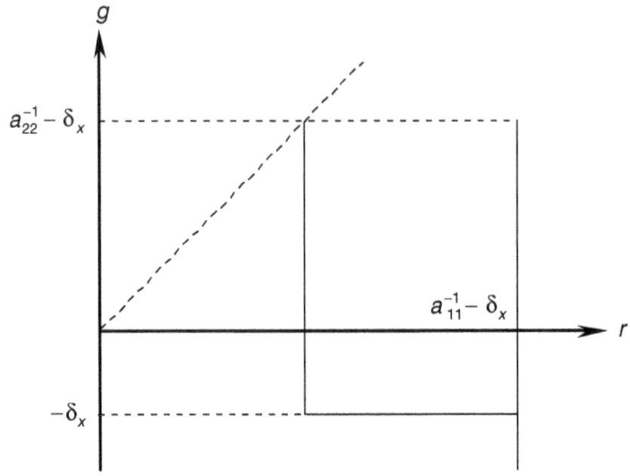

Figure 12.5 Single production and decomposable matrix **A**.

where

$$\mathbf{A} = \begin{bmatrix} a_{11} & a_{12} \\ 0 & a_{22} \end{bmatrix}, \ a_{11} < a_{22} \ \text{ and } \ \mathbf{c} = c \begin{bmatrix} 1 \\ 0 \end{bmatrix}.$$

It is easily verified that the steady-state optimal solutions can be represented in four regimes which are depicted in Figure 12.5. Three regimes are the same mentioned in the Classification Theorem. The fourth regime is characterized by $r = a_{11}^{-1} - \delta_x$ and $-\delta_x < g < a_{22}^{-1} - \delta_x$. In this regime commodity 2 is (over)produced and its price equals 0. The growth rate cannot be equal or larger than $a_{22}^{-1} - \delta_x$ because otherwise the intensity of operation of the process producing commodity 1 would be nought or negative (and therefore consumption would be nought or negative).

Process 2 in the example can be interpreted as a storage process for commodity 2 with a *negative* rate of decay. The existence of the fourth regime, however, does not depend on the sign of the rate of decay, but on the fact that $a_{22}^{-1} - \delta_x > -\delta_x$. It is clear therefore that something similar to the fourth regime contemplated in this example comes into existence whenever assumption [HP4] does not hold.

Notes

1 Champernowne (1945, p. 12) used this expression for the von Neumann (1945) model. In the following we will borrow other expressions from this paper by Champernowne to emphasize some similarities with the von Neumann model and the literature devoted to it.

2 Some theorists even came to the conclusion that unbounded growth is more an assumption about the linearity of the technology than a result of the models; see for instance Romer (1990b, p. S84).

3 This is not the usual interpretation found in the recent literature. On the contrary it has been suggested that the AK model 'becomes more plausible if we think of K in a

broad sense to include human capital' (Barro and Sala-i-Martin, 1995, p. 39). Such two interpretations are not so different as they seem at first sight. We will come back on this in note 4. It also possible to assume that the necessary subsistence of workers (or the inputs to produce human capital) are included in the A of the AK model, whereas another part of wages, which exceeds the necessaries, are subject to the choice of the 'representative agent', who, in this case, does not need to be any more a 'representative capitalist'.

4 In this description of technology, labour was not explicitly considered. On the contrary a process can be represented as

$$\mathbf{a}_j^T \oplus l_j \to \mathbf{b}_j^T,$$

where l_j refers to labour input. Then there are two ways to obtain the symbolism used in the text, in the assumption that the real wage rate per unit of labour is defined by the vector w. Let $\hat{\mathbf{A}}$ be the usual material input matrix used in input–output analysis and let $\mathbf{l}$ be the input vector of (simple) labour. Then the matrix $\mathbf{A}$ in the text can be seen as either of the following:

$$\mathbf{A} = \hat{\mathbf{A}} + \mathbf{l}\mathbf{w}^T, \mathbf{A} = \begin{bmatrix} \hat{\mathbf{A}} & \mathbf{l} \\ \mathbf{w} & 0 \end{bmatrix}.$$

In the latter alternative the last process referes to production' of 'labour' or 'human capital'.

5 The use of iso-elastic utility functions goes back to Ramsey (1928) who studied this 'interesting special case' in section II of his 1928 paper.

6 Cases with multiple consumption goods are considered by Gozzi and Freni (2001).

7 We note that the utility function u is unbounded above or below or, in the log case, both above and below. Moreover, the boundedness of feasible paths is not assumed. This generates a non-trivial existence problem for (P) which is usually solved by the introduction of an existence condition linking the technology with the preferences (see for example McFadden, 1967).

8 An example can clarify the issue. Let

$$\rho = \frac{1}{3}, u\left(\mathbf{c}(t)\right) = c_t^{1/2}, \mathbf{B} = \mathbf{I}, \delta_x = \delta_z = 1/2,$$

$$\mathbf{A} = \begin{bmatrix} \frac{1}{3} & \frac{1}{3} & \frac{1}{3} \\ \frac{1}{6} & \frac{2}{3} & \frac{1}{6} \\ \frac{1}{6} & \frac{1}{6} & \frac{2}{3} \end{bmatrix}, \hat{\mathbf{c}} = c\mathbf{e}_1 \text{ and } \mathbf{s}^* = \begin{bmatrix} \frac{42}{31} \\ \frac{72}{31} \\ \frac{72}{31} \end{bmatrix}$$

in the (P) problem. It is easily checked that

$$\mathbf{s} = \mathbf{s}^* e^{\frac{1}{3}t}, \ \mathbf{v} = \begin{bmatrix} 1 \\ 1 \\ 1 \end{bmatrix} e^{-\frac{1}{6}t} + h \begin{bmatrix} 0 \\ -1 \\ 1 \end{bmatrix} e^{-\frac{7}{6}t}, \ c = e^{\frac{1}{3}t},$$

$$\mathbf{x} = \begin{bmatrix} \frac{66}{31} \\ \frac{60}{31} \\ \frac{60}{31} \end{bmatrix}, \mathbf{q} = \begin{bmatrix} 1 \\ 1 \\ 1 \end{bmatrix} e^{\frac{1}{6}t} + 2h \begin{bmatrix} 0 \\ -1 \\ 1 \end{bmatrix} e^{-\frac{7}{6}t}$$

for $-1/2 < h < 1/2$ is a steady-state optimal solution to problem (P) supported by a competitive rental-price path, so that despite the fact that the quantity side grows at rate 1/3, the relative prices and relative rentals do not need to be constant (they are so if and only if $h = 0$).

9 This formula is clearly a reminiscence of Fisher formula, when the own rate of return is interpreted as a 'real' rate of profit, the discount rate as a 'nominal' rate, and the fraction in the RHS as an inflation rate.

10 Evans et al. (1998) refer to this relationship as a 'technological' relationship whereas they refer to equation (5) as a 'preferences' relationship. However, as shown in the example of Appendix C, the former relationship depends not only on technology, but also on preferences concerning consumption at a given moment in time.

11 It is easily checked that the Classification Theorem can be generalized to allow the existence of several processes for the production of each commodity (even a continuous number). If Assumptions [FGS1], [FGS3], [FGS5], [FGS6] hold and if it is further assumed that each process producing commodity 1 uses commmodity 1 as an input, the Classification Theorem holds with the following differences. In the first regime the rate of profit is $\lambda - \delta_x$, where λ is the minimum of all the Perron–Frobenius eigenvalues of possible input square matrices which can be obtained by peaking up for each commodity a process producing it; in the third regime the rate of profit is $a^{-1} - \delta_x$, where a is the minimum of all coefficients relative to inputs of commodity 1 used in the production of commodity 1.

12 The case of decomposable matrices is not uncommon in the new growth literature: the model by Lucas (1988), for instance, is of this type (for a similar remark, see also McKenzie, 1998, p. 11).

References

Atsumi, H. (1969), 'The efficient capital programme for a maintainable utility level', *Review of Economic Studies*, **36**, 263–87.

Boldrin, M. and D.K. Levine (2002), 'Factor saving innovation', *Journal of Economic Thoery*, **105**(1), 18–41.

Bose, S. (1968), 'Optimal growth and investment allocation', *Review of Economic Studies*, **35**, 465–80.

Burgstaller, A. (1994), *Property and Prices: Towards a Unified Theory of Value*, Cambridge: Cambridge University Press.

Cass, D. and K. Shell (1976), 'The structure and stability of competitive dynamical systems', *Journal of Economic Theory*, **12**, 10–18.

Champernowne, D.G. (1945–56), 'A note on J. v. Neumann's Article "A model of economic equilibrium" ', *Review of Economic Studies*, **13**, 1–9.

Dasgupta, S. and T. Mitra (1988), 'Intertemporal optimality in a closed linear model of production', *Journal of Economic Theory*, **45**, 288–315.

Dolmas, J. (1996), 'Endogenous growth in multisector Ramsey models', *International Economic Review*, **37**, 403–21.

Evans, G.W., S. Honkapohja and P.M. Romer (1998), 'Growth cycles', *American Economic Review*, **88**, 495–515.

Frankel, M. (1962), 'The production function in allocation and growth: a synthesis', *American Economic Review*, **52**, 995–1022.

Freni, G., F. Gozzi and N. Salvadori (2001), 'A multisector "Ak model" with endogenous growth: existence and characterization of optimal paths and steady state analysis', *Studi e Ricerche del Dipartimento di Scienze Economiche dell'Università di Pisa*, n. 75, http://www.dse.ec.unipi.it/ricerca/collana_studi.asp# FSG

Gale, D. (1960), *The Theory of Linear Economic Models*, New York: McGraw-Hill.

Gozzi, F. and G. Freni (2001), 'On a dynamic non-substitution theorem and other issues in Burgstaller's "Property and Prices" ', *Metroeconomica*, **52**(2), 181–96.

Jones, L. and R. Manuelli (1990), 'A convex model of equilibrium growth: theory and policy implications', *Journal of Political Economy*, **98**, 1008–38.

Jones, L.E. and R. Manuelli (1997), 'The sources of growth', *Journal of Economic Dynamics and Control*, **21**, 75–114.

Kaganovich, M. (1998), 'Sustained endogenous growth with decreasing returns and heterogenous capital', *Journal of Economic Dynamics and Control*, **22**, 1575–603.

Kurz, H.D. and N. Salvadori (1995), *Theory of Production: A Long-Period Analysis*, Cambridge: Cambridge University Press.

Kurz, H.D. and N. Salvadori (1998), 'Postscript (to "The non-substitution theorem: making good a lacuna")' in H.D. Kurz and N. Salvadori, *Understanding 'Classical' Economics. Studies in Long-period Theory*, London and New York: Routledge, pp. 95–9.

Ladron-de-Guevara, A., S. Ortigueira and M.S. Santos (1999), 'A two-sector model of endogenous growth with leisure', *Review of Economic Studies*, **66**, 609–31.

Lucas, R.E. (1988), 'On the mechanics of economic development', *Journal of Monetary Economics*, **22**(1), 3–42.

McFadden, D. (1967), 'The evaluation of development programmes', *Review of Economic Studies*, **34**, 25–50.

McKenzie, L.W. (1998), 'Turnpikes', *American Economic Review*, **88**, 1–14.

Neumann, J. von (1945), 'A model of general economic equilibrium', *Review of Economic Studies*, **13**, 1–9. English translation of 'Über ein ökonomisches Gleichungssystem und eine Verallgemeinerung des Brouwerschen Fixpunksatzes', in *Ergebnisse eines mathematischen Kolloquiums*, **8** (1937), 73–83.

Ossella, I. (1999), 'A turnpike property of optimal programs for a class of simple linear models of production', *Economic Theory*, **14**, 597–607.

Ramsey, F.P. (1928), 'A mathematical theory of saving', *Economic Journal*, **38**, 543–59.

Rebelo, S. (1991), 'Long run policy analysis and long run growth', *Journal of Political Economy*, **99**, 500–21.

Romer, P.M. (1986), 'Increasing returns and long-run growth', *Journal of Political Economy*, **94**(5), 1002–37.

Romer, P.M. (1987), 'Growth based on increasing returns due to specialization', *American Economic Review*, **77**, 56–62.

Romer, P.M. (1990), 'Endogenous technological change', *Journal of Political Economy*, **98**, 71–102.

Salvadori, N. (1998), 'A linear multisector model of "endogenous" growth and the problem of capital', *Metroeconomica*, **49**, 319–35.

Weitzman, M.L. (1971), 'Shiftable versus non-shiftable capital: a synthesis', *Econometrica*, **39**, 511–29.

Index

For Product Safety Concerns and Information please contact our EU representative GPSR@taylorandfrancis.com
Taylor & Francis Verlag GmbH, Kaufingerstraße 24, 80331 München, Germany

www.ingramcontent.com/pod-product-compliance
Ingram Content Group UK Ltd.
Pitfield, Milton Keynes, MK11 3LW, UK
UKHW020014200926
475702UK00014B/1875

* 9 7 8 1 1 3 8 0 1 0 6 3 5 *